McGRAW-HILL

5 Steps to a 5

AP Chemistry

John T. Moore
Richard Langley

McGRAW-HILL

New York   Chicago   San Francisco   Lisbon   London   Madrid   Mexico City
Milan   New Delhi   San Juan   Seoul   Singapore   Sydney   Toronto

The **McGraw·Hill** Companies

1 2 3 4 5 6 7 8 9 10 QPD/QPD 0 9 8 7 6 5 4 3

ISBN 0-07-141275-1

McGraw-Hill books are available at special quantity discounts to use as premiums and sales promotions, or for use in corporate training programs. For more information, please write to the Director of Special Sales, Professional Publishing, McGraw-Hill, Two Penn Plaza, New York, NY 10121-2298. Or contact your local bookstore.

 This book is printed on recycled, acid-free paper containing a minimum of 50% recycled, de-inked fiber.

Contents

Chapter 4   Reactions and Periodicity / 69

Chapter 13

Equilibrium / 232

Chapter 14

Electrochemistry / 266

Preface

Welcome to the AP Chemistry Five-Step Program. The fact that you are reading this preface suggests that you will be taking the AP exam in chemistry. The exam certainly isn't easy, but the rewards are worth it—college credit and the satisfaction of a job well done. You will have to work hard and study hard to do well, but we will, through this book, help you master the material and get ready for the exam.

Both of us have many years experience in teaching introductory general chemistry at the university level, but each of us has certain skills and experiences that will be of special help in presenting the material in this book. Richard "Doc" Langley has taught high school chemistry and has been a grader for the AP Chemistry exam free-response questions for years. He has a firsthand knowledge of how the AP exam is graded and scored. John Moore has years of grant experience teaching chemistry to both public school teachers and students and is the author of *Chemistry for Dummies*. We have tried not only to make the material understandable but also to present the problems in the format of the AP Chemistry exam. By faithfully working the problems you will increase your familiarity with the AP exam format, so when the time comes to take the exam there will be no surprises.

Use this book in addition to your regular chemistry text. If you are in the year-long program, use it as you are taking your AP Chemistry course. It will provide additional problems in the AP format. If you are in one of the other programs, still use a chemistry textbook, but you may need to lean a little more on this review book. Either way, if you put in the time and effort, you will do well.

Now it's time to start. Take the Diagnostic Exam at the end of Chapter 2. Your score will tell how well you understand the material right now and point out weak areas that may need a little extra attention. Use the review exams at the end of the chapters to check your comprehension. Also pay attention to the free-response questions. That is where you can really shine, and they are worth almost as much as the multiple-choice part. Use the Rapid Reviews to brush up on the important points in the chapters. Keep this book handy—it is going to be your friend for the next few weeks or months. Good luck, but remember that luck favors the prepared mind.

Acknowledgments

The authors would like to thank Grace Freedson, who believed in our abilities and gave us this project. Many thanks also to Donald Reis, whose editing polished up the manuscript and helped its readability. John would like to especially thank his dear wife, Robin, who put up with his late nights, tight deadlines, and foul moods.

INTRODUCTION

Chapter 1

How to Use This Book

THE BASICS

The Philosophy of This Book: In the Beginning

The key to doing well on the Advanced Placement (AP) Chemistry exam is to outline a method of attack and not to deviate from this attack. You will need to focus on each step. You have taken the first step with the purchase of this book, and we will work with you to make sure you take the best path toward the test. This book will serve as a tool to guide your steps. But do not forget—no tool is useful if you do not use it.

Why This Book?

We believe this book has something unique to offer you. We have worked with many AP Chemistry students, teachers, and free-response graders, and have incorporated many of their ideas. Consequently, this book represents not only student concerns, but also problems noted by teachers and graders. This book is directed toward you—the student. We will try to direct you toward the exam and not to present extraneous material. If you feel that you need a stronger background, do not be afraid to look in your regular chemistry textbook. This book is designed to help you review the chemistry you need for the exam; it is not designed to teach you chemistry.

This book serves many purposes. It should:

- clarify the requirements for the AP Chemistry exam
- give you the opportunity to practice for the exam
- provide you with a reasonable study schedule

- help you avoid common errors on the exam
- make you aware of the five steps to mastering the AP Chemistry exam

ORGANIZATION OF THE BOOK

We know your primary goal is to learn about the AP Chemistry exam. We start by introducing the basic five-step plan used in this book. Next, we present three different approaches to exam preparation. We then give you an overview of the AP exams. Many tips and suggestions are offered, and a Diagnostic Exam is presented to help you customize your study.

The volume of material to be mastered can be intimidating. Part III of this book provides a comprehensive review. Since not all of this material appears in every AP Chemistry class, this book will also help you to fill in gaps in your chemistry background.

Part IV of this book contains practice exams. This section will allow you to test your skills. The multiple-choice questions will provide practice on questions similar to those asked on past AP exams. These are not the exact questions, but ones that will focus you on the key AP Chemistry topics. There are also examples of free-response questions; there are fewer of these because they take much longer to answer. After you take an exam, you should review each question. Ask yourself, why was this question present? Why do I need to know this? Make sure you check your answers against the explanations. Do not just read the explanations for the questions you missed. If necessary, use the index to locate a particular topic and reread the review material.

The appendices provide supplemental information. You should use each part throughout your review.

INTRODUCTION TO THE FIVE-STEP PROGRAM

The purpose of the five-step program is to give you the skills and methodology to do well on the exam. There are also many opportunities to practice. Each step will bring you closer to the perfect 5.

 STEP ONE will lead you through a simple diagnostic process to determine your best method of preparation. There are three general approaches:

1. A month-to-month schedule—you work for the entire school year.
2. An abbreviated schedule—you work from January through May.
3. An intensive review schedule—you work for the six weeks prior the exam.

 STEP TWO will help you with the knowledge required for the exam.

1. A review of the exam is given.
2. A Diagnostic Exam, with answers, gives you a better understanding of the exam and your strengths and weaknesses. This will build your confidence.

3. Terms relating to the AP Chemistry exam appear in the Glossary.
4. You may also benefit from the list of websites.

 STEP THREE will help you develop the skills needed to do well on the exam.

1. There are practice multiple-choice questions.
2. There are practice free-response questions.

 STEP FOUR presents test-taking strategies.

1. You will learn about the test.
2. You will learn what to look for in a multiple-choice question.
3. You will learn strategies for multiple-choice questions, including a caveat on guessing.
4. You will learn what to look for in a free-response question.
5. You will learn strategies for answering free-response questions.

 STEP FIVE will help build your confidence in using the various skills developed in the first four steps.

1. A Practice Exam will help you gain confidence and practice.
2. Time management skills will help you prepare for the exam.
3. You will have the opportunity to hone your skills with two practice exams.

GRAPHICS USED IN THIS BOOK

To emphasize particular skills, strategies, and practices, we use seven sets of icons throughout this book.

The first icon is an hourglass, which indicates the passage of time during the school year. This hourglass icon will appear in the margin next to an item that may be of interest to one of the three types of students using this book (mode A, B, or C students).

For the student who plans to prepare for the AP Chemistry exam during the entire school year—September through May—we use an hourglass that is full on the top.

For the student who decides to begin preparing for the exam in January, we use an hourglass that is half-full on the top and half-full on the bottom.

For the student who wishes to prepare during the final six weeks before the exam, we use an hourglass that is almost empty on the top and almost full on the bottom.

The second icon is a footprint, indicating which step in the five-step program is being emphasized in an analysis, technique, or practice activity.

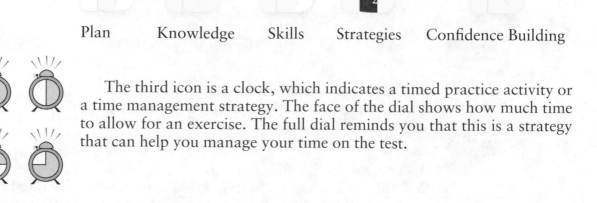

| Plan | Knowledge | Skills | Strategies | Confidence Building |

The third icon is a clock, which indicates a timed practice activity or a time management strategy. The face of the dial shows how much time to allow for an exercise. The full dial reminds you that this is a strategy that can help you manage your time on the test.

The fourth icon is an exclamation point, which will point to a very important idea, concept, or strategy that you should not pass over.

The fifth icon is a checkmark, which will alert you to pay close attention. This activity will be most helpful if you go back and check your work, your calendar, or your progress.

The sixth icon is a light bulb, which indicates strategies you may want to try.

The seventh icon is the sun, which indicates a tip that you might find useful.

Boldfaced words indicate terms that are included in the Glossary at the end of the book.

Throughout the book, you will find marginal notes, boxes, and starred areas. Pay close attention to these areas because they can provide tips, hints, strategies, and further explanations to help you reach your full potential.

THREE APPROACHES TO PREPARING FOR THE AP CHEMISTRY EXAM

Overview of the Three Plans

You are the best judge of your study habits. Good intentions and wishes will not prepare you for the exam. You should make a realistic decision of what will work best for you. Do not feel that you must follow one of these schedules exactly; you can fine-tune any one of them to your needs.

Do not make the mistake of forcing yourself to follow someone else's method. Look at the following descriptions, and see which best describes you. This will help you pick a prep mode.

You're a full-year prep student (Approach A) if:

1. You are the kind of person who likes to plan for everything far in advance.
2. You arrive early for appointments.
3. You like detailed planning and everything in its place.
4. You feel that you must be thoroughly prepared.
5. You hate surprises.

You're a one-semester prep student (Approach B) if:

1. You are always on time for appointments.
2. You are willing to plan ahead to feel comfortable in stressful situations, but are okay with skipping some details.
3. You feel more comfortable when you know what to expect, but a surprise or two is good.

You're a 6-week prep student (Approach C) if:

1. You get to appointments at the last second.
2. You work best under pressure and tight deadlines.
3. You feel very confident with the skills and background you learned in your AP Chemistry class.
4. You decided late in the year to take the exam.
5. You like surprises.

General Outline of Three Different Study Schedules

Month	Year-Long Plan	Calendar Year Plan	6-Week Plan
September– October	Introduction to material and Chapter 3		
November	Chapters 4–5		
December	Chapters 6–7		
January	Chapters 8–9	Chapters 3–5	
February	Chapters 10–11	Chapters 6–8	
March	Chapters 12–14	Chapters 9–12	
April	Chapters 15–17; Practice Exam 1	Chapters 13–17; Practice Exam 1	Skim Chapters 3–12; all rapid reviews; Practice Exam 1
May	Review everything; Practice Exam 2	Review everything; Practice Exam 2	Skim Chapters 13–17; Practice Exam 2

CALENDAR FOR EACH PLAN

A Calendar for Approach A:
Year-Long Preparation for the AP Chemistry Exam

The main reason for you to use this book is as a preparation for the
AP Chemistry exam. This book can fill other roles: it can broaden your study
of chemistry, help your analytical skills, and aid your scientific writing abilities.
These will help in a college chemistry course.

SEPTEMBER–OCTOBER (Check off the
activities as you complete them.)

_____ Determine your best study
schedule.

_____ Read Parts I and II of this book.
Highlight material that applies
to you.

_____ Pay careful attention to the
Diagnostic Exam.

_____ Take a look at the AP and other
websites.

_____ Skim Part III, the Comprehensive
Review section. The major part of
your preparation is in this part of
this book.

_____ Buy a few color highlighters.

_____ Look through the entire book.
You need to get some idea of the
layout, and break it in.

_____ You need to have a clear picture
of your school's AP Chemistry
curriculum.

_____ Use this book as a supplement to
your classroom experience.

NOVEMBER (The first 10 weeks have
elapsed.)

_____ Read and study Chapter 3,
Basics.

_____ Read and study Chapter 4,
Reactions and Periodicity.

_____ Read and study Chapter 5,
Stoichiometry.

DECEMBER

_____ Read and study Chapter 6, Gases.

_____ Read and study Chapter 7,
Thermodynamics.

_____ Review Chapters 3–5.

JANUARY (20 weeks have elapsed.)

_____ Read and study Chapter 8,
Spectroscopy, Light, and Electrons.

_____ Read and study Chapter 9,
Bonding.

_____ Review Chapters 3–7.

FEBRUARY

_____ Read and study Chapter 10,
Solids, Liquids, and
Intermolecular Forces.

_____ Read and study Chapter 11,
Solutions and Colligative
Properties.

_____ Review Chapters 3–9.

MARCH (30 weeks have now elapsed.)

_____ Read and study Chapter 12,
Kinetics.

_____ Read and study Chapter 13,
Equilibrium.

_____ Read and study Chapter 14,
Electrochemistry.

_____ Review Chapters 3–11.

APRIL

_____ Take Practice Exam 1 in the first week of April.

_____ Evaluate your strengths and weaknesses. Review the appropriate chapters to correct any weaknesses.

_____ Read and study Chapter 15, Nuclear Chemistry.

_____ Read and study Chapter 16, Organic Chemistry.

_____ Read and study Chapter 17, Experimental.

_____ Review Chapters 3–14.

MAY (First 2 weeks)

_____ Review Chapters 3–17—all the material.

_____ Take Practice Exam 2.

_____ Score your exam.

_____ Get a good night's sleep before the exam. Fall asleep knowing you are well prepared.

GOOD LUCK ON THE TEST!

A Calendar for Approach B:
Semester-Long Preparation for the AP Chemistry Exam

This approach uses the assumption that you have completed at least one semester of chemistry. This calendar begins in mid-year and prepares you for the mid-May exam.

JANUARY–FEBRUARY

_____ Read Parts I and II in this book.
_____ Pay careful attention to the Diagnostic Exam.
_____ Pay close attention to your walk-through.
_____ Read and study Chapter 3, Basics.
_____ Read and study Chapter 4, Reactions and Periodicity.
_____ Read and study Chapter 5, Stoichiometry.
_____ Read and study Chapter 6, Gases.
_____ Read and study Chapter 7, Thermodynamics.

MARCH (10 weeks to go)

_____ Read and study Chapter 8, Spectroscopy, Light, and Electrons.
_____ Review Chapters 3–5.
_____ Read and study Chapter 9, Bonding.
_____ Read and study Chapter 10, Solids, Liquids, and Intermolecular Forces.
_____ Review Chapters 6 and 7.
_____ Read and study Chapter 11, Solutions and Colligative Properties.
_____ Read and study Chapter 12, Kinetics.

APRIL

_____ Take Practice Exam 1 in the first week of April.
_____ Evaluate your strengths and weaknesses.
_____ Study appropriate chapters to correct your weaknesses.
_____ Read and study Chapter 13, Equilibrium.
_____ Review Chapters 3–7.
_____ Read and study Chapter 14, Electrochemistry.
_____ Read and study Chapter 15, Nuclear Chemistry.
_____ Review Chapters 8–12.
_____ Read and study Chapter 16, Organic Chemistry.
_____ Read and study Chapter 17, Experimental.

MAY (First 2 weeks)

_____ Review Chapters 3–17, all the material.
_____ Take Practice Exam 2.
_____ Score your exam.
_____ Get a good night's sleep before the exam. Fall asleep knowing you are well prepared.

GOOD LUCK ON THE TEST!

A Calendar for Approach C:
6-Week Preparation for the AP Chemistry Exam

This approach is for students who have already studied most of the material that may be on the exam. Your best use of this book is as a specific guide toward the AP Chemistry exam. There are time constraints to this approach; the exam is only a short time away. This is not the best time to try to learn new material.

APRIL 1–15

_____ Skim Parts I and II of this book.
_____ Go over Chapter 3.
_____ Skim Chapters 4–7.
_____ Carefully go over the Rapid Review sections of Chapters 3–7.
_____ Complete Practice Exam 1.
_____ Score the exam and analyze your mistakes.
_____ Skim and highlight the Glossary.

APRIL 16–MAY 1

_____ Skim Chapters 8–12.
_____ Carefully go over the Rapid Review sections of Chapters 8–12.
_____ Carefully go over the Rapid Review sections of Chapters 3–7.
_____ Continue to skim and highlight the Glossary.

MAY (First 2 weeks)

_____ Skim Chapters 13–17.
_____ Carefully go over the Rapid Reviews for Chapters 13–17.
_____ Complete Practice Exam 2.
_____ Score the exam and analyze your mistakes.
_____ Get a good night's sleep before the exam. Fall asleep knowing that you are well prepared.

GOOD LUCK ON THE TEST!

PART II

GETTING STARTED

Chapter 2

What You Need to Know About the AP Chemistry Exam

BACKGROUND OF THE ADVANCED PLACEMENT PROGRAM

 The College Board began the Advanced Placement program in 1955 to construct standard achievement exams that would allow highly motivated high school students the opportunity to receive advanced placement as first-year students in U.S. colleges and universities. Today there are 33 courses and exams, with more than a million students from every state and from foreign countries taking the exams each May.

The AP programs are for high school students who wish to take college-level courses. In our case, the AP Chemistry course and exam are designed to involve high school students in college-level chemistry studies.

WHO WRITES THE AP CHEMISTRY EXAM?

A group of college and high school chemistry instructors known as the AP Development Committee creates the AP Chemistry exam. The committee's job is to ensure that the annual AP Chemistry exam reflects what is in college-level chemistry classes at high schools.

This committee writes a large number of multiple-choice questions, which are pretested and evaluated for clarity, appropriateness, and range of possible answers. The committee also generates a pool of essay questions, pretests them, and chooses questions that best represent the full range of the scoring scale, allowing the AP readers to evaluate the essays equitably.

It is important to remember that the AP Chemistry exam is thoroughly evaluated after it is administered each year. This way, the College Board can use the results to make course suggestions and to plan future tests.

THE AP GRADES AND WHO RECEIVES THEM

Once you have taken the exam and it has been scored, your test will be graded with one of five numbers by the College Board:

- A 5 indicates that you are extremely well qualified.
- A 4 indicates that you are well qualified.
- A 3 indicates that you are adequately qualified.
- A 2 indicates that you are possibly qualified.
- A 1 indicates that you are not qualified to receive college credit.

Grades usually are reported by early July.

REASONS FOR TAKING THE AP CHEMISTRY EXAM

Why put yourself through a year of intensive study, pressure, stress, and preparation? Only you can answer that question. Following are some reasons that students have indicated to us for taking the AP exam:

- because colleges look favorably on the applications of students who enroll in AP courses
- to receive college credit or advanced standing at their colleges or universities
- to compare themselves with other students across the nation
- for personal satisfaction
- because they love the subject
- so that their families will be proud of them

There are other reasons, but no matter what they are, the primary reason for your enrolling in the AP Chemistry course and taking the exam in May is to feel good about yourself and the challenges that you have met.

4 QUESTIONS FREQUENTLY ASKED ABOUT THE AP CHEMISTRY EXAM

Here are some common questions and answers about the AP Chemistry exam.

If I Do Not Take an AP Chemistry Course, Can I Still Take the AP Chemistry Exam?

Yes, you may take the AP Chemistry exam. While the exam is designed for students who have completed a year-long course in AP Chemistry, anyone may take the test, including students whose high school does not offer the course. Students have done well on the exam without taking the course. It is to your advantage to take an AP Chemistry course if you are planning to take the exam.

How Is the Advanced Placement Chemistry Exam Organized?

The two-part exam is designed to take three hours. The first section has 75 multiple-choice questions. You will have 90 minutes to complete this section.

The second part of the exam is the free-response section. You will begin this section after completing and turning in your multiple-choice scan sheet. There will be a break before you begin the second section. You will not be able to go back to the multiple-choice questions.

You will be given a test booklet for the free-response section of the test. You will have 90 minutes to answer six out of eight questions. As a rule, you may answer either question 2 or 3, and either question 7 or 8. You are required to answer questions 1, 4, 5, and 6. This format may vary slightly, so make sure you answer the appropriate questions. Free-response questions may cover any of the material in the AP Chemistry course. Each of the chapters in Part III of this book covers one of these topics. During the past few years there has been a required question concerning reactions and a required question concerning an experiment.

Must I Check the Box at the End of the Essay Booklet that Allows AP Staff to Use My Essays as Samples for Research?

It does not matter what you check. Your choice will have no bearing upon your grade. This only allows the College Board to use your answer as a model.

How Is the Multiple-Choice Section Scored?

You will place your answers to the multiple-choice questions on a scan sheet, which will be computer graded. The computer counts the number of correct response and subtracts one-fourth of the wrong answers. A blank response is neither right nor wrong. If N is the number of answers, the formula is:

$N_{right} - (N_{wrong} \times 0.25) =$ raw score rounded up or down to the nearest whole number

How Are My Free-Response Answers Scored?

A trained AP reader, called a faculty consultant, grades each free-response answer. The AP/College Board members have developed a highly successful training program for their readers. Many opportunities for checks and double checks of essays ensure a fair and equitable reading of each essay.

A chief faculty consultant, a question leader, table leaders, and content experts carefully develop the scoring guides. All faculty consultants are then trained to read and score just one essay question on the exam. They actually become experts in that one essay question. No one knows the identity of any writer. The identification numbers and names are covered, and the exam booklets are randomly distributed to the readers in packets of 25 randomly chosen essays. Table leaders and the question leader review samples of each reader's scores to ensure that quality standards are constant.

Each essay is scored on a scale that varies from question to question. Once your essay is graded on this scale, the next set of calculations is completed.

How Is My Composite Score Calculated?

This is where fuzzy math comes into play. The free-response section represents 55 percent of this score. The multiple-choice section makes up 45 percent of the composite score.

Take your essay results and plug them into this formula:

- (points earned for question 1)(2.00) = score for question 1
- (points earned for question 2 or 3)(2.00) = score for question 2 or 3
- (points earned for question 4)(1.50) = score for question 3
- (points earned for question 5)(1.50) = score for question 4
- (points earned for question 6)(1.50) = score for question 6
- (points earned for question 7 or 8)(1.50) = score for question 7 or 8

total weighted score for the free-response section = sum of scores for all the questions

Your composite score for the exam is determined by adding the score from the multiple-choice section to the score from the free-response section and rounding that sum to the nearest whole number.

How Is My Composite Score Turned into the Grade that Is Reported to My College?

Keep in mind that the composite scores needed to earn a 5, 4, 3, 2, or 1 change each year. A committee of AP, College Board, and Educational Testing Service (ETS) directors, experts, and statisticians determines these cutoffs. The same exam that is given to AP Chemistry high school students is given to college students. College professors report how the college students fared on the exam. This provides information for the chief faculty consultant on where to draw the lines for a 5, 4, 3, 2, or 1 score. A score of 5 on this AP exam is set to represent the average score received by the college students who scored an A on the exam. A score of a 3 or a 4 is the equivalent of a college grade B, and so on.

Over the years there has been an observable trend indicating the number of points required to achieve a specific grade. Data released from a particular AP Chemistry exam show that the *approximate* range for the five different scores is:

- low 100s–150 points = 5
- low 80s–low 100s points = 4
- low 60s–low 80s points = 3
- low 40s–low 60s points = 2
- 0–low 40s points = 1

What Should I Bring to the Exam?

Here are some suggestions:

- several pencils
- an eraser
- a calculator
- several black pens (black ink is easier on the eyes)
- a watch
- something to drink—water is best
- a quiet snack, such as Lifesaver candies
- your brain
- tissues

What Should I Avoid Bringing to the Exam?

You should not bring:

- anything distracting
- loud stereo
- "Pop rocks" candy
- your parents

Should I Be Aware of Anything Else?

You should:

- allow plenty of time to get to the test site
- wear comfortable clothing
- eat a light breakfast and/or lunch
- remind yourself that you are well prepared and that the test is an enjoyable challenge and a chance to share your knowledge
- be proud of yourself! You worked hard.

Once test day comes, there is nothing further you can do. Do not worry about what you could have done differently. It is out of your hands, and your only job is to answer as many questions correctly as you possibly can. The calmer you are, the better your chances of doing well.

What Should I Do the Night Before the Exam?

Last-minute cramming of massive amounts of material will not help you. It takes time for your brain to organize material. There is some value to a last-minute review of material. This may involve looking over the Rapid Review portions of a few (not all) chapters, or looking through the Glossary. The night before the test should include a light review, and various relaxing activities. **A full night's sleep is one of the best preparations for the test.** If you have trouble falling asleep, review Chapter 3 until you fall asleep.

 TIPS FOR TAKING THE AP CHEMISTRY EXAM

Following are some suggestions for taking the multiple-choice and free-response parts of the exam:

Multiple-Choice Questions

Here are some basic rules:

1. Do not try to outthink the test. The multiple-choice questions are straightforward; do not overanalyze them. If you find yourself doing this, pick the simplest answer. If you know the answer to a difficult question, give yourself credit for preparing well; do not think it is too easy and you must have missed something. There are easy questions and difficult questions on the exam.
2. If you absolutely do not know the answer, leave it blank. You can come back to it if you have time. The grading of the exam has a built-in penalty for random guessing. You get a 0 for a question you leave blank and a $-\frac{1}{4}$ for a wrong answer. You can get a lower grade by guessing instead of leaving the answers blank. If you can eliminate one or more of the choices, it may be possible for you to guess and come out ahead.
3. Be very careful about each question's wording. It is easy to skip over small words like "not," "least," or "most." You must make sure you are answering the correct question. Many students make this type of mistake—do not add your name to the list.
4. Pace yourself. If you do not know the answer to a question immediately, skip it. You can come back to it later. You have approximately 70 seconds per question. You can get a good grade on the test even if

you do not finish all the questions. If you spend too much time on a question, you may get it correct; however, if you had gone on, you might have answered several questions correctly in the same amount of time. The more questions you read, the more likely you are to find the ones you can answer. Practice this timing. Times are given for the various tests in this book. If you try to adhere strictly to these times, you will learn how to pace yourself.

5. Change answers only as a last resort. You can mark your test and come back later to a problem. When you come back to a problem, make sure you have a definite reason for changing the answer.

Free-Response Questions

Here are some basic rules:

1. Read the question carefully. The free-response questions tend to be multipart questions. If you do not understand one part of the question, go on to the next part. The parts tend to be stand-alone. If you make a mistake in one part, you will not be penalized for the same mistake a second time.

2. Budget your time carefully. Spend 1–2 minutes reading the question and mentally outlining your response. Spend the next 3–5 minutes outlining your response. Finally, spend about 15 minutes answering the question. A common mistake is to overdo the answer. The question is worth a limited number of points. If your answer is twice as long, you will not get more points. Instead, you will lose time you could have spent on the remainder of the test. Make sure your answer goes directly to the point. There should be no deviations or extraneous material.

3. Make sure you spend some time on each section. A question's part is normally worth 1 to 3 points. You will receive only a set maximum number of points. Make sure you make an attempt to answer each part. You cannot compensate for leaving one part blank by doubling the length of the answer to another part.

   Make sure the grader is able to find the answer to each part. This will help make sure you get all the points you deserve. There will be at least a full page for your answer. Some questions will have multiple pages available for the answer; you are not expected to use them all. In some cases, the extra pages are there simply because the test booklet has a certain number of pages.

4. Outlines are very useful. They not only organize your answer, but they also can point to parts of the question you may need to reread. Your outline does not need to be detailed, just a few keywords to organize your thoughts. As you make the outline, refer back to the question, so you don't miss any important points. Use your outline to write a well-organized answer. The grader is not grading on how well your answer is written, but a well-written answer makes it easier for

the grader to understand your answer and give you all the points you deserve.

5. Grading depends on what you get right in your answer. If you say something that is wrong, it is not counted against you. Always try to say something; this will give you a chance for partial credit. Do not try too hard and negate something you have already said. The grader needs to know what you mean; if you say something and negate it later, there will be doubt.

2 GETTING STARTED: THE DIAGNOSTIC EXAM

The following problems refer to different chapters in the book. It is not important whether you get the correct answers. If you have a problem with one or more questions from a chapter, review the chapter.

Chapter 3

1. In most of its compounds, this element exists as a monatomic cation.

   A. F
   B. S
   C. N
   D. Ca
   E. Cl

2. Which of the following groups has the species correctly listed in order of decreasing radius?

   A. Cu^{2+}, Cu^+, Cu
   B. V, V^{2+}, V^{3+}
   C. F^-, Br^-, I^-
   D. B, Be, Li
   E. Li^+, K^+, Cs^+

3. Which of the following elements has the lowest electronegativity?

   A. F
   B. I
   C. Ba
   D. Al
   E. C

4. Which of the following represents the correct formula for hexaamminecobalt (III) nitrate?

   A. $[Co_3(NH_3)_6](NO_3)_3$
   B. $[Co(NH_3)_6](NO_2)_3$
   C. $Am_6Co(NO_3)_3$
   D. $(NH_3)_6Co_3(NO_3)$
   E. $[Co(NH_3)_6](NO_3)_3$

5. The discovery that atoms have small, dense nuclei is credited to which of the following?

   A. Einstein
   B. Dalton
   C. Bohr
   D. Rutherford
   E. Becquerel

Chapter 4

6. Choose the strongest Lewis acid from the following.

   A. BF_3
   B. F^-
   C. OH^-
   D. CH_4
   E. S^{2-}

7. ___ $Mn(OH)_2(s)$ + ___ $H_3AsO_4(aq)$ → ___ $Mn_3(AsO_4)_2(s)$ + ___ $H_2O(l)$

   After the above chemical equation is balanced, the lowest whole-number coefficient for water is:

   A. 6
   B. 2
   C. 12
   D. 3
   E. 9

Choose one of the following for questions 8–10.

   A. Cu^{2+}
   B. CO_3^{2-}
   C. Fe^{3+}
   D. Al^{3+}
   E. Pb^{2+}

8. This ion will form a precipitate when added to a sodium sulfate solution.

9. This ion gives a deep blue color when excess aqueous ammonia is added to a solution containing it.

10. Aqueous solutions of this ion give a reddish precipitate when excess hydroxide ion is added.

11. Which of the following best represents the net ionic equation for the reaction of calcium hydroxide with an aqueous sodium carbonate solution?

   A. $Ca^{2+} + Na_2CO_3 \rightarrow CaCO_3 + 2\ Na^+$
   B. $2\ Ca(OH) + Na_2CO_3 \rightarrow Ca_2CO_3 + 2\ NaOH$
   C. $Ca(OH)_2 + CO_3^{2-} \rightarrow CaCO_3 + 2\ OH^-$
   D. $Ca^{2+} + CO_3^{2-} \rightarrow CaCO_3$
   E. $Ca(OH)_2 + Na_2CO_3 \rightarrow CaCO_3 + 2\ NaOH$

12. A student mixes 50.0 mL of 0.10 M $Fe(NO_3)_2$ solution with 50.0 mL of 0.10 M KOH. A green precipitate forms, and the concentration of the hydroxide ion becomes very small. Which of the following correctly places the concentrations of the remaining ions in order of decreasing concentration?

   A. $[Fe^{2+}] > [NO_3^-] > [K^+]$
   B. $[Fe^{2+}] > [K^+] > [NO_3^-]$
   C. $[NO_3^-] > [K^+] > [Fe^{2+}]$
   D. $[Fe^{2+}] > [K^+] > [NO_3^-]$
   E. $[NO_3^-] > [Fe^{2+}] > [K^+]$

Chapter 5

13. $14\ H^+ + 6\ Fe^{2+} + Cr_2O_7^{2-} \rightarrow 2\ Cr^{3+} + 6\ Fe^{3+} + 7\ H_2O$

   The above reaction is used in the titration of an iron solution. What is the concentration of the iron solution if it takes 45.20 mL of 0.1000 M $Cr_2O_7^{2-}$ solution to titrate 75.00 mL of an acidified iron solution?

   A. 0.1000 M
   B. 0.4520 M

   C. 0.3616 M
   D. 0.7232 M
   E. 0.1808 M

14. Manganese, Mn, forms a number of oxides. A particular oxide is 49.5% mass Mn. What is the simplest formula for this oxide?

   A. MnO
   B. Mn_2O_3
   C. Mn_3O_4
   D. MnO_2
   E. Mn_2O_7

15. $2\ KMnO_4 + 5\ H_2C_2O_4 + 3\ H_2SO_4 \rightarrow K_2SO_4 + 2\ MnSO_4 + 10\ CO_2 + 8\ H_2O$

   How many moles of $MnSO_4$ are produced when 2.0 mol of $KMnO_4$, 2.5 mol of $H_2C_2O_4$, and 3.0 mol of H_2SO_4 are mixed?

   A. 1.0 mol
   B. 3.5 mol
   C. 2.0 mol
   D. 2.5 mol
   E. 3.0 mol

16. $Ba + 2\ H_2O \rightarrow Ba(OH)_2 + H_2$

   Barium reacts with water according to the above reaction. What volume of hydrogen gas, at standard temperature and pressure, is produced from 0.400 mol of barium?

   A. 8.96 L
   B. 5.60 L
   C. 4.48 L
   D. 3.36 L
   E. 2.24 L

Chapter 6

17. A sample of chlorine gas is placed in a container of constant pressure. The sample is heated until the absolute temperature is doubled. This will also double which of the following?

A. potential energy
B. moles
C. density
D. number of molecules
E. volume

18. A balloon contains 2.0 g of hydrogen gas. A second balloon contains 4.0 mol of helium gas. Both balloons are at the same temperature and pressure. Pick the **false** statement from the following list.

    A. The number of hydrogen molecules is the same as the number of helium atoms in each balloon.
    B. The density of the helium in its balloon is greater than the density of the hydrogen in its balloon.
    C. The volume of each balloon is the same.
    D. The average speed of the molecules/atoms in each balloon is the same.
    E. The average kinetic energy of the molecules/atoms in each balloon is the same.

19. The volume and pressure of a real gas are not the same as those calculated from the ideal gas equation, because the ideal gas equation does NOT take into account:

    A. the attraction between the molecules and the speed at which the molecules are moving
    B. the volume of the molecules and the mass of the molecules
    C. the attraction between the molecules and the mass of the molecules
    D. the volume of the molecules and variations in the absolute temperature
    E. the volume of the molecules and the attraction between the molecules

20. Aluminum metal reacts with HCl to produce aluminum chloride and hydro-gen gas. What volume of hydrogen gas, at STP, is produced when 13.5 g of aluminum is mixed with an excess of HCl?

    A. 22.4 L
    B. 33.6 L
    C. 11.2 L
    D. 16.8 L
    E. 7.47 L

21. A sample containing the gases carbon dioxide, carbon monoxide, and water vapor was analyzed and found to contain 4.5 mol of carbon dioxide, 4.0 mol of carbon monoxide, and 1.5 mol of water vapor. The mixture had a total pressure of 1.2 atm. What was the partial pressure of the carbon monoxide?

    A. 0.48 atm
    B. 0.18 atm
    C. 5.4 atm
    D. 0.54 atm
    E. 0.98 atm

22. An ideal gas sample weighing 0.548 g at 100°C and 0.993 atm has a volume of 0.237 L. Determine the molar mass of the gas.

    A. 71.3 g/mol
    B. 143 g/mol
    C. 19.1 g/mol
    D. 0.0140 g/mol
    E. 35.7 g/mol

23. If a sample of He effuses at a rate of 30 mol per hour at 45°C, which of the gases below will effuse at approximately one-half the rate under the same conditions?

    A. CH_4
    B. O_3
    C. N_2
    D. H_2
    E. CO

Chapter 7

Choose from the following types of energy for questions 24–27.

    A. free energy
    B. lattice energy
    C. kinetic energy
    D. activation energy
    E. ionization energy

24. The energy required to produce a gaseous cation from a gaseous atom in the ground state

25. The average _____ is the same for any ideal gas at a given temperature.

26. The maximum energy available for useful work from a spontaneous reaction

27. The energy required to completely separate the ions from a solid is

28. Oxidation of ClF by F_2 yields ClF_3, an important fluorinating agent formerly used to produce the uranium compounds in nuclear fuels: $ClF(g) + F_2(g) \rightarrow ClF_3(l)$ Use the following thermochemical equations to calculate $\Delta H°_{rxn}$ for the production of ClF_3:

  1. $2\ ClF(g) + O_2(g)$ $\Delta H° = 167.5\ kJ$
      $\rightarrow Cl_2O(g) + OF_2(g)$

  2. $2\ F_2(g) + O_2(g)$ $\Delta H° = -43.5\ kJ$
      $\rightarrow 2\ OF_2(g)$

  3. $2\ ClF_3(l) + 2\ O_2(g)$ $\Delta H° = 394.1\ kJ$
      $\rightarrow Cl_2O(g) + 3\ OF_2(g)$

    A. +270.2 kJ
    B. −135.1 kJ
    C. 0.0 kJ
    D. −270.2 kJ
    E. +135.1 kJ

29. Choose the reaction expected to have the greatest increase in entropy.

    A. $N_2(g) + O_2(g) \rightarrow 2\ NO(g)$
    B. $CO_2(g) \rightarrow CO_2(s)$
    C. $2\ XeO_3(s) \rightarrow 2\ Xe(g) + 3\ O_2(g)$
    D. $2\ K(s) + F_2(g) \rightarrow 2\ KF(s)$
    E. $C(s) + O_2(g) \rightarrow CO_2(g)$

30. A certain reaction is nonspontaneous under standard conditions, but becomes spontaneous at lower temperatures. What conclusions may be drawn under standard conditions?

    A. $\Delta H > 0$, $\Delta S > 0$ and $\Delta G > 0$
    B. $\Delta H < 0$, $\Delta S < 0$ and $\Delta G = 0$
    C. $\Delta H < 0$, $\Delta S > 0$ and $\Delta G > 0$
    D. $\Delta H < 0$, $\Delta S < 0$ and $\Delta G > 0$
    E. $\Delta H > 0$, $\Delta S < 0$ and $\Delta G > 0$

Chapter 8

31. Which of the following groups contains only atoms that are paramagnetic in their ground-state?

    A. Be, O, and N
    B. Mg, He, and Rb
    C. K, C, and Fe
    D. Br, Sb, and Kr
    E. S, Zn, and F

The following ground-state electron configurations are to be used for questions 32–35:

    A. $1s^2 1p^6 2s^2 2p^3$
    B. $1s^2 2s^2 2p^6 3s^2 3p^6 4s^2 3d^{10} 4p^6 5s^2 4d^1$
    C. $1s^2 2s^2 2p^6 3s^2 3p^6 3d^3$
    D. $1s^2 2s^2 2p^5$
    E. $1s^2 2s^2 2p^6 3s^2 3p^6 4s^2 3d^{10} 4p^6$

32. This is the configuration of a transition metal ion.

33. This is the configuration of a Noble gas.

34. The halogen in this group.

35. This is an impossible electron configuration.

The following answers are to be used for questions 36–39:

   A. Pauli exclusion principle
   B. electron shielding
   C. the wave properties of matter
   D. Heisenberg uncertainty principle
   E. Hund's rule

36. The exact position of an electron is not known.

37. Nitrogen atoms, in their ground state, are paramagnetic.

38. An atomic orbital can hold no more than two electrons.

39. The 4s orbital fills before the 3d.

40. Magnesium reacts with element X to form an ionic compound. If the ground-state electron configuration of X is $1s^2 2s^2 2p^3$, what is the simplest formula for this compound?

   A. MgX_2
   B. Mg_2X_3
   C. Mg_3X_2
   D. MgX
   E. Mg_2X

Chapter 9

41. VSEPR predicts that an IF_5 molecule will be which of the following shapes?

   A. tetrahedral
   B. trigonal bipyramidal
   C. square pyramid
   D. trigonal planar
   E. square planar

42. Which of the following does not have one or more π bonds?

   A. SO_2
   B. SF_6
   C. O_2
   D. SO_3
   E. O_3

43. Which of the following is nonpolar?

   A. IF_5
   B. BrF_3
   C. CF_4
   D. SF_4
   E. OF_2

44. The only substance listed below that contains ionic, σ, and π bonds is:

   A. Na_3N
   B. NO_2
   C. $NaNO_3$
   D. NH_3
   E. HNO_3

45. Which molecule or ion in the following list has the greatest number of unshared electron pairs around the central atom?

   A. SO_2
   B. CO_3^{2-}
   C. XeF_2
   D. CF_4
   E. H_2O

46. What types of hybridization of carbon are in the compound acetic acid, CH_3COOH?

   I. sp^3
   II. sp^2
   III. sp

   A. I, II, and III
   B. I only
   C. I and II
   D. II and III
   E. II only

Chapter 10

Choose from the following descriptions of solids for questions 47–50.

    A. composed of atoms held together by delocalized electrons

    B. composed of molecules held together by intermolecular dipole–dipole interactions

    C. composed of positive and negative ions held together by electrostatic attractions

    D. composed of macromolecules held together by strong bonds

    E. composed of molecules held together by intermolecular London forces

47. Graphite

48. $Ca(s)$

49. $CaCO_3(s)$

50. $SO_2(s)$

51. The critical point on a phase diagram represents

    A. the highest temperature and pressure where a substance can sublime

    B. the highest temperature and pressure where the substance may exist as discrete solid and gas phases

    C. the temperature and pressure where the substance exists in equilibrium as solid, liquid, and gas phases

    D. the highest temperature and pressure where the substance may exist as discrete liquid and gas phases

    E. the highest temperature and pressure where the substance may exist as discrete liquid and solid phases

Choose the appropriate answer from the following list for questions 52 and 53.

    A. London dispersion forces
    B. covalent bonding
    C. hydrogen bonding
    D. metallic bonding
    E. ionic bonding

52. This is why copper is ductile.

53. This is why acetic acid molecules exist as dimers in the gaseous phase.

54. For the following, pick the answer that most likely represents their relative solubilities in water.

    A. $CH_3CH_2CH_2OH < HOCH_2CH_2OH < CH_3CH_2CH_2CH_3$

    B. $CH_3CH_2CH_2CH_3 < HOCH_2CH_2OH < CH_3CH_2CH_2OH$

    C. $CH_3CH_2CH_2CH_3 < CH_3CH_2CH_2OH < HOCH_2CH_2OH$

    D. $CH_3CH_2CH_2OH < CH_3CH_2CH_2CH_3 < HOCH_2CH_2OH$

    E. $HOCH_2CH_2OH < CH_3CH_2CH_2OH < CH_3CH_2CH_2CH_3$

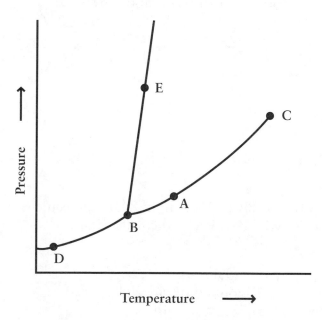

55. Which point on the above diagram represents the triple point?

Chapter 11

56. A solution is prepared by dissolving 0.500 mol of NaCl in 500.0 g of water. Which of the following would be the best procedure to determine the molarity of the solution?

A. Measure the volume of the solution.
B. Titrate the solution with standard silver nitrate solution.
C. Determine the freezing point of the solution.
D. Determine the osmotic pressure of the solution.
E. Measure the mass of the solution.

57. A chemist needs 800 mL of a 0.50 M bromide ion, Br$^-$, solution. She has 800 mL of a 0.20 M KBr solution. How many moles of solid MgBr$_2$ will she need to add to increase the concentration to the desired value?

A. 0.24
B. 0.50
C. 0.30
D. 0.12
E. 0.15

58. A solution of pentane, C$_5$H$_{12}$, in carbon tetrachloride, CCl$_4$, is nearly ideal. The vapor pressure of pentane is 450 mm Hg at 20°C, and the vapor pressure of carbon tetrachloride is 87 mm Hg at this temperature. What is the mole fraction of carbon tetrachloride in the vapor over an equimolar solution of these two liquids?

A. 0.16
B. 0.84
C. 0.19
D. 0.87
E. 0.50

59. How many grams of HNO$_3$ (molecular weight 63.0) are in 500.0 mL of a 5.00 M solution?

A. 31.5 g
B. 63.0 g

C. 5.00 g
D. 315 g
E. 158 g

60. Which of the following aqueous solutions would have the greatest freezing point depression?

A. 0.15 m NH$_4$Br
B. 0.15 m Ca(C$_2$H$_3$O$_2$)$_2$
C. 0.15 m KIO$_3$
D. 0.15 m KC$_2$H$_3$O$_2$
E. 0.15 m C$_2$H$_4$(OH)$_2$

Chapter 12

61. Step 1: 2 NO$_2$(g) → N$_2$(g) + 2 O$_2$(g)
Step 2: 2 CO(g) + O$_2$(g) → 2 CO$_2$(g)
Step 3: N$_2$(g) + O$_2$(g) → 2 NO(g)

The above represents a proposed mechanism for the reaction of NO$_2$ with CO. What are the overall products of the reaction?

A. N$_2$ and O$_2$
B. O$_2$ and CO$_2$
C. N$_2$ and NO
D. NO only
E. NO and CO$_2$

62. The difference in energy between the transition state and the reactants is

A. the kinetic energy
B. the activation energy
C. the free energy
D. the reaction energy
E. the heat of reaction

63. The table below gives the initial concentrations and rates for three experiments.

Experiment	Initial [ClO$_2$] (mol L^{-1})	Initial [OH$^-$] (mol L^{-1})	Initial rate of formation of ClO$_2^-$ (mol L^{-1} s^{-1})
1	0.100	0.100	2.30 × 10^5
2	0.200	0.100	9.20 × 10^5
3	0.200	0.200	1.84 × 10^6

The reaction is $2ClO_2(aq) + 2OH^-(aq)$ $\rightarrow ClO_2^-(aq) + ClO_3^-(aq) + H_2O(l)$. What is the rate law for this reaction?

A. Rate = $k[ClO_2]^2[OH^-]^2$
B. Rate = $k[ClO_2]$
C. Rate = $k[ClO_2]^2[OH^-]$
D. Rate = $k[OH^-]^2$
E. Rate = $k[ClO_2][OH^-]$

Chapter 13

64. Which of the following CANNOT behave as both a Brønsted base and a Brønsted acid?

A. HCO_3^-
B. HPO_4^{2-}
C. HSO_4^-
D. CO_3^{2-}
E. $HC_2O_4^-$

65. A species, molecule, or ion, is called a Lewis base if it does which of the following?

A. It donates an H^+.
B. It accepts an H^+.
C. It increases the $H^+(aq)$ in water.
D. It donates a pair of electrons.
E. It accepts a pair of electrons.

66.

Acid	K_a, acid dissociation constant
H_3PO_4	7.2×10^{-3}
$H_2PO_4^-$	6.3×10^{-8}
HPO_4^{2-}	4.2×10^{-13}

Using the above information, choose the best answer for preparing a pH = 8.5 buffer.

A. $K_2HPO_4 + K_3PO_4$
B. $H_3PO_4 + KH_2PO_4$
C. K_3PO_4
D. K_2HPO_4
E. $K_2HPO_4 + KH_2PO_4$

67. What is the ionization constant, K_a, for a weak monoprotic acid if a 0.5-molar solution has a pH of 5.0?

A. 3×10^{-4}
B. 2×10^{-10}
C. 7×10^{-8}
D. 1×10^{-6}
E. 5×10^{-5}

Questions 68–71 refer to the following aqueous solutions. All concentrations are 1 M.

A. KBr (potassium bromide) and HBr (hydrobromic acid)
B. $H_2C_2O_4$ (oxalic acid) and KHC_2O_4 (potassium hydrogen oxalate)
C. NH_3 (ammonia) and NH_4NO_3 (ammonium nitrate)
D. $(CH_3)_2NH$ (dimethylamine) and $HC_2H_3O_2$ (acetic acid)
E. $(CH_3)_2NH$ (dimethylamine) and $Ca(OH)_2$ (calcium hydroxide)

68. The most acidic solution (lowest pH)

69. The solution with a pH nearest 7

70. A buffer with a pH > 7

71. A buffer with a pH < 7

72. Determine the $OH^-(aq)$ concentration in 0.0010 M pyridine (C_5H_5N) solution. (The K_b for pyridine is 9×10^{-9}.)

A. 5×10^{-6} M
B. 1×10^{-3} M
C. 3×10^{-6} M
D. 9×10^{-9} M
E. 7×10^{-7} M

73. $SnS(s) + 2 H^+(aq) \rightleftharpoons Sn^{2+}(aq) + H_2S(aq)$

What is the equilibrium constant for the above reaction? The successive acid dissociation constants for H_2S are 9.5×10^{-8} (K_{a1}) and 1×10^{-19} (K_{a2}). The

K_{sp}, the solubility product constant, for SnS equals 1.0×10^{-25}.

A. $9.5 \times 10^{-8} / 1.0 \times 10^{-25}$
B. $9.5 \times 10^{-27} / 1.0 \times 10^{-25}$
C. $1.0 \times 10^{-25} / 9.5 \times 10^{-27}$
D. $1 \times 10^{-19} / 1.0 \times 10^{-25}$
E. $1.0 \times 10^{-25} / 9.5 \times 10^{-8}$

74. $N_2O_4(g) \rightleftharpoons 2\ NO_2(g)$
endothermic

An equilibrium mixture of the compounds is placed in a sealed container at $150°C$. The amount of the product may be increased by which of the following changes?

I.   Adding 1 mole of Ar(g) to the container
II. Increasing the volume of the container
III. Raising the temperature of the container

A. III only
B. II and III
C. II only
D. II and III
E. I only

75. The K_{sp} for LaF_3 is 2×10^{-19}. What is the molar solubility of this compound in water?

A. 7.4×10^{-21}
B. $\sqrt[4]{2 \times 10^{-19}}$
C. $\sqrt[2]{2 \times 10^{-19}}$
D. $\sqrt[4]{7.4 \times 10^{-21}}$
E. 2×10^{-19}

Chapter 14

76. $I^-(aq) + H^+(aq) + MnO_4^-(aq) \rightarrow$
$Mn^{2+}(aq) + H_2O(l) + I_2(s)$

What is the coefficient of H^+ when the above reaction is balanced?

A. 12
B. 32
C. 16
D. 8
E. 2

77. How many moles of Au may be deposited on the cathode when 0.60 Faradays of electricity is passed through a 1.0 M solution of Au^{3+}?

A. 0.60 mol
B. 0.30 mol
C. 0.40 mol
D. 0.20 mol
E. 1.0 mol

78. $Sn^{2+} + 2\ Fe^{3+} \rightarrow Sn^{4+} + 2\ Fe^{2+}$

The reaction shown above was used in an electrolytic cell. The voltage measured for the cell was not equal to the calculated $E°$ for the cell. This discrepancy could be caused by which of the following?

A. Both of the solutions were at $25°C$ instead of $0°C$.
B. The anode and cathode were different sizes.
C. The anion in the anode compartment was chloride instead of nitrate, as in the cathode compartment.
D. One or more of the ion concentrations was not 1 M.
E. The solution in the salt bridge was Na_2SO_4 instead of KNO_3.

Questions 79–80 are concerned with the following half-reaction in an electrolytic cell:

$$2\ SO_4^{2-} + 10\ H^+ + 8\ e^- \rightarrow S_2O_3^{2-} + 5\ H_2O$$

79. Choose the correct statement from the following list.

A. The sulfur is oxidized.
B. This is the cathode reaction.
C. The oxidation state of sulfur does not change.

D. The H^+ serves as a catalyst.

E. This is the anode reaction.

80. If a current of 0.60 amperes is passed through the electrolytic cell for 0.75 hours, how should you calculate the grams of $S_2O_3^{2-}$ formed?

A. $(0.60)(0.75)(3600)(112) / (96500)(8)$

B. $(0.60)(0.75)(3600)(112) / (96500)(10)$

C. $(0.60)(0.75)(60)(32) / (96500)(8)$

D. $(0.60)(0.75)(3600)(112) / (10)$

E. $(0.60)(0.75)(32) / (96500)(8)$

Chapter 15

81. When $^{226}_{88}Ra$ decays, it emits 2 α particles, then a β particle, followed by an α particle. The resulting nucleus is:

A. $^{212}_{83}Bi$

B. $^{222}_{86}Rn$

C. $^{214}_{82}Pb$

D. $^{214}_{83}Bi$

E. $^{212}_{85}At$

82. Which of the following lists the types of radiation in the correct order of increasing penetrating power?

A. α, γ, β

B. β, α, γ

C. α, β, γ

D. β, γ, α

E. γ, β, α

83. What is the missing product in the following nuclear reaction?

$$^{236}_{92}U \rightarrow 4\,^{1}_{0}n + ^{136}_{53}I + \underline{\quad}$$

A. $^{99}_{39}Y$

B. $^{96}_{38}Sr$

C. $^{96}_{39}Y$

D. $^{98}_{40}Zr$

E. $^{98}_{41}Nb$

84. If 75% of a sample of pure $^{3}_{1}H$ decays in 24.6 yr, what is the half-life of $^{3}_{1}H$?

A. 24.6 yr

B. 18.4 yr

C. 12.3 yr

D. 6.15 yr

E. 3.07 yr

Chapter 16

85. Alkenes are hydrocarbons with the general formula C_nH_{2n}. If a 1.40-g sample of any alkene is combusted in excess oxygen, how many moles of water will form?

A. 0.2

B. 0.1

C. 1.5

D. 0.7

E. 0.05

86. What type of compound is shown below?

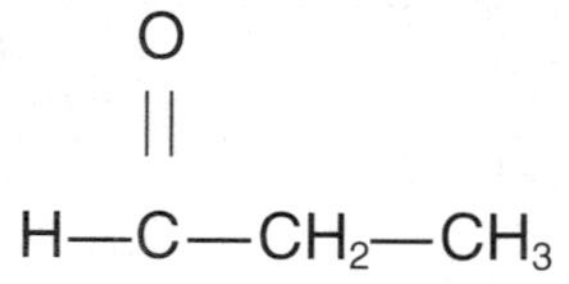

$$\overset{\displaystyle O}{\underset{\displaystyle ||}{}}$$
$$H-C-CH_2-CH_3$$

A. an alcohol

B. an aldehyde

C. a ketone

D. an ester

E. an alkane

Chapter 17

Questions on this chapter are incorporated into the chapters concerning the specific experiments.

ANSWERS AND EXPLANATIONS

Chapter 3

1. **D.** The others form anions.

2. **B.** Decreasing radii for increasing charges, or for going up a column (with equal charges), or moving towards the right in a period of the periodic table.

3. **C.** The element that is furthest from F.

4. **E.** Hexaammine = $(NH_3)_6$; cobalt(III) = Co^{3+}; and nitrate = NO_3^-.

5. **D.** This was determined by bombarding gold foil with alpha particles.

Chapter 4

6. **A.** All others, except D, are Lewis bases. D is neither a Lewis acid nor a Lewis base.

7. **A.**

$$3\ Mn(OH)_2(s) + 2\ H_3AsO_4(aq)$$
$$\rightarrow Mn_3(AsO_4)_2(s) + 6\ H_2O(l)$$

8. **E.** $PbSO_4$ forms.

9. **A.** $[Cu(NH_3)_4]^{2+}$ forms.

10. **C.** $Fe(OH)_3$ forms.

11. **D.** $Ca(OH)_2$, $NaOH$, and Na_2CO_3 are strong electrolytes and should be separated. Cancel all spectator ions.

12. **C.** The hydroxide took some of the iron with it, so Fe^{2+} will be low. The nitrate is double the potassium because there are two nitrates per iron(II) nitrate instead of one, as in potassium hydroxide.

Chapter 5

13. **C.** $(0.1000\ mol\ Cr_2O_7^{2-}/1000\ mL)$
$(45.20\ mL)(6\ mol\ Fe^{2+}/1\ mol\ Cr_2O_7^{2-})$
$(1/75.00\ mL)(1000\ mL/L)$

14. **E.** Percent Mn in each oxide: (A)77.4; (B) 69.6; (C) 79.9; (D) 63.2; (E) 49.5.

15. **A.** $H_2C_2O_4$ is the limiting reagent.

16. **A.** $(0.400\ mol\ Ba)(1\ mol\ H_2/1\ mol\ Ba)$
$(22.4\ L/mol)$

Chapter 6

17. **E.** This is an application of Charles's Law.

18. **D.** Two grams of H_2 is 1 mol of H_2.

19. **E.** The basic difference between ideal and real gases.

20. **D.** $(13.5\ g\ Al)(1\ mol\ Al/27.0\ g\ Al)$
$(3\ mol\ H_2/2\ mol\ Al)(22.4\ L/mol\ H_2)$

21. **A.** The mole fraction of CO times the total pressure yields the partial pressure. The mole fraction of CO is the moles of CO divided by the total moles.

22. **A.** $n = PV/RT = (0.993\ atm)(0.237\ L)/$
$(0.0821\ L\ atm/K\ mol)(373\ K)$
$= 7.69 \times 10^{-3}\ mol$
molar mass $= 0.548\ g/7.69 \times 10^{-3}\ mol$
$= 71.3\ g/mol$

23. **A.** The molar mass of the gas must be the square of the molar mass of helium.

Chapter 7

24. **E.** Definition.

25. **C.** Basic postulate of kinetic molecular theory.

26. **A.** One of the properties of free energy.

27. **B.** Definition.

28. **B.**

$$\frac{1}{2}[2\ ClF(g) + O_2(g) \qquad \frac{1}{2}(167.5\ kJ)$$
$$\to Cl_2O(g) + OF_2(g)]$$

$$\frac{1}{2}[2\ F_2(g) + O_2(g) \qquad \frac{1}{2}(-43.5\ kJ)$$
$$\to 2\ OF_2(g)]$$

$$\frac{1}{2}[Cl_2O(g) + 3\ OF_2(g) \qquad -\frac{1}{2}(394.1\ kJ)$$
$$\to 2\ ClF_3(l) + 2\ O_2(g)]$$

_____

$$ClF(g) + F_2(g) \to ClF_3(l) \qquad -135.1 kJ$$

29. **C.** The one with the greatest increase in the moles of gas.

30. **D.** Nonspontaneous means $\Delta G > 0$. Becoming spontaneous at lower temperature means $\Delta H < 0$ and $\Delta S < 0$.

Chapter 8

31. **C.** Atoms with completely filled shells or subshells are not paramagnetic. These are: Be, Mg, He, Kr, and Zn.

32. **C.** Transition metal ions are s^0. C could be Cr^{3+}.

33. **E.** Noble gases, except helium, are ns^2np^6. In this case, $n = 4$.

34. **D.** Halogens are ns^2np^5. In this case, the halogen is F.

35. **A.** There is no such thing as a 1p.

36. **D.** Definition.

37. **E.** The electrons fill the 2p orbitals individually.

38. **A.** Definition.

39. **B.** The d orbitals are less effectively shielded than the s orbitals.

40. **C.** Mg becomes Mg^{2+}. The element is N which can become N^{3-}.

Chapter 9

41. **C.** The iodine has five bonding pairs and one lone pair.

42. **B.** This is the only one with only single bonds.

43. **C.** Use VSEPR.

44. **C.** The only ionic bonds are the sodium compounds. The nitride ion has no internal bonding, but the nitrate ion has σ and π bonds.

45. **C.** Numbers of unshared pairs: (A) 1; (B) 0; (C) 3; (D) 0; (E) 2

46. **C.** The carbon on the left is sp^3, and the other is sp^2.

Chapter 10

47. **D.** Both graphite and diamond are covalent-network solids.

48. **A.** Calcium is a metal, and answer A applies to metallic bonding.

49. **C.** Calcium carbonate is ionic.

50. **B.** This is a polar molecule.

51. **D.** Definition.

52. **D.** This is a consequence of metallic bonding.

53. **C.** The carbonyl and –OH groups are capable of participating in hydrogen bonds.

54. **C.** The more –OH groups, the more hydrogen bonding, and the more soluble in water.

55. **B.** Definition.

Chapter 11

56. **A.** Molarity is moles over liters, and the moles are already known.

57. **D.** (0.800 L)(0.50 mol Br^-/L) = 0.40 mol needed.

    (0.800 L)(0.20 mol Br^-/L) = 0.16 mol present.

    (0.24 mol Br^- to be added) (1 mol $MgBr_2$/2 mol Br^-0)

58. **A.** Mole fraction of each = 0.5 since the solution is equimolar.

    Vapor pressure of CCl_4 = 0.5 (87 mm Hg) = 43.5 mm Hg

    Vapor pressure of pentane = 0.5 (450 mm Hg) = 225 mm Hg

    Mole fraction of CCl_4 in vapor = 43.5 mm Hg/(43.5 + 225) mm Hg

59. **E.** (0.5000 L)(5.00 mol/L)(63.0 g/mol) = 158 g

60. **B.** Since all the molalities are the same, look for the one that produces the most ions.

Chapter 12

61. **E.** Add the equations and cancel anything that appears on both sides of the reaction arrows.

62. **B.** Definition.

63. **C.** The table shows second order in chlorine dioxide and first order in hydroxide ion.

Chapter 13

64. **D.** The carbonate ion has no H^+ to donate.

65. **D.** Definition.

66. **E.** Start with the one with a pK_a as near 8.5 as possible ($H_2PO_4^-$). To go to a higher pH, the HPO_4^{2-} ion is needed.

67. **B.** This is an approximation.

    $$K_a = (10^{-5})^2/0.5.$$

68. **A.** HBr is a strong acid.

69. **D.** The weak acid and weak base give a nearly neutral solution.

70. **C.** Only B and C are buffers. B is acidic and C is basic.

71. **B.** Only B and C are buffers. B is acidic and C is basic.

72. **C.** $[OH^-] = (0.0010 \times 9 \times 10^{-9})^{1/2} = (9 \times 10^{-12})^{1/2}$

73. **C.** $K = K_{sp}/K_{a1}K_{a2}$

74. **B.** I yields no change.

75. **D.** $K_{sp} = [La^{3+}][F^-]^3 = [\times][3\times]^3 = 27 \times^4$

Chapter 14

76. **C.** 10 I^-(aq) + 16 H^+(aq) + 2 MnO_4^-(aq) → 2 Mn^{2+}(aq) + 8 H_2O(l) + 5 I_2(s)

77. **D.** (0.60 F)(1 mol Au/3 F) = 0.20 moles

78. **D.** The cell must be nonstandard. This could be due to variations in temperature or concentrations that are not standard.

79. B. A reduction is shown. Reductions take place at the cathode.

80. A. Use dimensional analysis:
$(0.60 \text{ coul/s})(0.75 \text{ h})(3600 \text{ s/h})$
$(112 \text{ g } S_2O_3{}^{2-}/\text{mol } S_2O_3{}^{2-})/(96500 \text{ coul/F})$
$(8 \text{ F/mol } S_2O_3{}^{2-})$

Chapter 15

81. D. The mass should be $226 - (4 + 4 + 0 + 4) = 214$. The atomic number should be $88 - (2 + 2 - 1 + 2) = 83$.

82. C. Alpha particles are the least penetrating, and gamma rays are the most penetrating.

83. C. Mass difference = $236 - 4(1) - 136 = 96$. Atomic number difference = $92 - 4(0) - 53 = 39$.

84. C. After one half-life, 50% would remain. After another half-life this would be reduced by ½ to 25%. The total amount decayed is 75%. Thus, 24.6 years must be two half-lives of 12.3 years each.

Chapter 16

85. B. $(1.40 \text{ g})(1 \text{ mol}/14 \text{ g})$

86. B.

Scoring and Interpretation

Now that you have finished and scored the Diagnostic Exam, it is time for you to learn what it all means. First, note any part where you had difficulty. This should not be limited to unfamiliar material. Do this even if you got the correct answer. Determine where this material is covered in the book. Plan to spend additional time on this chapter. There is material you may not recognize because you have not gotten that far in class.

The following relation determines the baseline score. N represents the number of answers. Ignore those you left blank.

$$(N_{correct} - \tfrac{1}{4} N_{incorrect}) = \text{raw score for the multiple-choice section}$$

There are no free-response questions on this Diagnostic Exam. They are not useful at this point. We will use the multiple-choice questions to provide an estimate of your preparation. Use these results as a guide.

Raw Score	Approximate AP Score
50–86	5
37–49	4
27–36	3
16–26	2
0–15	1

If you did better than you expected—great. Be careful not to become overconfident. You will need to prepare much more before you take the AP Chemistry exam.

If you did not do as well as you hoped, don't panic. There is plenty of time for you to prepare for the exam.

No matter what your results were, you are about to begin your Five Steps to a Five.

Good luck!

PART III

COMPREHENSIVE REVIEW

Chapter 3

Basics

 2 **KEYWORDS AND EQUATIONS**

✓ This section of each chapter will contain the mathematical equations and constants that are supplied to you on the AP exam. We have tried to use, as much as possible, the exact format that is used on the test.

T = temperature	n = moles	m = mass	P = pressure
V = volume	D = density	v = velocity	**M** = molar mass
KE = kinetic energy	t = time		

Boltzmann's constant, $k = 1.38 \times 10^{-23}$ J K^{-1}
electron charge $= -1.6022 \times 10^{-19}$ coulombs
1 electron volt per atom $= 96.5$ kJ mol^{-1}

$K = {}^{\circ}C + 273$ $\qquad$ $D = m/V$

INTRODUCTION

 This chapter on basic chemical principles should serve as a review if you have had a pre-AP chemistry course in school. We assume (and we all know about assumptions) that you know about such things as the scientific method, elements, compounds, and mixtures. We may mention elementary chemistry topics like this, but we will not spend a lot of time discussing them. When you are using this book, have your textbook handy. If we mention a topic and it doesn't sound familiar, go to your textbook and review it in depth. We will be covering topics that are on the AP exam. There is a lot of good information in your text that is not covered on the AP exam, so if you want more, read your text.

UNITS AND MEASUREMENTS

Almost all calculations in chemistry involve both a number and a unit. One without the other is useless. Every time you complete a calculation, be sure that your units have cancelled and that the desired unit is written with the number.

√ **Always show your units!**

Units

The system of units used in chemistry is the SI system (Système International), which is related to the metric system. There are base units for length, mass, etc. and decimal prefixes that modify the base unit. Since most of us do not tend to think in these units, it is important to be able to convert back and forth from the English system to the SI system. These three conversions are the most useful ones, although knowing the others might allow you to simplify your calculations:

mass: 1 pound = 0.4536 kg (453.6 g)
volume: 1 quart = 0.9464 dm³ (0.9464 L)
length: 1 inch = 2.54 cm (exact)

As shown above, the SI unit for volume is the cubic decimeter (dm³), but most chemists use the liter (L, which is equal to 1 dm³) or milliliter (mL). Appendix A lists the SI base units and prefixes, as well as some English–SI equivalents.

We in the United States are used to thinking of temperature in Fahrenheit, but most of the rest of the world measures temperature in Celsius. On the Celsius scale water freezes at 0°C and boils at 100°C. Here are the equations needed to convert from Fahrenheit to Celsius and vice versa:

$$°C = \frac{5}{9}\left[°F - 32\right]$$

$$°F = \frac{9}{5}\left(°C\right) + 32$$

Many times, especially in working with gases, chemists use the Kelvin scale. Water freezes at 273.15 K and boils at 373.15 K. To convert from Celsius to Kelvin:

$$K = °C + 273.15$$

Absolute zero is 0 K and is the point at which all molecular motion ceases.

The density of a substance is commonly calculated in chemistry. The **density (D)** of an object is calculated by dividing the mass of the object by its volume. (Some authors will use a lowercase d to represent the density term; be prepared for either.) Since density is independent of the quantity of matter (a big piece of gold and a little piece have the same density), it can be used for identification purposes. The most common units for density in chemistry are g/cm^3 or g/mL.

Measurements

We deal with two types of numbers in chemistry—exact and measured. Exact values are just that—exact, by definition. There is no uncertainty associated with them. There are exactly 12 items in a dozen and 144 in a gross. Measured values, like the ones you deal with in the lab, have uncertainty associated with them because of the limitations of our measuring instruments. When those measured values are used in calculations, the answer must reflect that combined uncertainty by the number of significant figures that are reported in the final answer. The more significant numbers reported, the greater the certainty in the answer.

The measurements used in calculations may contain varying numbers of significant figures, so carry as many as possible until the end and then round off the final answer. The least precise measurement will determine the significant figures reported in the final answer. Determine the number of significant figures in each *measured* value (not the exact ones) and then, depending on the mathematical operations involved, round off the final answer to the correct number of significant figures. Here are the rules for determining the number of significant figures in a measured value:

1. All non-zero digits (1, 2, 3, 4, etc.) are significant.
2. Zeroes between non-zero digits are significant.
3. Zeroes to the left of the first non-zero digit are not significant.
4. Zeroes to the right of the last non-zero digit are significant if there is a decimal point present, but not significant if there is no decimal point.

Rule 4 is a convention that many of us use, but some teachers or books may use alternative methods.

By these rules, 0.230500 would contain 6 significant figures, but 230500 would contain only 4.

Another way to determine the number of significant figures in a number is to express it in scientific (exponential) notation. The number of digits shown is the number of significant figures. For example 2.305×10^{-5} would contain 4 significant figures. Review exponential notation.

In determining the number of significant figures to be expressed in the final answer, the following rules apply:

1. For addition and subtraction problems, the answer should be rounded off to the same number of decimal points as the measurement with the fewest decimal places.

2. For multiplication and division problems, round off the answer to the same number of significant figures in the measurement with the fewest significant figures.

Remember: Carry as many numbers as possible throughout the calculation and only round off the final answer.

DIMENSIONAL ANALYSIS—THE FACTOR LABEL METHOD

Dimensional analysis, sometimes called the factor label method, is a method for setting up mathematical problems. Mathematical operations are conducted with the units associated with the numbers, and these units are cancelled until only the unit of the desired answer is left. This results in a setup for the problem. Then the mathematical operations can efficiently be conducted and the final answer calculated and rounded off to the correct number of significant figures. For example, to determine the number of centimeters in 2.3 miles:

First, write down the initial data as a fraction:

$$\frac{2.3 \text{ mi}}{1}$$

Convert from miles to feet:

$$\frac{2.3 \text{ mi}}{1} \times \frac{5280 \text{ ft}}{1 \text{ mi}}$$

Convert from feet to inches:

$$\frac{2.3 \text{ mi}}{1} \times \frac{5280 \text{ ft}}{1 \text{ mi}} \times \frac{12 \text{ in}}{1 \text{ ft}}$$

Finally, convert from inches to centimeters:

$$\frac{2.3 \text{ mi}}{1} \times \frac{5280 \text{ ft}}{1 \text{ mi}} \times \frac{12 \text{ in}}{1 \text{ ft}} \times \frac{2.54 \text{ cm}}{1 \text{ in}}$$

The answer will be rounded off to 2 significant figures based upon the 2.3 miles, since all the other numbers are exact:

$$\frac{2.3 \text{ mi}}{1} \times \frac{5280 \text{ ft}}{1 \text{ mi}} \times \frac{12 \text{ in}}{1 \text{ ft}} \times \frac{2.54 \text{ cm}}{1 \text{ in}} = 3.7 \times 10^5 \text{ cm}$$

Sometimes on the AP exam, only setups will be given as possible answers. Write the correct setup to the problem and then see which one of the answers represents your answer.

Remember: The units must cancel!

Also: Make sure that the answer is a reasonable one!

THE STATES OF MATTER

Matter can exist in one of three states: solid, liquid, or gas. A **solid** has both a definite shape and a definite volume. At the molecular level, the particles that make up a solid are close together and many times are locked into a very regular framework called a crystal lattice. Molecular motion exists, but it is slight.

A **liquid** has a definite volume but no definite shape. It conforms to the container in which it is placed. The particles are moving much more than in the solid. There are usually clumps of particles moving relatively freely among other clumps.

A **gas** has neither definite shape nor volume. It expands to fill the container in which it is placed. The particles move rapidly with respect to each other and act basically independently of each other.

We will indicate the state of matter that a particular substance is in by a parenthetical s, l, or g. Thus, $H_2O(s)$ would represent solid water (ice), while $H_2O(g)$ would represent gaseous water (steam). For a more detailed discussion of solids, liquids and gases see Chapter 10.

THE STRUCTURE OF THE ATOM

Historical Development

The first modern atomic theory was developed by John Dalton and first presented in 1808. Dalton used the term atom (first used by Democritus) to describe the tiny, indivisible particles of an element. Dalton also thought that atoms of an element are the same and atoms of different elements are different. In 1897, J. J. Thompson discovered the existence of the first subatomic particle, the electron, by using magnetic and electric fields. In 1909 Robert Millikan measured the charge on the electron in his oil drop experiment (electron charge = -1.6022×10^{-19} coulombs), and from that he calculated the mass of the electron. Thompson developed an atomic model, the raisin pudding model, which described the atom as being a diffuse positively charged sphere with electrons scattered throughout.

Ernest Rutherford in 1910 was investigating atomic structure by shooting positively charged alpha particles at a thin gold foil. Most of the particles passed through with no deflection, a few were slightly deflected, and every once in a while an alpha particle was deflected back towards the alpha source. Rutherford concluded from this scattering experiment that the atom was mostly empty space where the electrons were, and that there was a dense core of positive charge at the center of the atom that contained most of the atom's mass. He called that dense core the **nucleus.**

Subatomic Particles

Our modern theory of the atom describes it as an electrically neutral sphere with a tiny nucleus at the center, which holds the positively charged protons and the neutral neutrons. The negatively charged electrons move around the nucleus in complex paths, all of which comprise the electron cloud. Table 3.1 summarizes the properties of the three fundamental subatomic particles:

Table 3.1 The Three Fundamental Subatomic Particles

Name	Symbol	Charge	Mass (amu)	Mass (g)	Location
proton	p^+	1+	1.007	1.673×10^{-24}	nucleus
neutron	n^0	0	1.009	1.675×10^{-24}	nucleus
electron	e^-	1−	5.486×10^{-4}	9.109×10^{-28}	outside nucleus

Many teachers and books omit the charges on the symbols for the proton and neutron.

The **amu (atomic mass unit)** is commonly used for the mass of subatomic particles and atoms. An amu is $\frac{1}{12}$ the mass of a carbon atom, which contains 6 protons and 6 neutrons (C-12).

Since the atom itself is neutral, the number of electrons must equal the number of protons. However, the number of neutrons in an atom may vary. Atoms of the same element (same number of protons) that have differing numbers of neutrons are called **isotopes.** A specific isotope of an element can be represented by the following symbolization:

$$^A_Z X$$

X represents the element symbol taken from the periodic table. Z is the **atomic number** of the element, the number of protons in the nucleus. A is the **mass number,** the sum of the protons and neutrons. By subtracting the atomic number (p) from the mass number ($p + n$), the number of neutrons may be determined. For example, $^{288}_{92}U$ (U-238) contains 92 protons, 92 electrons, and (238 − 92) 146 neutrons.

Electron Shells, Subshells, and Orbitals

According to the latest atomic model, the electrons in an atom are located in various energy levels or **shells** that are located at different distances from the nucleus. The lower the number of the shell, the closer to the nucleus the electrons are found. Within the shells, the electrons are grouped in **subshells** of slightly different energies. The number associated with the shell is equal to the number of subshells found at that energy level. For example,

Table 3.2 Summary of Atomic Shell, Subshells, and Orbitals for Shells 1–4

Shell (Energy Level)	Subshell	Number of Orbitals	Electron Capacity
1	s	1	2 total
2	s	1	2
	p	3	<u>6</u>
			8 total
3	s	1	2
	p	3	6
	d	5	<u>10</u>
			18 total
4	s	1	2
	p	3	6
	d	5	10
	f	7	<u>14</u>
			32 total

energy level 2 (shell 2) has two subshells. The subshells are denoted by the symbols s, p, d, f, etc. and correspond to differently shaped volumes of space in which the probability of finding the electrons are high. The electrons in a particular subshell may be distributed among volumes of space of equal energies, **orbitals.** There is one orbital for an s subshell, three for a p, five for a d, seven for an f, etc. Only two electrons may occupy an orbital. Table 3.2 summarizes the shells, subshells, and orbitals in an atom. Chapter 8 has a discussion of the origin of this system.

Energy Level Diagrams

The information above can be shown in graph form as an energy level diagram, as shown in Figure 3.1:

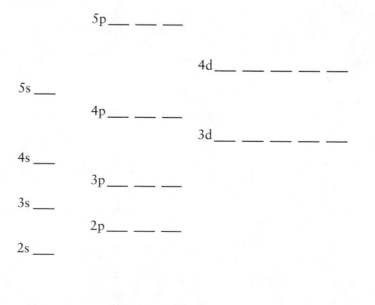

Figure 3.1 Energy level diagram of an atom.

Be sure to fill the lowest energy levels first (**Aufbau principle**) when using the diagram above. In filling the orbitals (having equal energy), electrons are added to the orbitals, half filling them all before pairing (**Hund's rule**). Sometimes it is difficult to remember the relative energy position of the orbitals. Notice that the 4s fills before the 3d. Figure 3.2 may help you remember the pattern in filling. Study the pattern and be able to reproduce it during the exam.

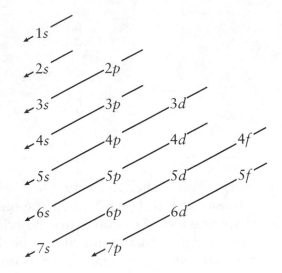

Figure 3.2 Orbital filling pattern.

Following these rules, the energy level diagram for silicon (Z=14) can be written as shown in Figure 3.3:

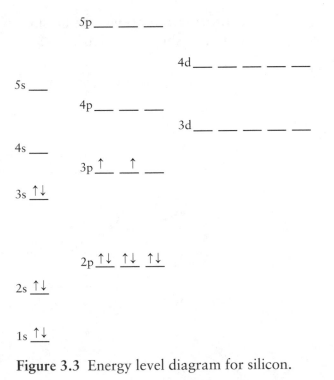

Figure 3.3 Energy level diagram for silicon.

Although this filling pattern conveys a lot of information, it is bulky. A shorthand method for giving the same information has been developed— the electronic configuration.

Electronic Configurations

The **electronic configuration** is a condensed way of representing the pattern of electrons in an atom. Using the Aufbau build-up pattern that was used in writing the energy level diagram, consecutively write the number of the shell (energy level), the type of orbital (s, p, d, etc.), and then the number of electrons in that orbital shown as a superscript. For example, $1s^2 2s^1$ would indicate that there are two electrons in the s-orbital in energy level (shell) 1, and one electron in an s-orbital in energy level 2. Looking at the energy level diagram for silicon above, the electronic configuration would be written as:

$$\text{silicon: } 1s^2 2s^2 2p^6 3s^2 3p^2$$

The sum of all the superscripts should be equal to the number of electrons in the atom (the atomic number, Z). Electronic configurations can also be written for cations and anions.

PERIODIC TABLE

If chemistry students had to learn the individual properties of the 100+ elements that are now known, it would be a monumental and frustrating task. Early scientists had to do just that. Then several scientists began to notice trends in the properties of the elements and began grouping them in various ways. In 1871 a Russian chemist, Dmitri Mendeleev, introduced the first modern periodic table. He arranged the elements in terms of increasing atomic mass. He then arranged columns so that elements that had similar properties were in the same column. Mendeleev was able to predict the existence and properties of elements that were then unknown. Later, when they were discovered, Mendeleev's predictions were remarkably accurate. Later the periodic table was rearranged to sequence the elements by increasing atomic number, not mass. The result is the modern periodic table shown in Figure 3.4.

This is not the periodic table supplied on the AP exam. This one has family and period labels. Become familiar with these labels so that you can effectively use the unlabeled one.

Each square on this table represents a different element and contains three bits of information. The first is the element symbol. You should become familiar with the symbols of the commonly used elements. Secondly, the square lists the atomic number of the element, usually centered above the element. This number represents the number of protons in the element's nucleus. The atomic number will always be a

Periodic Table of the Elements

Classical group numbers	IA	IIA	IIIB	IVB	VB	VIB	VIIB	VIII			IB	IIB	IIIA	IVA	VA	VIA	VIIA	0
Modern group numbers	1	2	3	4	5	6	7	8	9	10	11	12	13	14	15	16	17	18

Periods

Period																		
1	1 H 1.0080																	2 He 4.00260
2	3 Li 6.941	4 Be 9.01218											5 B 10.81	6 C 12.011	7 N 14.0067	8 O 15.9994	9 F 18.9984	10 Ne 20.179
3	11 Na 22.9898	12 Mg 24.305											13 Al 26.9815	14 Si 28.086	15 P 30.9738	16 S 32.06	17 Cl 35.453	18 Ar 39.948
4	19 K 39.102	20 Ca 40.08	21 Sc 44.9559	22 Ti 47.90	23 V 50.9414	24 Cr 51.996	25 Mn 54.9380	26 Fe 55.847	27 Co 58.9332	28 Ni 58.71	29 Cu 63.546	30 Zn 65.37	31 Ga 69.72	32 Ge 72.59	33 As 74.9216	34 Se 78.96	35 Br 79.904	36 Kr 83.80
5	37 Rb 85.4678	38 Sr 87.62	39 Y 88.9059	40 Zr 91.22	41 Nb 92.9064	42 Mo 95.94	43 Tc 98.9062	44 Ru 101.07	45 Rh 102.9055	46 Pd 106.4	47 Ag 107.868	48 Cd 112.40	49 In 114.82	50 Sn 118.69	51 Sb 121.75	52 Te 127.60	53 I 126.9045	54 Xe 131.30
6	55 Cs 132.9055	56 Ba 137.34	* 57 La 138.9055	72 Hf 178.49	73 Ta 180.9479	74 W 183.85	75 Re 186.2	76 Os 190.2	77 Ir 192.22	78 Pt 195.09	79 Au 196.9665	80 Hg 200.59	81 Tl 204.37	82 Pb 207.2	83 Bi 208.9806	84 Po (210)	85 At (210)	86 Rn (222)
7	87 Fr (223)	88 Ra 226.0254	† 89 Ac (227)	104 Unq (261)	105 Unp (262)	106 Unh (263)												

Atomic number — 1 H (Symbol) 1.0080 (Atomic Mass)

*	58 Ce 140.12	59 Pr 140.9077	60 Nd 144.24	61 Pm (145)	62 Sm 150.4	63 Eu 151.96	64 Gd 157.25	65 Tb 158.9254	66 Dy 162.50	67 Ho 164.9303	68 Er 167.26	69 Tm 168.9342	70 Yb 173.04	71 Lu 174.97
†	90 Th 232.0381	91 Pa 231.0359	92 U 238.029	93 Np 237.0482	94 Pu (242)	95 Am (243)	96 Cm (247)	97 Bk (249)	98 Cf (251)	99 Es (254)	100 Fm (253)	101 Md (256)	102 No (254)	103 Lr (257)

Figure 3.4 The periodic table.

whole number. Thirdly, the square lists the element's mass, normally centered underneath the element symbol. This number is not a whole number because it is the weighted average (taking into consideration abundance) of all the masses of the naturally occurring isotopes of that element. The mass number can never be less than the atomic number.

Arrangement of Elements

There are a number of different groupings of elements on the periodic table that may be utilized. One system involves putting the elements into three main groups—metals, nonmetals, and metalloids (semimetals). Look at Figure 3.4. Notice the heavy stair-stepped line starting at boron (B) and going downward and to the right. The elements to the left of that line (except for H, Ge, and Sb) are classified as metals. **Metals** are normally solids (mercury being an exception), shiny, and good conductors of heat and electricity. They can be hammered into thin sheets (malleable) and extruded into wires (ductile). Chemically, metals tend to lose electrons in reactions.

Elements bordering the stair-stepped line (B, Si, Ge, As, Sb, Te) are classified as metalloids. **Metalloids** have properties of both metals and nonmetals. Their unusual electrical properties make them valuable in the semiconductor and computer industry.

The rest of the elements, to the right of the metalloids, are called nonmetals. **Nonmetals** have properties that are often the opposite of metals. Some are gases, are poor conductors of heat and electricity, are neither malleable nor ductile and tend to gain electrons in their chemical reactions.

Another way to group the elements on the periodic table is in terms of periods and groups (families). **Periods** are the horizontal rows which have consecutive atomic numbers. The periods are numbered from 1 to 7. Elements in the same period do not have similar properties in terms of reactions.

The vertical rows on the periodic table are called **groups** or **families.** They may be labeled in one of two ways. An older and still more widely used system is to label each group with a Roman numeral and a letter, A or B. The groups that are labeled with an A are called the main-group elements, while the B groups are called the **transition elements.** Two other horizontal groups, the **inner transition elements,** have been pulled out of the main body of the periodic table. The Roman numeral at the top of the main-group families indicates the number of **valence** (outermost shell) electrons in that element. Valence electrons are normally considered to be only the s and p electrons in the outermost energy level. The transition elements (B groups) are filling d-orbitals, while the inner transition elements are filling f-orbitals.

Four main-group families are given special names, which you should remember:

!

- IA group   alkali metals
- IIA group   alkaline earth metals
- VIIA group   halogens
- VIIIA group   noble gases

A new way to label the groups is to number consecutively the groups from left to right, 1–18. This method is newer than the other labeling method, and it has not gained wide use. Most teacher and chemists still prefer and use the older method.

Trends in Periodic Properties

The size of an atom is generally determined by the number of energy levels occupied by electrons. This means that as we move from top to bottom within a group, the size of the atom increases due to the increased number of shells containing electrons. As we move from left to right within a period (within the same valence shell), the atomic size decreases somewhat due to the increased attraction of the nucleus for the electrons. This increased attraction is related to the increasing number of protons within the nucleus. A cation is smaller than the neutral atom because, in many cases, an entire energy shell has been removed. An anion is larger than the corresponding neutral atom because the nuclear attraction is spread over additional electrons. As the number of electrons changes, so will the electron–electron repulsion. The greater the electron–electron repulsion, the larger the species becomes, and vice versa.

The overall attraction that an electron experiences is called the **effective nuclear charge.** This is less than the actual nuclear charge because other electrons interfere with attraction of the protons.

The **ionization energy** (**IE**) is the energy needed to remove completely an electron from an atom. It may be expressed in terms of 1 atom or a mole of atoms. Energy is required in this process to overcome the attraction of the nucleus for the electrons. The closer the electrons are to the nucleus, the more energy is required to break the attraction. Therefore, ionization energy tends to decrease from top to bottom within a group, since the valence electrons (the first ones to be lost) are farther away from the nucleus. Ionization energies increase from left to right in a period because the atoms are getting slightly smaller and, therefore, the nucleus has a greater attraction for the electrons. The ionization potential for the removal of a second electron is greater in all cases than the first because the electron is being pulled away from a positively charged ion, and the attraction is greater than from a neutral atom.

The **electron affinity** is the energy change that results from adding an electron to an atom or ion. The trends in electron affinity are not quite as regular as size or ionization energy. In general, electron affinity increases from left to right within a period and decreases from top to bottom within a group.

OXIDATION NUMBERS

Oxidation numbers are bookkeeping numbers that allow chemists to do things like balance redox equations. Don't confuse oxidation numbers with the charge on an ion. Oxidation numbers are assigned to elements in their natural state or in compounds using the following rules:

• The oxidation number of an element in its elemental form (i.e., H_2, Au, Ag, N_2) is zero.
• The oxidation number of a monoatomic ion is equal to the charge on the ion. The oxidation number of Mg^{2+} is +2. Note that the charge is written with number first, then sign; for oxidation numbers it is sign, then number.
• The sum of all the oxidation numbers of all elements in a neutral molecule is zero. The sum of all oxidation numbers of a polyatomic ion is equal to the charge on the ion.
• The alkali metal ions have an oxidation number of +1 in compounds.
• The alkaline earth metals have an oxidation number of +2 in compounds.
• The oxidation number of hydrogen in compounds is +1, except it is −1 when combined with metals or boron in binary compounds.

- The oxidation number of halogens in their compounds is −1 except when combined with another halogen above it on the periodic table, or with oxygen.
- The oxidation number of oxygen is −2 except for peroxides, in which it is −1.

Determine the oxidation number of sulfur in sulfuric acid, H_2SO_4. The sum of all the oxidation numbers must equal zero, since this is a neutral compound. The oxidation numbers of hydrogen (+1) and oxygen (−2) are known, so the oxidation number of sulfur can be determined:

$$2(+1) + ? + 4(-2) = 0$$
$$H_2SO_4$$

The oxidation number of sulfur in this compound must be +6.

NOMENCLATURE OVERVIEW

This overview covers some of the rules for naming simple inorganic compounds. There are additional rules, and some exceptions to these rules. The first part of this overview discusses the rules for deriving a name from a chemical formula. In many cases, the formula may be determined from the name by reversing this process. The second part examines situations in which additional information is needed to generate a formula from the name of a compound. The transition metals present some additional problems; thus, there is a section covering transition metal nomenclature and coordination compounds.

Binary Compounds

Binary compounds are compounds that consist of only two elements. Some binary compounds have special names, and these special names supersede any of the rules given below. H_2O is water, NH_3 is ammonia, and CH_4 is methane. All other binary compounds have a name with a suffix *ide*. Binary compounds may be subdivided into metal type, nonmetal type, and acid type.

(a) **Metal type** These binary compounds begin with metals. The metal is given first in the formula. In general, metals are the elements on the left-hand side of the periodic table, and the nonmetals are on the right-hand side. Hydrogen, a nonmetal, is an exception to this generalization.

First name the metal, then name the nonmetal with the suffix *ide*. Examples:

Formula	Name
Na_2O	sodium oxide
$MgCl_2$	magnesium chloride

The ammonium ion (NH_4^+) is often treated as a metal, and its compounds are named under this rule. Thus, NH_4Cl is named ammonium chloride.

(b) **Nonmetal type** These binary compounds have formulas that begin with a nonmetal. Prefixes are used to indicate the number of each atom present. No prefixes are used for hydrogen. Naming the compounds can best be explained using the following examples:

Formula	Name
CO	carbon monoxide
SO_3	sulfur trioxide
P_4O_{10}	tetraphosphorus decoxide

Carbon monoxide is one of the very few cases where the prefix *mono* is used. In general, you should not use *mono* in any other compound.

Some of the prefixes used to denote the numbers of atoms in the compound are listed below:

Number of atoms	Prefix
1	mono
2	di
3	tri
4	tetra
5	penta
6	hexa
7	hepta
8	octa
9	nona
10	deca

On many occasions the *a* or *o* is dropped for oxides, so they read as pentoxide, heptoxide, or monoxide.

In normal nomenclature, the nonmetal prefixes are not used if a metal present. One of the few exceptions to this is MnO_2, sometimes called manganese dioxide.

(c) **Acid type** These binary compounds have formulas that begin with hydrogen. If the compound is not in solution, the naming is similar to that of the metal type. If the compound is dissolved in H_2O, indicated by (*aq*), the compound takes on the prefix *hydro* and the suffix *ic*. If the compound is not in solution, the state of matter should be shown as follows:

$$HCl(g), \quad HF(l)$$

If the formula has no designation of phase or water, either name may be used. Examples for naming these compounds are:

Formula	Name
$HCl(g)$	hydrogen chloride
$H_2S(g)$	hydrogen sulfide
$HCl(aq)$	*hydro*chlor*ic* acid
$H_2S(aq)$	*hydro*sulfur*ic* acid
HCl	hydrogen chloride or *hydro*chlor*ic* acid
H_2S	hydrogen sulfide or *hydro*sulfur*ic* acid

HCN (hydrocyanic acid) is named using these rules. However, in this case, it does not matter if the phase or water is indicated.

Ternary Compounds

Ternary compounds are those containing three or more elements. If the first element in the formula is hydrogen, it is usually classified as an acid. If the formula contains oxygen in addition to the hydrogen, the compound is usually classified as an oxyacid. In general, if the first element in the formula is not hydrogen, the compound is classified as a salt.

Ternary acids are usually named with the suffixes *ic* or *ous*. The exceptions are the acids derived from ions with an *ide* suffix (see HCN in the preceding section). These acids undergo many reactions to form salts, compounds of a metal, and the ion of an acid. The ions from the acids H_2SO_4 and HNO_3 are SO_4^{2-}, NO_3^-. If an acid name has the suffix *ic,* the ion of this acid has a name with the suffix *ate*. If an acid name has the suffix *ous*, the ion has a name with the suffix *ite*. Salts have the same suffixes as the suffixes of the ions. The difference between the acid with a suffix *ic* and the acid with the suffix *ous* can many times be determined by visual inspection of the formula. The acid with the suffix *ous* usually has one less oxygen atom than the acid with the suffix *ic*. Examples:

Formula	Name of the acid	Formula	Name of the acid
H_2SO_4	sulfuric acid	HNO_3	nitric acid
H_2SO_3	sulfurous acid	HNO_2	nitrous acid

When the ternary compound is not an acid, the first element is usually a metal. In these cases, the name of the compound is simply the name of the metal followed by the name of the ion. The ammonium ion is treated as a metal in these cases.

The following are examples:

Acid formula	Acid name	Ion name	Salt formula	Salt name
H_2SO_4	sulfuric acid	sulfate ion	Na_2SO_4	sodium sulfate
H_2SO_3	sulfurous acid	sulfite ion	Na_2SO_3	sodium sulfite
HNO_3	nitric acid	nitrate ion	KNO_3	potassium nitrate
HNO_2	nitrous acid	nitrite ion	KNO_2	potassium nitrite
H_3PO_4	phosphoric acid	phosphate ion	$(NH_4)_3PO_4$	ammonium phosphate

Writing Formulas

To write the formula from the name of a binary compound containing only nonmetals, simply write the symbols for the separate atoms with the prefixes converted to subscripts.

In all compounds, the total charge must be zero. There are NO exceptions. Thus, to determine the formula in those cases where no prefixes are given, it is necessary to have some idea what the individual charges are. The species with the positive charge is listed and named first; this is followed by the species with the negative charge. Subscripts may be needed to make sure the sum of the valences will equal zero. Examples:

1. Magnesium oxide

$$Mg^{2+}O^{2-} \quad = +2 - 2 = 0$$

2. Sodium oxide

$$Na^{+1}O^{2-} \quad = +1 - 2 = -1 \quad \text{thus a subscript is needed}$$
$$Na_2^{2(+1)}O^{-2} \quad = 2(+1) - 2 = 0$$

3. Aluminum oxide

$$Al^{3+}O^{2-} \quad = +3 - 2 = +1 \quad \text{thus a subscript is needed}$$
$$Al_2^{2(+3)}O_3^{3(-2)} \quad = 2(+3) + 3(-2) = 0$$

If a polyatomic ion must be increased to achieve zero charge, parentheses should be used. An example of this is shown as:

$$NH_4^{+}SO_4^{2-} \quad = +1 - 2 = -1$$
$$(NH_4)_2^{2(+1)}SO_4^{-2} \quad = 2(+1) - 2 = 0$$

One way of predicting the values of the subscripts is to crisscross the valences. This is not a rule of nomenclature, but for practice purposes in this exercise it will be referred to as the crisscross rule. It works most of the time and therefore is worth considering. Example:

$Al^{3+}O^{2-}$ crisscross the 2 from the oxygen charge to the aluminum and the 3 from the aluminum charge to the oxygen

$Al_2^{3+}O_3^{2-}$

If the crisscross rule is applied, you should reduce the formula if possible. For example:

$Mn^{4+}O^{2-}$ crisscrosses to
Mn_2O_4 this should be reduced to
MnO_2

If a formula is given, the crisscross rule can be reversed to give the valences:

Al_2O_3
$Al_2^{3+}O_3^{2-}$

As a first approximation, the valences of the representative elements may be predicted from their position on the periodic table. Hydrogen and the metals have positive charges beginning with +1 on the left and increasing by one as you proceed to the right on the periodic table (skipping the transition metals). Nonmetals begin with 0 in the rightmost column of the periodic table and decrease by 1 as you move to the left on the periodic table. Metalloids may be treated as metals or nonmetals. Examples are:

Na^+ Al^{3+} Pb^{4+} I^- Se^{2-} N^{3-}

Transition Metals

Many transition metals and the group of six elements centered around lead on the periodic table have more than one valence. The valence of these metals in a compound must be known before the compound can be named. Modern nomenclature rules indicate the valence of one of these metals with a Roman numeral suffix (Stock notation). Older nomenclature rules used different suffixes to indicate the charge. Examples:

1. $FeCl_3$

   $Fe^{3+}Cl_3^{1-}$ (crisscross rule)

   The compound is named iron(III) chloride or ferric chloride.

2. $FeCl_2$

If chloride is −1, two chloride ions are −2. Fe has a valence of +2, to give a total charge of zero. The name is iron(II) chloride or ferrous chloride.

3. MnO_2

Mn^{4+} (found previously)

The name would be manganese(IV) oxide, although it is often named manganese dioxide.

The Roman numeral suffix is part of the name of the metal. Thus iron(III) is one word.

Stock notation should be used for all metals that have a variable valence. This includes almost all the transition elements and the elements immediately around lead on the periodic table. Stock notation is often omitted for Zn, Cd, and Ag.

The valences of some common metals and acids are listed in Appendix C.

Coordination Compounds

Coordination compounds are a type of complex. In general, a complex may be recognized because it is enclosed in square brackets [ ]. The square brackets are omitted when the actual structure of the complex is uncertain.

A complex is composed of a central atom, normally a metal, surrounded by atoms or groups of atoms called ligands. One way of forming a complex is illustrated below:

$$Ni^{2+} + 6\,H_2O \rightarrow \left[Ni(H_2O)_6\right]^{2+}$$

In this reaction the metal behaves as a Lewis acid and accepts a pair of electrons from the Lewis base (ligand). In this case the ligand is water, with the oxygen atom donating one of its lone pairs to the nickel. The oxygen atom is called the donor atom. In this complex, there are six donor atoms.

A complex may be ionic or neutral. An ionic complex is called a complex ion. A neutral complex is a type of coordination compound. The only difference in naming coordination compounds or complex ions is that anionic complex ions have an *ate* suffix.

A coordination compound may contain more than one complex ion or material that is not part of the complex, but it must have an overall neutral charge. Examples of coordination compounds are: $[Pt(NH_3)_2Cl_2]$, $K_2[Mn(C_2O_4)_3]$, and $[Ni(H_2O)_6]SO_4$.

When writing formulas the metal (central atom) is *always* listed first within the brackets. However, when writing names the metal name is *always* given last. Any material not listed within the brackets is named separately.

Examples:

$[Ru(NH_3)_5(N_2)]Cl_2$	coordination compound
$[Ru(NH_3)_5(N_2)]^{2+}$	complex ion (cationic)
$[PtNH_3Cl_2(C_5H_5N)]$	coordination compound
$[IF_6]^-$	complex ion (anionic) (the name must end in -ate)
$K[IF_6]$	coordination compound (same -ate ending)

If everything in the formula is enclosed within one set of brackets, the entire name will be one word. If there is material outside the brackets, this outside material is named separately.

Just as with simpler compounds, cations are always named before anions. Thus, a cationic complex would be the first word in the name, and an anionic complex would be the last word in a name (with an *ate* ending).

Examples:

$[Ni(H_2O)_4Cl_2]$	tetraaquadichloronickel(II)
$[Co(NH_3)_6]Cl_3$	hexaamminecobalt(III) chloride
$K_2[PtCl_4]$	potassium tetrachloroplatinate(II)

When naming a complex, or when writing the formula for a complex, the ligands are listed alphabetically. Again, do not forget that metals are first in the formula and last in the name.

The names of anionic ligands always end in an *o*. Neutral ligands are basically unchanged. Two common exceptions in the case of neutral ligands are NH_3 = ammine (note the double m), and H_2O = aqua. Other common ligands and their names are listed in Appendix C.

Multiple identical ligands have prefixes added to designate the number of such ligands:

2	di-	5	penta-	8	octa-
3	tri-	6	hexa-	9	nona-
4	tetra-	7	hepta-	10	deca-

Examples:

$[Co(NH_3)_6]Cl_3$	hexamminecobalt(III) chloride
$[Cr(NO)_4]$	tetranitrosylchromium(0)

If the ligand name contains a prefix or begins with a vowel (except ammine and aqua), alternate prefixes should be used:

2	bis-	5	pentakis-	8	octakis-
3	tris-	6	hexakis-	9	nonakis-
4	tetrakis-	7	heptakis-	10	decakis-

When using the alternate prefixes, it is common practice to enclose the name of the ligand within parentheses. Either type of prefix is added after the ligands have been alphabetized.

Examples:

$[Cr(en)_3]Cl_3$	Tris(ethylenediamine)chromium(III) chloride
$K_2[Ge(C_2O_4)_3]$	Potassium tris(oxalato)germanate

Anionic complexes always have names ending in *ate*. This will require a change in the name of the metal. Thus, aluminum would become aluminate, and zinc would become zincate. The only exceptions to this are some of the metals whose symbols are based on Latin or Greek names. These exceptions are:

Metal (Greek or Latin name)	Symbol	Anionic name
copper (cuprum)	Cu	cuprate
silver (argentum)	Ag	argentate
gold (aurum)	Au	aurate
iron (ferrum)	Fe	ferrate
tin (stannum)	Sn	stannate
lead (plumbum)	Pb	plumbate

Examples:

$K[Au(CN)_4]$	potassium tetracyanoaurate(III)
$(NH_4)_2[PbCl_6]$	ammonium hexachloroplumbate(IV)

If the metal ion may exist in more than one oxidation state, this oxidation state should be listed, in Roman numerals, *immediately* after the name of the metal ion. The Roman numeral is enclosed in parentheses and is considered part of the same word, and not a separate grouping. If the metal only occurs in one oxidation state, no such indicator is used. This notation is known as the Stock system.

EXPERIMENTAL

Experiments involving the basic material covered in this chapter have been placed in the in-depth chapters throughout the remainder of this book.

COMMON MISTAKES TO AVOID

Between the two of us, we have almost 60 years of teaching experience. We've seen a lot of student mistakes. We will try to steer you clear of the most common ones.

1. Always show your units in mathematical problems.
2. In the conversion from °F to °C, be sure to subtract 32 from the Fahrenheit temperature first, then multiply by $\frac{5}{9}$.
3. In the conversion from °C to °F, be sure to multiply the Celsius temperature by $\frac{9}{5}$, then add 32.
4. There is no degree sign used for Kelvin.
5. Only consider measured values for significant figures.
6. When considering whether or not zeroes to the right of the last non-zero digit are significant, pay attention to whether or not there is a decimal point.
7. Only round off your final answer, not intermediate calculations.
8. In working problems, be sure that your units cancel.
9. If you are solving for cm, for example, be sure you end up with cm and not 1/cm.
10. Make sure your answer is a reasonable one.
11. Don't confuse the mass number (A) with the atomic number (Z).
12. When considering valence electrons, only the s and p electrons are considered.
13. Don't put more than 2 electrons in any individual orbital.
14. Always fill lowest energy levels first.
15. Half fill orbitals of equal energy before pairing up the electrons.
16. In writing the electronic configuration of an atom, make sure you use the correct filling order.
17. Don't confuse the periods with the groups on the periodic table.
18. Don't confuse ionization energy with electron affinity.
19. Don't confuse oxidation numbers with ionic charge.
20. In naming compounds, don't confuse metal and nonmetal type binary compounds. Prefixes are used only with nonmetal types.
21. Be careful when using the crisscross rule to reduce the subscripts to their lowest whole number ratio.

3 REVIEW QUESTIONS

This is where you get a chance to practice your multiple-choice test-taking skills. Take it as a test, within the specified time frame. We have attempted to word the questions as closely as possible to the way the questions will be worded on the AP Exam.

Answer the following questions. You have 25 minutes. You may not use a calculator.

1. In most of its compounds, this element exists as a monatomic cation.

   A. O
   B. Cl
   C. Na
   D. N
   E. I

2. This element may form a compound with the formula $CaXO_4$.

   A. Se
   B. Cl
   C. P
   D. Na
   E. He

3. Which of the following elements may occur in the largest number of different oxidation states?

   A. C
   B. F
   C. O
   D. Ca
   E. Na

4. Choose the group that does not contain isotopes of the same element.

		Number of protons	Number of neutrons
A.	Atom I	18	18
	Atom II	18	19
B.	Atom I	25	30
	Atom II	25	31
C.	Atom I	37	42
	Atom II	37	41
D.	Atom I	82	126
	Atom II	82	128
E.	Atom I	18	18
	Atom II	17	18

5. Which of the following groups has the species correctly listed in order of increasing radius?

   A. Mg^{2+}, Ca^{2+}, Ba^{2+}
   B. K^+, Na^+, Li^+
   C. Br^-, Cl^-, F^-
   D. Na, Mg, Al
   E. Fe, Fe^{2+}, Fe^{3+}

6. Which of the following elements has the lowest electronegativity?

   A. C
   B. K
   C. Al
   D. I
   E. F

7. Choose the ion with the largest ionic radius.

   A. F^-
   B. Al^{3+}
   C. K^+
   D. O^{2-}
   E. I^-

8. What is the name of the energy change when a gaseous atom, in the ground-state, adds an electron?

   A. ionization energy
   B. sublimation energy
   C. atomization energy
   D. electron affinity
   E. lattice energy

9. The following ionization energies are reported for element X. (All the values are in kJ/mol.)

First	Second	Third	Fourth	Fifth
500	4560	6910	9540	13400

   Based on the above information, the most likely identity of X is

   A. Mg
   B. Cl
   C. Al
   D. Na
   E. Si

10. In general, as the atomic numbers increase within a period, the atomic radius

    A. first increases and then decreases
    B. increases
    C. first decreases and then increases
    D. does not change
    E. decreases

Choose one of the following elements for questions 11 and 12.

    A. chlorine
    B. gold
    C. sodium
    D. radon
    E. radium

11. This element is a reactive gas.

12. This element is an unreactive metal.

13. Which of the following represents the correct formula for potassium trisoxalatoferrate(III)?

    A. $P_3[Fe(C_2O_4)_3]$
    B. $K_3[Fe(C_2O_4)_3]$
    C. $KFe_3(C_2O_4)_3$
    D. K_3FeO_3
    E. $K_3[Fe_3(C_2O_4)_3]$

14. Which of the following substances will produce a colorless aqueous solution?

    A. $Zn(NO_3)_2$
    B. $CuSO_4$
    C. $K_2Cr_2O_7$
    D. $Co(NO_3)_2$
    E. $NiSO_4$

15. This element is a liquid at room temperature.

    A. Hg
    B. Th
    C. Na
    D. Cl
    E. Co

Choose from the following elements for questions 16–18.

    A. K
    B. Ga
    C. Fe
    D. Mg
    E. Al

16. This element is present in chlorophyll.

17. This element forms a protective oxide coating.

18. This element is used to improve the conductivity of germanium.

19. Which of the following aqueous solutions is blue?

    A. $CuSO_4$
    B. $Cr_2(SO_4)_3$
    C. $NiSO_4$
    D. $ZnSO_4$
    E. $CoSO_4$

20. In order to separate two substances by fractional crystallization, the two substances must differ in which of the following?

    A. solubility
    B. specific gravity
    C. vapor pressure
    D. viscosity
    E. freezing point

21. In a flame test, copper compounds impart which of the following colors to a flame?

    A. red
    B. orange
    C. blue to green
    D. violet
    E. yellow

22. What should you do if you spill sulfuric acid on the countertop?

    A. Neutralize the acid with vinegar.
    B. Sprinkle solid NaOH on the spill.
    C. Neutralize the acid with $NaHCO_3$ solution.
    D. Neutralize the acid with an Epsom salt ($MgSO_4$) solution.
    E. Use paper towels to soak up the acid.

23. Which of the following can be achieved by using a visible-light spectrophotometer?

    I. Detecting the presence of isolated double bonds.
    II. Finding the concentration of a $KMnO_4$ solution.
    III. Running a flame test to determine if Na^+ or K^+ in a solution.

A. III only
B. II only
C. I only
D. II and III
E. I and II

24. You are given an aqueous solution of NaCl. The simplest method for the separation of NaCl from the solution is

A. evaporation of the solution to dryness
B. centrifuging the solution

C. osmosis of the solution
D. electrolysis of the solution
E. filtration of the solution

25. The determination that atoms have small, dense nuclei is attributed to

A. Rutherford
B. Becquerel
C. Einstein
D. Dalton
E. Bohr

ANSWERS AND EXPLANATIONS

Here are the answers and explanations to the review questions. Go through each one. Don't memorize; strive to understand.

1. **C.** All the other elements are nonmetals. Nonmetals usually form monatomic anions.

2. **A.** The element can not be a metal (Na) or a noble gas (He). A nonmetal that can have a +6 oxidation state is needed. P has a maximum of +5. Cl may be +5 or +7. Se, in column 6A, can easily be +6.

3. **A.** Based on their positions on the periodic table:

C	+4 to −4
F	−1 and 0 (element)
O	−2 to 0
Ca	+2 and 0
Na	+1 and 0

4. **E.** Isotopes MUST have the same number of protons. Different isotopes have different numbers of neutrons.

5. **A.** All the others are in decreasing order.

6. **B.** In general, the element furthest from F on the periodic table will have the lowest electronegativity. There are exceptions.

7. **E.** The very large iodine atom gains an electron to make it even larger.

8. **D.** The definition of electron affinity is: the energy change when a ground-state gaseous atom adds an electron.

9. **D.** The more electrons removed, the higher the values should be. The large increase between the first and second ionization energies indicates a change in electron shell. The element, X, only has 1 valence electron. This is true for Na. For the other elements the numbers of valence electrons are: Mg—2; Cl—7; Al—3; and Si—4.

10. **E.** The increase in the number of protons in the nucleus has a greater attraction for the electrons being added in the same energy level. Thus, the electrons are pulled closer to the nucleus and the size slightly decreases.

11. **A.** The only other gas is radon, and it is inert.

12. **B.** Sodium and radium are metals on the left side of the periodic table. Metals on the left side of the periodic table are very reactive.

13. **B.** Ferrate(III) means Fe^{3+}, while trisoxalato means $(C_2O_4)_3^{6-}$; three potassiums are needed to balance the charge.

14. **A.** B is blue; C is orange; D is pink to red; and Ni is green.

15. **A.** Chlorine is a gas; all the others are solids.

16. **D.**

17. **E.**

18. **B.**

19. **A.** B is purple; C is green; D is colorless; and E is pink to red.

20. **A.** Fractional crystallization works because the less soluble material separates first.

21. **C.** A could be Li or Sr; B is Ca; D is K; and E is Na.

22. **C.** A weak base with water to disperse the heat is the best choice.

23. **B.** A solution containing a colored substance is needed.

24. **A.** Separation of materials in solution is normally not simple. *Reverse osmosis* would also work.

25. **A.**

3 FREE-RESPONSE QUESTIONS

(One of the authors, Dr. Langley, has been an AP free-response grader for years. Here are some free-response questions for practice. You have 10 minutes. You may not use a calculator.)

Use the periodic table and other information concerning bonding and electronic structure to explain the following observations.

a. The radii of the iron cations are less than that of an iron atom, and Fe^{3+} is smaller than Fe^{2+}.

b. When moving across the periodic table from Li to Be to B, the first ionization energy increases from Li to Be, then drops for B. B is greater than Li.

c. The electron affinity of F is higher than the electron affinity of O.

d. The following observations have been made about the lattice energy and ionic radii of the compounds listed below. Compare NaF to CaO, and then compare CaO to BaO. All of the solids adopt the same crystal structure.

Compound	Ionic radius of cation (pm)	Ionic radius of anion (pm)	Lattice energy (kJ/mole)
NaF	116	119	911
CaO	114	126	3566
BaO	149	126	3202

ANSWERS AND EXPLANATIONS

✓ Notice that all the answers are very short. Do not try to fill all the space provided on the exam. You score points by saying specific things, not by the bulk of material. The graders look for certain keywords or phrases.

a. The observed trend of radii is: $Fe > Fe^{2+} > Fe^{3+}$. There is an increase in the effective nuclear charge in this series. As electrons are removed, the repulsion between the electrons decreases. The larger the effective nuclear charge, the more the electrons are pulled towards the nucleus and the smaller the atom or ion becomes. Give yourself 1 point for "effective nuclear charge," and 1 point for the rest of this argument.

b. When moving across a period on the periodic table, the value of the effective nuclear charge increases with atomic number. This causes a general increase from Li to Be to B. This effective nuclear charge argument is worth 1 point.

   The even higher value of Be (greater than B) is due to the increased stability of the electron configuration of Be. Beryllium has a filled s-subshell. Filled subshells have an increased stability, and additional energy is required to pull an electron away. Give yourself 1 point for the filled subshell discussion.

c. The effective nuclear charge in F is greater than the effective nuclear charge in O. This causes a greater attraction of the electrons. You get 1 point for this answer.

d. Because all the solids adopt the same structure, the structure is irrelevant. The sizes of the anions are similar; thus, anion size arguments are not important.

   Two factors, other than structure, are important here. The two compounds with the highest lattice energies contain divalent ions (+2 or −2) while NaF contains univalent ions (+1 or −1). The higher the charge is, the greater attraction between the ions is. The lattice energy increases as the attraction increases. You get 1 point for correctly discussing the charges.

The difference between the CaO and BaO values is because the larger the ion is, the lower the attraction (greater separation). The lower attraction leads to a lower lattice energy. This size argument will get you 1 point.

Total your points. The maximum is 7.

RAPID REVIEW

 Here is a brief review of the most important points in the chapter. If something sounds unfamiliar, study it in the chapter and your textbook.

- Know the metric measurement system and some metric/English conversions.

- Know how to convert from any one of the Fahrenheit/Celsius/Kelvin temperature scales to the other two.

- The density is mass per unit volume.

- Know how to determine the number of significant figures in a number, the rules for how many significant figures to be shown in the final answer, and the round-off rules.

- Know how to set up problems using the factor label method.

- Know the differences between a solid, liquid, and gas at both the macroscopic and microscopic levels.

- Know what part Dalton, Thompson, Millikan, and Rutherford had in the development of the atomic model.

- Know the three basic subatomic particles—proton, neutron, and electron—their symbols, mass in amu, and their location.

- Isotopes are atoms of the same element that have differing numbers of neutrons.

- Electrons are located in major energy levels called shells. Shells are divided into subshells, and there are orbitals for each subshell.

- Know the electron capacity of each orbital (always 2).

- Be able to write both the energy level diagram and the electronic configuration of an atom or ion by applying both the Aufbau build-up principle and Hund's rule.

- Know how the modern periodic table was developed, including the differences between Mendeleev's table and the current table.

- Periods are the horizontal rows on the periodic table; the elements have properties unlike the other members of the period.

- Groups or families are the vertical rows on the periodic table; the elements have similar properties.

- Know the properties of metals, nonmetals, and metalloids and which elements on the periodic table belong to each group.

- Valence electrons are outer-shell electrons.

- The IA family is known as the alkali metals; the IIAs are the alkaline earth metals; the VIIAs are the halogens; and the VIIIAs are the noble gases.

- Know why atoms get larger as we go from top to bottom in a group and slightly smaller as we move from left to right on the periodic table.

- Ionization energy is the energy it takes to remove an electron from a gaseous atom or ion. It decreases from top to bottom and increases from left to right on the periodic table. Much the same trend is noted for electron affinity, the energy change that takes place when an electron is added to a gaseous atom or ion.

- Oxidation numbers are bookkeeping numbers. Know the rules for assigning oxidation numbers.

- Be able to name binary metal type and nonmetal type compounds, as well as ternary compounds, oxyacids, simple coordination compounds, etc.

Chapter 4

Reactions and Periodicity

KEYWORDS AND EQUATIONS

There are no keywords or equations specific to this chapter on the AP exam.

INTRODUCTION

Chemistry is the world of chemical reactions. Chemical reactions power our society, our environment, and our bodies. Some chemical species called **reactants** get converted into different substances called **products.** During this process energy changes take place. It takes energy to break old bonds. Energy is released when new bonds are formed. Does it take more energy to break the bonds than is released in the formation of the new bonds? If so, energy will have to be supplied constantly to convert the reactants into products. This type of reaction is said to be **endothermic,** absorbing energy. If more energy is released than needed to break the old bonds, then the reaction is said to be **exothermic,** releasing energy. The chemical reactions that provide the energy for our world are exothermic reactions. In Chapter 7, Thermodynamics, you can read in more depth about the energy changes that occur during reaction.

Reactions occur because of collisions. One chemical species collides with another at the right place, transfers enough energy, and a chemical reaction occurs. Such reactions can be very fast or very slow. In Chapter 12, Kinetics, you can study how reactions occur and the factors that affect the speed of reactions. But in this chapter we will review the balancing of chemical equations and discuss the general types of chemical reactions that are commonly found on the AP exam.

GENERAL ASPECTS OF CHEMICAL REACTIONS AND EQUATIONS

Balancing Chemical Equations

The authors assume that because you are preparing to take the AP exam, you already have been exposed to balancing chemical equations. We will quickly review this topic and point out some specific aspects of balancing equations as the different types of chemical reactions are discussed.

The balanced chemical equation provides a lot of information. It shows what chemical species are the reactants and what species are the products. It may also indicate in what state of matter the reactants and products exist. Special conditions of temperature, catalysts, and the like may be placed over or under the reaction arrow. And, very importantly, the coefficients (the integers in front of the chemical species) indicate the number of each reactant that is used and the number of each product that is formed. These coefficients may stand for individual atoms or molecules, or they may represent large numbers of them called moles (see Chapter 5 for a discussion of moles). The basic idea behind the balancing of equations is the **Law of Conservation of Matter,** which says that in ordinary chemical reactions matter is neither created nor destroyed. The number of each type of atom that is put into the reaction as a reactant must equal the number of that type product atoms. This requires adjusting the reactant and product coefficient—balancing the equation. And when finished, the coefficients should be in the lowest whole number ratio.

Most equations are balanced by inspection. This means basically a trial-and-error, methodical approach to adjusting the coefficients. One procedure that works well is to balance the diatomic (two-atom) homonuclear (same nucleus) element last. Chemical species that fall into this category include O_2, H_2, N_2, Cl_2, etc.—in other words, the diatomic elements. This procedure is especially useful when balancing combustion reactions. Know the diatomic elements: H_2, O_2, N_2, F_2, Cl_2, Br_2, and I_2. If a problem states that oxygen gas was used, then knowing that oxygen exists as the diatomic element is absolutely necessary in balancing the equation correctly.

Periodic Relationships

The periodic table can give us many clues as to the type of reaction that is taking place. One general rule that is covered in more detail in Chapter 9, Bonding, is that metals react with nonmetals to form ionic compounds, and that nonmetals react with other nonmetals to form covalent compounds. Also, because of the wonderful arrangement of the periodic table, the members of a family or group (a vertical grouping) all react basically in the same fashion. Many times, in reactions that involve the loss of electrons, the reaction rates (speed) increase as we proceed from top to bottom in a family. Recall also that the noble gases (VIIIA) undergo very few reactions. Other specific periodic aspects will be discussed in the various reaction sections.

GENERAL PROPERTIES OF AQUEOUS SOLUTIONS

Many of the reactions that you will study occur in aqueous solution. Water is called the universal solvent because it dissolves so many substances. It readily dissolves ionic compounds as well as polar covalent compounds because of its polar nature. Ionic compounds that dissolve in water (dissociate) form **electrolyte** solutions—solutions that conduct electrical current due to the presence of ions. The ions can attract the polar water molecules to them and form a layer of bound waters. This process is called **solvation.**

Even though many ionic compounds dissolve in water, many do not. If the attraction of the oppositely charged ions in the solid is greater that the attraction of the polar water molecules to the ions, the salt will not dissolve to an appreciable amount.

As mentioned before, certain covalent compounds, like alcohols, readily dissolve in water if they are polar. Since water is polar and these covalent compounds are also polar, water will act as a solvent for them. (The general rule of solubility is "Like dissolves like.") Compounds like alcohols are called **nonelectrolytes,** substances that do not conduct an electrical current when dissolved in water. However certain covalent compounds, like acids, will **ionize** in water, that is, form ions:

$$HCl(aq) \rightarrow H^+(aq) + Cl^-(aq)$$

There are several ways of representing reactions that occur in water. Suppose, for example, that we were writing the equation to describe the mixing of a lead(II) nitrate with a sodium sulfate solution and showing the resulting formation of lead(II) sulfate solid. One type of equation that can be written is the **molecular equation,** in which both the reactants and products are shown in the undissociated form:

$$Pb(NO_3)_2(aq) + Na_2SO_4(aq) \rightarrow PbSO_4(s) + 2\,NaNO_3(aq)$$

Molecular equations are quite useful when doing reaction stoichiometry problems (see Chapter 5).

Showing the soluble reactants and products in the form of ions yields the **ionic equation** (sometimes called the total ionic equation):

$$Pb^{2+}(aq) + 2\,NO_3^-(aq) + 2\,Na^+(aq) + SO_4^{2-}(aq)$$

$$\rightarrow PbSO_4(s) + 2\,Na^+(aq) + 2\,NO_3^-(aq)$$

Writing the equation in the ionic form shows clearly which species are really reacting and which are not. In the example above, the Na⁺ and

NO_3^- appear on both sides of the equation. They do not react, but are simply there in order to maintain electrical neutrality of the solution. Ions like this, which are not actually involved in the chemical reaction taking place, are called **spectator ions.**

The **net ionic equation** is written by dropping out the spectator ions and showing only those chemical species that are involved in the chemical reaction:

$$Pb^{2+}(aq) + SO_4^{2-}(aq) \rightarrow PbSO_4(s)$$

This net ionic equation focuses on the reactants only. It indicates that an aqueous solution containing Pb^{2+} [any solution, not just $Pb(NO_3)_2(aq)$] will react with any solution containing the sulfate ion to form insoluble lead(II) sulfate. If this equation form is used, the spectator ions involved will not be known; in most cases this is not a problem because the focus is the general reaction and not the specific one.

PRECIPITATION REACTIONS

Precipitation reactions involve the formation of an insoluble compound, a **precipitate,** from the mixing of two soluble compounds. Precipitation reactions normally occur in aqueous solution. The example above that was used to illustrate molecular equations, ionic equations, etc. was a precipitation reaction. A solid, lead(II) sulfate was formed from the mixing of the two aqueous solutions. To predict whether precipitation will occur if two solutions are mixed you must:

1. be able to write the correct chemical formulas from the names. In the AP exam reaction section, names are given instead of formulas.
2. be able to write the reactants in their ionic form, as in the ionic equation example above. Be sure, however, that you do not try to break apart molecular compounds, such as most organic compounds.
3. know and be able to apply the following solubility rules, by combining the cation of one reactant with the anion of the other in the correct formula ratio and determining the solubility of the proposed product. Then do the same thing for the other anion/cation combination.

Learn the following solubility rules.

Salts containing the following ions are normally **soluble:**

- All salts of group IA (Li^+, Na^+, etc.) and the ammonium ion (NH_4^+) are *soluble.*
- All salts containing nitrate (NO_3^-), acetate (CH_3COO^-), and perchlorates (ClO_4^-) are *soluble.*

- All chlorides (Cl^-), bromides (Br^-), and iodides (I^-) are *soluble* <u>except</u> those of Cu^+, Ag^+, Pb^{2+}, and Hg_2^{2+}.
- All salts containing sulfate (SO_4^{2-}) are *soluble* <u>except</u> those of Pb^{2+}, Ca^{2+}, Sr^{2+}, and Ba^{2+}.

Salts containing the following ions are normally **insoluble:**

- Most carbonates (CO_3^{2-}) and phosphates (PO_4^{3-}) are *insoluble* <u>except</u> those of Group IA and the ammonium ion.
- Most sulfides (S^{2-}) are *insoluble* <u>except</u> those of Group IA and IIA and the ammonium ion.
- Most hydroxides (OH^-) are *insoluble* <u>except</u> those of Group IA, calcium, strontium, and barium.
- Most oxides (O^{2-}) are *insoluble* <u>except</u> for those of Group IA, and calcium, strontium, and barium, which react with water.

Let's see how one might apply these rules. Suppose a solution of lead(II) nitrate is mixed with a solution of sodium iodide. Predict what will happen.

Write the formulas:

$$Pb(NO_3)_2(aq) + NaI(aq) \rightarrow$$

Convert to the ionic form:

$$Pb^{2+}(aq) + 2\,NO_3^-(aq) + Na^+(aq) + I^-(aq) \rightarrow$$

Predict the possible products by combining the cation of one reactant with the anion of the other and vice versa:

$$PbI_2 + NaNO_3$$

Apply the solubility rules to the two possible products:

$PbI_2(s)$	*Insoluble,* therefore a precipitate will form
$NaNO_3(aq)$	*Soluble,* no precipitate will form

Complete the chemical equation and balance it:

$$Pb(NO_3)_2(aq) + 2\,NaI(aq) \rightarrow PbI_2(s) + 2\,NaNO_3(aq)$$

If neither possible product is insoluble, then the reaction would be listed as NR (No Reaction). If at least one insoluble product is formed, the reaction is sometimes classified as a **double displacement (replacement)** or **metathesis reaction.**

OXIDATION-REDUCTION REACTIONS

Oxidation-reduction reactions, commonly called **redox** reactions, are an extremely important category of reaction. Redox reactions include combustion, corrosion, respiration, photosynthesis, and the reactions involved in electrochemical cells (batteries). Chapter 14 goes into depth about electrochemistry and redox reactions.

The AP free-response booklet includes a table of half-reactions which you may use for help during this part of the exam. Alternatively, you may wish to memorize the common oxidizing and reducing agents.

Redox is a term that stands for reduction and oxidation. **Reduction** is the gain of electrons, and **oxidation** is the loss of electrons. For example, suppose a piece of zinc metal is placed in a solution containing the Cu^{2+} cation. Very quickly a reddish solid forms on the surface of the zinc metal. That substance is copper metal. At the molecular level the zinc metal is losing electrons to form the Zn^{2+} cation, and the Cu^{2+} cation is gaining electrons to form copper metal. These two processes can be shown as:

$$Zn \rightarrow Zn^{2+}(aq) + 2\ e^- \quad (oxidation)$$
$$Cu^{2+}(aq) + 2\ e^- \rightarrow Cu \quad (reduction)$$

The electrons that are being lost by the zinc metal are the same electrons that are being gained by the cupric ion. The zinc metal is being oxidized, and the cupric ion is being reduced.

Something must cause the oxidation (taking the electrons), and that substance is called the **oxidizing agent** (the reactant being reduced). In the example above, the oxidizing agent is the Cu^{2+} ion. The reactant undergoing oxidation is called the **reducing agent** because it is furnishing the electrons that are being used in the reduction half-reaction. Zinc metal is the reducing agent above. The two half reactions, oxidation and reduction, can be added together to give the overall redox reaction. The electrons must cancel—that is, there must be the same number of electrons lost as electrons gained:

$$Zn + Cu^{2+}(aq) + 2\ e^- \rightarrow Zn^{2+}(aq) + 2\ e^- + Cu \ or$$

$$Zn + Cu^{2+}(aq) \rightarrow Zn^{2+}(aq) + Cu$$

In these redox reactions there is a simultaneous loss and gain of electrons. In the oxidation reaction (commonly called a half-reaction) electrons are being lost, but in the reduction half-reaction those same electrons are being gained. So, in redox reactions electrons are being exchanged as reactants are being converted into products. This electron exchange may be direct, as when copper metal plates out on a piece of zinc, or it may be indirect, as in an electrochemical cell (battery).

Another way to determine what is being oxidized and what is being reduced is by looking at the change in oxidation numbers of the reactant species. (See Chapter 3 for a discussion of oxidation numbers and how to calculate them.) Oxidation is indicated by an increase in oxidation number. In the example above, the Zn metal went from an oxidation state of zero to +2. Reduction is indicated by a decrease in oxidation number. Cu^{2+} went from an oxidation state of +2 to zero. To figure out if a reaction is a redox reaction, write the net ionic equation. Then determine the oxidation numbers of each element in the reaction. If one or more elements have changed oxidation number, it is a redox reaction.

A number of specific categories of reactions that are commonly taught fall under the general category of redox reactions. We will discuss each of these in turn.

Combination Reactions

Combination reactions are reactions in which two or more reactants (elements or compounds) combine to form one product. Although these reactions may be of a number of different types, some types are definitely redox reactions. These include reactions of metals with nonmetals to form ionic compounds, and the reaction of nonmetals with other nonmetals to form covalent compounds.

$$2\ K(s) + Cl_2(g) \rightarrow 2\ KCl(s)$$

$$2\ C(s) + O_2(g) \rightarrow 2\ CO(g)$$

Decomposition Reactions

Decomposition reactions are reactions in which a compound breaks down into two or more simpler substances. Although not all decomposition reactions are redox reactions, many are. Examples include thermal decomposition reactions, such as the common laboratory experiment of generating oxygen by heating potassium chlorate:

$$2\ KClO_3(s) \xrightarrow{\ \Delta\ } 2\ KCl(s) + 3\ O_2(g)$$

and **electrolysis**, in which an electrical current is used to decompose a compound into its elements:

$$2\ H_2O(l) \xrightarrow{\ \text{electricity}\ } 2\ H_2(g) + O_2(g)$$

Single Displacement Reactions

Single displacement (replacement) reactions are reactions in which atoms of an element replace the atoms of another element in a compound. All single replacement reactions are redox reactions, since the element (in a zero oxidation state) becomes an ion. Most single displacement reactions can be categorized into one of three types of reactions:

- a metal displacing a metal ion from solution
- a metal displacing hydrogen gas (H_2) from an acid or from water
- one halogen replacing another halogen

For the first two types, a table of metals relating their ease of oxidation to each other is useful in predicting what displaces what. Table 4.1 shows the **activity series for metals,** which lists metals in order of decreasing ease of oxidation.

Elements on this activity series can displace ions of metals *lower* on the list. If, for example, one placed a piece of zinc metal into a solution containing $Cu(NO_3)_2(aq)$, the Zn would replace the Cu^{2+} cation:

$$Zn(s) + Cu(NO_3)_2(aq) \rightarrow Zn(NO_3)_2(aq) + Cu(s)$$

If a piece of copper metal was placed in a $Zn(NO_3)_2(aq)$ solution, there would be no reaction since copper is lower than zinc on the activity series. This table also allows us to predict that if sodium metal is placed in water, it will displace hydrogen, forming hydrogen gas.

$$2 Na(s) + 2 H_2O(l) \rightarrow 2 NaOH(aq) + H_2(g)$$

The group IA and IIA elements on the activity table will displace hydrogen from water, but not the other metals shown. All the metals above hydrogen will react with acid solution to produce hydrogen gas:

$$Co(s) + 2 HCl(aq) \rightarrow CoCl_2 + H_2(g)$$

Table 4.1 Activity Series of Metals in Aqueous Solution

Metal	Oxidation Reaction	
Lithium	$Li \rightarrow Li^+ + e^-$	
Potassium	$K \rightarrow K^+ + e^-$	
Barium	$Ba \rightarrow Ba^{2+} + 2e^-$	
Calcium	$Ca \rightarrow Ca^{2+} + 2e^-$	
Sodium	$Na \rightarrow Na^+ + e^-$	
Magnesium	$Mg \rightarrow Mg^{2+} + 2e^-$	
Aluminum	$Al \rightarrow Al^{3+} + 3e^-$	
Manganese	$Mn \rightarrow Mn^{2+} + 2e^-$	
Zinc	$Zn \rightarrow Zn^{2+} + 2e^-$	
Chromium	$Cr \rightarrow Cr^{3+} + 3e^-$	Ease of oxidation increases
Iron	$Fe \rightarrow Fe^{2+} + 2e^-$	
Cobalt	$Co \rightarrow Co^{2+} + 2e^-$	
Nickel	$Ni \rightarrow Ni^{2+} + 2e^-$	
Tin	$Sn \rightarrow Sn^{2+} + 2e^-$	
Lead	$Pb \rightarrow Pb^{2+} + 2e^-$	
Hydrogen	$H_2 \rightarrow 2H^+ + 2e^-$	
Copper	$Cu \rightarrow Cu^{2+} + 2e^-$	
Silver	$Ag \rightarrow Ag^+ + e^-$	
Mercury	$Hg \rightarrow Hg^{2+} + 2e^-$	
Platinum	$Pt \rightarrow Pt^{2+} + 2 e^-$	
Gold	$Au \rightarrow Au^{3+} + 3 e^-$	

Halogen reactivity decreases as one goes from top to bottom in the periodic table, so that a separate activity series for the halogens can be developed:

$$F_2$$
$$Cl_2$$
$$Br_2$$
$$I_2$$

The above series would indicate that if chlorine gas were bubbled through a KI(aq) solution, the chlorine would displace the iodide ion:

$$Cl_2(aq) + 2\ KI(aq) \rightarrow 2\ KCl(aq) + I_2(aq)$$

Combustion Reactions

Combustion reactions are redox reactions in which the chemical species rapidly combines with oxygen and usually emits heat and light. Reactions of this type are extremely important in our society as the sources of heat energy. Complete combustion of carbon yields carbon dioxide, and complete combustion of hydrogen yields water. The complete combustion of **hydrocarbons**—organic compounds containing only carbon and hydrogen—yields carbon dioxide and water:

$$2\ C_2H_6(g) + 7\ O_2(g) \rightarrow 4\ CO_2(g) + 6\ H_2O(g)$$

If the compound also contains oxygen, such as in alcohols, ethers, and the like, the products are still carbon dioxide and water:

$$2\ CH_3OH(l) + 3\ O_2(g) \rightarrow 2\ CO_2(g) + 4\ H_2O(g)$$

If the compound contains sulfur, the complete combustion produces sulfur dioxide, SO_2:

$$2\ C_2H_6S(g) + 9\ O_2(g) \rightarrow 4\ CO_2(g) + 6\ H_2O(g) + 2\ SO_2(g)$$

If nitrogen is present, it will normally form nitrogen gas, N_2.
In balancing any of these combustion reactions, it is helpful to balance the oxygen last.

COORDINATION COMPOUNDS

When a salt is dissolved in water, the metal ions, especially transition metal ions, form a complex ion with water molecules. A complex ion is composed of a metal ion bonded to two or more molecules or ions called ligands. For example, suppose $Cr(NO_3)_3$ is dissolved in water. The Cr^{3+} cation attracts water molecules to form the complex ion $Cr(H_2O)_6^{3+}$. In this complex ion, water acts as the ligand. If ammonia is added to this solution, the ammonia can displace the water molecules from the complex:

$$Cr(H_2O)_6^{3+}(aq) + 6\ NH_3(aq) \Leftrightarrow Cr(NH_3)_6^{3+}(aq) + 6\ H_2O(l)$$

The **coordination number** is the number of ligands that can bond covalently to the metal ion in the complex ion. As seen above, the coordination number for Cr^{3+} is 6. Coordination numbers are normally 2, 4, or 6.

ACID–BASE REACTIONS

Acids and bases are extremely common, as are the reactions between acids and bases. Chapter 13, Equilibrium, describes the equilibrium reactions of acids and bases as well as some information concerning acid–base titration. After you finish this section, you may want to review the acid–base part of Chapter 13.

Properties of Acids, Bases, and Salts

At the macroscopic level acids taste sour, may be damaging to the skin, react with substances called **indicators** to change their color, and react with bases to yield salts. Bases taste bitter, feel slippery, also react with indicators to change their color, and react with acids to form salts.

At the microscopic level, **acids** are defined as proton (H^+) donors (Brønsted-Lowry Theory) or electron-pair acceptors (Lewis theory). **Bases** are defined as proton (H^+) acceptors (Brønsted-Lowry Theory) or electron-pair donors (Lewis Theory). Consider the gas-phase reaction between hydrogen chloride and ammonia:

$$HCl(g) + :NH_3(g) \rightarrow HNH_3^+Cl^-$$

HCl is the acid because it is donating an H^+, and the H^+ will accept an electron pair from ammonia. Ammonia is the base, accepting the H^+ and furnishing an electron pair with which the H^+ will bond via coordinate covalent bonding. **Coordinate covalent bonds** are covalent bonds in which one of the atoms furnishes both of the electrons for the bond. After the bond is formed, it is identical to a covalent bond formed by donation of one electron by both of the bonding atoms.

Acids and bases may be **strong,** dissociating completely, or **weak,** partially dissociating and forming an equilibrium system. (See Chapter 13 for the details on weak acids and bases.) Strong acids include:

1. chloric, $HClO_3$
2. hydrobromic, HBr

3. hydrochloric, HCl
4. hydroiodic, HI
5. nitric, HNO_3
6. perchloric, $HClO_4$
7. sulfuric, H_2SO_4

Strong bases include:

!

1. alkali metal (Group IA) hydroxides (LiOH, NaOH, etc.)
2. calcium, strontium, and barium hydroxides

Most acids and bases not on the lists above are weak and will establish an equilibrium system when placed into water.

Some salts have acid–base properties. When dissolved in water ammonium chloride, NH_4Cl, will dissociate, and the ammonium ion will act as a weak acid, donating a proton. The strong bases listed above are all compunds that dissolve yielding the hydroxide ion (which is really the base, not the salt).

Certain oxides can have acid or basic properties. Many oxides of metals that have a +1 or +2 charge are called basic oxides because they will react with water to form a basic solution:

$$Na_2O(s) + H_2O(l) \rightarrow 2\,NaOH(aq)$$

Many nonmetal oxides are called acidic oxides because they react with water to form an acidic solution:

$$CO_2(g) + H_2O(l) \rightarrow H_2CO_3(aq)$$

$H_2CO_3(aq)$, named carbonic acid, is the reason that most carbonated beverages are slightly acidic. It is also the reason that soft drinks have fizz, because carbonic acid can revert to carbon dioxide and water.

Another salt-like group of compounds that have acid–base properties are the hydrides of the alkali metals and calcium, strontium, and barium. These hydrides will react with water to form the hydroxide ion and hydrogen gas:

$$NaH(s) + H_2O(l) \rightarrow NaOH(aq) + H_2(g)$$

Acid–Base Reactions

In general, strong acids react with strong bases to form water and a salt. The salt will depend upon what acid and base are used:

$$HCl(aq) + NaOH(aq) \rightarrow H_2O(l) + NaCl(aq)$$

$$HNO_3(aq) + KOH(aq) \rightarrow H_2O(l) + KNO_3(aq)$$

Reactions of this type are called **neutralization reactions.**

Acids will react with carbonates and acid carbonates to form carbonic acid, which then decomposes to carbon dioxide and water:

$$2\,HCl(aq) + Na_2CO_3(aq) \rightarrow 2\,NaCl(aq) + H_2CO_3(aq)$$

$$\downarrow$$

$$CO_2(g) + H_2O(l)$$

Sulfites behave similarly, producing sulfur dioxide and water. Sulfides will yield hydrogen sulfide gas.

Ammonia gas may be generated by the reaction of a compound containing the ammonium ion, NH_4^+, with a base.

Acid–Base Titrations

A common laboratory application of acid–base reactions is a titration. A **titration** is a laboratory procedure in which a solution of known concentration is used to determine the concentration of an unknown solution. For strong acid/strong base titration systems, the net ionic equation is:

$$H^+(aq) + OH^-(aq) \rightarrow H_2O(l)$$

For example, suppose you want to determine the molarity of an HCl solution. You would pipette a known volume of the acid into a flask and add a couple drops of a suitable acid–base indicator. An indicator that is commonly used is phenolphthalein, which is colorless in an acid solution and pink in a base solution. You would then fill a buret with a strong base solution (NaOH is commonly used) of known concentration. The buret allows you to add small amounts of the base solution to the acid solution in the flask. The course of the titration can also be followed by the use of a pH meter. Initially the pH of the solution will be low since it is an acid solution. As the base is added and neutralization of the acid takes place, the pH will slowly rise. Small amounts of the base are added until one reaches the equivalence point. The **equivalence point** is that point in the titration where the moles of H^+ in the acid solution have been exactly neutralized with the same number of moles of OH^-:

$$\text{moles } H^+ = \text{moles } OH^- \qquad \text{at the equivalence point}$$

For the titration of a strong acid with a strong base, the pH rapidly rises in the vicinity of the equivalence point. Then, as the tiniest amount of bases is added in excess, the indicator turns pink. This is called the **endpoint** of the titration. In an accurate titration the endpoint will be as close to the equivalence point as possible. For simple titrations that do not use a pH meter, it is assumed that the endpoint and the equivalence point are the same, so that:

$$\text{moles } H^+ = \text{moles } OH^- \qquad \text{at the endpoint}$$

After the equivalence point has been passed, the pH is greater than 7 (basic solution) and begins to level out somewhat. Figure 4.1 shows the shape of the curve for this titration.

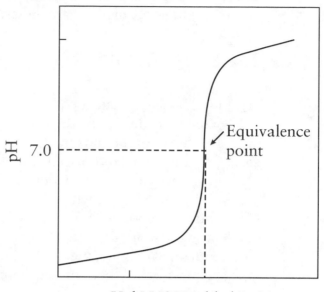

pH 7.0

Equivalence point

Vol NaOH added (mL)

Figure 4.1 Titration of a strong acid with a strong base.

Reaction stoichiometry can then be used to solve for the molarity of the acid solution. See Chapter 5 for a discussion of solution stoichiometry.

An unknown base can be titrated with an acid solution of known concentration. A major difference is that the pH will be greater than 7 initially and will decrease as the titration proceeds. Another major difference is that the indicator will start off pink and the color will vanish at the endpoint.

EXPERIMENTAL

Laboratory experiments involving reactions are usually concerned with both the reaction and the stoichiometry.

You need some idea of the balanced chemical equation. In the case of an acid–base reaction, an acid reacts with a base. The acid supplies H^+ and the base accepts the H^+. If the acid is diprotic, such as H_2SO_4, it can donate two H^+ to two bases.

The key to any reaction experiment is the moles. The moles may be calculated from various measurements. A sample may be weighed on a balance to give the mass, and the moles calculated with the formula weight. The mass of a substance may also be determined using a volume measurement combined with the density. The volume of a solution may be measured with a pipette, or calculated from the final and initial readings from a buret. This volume, along with the molarity, may be used to calculate the moles present. The volume, temperature, and pressure of a gas may be measured and used to calculate the moles of a gas. You should be very careful on the AP exam to distinguish the values that you measure and those that you calculate.

The moles of any substance in a reaction may be converted to the moles of any other substance through a calculation using the balanced chemical equation. Other calculations are presented in the stoichiometry chapter.

COMMON MISTAKES TO AVOID

1. In balancing chemical equations <u>don't</u> change the subscripts in the chemical formula, just the coefficients.
2. Molecular compounds may ionize; ionic compounds dissociate.
3. In writing ionic and net ionic equations, show the chemical species as they actually exist in solution.
4. In writing ionic and net ionic equations, don't break apart covalently bonded compounds unless they are acids that are ionizing.
5. Know the solubility rules.
6. Oxidizing and reducing agents are reactants, not products.
7. The products of the complete combustion of a hydrocarbon are carbon dioxide and water. This is also true if oxygen is also present, but if there is some other element present, such as sulfur, you will have something in addition to carbon dioxide and water.
8. If a substance that does not contain carbon, such as elemental sulfur, undergoes complete combustion, <u>no</u> carbon dioxide can be formed.
9. If an alcohol like methanol, CH_3OH, is dissolved in water, no hydroxide ion, OH^-, will be formed.
10. Know the strong acids and bases.
11. HF is not a strong acid.
12. In titration calculations, you must consider the reaction stoichiometry.
13. Be sure to indicate the charges on ions correctly.

3 REVIEW QUESTIONS

You have 20 minutes. You may not use a calculator.

1. ___ $Fe(OH)_2(s)$ + ___ $H_3PO_4(aq)$
→ ___ $Fe_3(PO_4)_2(s)$ + ___ $H_2O(l)$

After the above chemical equation is balanced, the lowest whole-number coefficient for water is:

A. 3
B. 1
C. 9
D. 6
E. 12

Choose one of the following for questions 2–4.

A. Cu^{2+}
B. CO_3^{2-}
C. Fe^{3+}
D. Al^{3+}
E. Pb^{2+}

2. This ion will generate gas bubbles when hydrochloric acid is added.

3. When dilute sodium hydroxide is added to a solution containing this ion, the ion initially gives a white precipitate. The precipitate will dissolve in excess sodium hydroxide.

4. Aqueous solutions of this ion are blue.

5. Which of the following best represents the net ionic equation for the reaction of lead(II) carbonate with concentrated hydrochloric acid?

   A. $Pb_2CO_3 + 2 H^+ + Cl^- \rightarrow Pb_2Cl + CO_2 + H_2O$
   B. $PbCO_3 + 2 H^+ + 2 Cl^- \rightarrow PbCl_2 + CO_2 + H_2O$
   C. $PbCO_3 + 2 H^+ \rightarrow Pb^{2+} + CO_2 + H_2O$
   D. $PbCO_3 + 2 Cl^- \rightarrow PbCl_2 + CO_3^{2-}$
   E. $PbCO_3 + 2 HCl \rightarrow PbCl_2 + CO_2 + H_2O$

6. A sample of copper metal is reacted with dilute nitric acid in the absence of air. After the reaction, which of the final products are present?

   A. $CuNO_3$ and H_2O
   B. $Cu(NO_3)_3$, NO, and H_2O
   C. $Cu(NO_3)_2$, NO, and H_2O
   D. $CuNO_3$, H_2O, and H_2
   E. $Cu(NO_3)_2$, NO, and H_2

7. Which of the following is the correct net ionic equation for the reaction of acetic acid with potassium hydroxide?

   A. $HC_2H_3O_2 + OH^- \rightarrow C_2H_3O_2^- + H_2O$
   B. $HC_2H_3O_2 + K^+ \rightarrow KC_2H_3O_2 + H^+$
   C. $HC_2H_3O_2 + KOH \rightarrow KC_2H_3O_2 + H_2O$
   D. $H^+ + OH^- \rightarrow H_2O$
   E. $C_2H_3O_2^- + KOH \rightarrow KC_2H_3O_2 + OH^-$

8. Which of the following is the correct net ionic equation for the addition of aqueous ammonia to a precipitate of silver chloride?

   A. $AgCl + 4 NH_3 \rightarrow [Ag(NH_3)_4]Cl$
   B. $AgCl + 2 NH_4^+ \rightarrow [Ag(NH_4)_2]^{3+} + Cl^-$
   C. $AgCl + NH_4^+ \rightarrow Ag^+ + NH_4Cl$
   D. $AgCl + NH_3 \rightarrow Ag^+ + NH_3Cl$
   E. $AgCl + 2 NH_3 \rightarrow [Ag(NH_3)_2]^+ + Cl^-$

9. Potassium metal will react with water to release a gas and a potassium compound. Which of the following statements is false?

   A. The solution is acidic.
   B. The gas is hydrogen.
   C. The potassium compound is water-soluble.
   D. The potassium compound will react with hydrochloric acid.
   E. A solution of the potassium compound will form a precipitate when added to a $FeCl_2$ solution.

10. A sample is tested for the presence of the Hg_2^{2+} ion. This ion, along with others, may be precipitated with chloride ion. If Hg_2^{2+} is present in the chloride precipitate, a black color will form upon treatment with aqueous ammonia. The net ionic equation for the formation of this black color is:

    A. $Hg_2Cl_2 + 2 NH_3 + 2 H_2O \rightarrow 2 Hg + 2 NH_4^+ + 2 Cl^- + 2 OH^-$
    B. $Hg_2Cl_2 + 2 NH_3 \rightarrow 2 Hg + 2 NH_3Cl$
    C. $Hg_2Cl_2 + 2 NH_4^+ \rightarrow 2 Hg + 2 NH_4Cl$
    D. $Hg_2Cl_2 + NH_4^+ \rightarrow 2 Hg + NH_4Cl + Cl^-$
    E. $Hg_2Cl_2 + 2 NH_3 \rightarrow Hg + HgNH_2Cl + NH_4^+ + Cl^-$

11. Which of the following solids is not soluble in water, but soluble in dilute nitric acid (HNO_3)?

    A. NaOH
    B. $BaCO_3$
    C. AgCl
    D. $(NH_4)_3PO_4$
    E. $FeCl_2$

12. How many moles of $Pb(NO_3)_2$ must be added to 0.10 L of a solution that is 1.0 M in $MgCl_2$ and 1.0 M in KCl to precipitate the compound $PbCl_2$?

    A. 1.0 mol
    B. 0.20 mol
    C. 0.50 mol
    D. 0.15 mol
    E. 0.30 mol

13. When 50.0 mL of 1.0 M $AgNO_3$ is added to 50.0 mL of 0.50 M HCl, a precipitate of AgCl forms. After the reaction is complete, what is the concentration of silver ions in the solution?

    A. 0.50 M
    B. 0.0 M
    C. 1.0 M
    D. 0.25 M
    E. 0.75 M

14. A student mixes 50.0 mL of 0.10 M $Pb(NO_3)_2$ solution with 50.0 mL of 0.10 M KCl. A white precipitate forms, and the concentration of the chloride ion becomes very small. Which of the following correctly places the concentrations of the remaining ions in order of decreasing concentration?

    A. $[NO_3^-] > [Pb^{2+}] > [K^+]$
    B. $[NO_3^-] > [K^+] > [Pb^{2+}]$
    C. $[K^+] > [NO_3^-] > [Pb^{2+}]$
    D. $[Pb^{2+}] > [NO_3^-] > [K^+]$
    E. $[Pb^{2+}] > [K^+] > [NO_3^-]$

15. A solution is prepared for qualitative analysis. The solution contains the following ions: Co^{2+}, Pb^{2+}, and Al^{3+}. Which of the following will cause no observable reaction?

    A. Dilute $NH_3(aq)$ is added.
    B. Dilute $K_2CrO_4(aq)$ is added.
    C. Dilute $HNO_3(aq)$ is added.
    D. Dilute $K_2S(aq)$ is added.
    E. Dilute $HCl(aq)$ is added.

16. Chlorine gas is bubbled through a colorless solution, and the solution turns reddish. Adding a little methylene chloride to the solution extracts the color into the methylene chloride layer. Which of the following ions may be present in the original solution?

    A. Cl^-
    B. F^-
    C. SO_4^{2-}
    D. Na^+
    E. Br^-

17. The addition of concentrated NaOH(aq) to a 1.0 M $(NH_4)_2SO_4$ solution will result in which of the following observations?

    A. The solution becomes neutral.
    B. The formation of a brown precipitate takes place.
    C. Nothing happens because the two solutions are immiscible.
    D. The odor of ammonia will be detected.
    E. An odorless gas forms and bubbles out of the mixture.

18. Which of the following solutions will give a yellow precipitate when a 0.1 M Na_2CrO_4 solution is added to a 0.1 M solution of the ion listed?

    A. $K^+(aq)$
    B. $Pb^{2+}(aq)$
    C. $NO_3^-(aq)$
    D. $OH^-(aq)$
    E. $NH_4^+(aq)$

ANSWERS AND EXPLANATIONS

1. **D.** The balanced equation is:

$$3\ Fe(OH)_2(s) + 2\ H_3PO_4(aq) \rightarrow Fe_3(PO_4)_2(s) + 6\ H_2O(l)$$

2. **B.** Carbonates produce carbon dioxide gas in the presence of an acid.

3. **D.** Aluminum hydroxide initially forms, and then it dissolves to form the $Al(OH)_4^-$ ion.

4. **A.** Aqueous solutions of Cu^{2+} are normally blue. Iron ions give a variety of colors, but are normally colorless, or nearly so, in the absence of complexing agents. All the others are colorless.

5. **B.** Lead(II) carbonate is insoluble, so its formula should be left as $PbCO_3$. Hydrochloric acid is a strong acid, so it should be written as separate H^+ and Cl^- ions. Lead(II) chloride, $PbCl_2$, is insoluble, and carbonic acid, H_2CO_3, quickly decomposes to CO_2 and H_2O.

6. **C.** The balanced chemical equation is:

$$3\ Cu + 8\ HNO_3 \rightarrow 3\ Cu(NO_3)_2 + 2\ NO + 4\ H_2O$$

Copper is below hydrogen on the activity series, so H_2 cannot be formed by this acid metal reaction. Nitric acid is an oxidizing agent that will oxidize copper to Cu^{2+} giving $Cu(NO_3)_2$.

7. **A.** Acetic acid is a weak acid; it should appear as $HC_2H_3O_2$. Potassium hydroxide is a strong base, so it will separate into K^+ and OH^- ions. The potassium ion is a spectator ion, and is left out of the net ionic equation.

8. **E.** Aqueous ammonia contains NH_3. The reaction produces the silver–ammonia complex, $[Ag(NH_3)_2]^+$.

9. **A.** The reaction is:

$$2\ K + 2\ H_2O \rightarrow 2\ KOH + H_2$$

KOH is a water soluble strong base, not an acid. As a strong base, it will react with an acid. Iron(II) hydroxide, $Fe(OH)_2$, is insoluble and will precipitate.

10. **E.** Aqueous ammonia contains NH_3. The charges on each side of the reaction arrow must be equal.

11. **B.** Neither B nor C is soluble in water. Only B will react will nitric acid, and dissolve.

12. **D.** The magnesium chloride gives 0.20 mol of chloride ion, and the potassium chloride gives 0.10 mol of chloride ion. A total of 0.30 mol of chloride will react with 0.15 mol of lead, because two Cl^- require 1 Pb^{2+}.

13. **D.** The HCl will react with one-half the silver to halve the concentration. The doubling of the volume halves the concentration a second time.

14. **B.** All the potassium and nitrate ions remain in solution. However, two nitrate ions are produced per solute formula as opposed to only one potassium ion. The lead and potassium would be equal, but some of the lead is precipitated as $PbCl_2$.

15. **C.** Ammonia, as a base, will precipitate the metal hydroxides. Chromate, sulfide, and chloride ions will precipitate one or more of the ions.

16. **E.** Chlorine is an oxidizing agent. It is capable of oxidizing Br^-, giving reddish Br_2.

17. **D.** The following reaction occurs: $NH_4^+(aq) + OH^-(aq) \rightarrow NH_3(g) + H_2O(l)$

18. **B.** The precipitate is $PbCrO_4$.

FREE-RESPONSE QUESTIONS

You have 5 minutes. You may not use a calculator.

Choose FIVE of the following eight questions. Place your answers in the appropriate boxes. There is no extra credit for answering more than five. Formulas for reactants and products are needed. Do not include formulas for substances that remain unchanged during the reaction. It is not necessary to balance the equations. Unless otherwise noted, assume all the reactions occur in aqueous solution. If a substance is present as ions in solution, write its formula as an ion.

Example: Hydrochloric acid is added to a lead(II) nitrate solution.

$$Pb^{2+} + Cl^- \rightarrow PbCl_2$$

a. Excess sodium hydroxide is added to an aluminum sulfate solution.

b. An acidified iron(II) sulfate solution is added to a potassium permanganate solution.

c. Metallic strontium is added to warm water.

d. Solid manganese(IV) oxide is added to concentrated hydrochloric acid.

e. Gaseous sulfur dioxide is passed over solid calcium oxide.

f. Potassium chlorate is heated strongly.

g. Dichlorine heptaoxide is mixed with water.

h. A lead(II) nitrate solution is mixed with an ammonium sulfate solution.

ANSWERS AND EXPLANATIONS

Only five answers will be graded. If you do more than five, only the first five will be graded. No extra points will be given for doing more than five. There are no extra points for balancing.

a. $OH^- + Al^{3+} \rightarrow Al(OH)_4^-$

You get 1 point for the correct formulas for the reactants and 2 points for the correct formula for the product. No variations are allowed.

b. $Fe^{2+} + H^+ + MnO_4^- \rightarrow Fe^{3+} + Mn^{2+} + H_2O$

You get 1 point if you have the correct formula for one of the reactants. You get 2 points for the correct formulas of ALL the products, but only 1 point if any formula is missing or wrong. No variations are allowed.

c. $Sr + H_2O \rightarrow Sr^{2+} + OH^- + H_2$

You get 1 point if you have the correct formula for one of the reactants. You get 2 points for the correct formulas of ALL the products, but only 1 point if any formula is missing or wrong. No variations are allowed.

d. $MnO_2 + H^+ + Cl^- \rightarrow Mn^{2+} + Cl_2 + H_2O$

You get 1 point if you have the correct formula for one of the reactants. You get 2 points for the correct formulas of ALL the products, but only 1 point if any formula is missing or wrong. No variations are allowed.

e. $SO_2 + CaO \rightarrow CaSO_3$

You get 1 point for the correct formulas for the reactants and 2 points for the correct formula for the product. No variations are allowed.

f. $KClO_3 \rightarrow KCl + O_2$

You get 1 point if you have the correct formula for the reactant. You get 2 points for the correct formulas of ALL the products, but only 1 point if any formula is missing or wrong. No variations are allowed.

g. $Cl_2O_7 + H_2O \rightarrow HClO_4$

You get 1 point for the correct formulas for the reactants and 2 points for the correct formula for the product. No variations are allowed.

h. $Pb^{2+} + SO_4^{2-} \rightarrow PbSO_4$

You get 1 point for the correct formulas for the reactants and 2 points for the correct formula for the product. No variations are allowed.

There are a maximum of 15 points possible.

RAPID REVIEW

- In chemical reactions, reactants get converted into new substances called products.
- Energy may be released in a reaction (exothermic) or absorbed (endothermic).
- Chemical equations are balanced by adding coefficients in front of the chemical species; the number of each type of atom must be the same on both the right and left sides of the arrow.
- Water is the universal solvent, dissolving a wide variety of polar substances.

- Electrolytes are substances that conduct an electrical current when dissolved in water or melted; nonelectrolytes do not.

- Most ions in solution attract and bind a layer of water molecules in a process called solvation.

- Some molecular compounds, like acids, ionize in water, forming ions.

- In the molecular equation the reactants and products are shown in their undissociated/unionized form; the ionic equation shows the reactants and products in the form of ions; the net ionic equation drops out all spectator ions and only shows those species that are undergoing chemical change.

- Precipitation reactions form an insoluble compound, a precipitate, from the mixing of two soluble compounds.

- Learn and be able to apply the solubility rules.

- Redox reactions are those reactions in which a simultaneous oxidation and reduction takes place.

- Oxidation is the loss of electrons, and reduction is the gain of electrons.

- Oxidizing agents are reactants that cause oxidation to take place (the reactant being reduced) and reducing agents are reactant species that cause reduction to take place (the reactant being oxidized).

- Combination reactions are reactions in which two or more reactants (elements or compounds) combine to form one product.

- Decomposition reactions are reactions in which a compound breaks down into two or more simpler substances.

- Single displacement reactions are reactions in which atoms of an element replace the atoms of another element in a compound.

- Know how to use the activity series to predict whether or not an element will displace another element.

- Combustion reactions are redox reactions in which the chemical species rapidly combines with diatomic oxygen gas, emitting heat and light. The products of the complete combustion of a hydrocarbon are carbon dioxide and water.

- Indicators are substances that have a different color in an acid or base solution.

- Acids are proton donors (electron pair acceptors).

- Bases are proton acceptors (electron pair donors).

- Coordinate covalent bonds are covalent bonds in which one atom furnishes both of the electrons for the bond.

- Strong acids and bases completely ionize/dissociate; weak acids and bases only partially ionize/dissociate.

- Know the strong acids and bases.

- Acids react with bases to form a salt and water in a neutralization reaction.

- Many hydrides react with water to form hydroxide and hydrogen gas.

- A titration is a laboratory procedure for determining the concentration of an unknown solution using a solution of known concentration.

- The equivalence point of an acid-base titration is the point at which the moles of H^+ from the acid equal the moles of OH^- added from the base. The endpoint is the point at which the indicator changes color, indicating the equivalence point.

- A complex ion is composed of a metal ion covalently bonded to two or more molecules or anions called ligands.

- The coordination number is the number of ligands that can surround a metal ion in an aqueous complex.

Chapter 5

Stoichiometry

KEYWORDS AND EQUATIONS

✓ There are no specific keywords or equations on the AP exam directly related to this chapter.

INTRODUCTION

The previous chapter on chemical reactions discussed reactants and products in terms of individual atoms and molecules. But an industrial chemist is not interested in the number of molecules being produced; she or he is interested in kilograms or pounds or tons of products being formed per hour or day. How many kilograms of reactants will it take? How many kilograms of products will be formed? These are the questions of interest. A production chemist is interested primarily in the macroscopic world, not the microscopic one of atoms and molecules. Even a chemistry student working in the laboratory will not be weighing out individual atoms and molecules, but large numbers of them in grams. There must be a way to bridge between the microscopic world of individual atoms and molecules and the macroscopic world of grams and kilograms. There is—it is called the mole concept, and it is one of the most central concepts in the world of chemistry.

MOLES AND MOLAR MASS

The **mole (mol)** is the amount of a substance that contains the same number of particles as atoms in exactly 12 grams of carbon-12. This number of particles (atoms or molecules or ions) per mole is called **Avogadro's number** and is numerically equal to 6.022×10^{23} particles. The mole is simply a term that represents a certain number of particles, like a dozen or a pair. That relates it to the microscopic world, but what about the macroscopic world? The mole also represents a certain mass of a chemical substance. That mass is the substance's atomic or molecular weight expressed in grams. In Chapter 3 we described the atomic mass of an element in terms of atomic mass units (amu). This was the mass associated with an individual atom. Then we described how one could calculate the mass of a compound by simply adding together the masses in amu of the individual elements in the compound. This is still the case, but at the macroscopic level the unit of grams is used to represent the quantity of a mole. Thus, the following relationships apply:

!

$$6.022 \times 10^{23} \text{ particles} = \underline{1 \text{ mol}}$$

$$= \text{atomic (molecular, formula) mass in grams}$$

The relationship above gives a way of converting from grams to moles to particles, and vice versa. If you have any one of the three quantities, you can calculate the other two. This becomes extremely useful in working with chemical equations, as we will see later, because the coefficients in the balanced chemical equation are not only the number of individual atoms or molecules at the microscopic level, but also the number of moles at the macroscopic level.

How many moles are present in 1.20×10^{25} silver atoms?

Answer:

$$\frac{(1.20 \times 10^{25} \text{ Ag atoms})(1 \text{ mol Ag})}{(6.022 \times 10^{23} \text{ Ag atoms})} = 19.9 \text{ mol Ag}$$

PERCENT COMPOSITION AND EMPIRICAL FORMULAS

If the formula of a compound is known, it is a fairly straightforward task to determine the percent composition of each element in the compound. For example, suppose you want to calculate the percentage hydrogen and oxygen in water, H_2O. First calculate the molecular mass of water:

$$1 \text{ mol } H_2O = 2 \text{ mol } H + 1 \text{ mol } O$$

Substituting the masses involved:

$$1 \text{ mol } H_2O = 2 \left(1.0079 \text{ g/mol}\right) + 16.00 \text{ g/mol} = 18.0158 \text{ g/mol}$$

(intermediate calculation—don't worry about significant figures yet)

$$\text{percentage hydrogen} = [\text{mass H/mass } H_2O] \times 100$$

$$= [2(1.0079 \text{ g/mol})/18.0158 \text{ g/mol}] \times 100$$

$$= 11.19\% \text{ H}$$

$$\text{percentage oxygen} = [\text{mass O/mass H}_2\text{O}] \times 100$$
$$= [16.00 \text{ g/mol}/18.0158 \text{ g/mol}] \times 100$$
$$= 88.81\% \text{ O}$$

As a good check, add the percentages together. They should equal to 100% or be very, very close.

Determine the mass percent of each
of the elements in $C_6H_{12}O_6$ $\qquad$ FW = 180.158 amu

Answer:

$$\% \text{ C} = \frac{(6 \text{ C atoms})(12.011 \text{ amu/atom})}{(180.158 \text{ amu})} \times 100\% = 40.002\%$$

$$\% \text{ H} = \frac{(12 \text{ H atoms})(1.008 \text{ amu/atom})}{(180.158 \text{ amu})} \times 100\% = 6.714\%$$

$$\% \text{ O} = \frac{(6 \text{ O atoms})(15.9994 \text{ amu/atom})}{(180.158 \text{ amu})} \times 100\% = 53.2846\%$$

$$\text{Total } = 100.001\%$$

The total is a check. It should be *very* close to 100%.

In the problems above, the percentage data was calculated from the chemical formula, but the empirical formula can be determined if the percent compositions of the various elements are known. The **empirical formula** tells us what elements are present in the compound and the simplest whole-number ratio of elements. The data may be in terms of percentage or mass or even moles. But the procedure is still the same: convert each to moles, divide each by the smallest, then use an appropriate multiplier if needed. The empirical formula mass can then be calculated. If the actual molecular mass is known, dividing the molecular mass by the empirical formula mass gives an integer (rounded if needed) that is used to multiply each of the subscripts in the empirical formula. This gives the **molecular (actual) formula,** which tells what elements are in the compound and the actual number of each.

A sample of a gas was analyzed and found to contain 2.34 g of nitrogen and 5.34 g of oxygen. What was the formula of this gas?

Answer:

$$\frac{(2.34 \text{ g N})(1 \text{ mol N})}{(14.0 \text{ g N})} = 0.167 \text{ mol N} \quad \frac{0.167}{0.167} = 1$$

$$\frac{(5.34 \text{ g O})(1 \text{ mol O})}{(16.0 \text{ g O})} = 0.334 \text{ mol O} \quad \frac{0.334}{0.167} = 2$$

empirical formula $= NO_2$

REACTION STOICHIOMETRY

As we have discussed previously, the balanced chemical equation not only indicates what chemical species are the reactant and what the products are, but also indicates the relative ratio of reactants and products. Consider the balanced equation of the Haber process for the production of ammonia:

$$N_2(g) + 3 H_2(g) \rightarrow 2 NH_3(g)$$

This balanced equation can be read as: *1 nitrogen molecule reacts with 3 hydrogen molecules to produce 2 ammonia molecules*. But as indicated previously, the coefficients can stand not only for the number of atoms or molecules (microscopic level); they can also stand for the number of <u>moles</u> of reactants or products. The equation can also be read as: *1 mol of nitrogen molecules reacts with 3 mol of hydrogen molecules to produce 2 mol of ammonia molecules*. And if the number of moles is known, the number of grams or molecules can be calculated. This is **stoichiometry,** the calculation of the amount (mass, moles, particles) of one substance in a chemical reaction through the use of another. The coefficients in the balanced chemical equation define the mathematical relationship between the reactants and products, and allow the conversion from moles of one chemical species in the reaction to another.

Consider the Haber process above. How many moles of ammonia could be produced from the reaction of 20.0 mol of nitrogen with excess hydrogen?

Before any calculation can be done you <u>must</u> have a balanced chemical equation!

You are starting with moles of nitrogen and want moles of ammonia, so we'll convert from moles of nitrogen to moles of ammonia by using the ratio of moles of ammonia to moles of nitrogen as defined by the balanced chemical equation:

$$\frac{20.0 \text{ mol N}_2}{1} \times \frac{2 \text{ mol NH}_3}{1 \text{ mol N}_2} = 40.0 \text{ mol NH}_3$$

The ratio of 2 mol NH_3 to 1 mol N_2 is called the stoichiometric ratio and comes from the balanced chemical equation.

Suppose you also wanted to know how many moles of hydrogen it would take to fully react with the 20.0 mol of nitrogen. Just change the stoichiometric ratio:

$$\frac{20.0 \text{ mol N}_2}{1} \times \frac{3 \text{ mol NH}_2}{1 \text{ mol N}_2} = 60.0 \text{ mol H}_2$$

Notice that this new stoichiometric ratio came from the balanced chemical equation.

Suppose instead of moles you had grams and wanted grams. How many grams of ammonia could be produced from the reaction of 85.00 g of hydrogen gas with excess nitrogen?

 In working problems that involve something other than moles, you will need to convert eventually to moles. And you will need the balanced chemical equation.

In this problem we will convert from grams of hydrogen to moles of hydrogen to moles of ammonia using the correct stoichiometric ratio, and finally to grams of ammonia. And we will need the molar mass of H_2 (2.0158 g/mol) and ammonia (17.0307 g/mol):

$$\frac{85.0 \text{ g } H_2}{1} \times \frac{1 \text{ mol } H_2}{2.0158 \text{ g}} \times \frac{2 \text{ mol } NH_3}{3 \text{ mol } H_2} \times \frac{17.0307 \text{ g}}{1 \text{ mol } NH_3} = 478.9 \text{ g } NH_3$$

Actually, you could have calculated the actual number of ammonia atoms produced if you had gone from moles of ammonia to molecules (using Avogadro's number):

$$\frac{85.0 \text{ g } H_2}{1} \times \frac{1 \text{ mol } H_2}{2.0158 \text{ g}} \times \frac{2 \text{ mol } NH_3}{3 \text{ mol } H_2} \times \frac{6.022 \times 10^{23} \text{ molecules } NH_3}{1 \text{ mol } NH_3}$$

$$= 1.673 \times 10^{25} \text{ molecules } NH_3$$

If 40.0 g of Cl_2 and excess H_2 are combined, HCl will be produced. How many grams of HCl will form?

$$H_2 + Cl_2 \rightarrow 2 \text{ HCl}$$

Answer:

$$\frac{(40.0 \text{ g } Cl_2)(1 \text{ mol})(2 \text{ mol HCl})(36.461 \text{ g HCl})}{(70.906 \text{ g } Cl_2)(1 \text{ mol } Cl_2)(1 \text{ mol HCl})} = 41.1 \text{ g HCl}$$

LIMITING REACTANTS

In the examples above, one reactant was present in excess. The other reactant was being used up, and some of the reactant in excess would be left over. The reactant that is used up first is called the **limiting reactant** (L.R.). This reactant really determines the amount of product being formed. How is the limiting reactant determined? You can't assume it is the reactant in the smallest amount, since the reaction stoichiometry must be considered. There are, in general, two ways to determine which reactant is the limiting reactant:

1. Each reactant, in turn, is assumed to be the limiting reactant, and the amount of product that would be formed is calculated. The reactant

that yields the *smallest* amount of product is the limiting reactant. The advantage of this method is that you get to practice your calculation skills; the disadvantage is that you have to do a lot of calculations.

2. The moles of reactant per coefficient of that reactant in the balanced chemical equation is calculated. The reactant that has the smallest mole-to-coefficient ratio is the limiting reactant. This is the method that many use.

Let us consider the Haber reaction once more. Suppose that 50.0 g of nitrogen and 40.0 g of hydrogen were allowed to react. Calculate the number of grams of ammonia that could be formed.

First, write the balanced chemical equation:

$$N_2(g) + 3 H_2(g) \rightarrow 2 NH_3(g)$$

Next, convert the grams of each reactant to moles:

$$\frac{50.0 \text{ g N}_2}{1} \times \frac{1 \text{ mol N}_2}{28.014 \text{ g N}_2} = 1.7848 \text{ mol N}_2$$

$$\frac{40.0 \text{ g H}_2}{1} \times \frac{1 \text{ mol H}_2}{2.0158 \text{ g H}_2} = 19.8432 \text{ mol H}_2$$

Divide each by the coefficient in the balanced chemical equation. The smallest is the limiting reactant:

For N_2: 1.7848 mol N_2/1 = 1.7848 mol/coefficient *limiting reactant*

For H_2: 19.8432 mol H_2/3 = 6.6144 mol/coefficient

Finally, base the stoichiometry of the reaction on the limiting reactant:

$$\frac{50.0 \text{ g N}_2}{1} \times \frac{1 \text{ mol N}_2}{28.014 \text{ g N}_2} \times \frac{2 \text{ mol NH}_3}{1 \text{ mol N}_2} \times \frac{17.0307 \text{ g}}{1 \text{ mol NH}_3} = 60.8 \text{ g NH}_3$$

To carry out the following reaction: $P_2O_5 + 3 H_2O \qquad 2 H_3PO_4$

125 g of P_2O_5 and 50.0 g of H_2O were supplied. How many grams of H_3PO_4 may be produced?

Answer:

HINT: *Anytime the quantities of more than one reactant are given it is probably a L.R. problem.*

1. Convert to moles:

$$\frac{(125 \text{ g P}_2\text{O}_5)(1 \text{ mol})}{(142 \text{ g P}_2\text{O}_5)} = 0.880 \text{ mol P}_2\text{O}_5$$

$$\frac{(50.0 \text{ g H}_2\text{O})(1 \text{ mol})}{(18.0 \text{ g H}_2\text{O})} = 2.78 \text{ mol H}_2\text{O}$$

2. Find the limiting reactant

$$\frac{0.880 \text{ mol}}{1 \text{ mol}} = 0.880 \text{ P}_2\text{O}_5$$

$$\frac{2.78 \text{ mol}}{3 \text{ mol}} = 0.927 \text{ H}_2\text{O}$$

The 1 mol and the 3 mol come from the balanced chemical equation. The 0.880 is smaller, so this is the L.R.

3. Finish using the L.R.

$$\frac{\left(0.880 \text{ mol P}_2\text{O}_5\right)\left(2 \text{ mol H}_3\text{PO}_4\right)\left(98.0 \text{ g}\right)}{\left(1 \text{ mol P}_2\text{O}_5\right)\left(1 \text{ mol H}_3\text{PO}_4\right)} = 172 \text{ g}$$

PERCENT YIELD

In the problems above, the amount of product calculated based on the limiting reactant concept is the maximum amount of product that could be formed from the given amount of reactants. This maximum amount of product formed is called the **theoretical yield.** However, rarely is the amount that is actually formed (the **actual yield**) the same as the theoretical yield. Normally it is less. There are many reasons for this, but the principal reason is that most reactions do not go to completion; they establish an equilibrium system (see Chapter 13 for a discussion on chemical equilibrium). For whatever reason, not as much as expected is formed. The efficiency of the reaction can be judged by calculating the percent yield. The **percent yield (% yield)** is the actual yield divided by the theoretical yield, and the resultant multiplied by 100 to generate percentage:

$$\% \text{ yield} = \frac{\text{actual yield}}{\text{theoretical yield}} \times 100$$

Consider the problem in which it was calculated that 60.8 g NH_3 could be formed. Suppose that reaction was carried out, and only 52.3 g NH_3 was formed. Calculate the percent yield.

$$\% \text{ yield} = \frac{52.3 \text{ g}}{60.8 \text{ g}} \times 100 = 86.0\%$$

A 25.0-g sample of calcium oxide is heated with excess hydrogen chloride to produce water and 37.5 g of calcium chloride. What is the percent yield?

$$CaO + 2 \text{ HCl} \rightarrow CaCl_2 + H_2O$$

Answer:

$$\frac{(25.0 \text{ g CaO})(1 \text{ mol CaO})(1 \text{ mol})(110.984 \text{ g})}{(56.077 \text{ g CaO})(1 \text{ mol CaO})(1 \text{ mol CaCl}_2)} = 49.478 \text{ g CaCl}_2$$

The theoretical yield is 49.5 g.

$$\frac{37.5 \text{ g} \times 100\%}{49.478 \text{ g}} = 75.8\%$$

Note: All the units but % cancel.

MOLARITY AND SOLUTION CALCULATIONS

We discuss solutions in Chapter 11, but solution stoichiometry is so common on the AP exam, that we will discuss it here briefly also. **Solutions** are homogeneous mixtures composed of a **solute** (substance present in smaller amount) and a **solvent** (substance present in larger amount). If sodium chloride is dissolved in water, the NaCl is the solute and the water the solvent.

One important aspect of solutions is their **concentration,** the amount of solute dissolved in the solvent. In Chapter 11 we will cover several concentration units, but for the purpose of stoichiometry, the only concentration unit we will use is molarity. **Molarity (M)** is defined as the moles of solute per liters of solution:

$$M = \text{mol solute}/\text{L solution}$$

A solution of NaCl contains 39.12 g of this compound in 100.0 mL of solution. Calculate the molarity of NaCl.

Answer:

$$\frac{(39.12 \text{ g NaCl}) \dfrac{[1 \text{ mol NaCl}]}{[58.45 \text{ g NaCl}]}}{(100.0 \text{ mL}) \dfrac{[1 \text{ L}]}{[1000 \text{ mL}]}} = 6.693 \text{ M NaCl}$$

Knowing the volume of the solution and the molarity allows you to calculate the moles or grams of solute present.

How many moles of ammonium ions are in 0.100 L of a 0.20 M ammonium sulfate solution?

Answer:

$$\left[\frac{0.20 \text{ mol}(NH_4)_2SO_4}{L}\right]\left[\frac{2 \text{ mol } NH_4^+}{1 \text{ mol}(NH_4)_2SO_4}\right](0.100 \text{ L}) = 0.040 \text{ mol}$$

Stoichiometry problems (including limiting reactant problems) involving solutions can be worked in the same fashion as before, except that the volume and molarity of the solution must first be converted to moles.

If 35.00 mL of a 0.1500 M KOH solution is required to titrate 40.00 mL of a phosphoric acid solution, what is the concentration of the acid? The reaction is:

$$2\ KOH + H_3PO_4 \rightarrow K_2HPO_4 + 2\ H_2O$$

Answer:

$$\frac{(35.00\ \text{mL})\ \dfrac{(1500\ \text{mol KOH})(1\ \text{mol } H_3PO_4)}{(1000\ \text{mL})(2\ \text{mol KOH})}}{(40.00\ \text{mL})\ \dfrac{(1\ \text{L})}{(1000\ \text{mL})}} = 0.06562\ \text{M}$$

EXPERIMENTAL

Stoichiometry experiments must involve moles. They nearly always use a balanced chemical equation.

Measurements include initial and final masses, and initial and final volumes. Calculations may include the difference between the initial and final values. Using the formula weight and the mass, moles may be calculated. Moles may also be calculated from the volume of a solution and its molarity.

Once the moles have been calculated (they are never measured), the experiment will be based on further calculations using these moles.

COMMON MISTAKES TO AVOID

1. Avogadro's number is 6.022×10^{23}, not 10^{-23}.
2. Be sure to know the difference between molecules and moles.
3. In empirical formula problems, be sure to get the lowest ratio of whole numbers.
4. In stoichiometry problems, be sure to use the <u>balanced chemical equation.</u>
5. The stoichiometric ratio comes from the <u>balanced chemical equation.</u>
6. When in doubt, convert to moles.
7. In limiting reagent problems, don't just consider the number of grams or even moles to determine the limiting reactant—use the mol/coefficient ratio.
8. The limiting reactant is a reactant, a chemical species to the left of the reactant arrow.
9. <u>Use the balanced chemical equation.</u>
10. Percent yield is actual yield over the theoretical yield times 100.

11. Molarity is moles of <u>solute</u> per liters of <u>solution</u>, not solvent.
12. Be careful when using Avogadro's number—use it when you need atoms or molecules.

 3 **REVIEW QUESTIONS**

Answer the following questions. You have 20 minutes, and you may not use a calculator.

1. How many milliliters of 0.100 M H_2SO_4 are required to neutralize 50.0 mL of 0.200 M KOH?

   A. 25.0 mL
   B. 30.0 mL
   C. 20.0 mL
   D. 50.0 mL
   E. 60.0 mL

2. A sample of oxalic acid, $H_2C_2O_4$, is titrated with standard sodium hydroxide, NaOH, solution. A total of 45.20 mL of 0.1200 M NaOH is required to neutralize completely 20.00 mL of the acid. What is the concentration of the acid?

   A. 0.2712 M
   B. 0.1200 M
   C. 0.1356 M
   D. 0.2400 M
   E. 0.5424 M

3. A solution is prepared by mixing 50.0 mL of 0.20 M arsenic acid, H_3AsO_4, and 50.0 mL of 0.20 M sodium hydroxide, NaOH. Which anion is present in the highest concentration?

   A. $HAsO_4^{2-}$
   B. OH^-
   C. $H_2AsO_4^-$
   D. Na^+
   E. AsO_3^{3-}

4. $14\,H^+ + 6\,Fe^{2+} + Cr_2O_7^{2-}$

   $\rightarrow 2\,Cr^{3+} + 6\,Fe^{3+} + 7\,H_2O$

This reaction is used in the titration of an iron solution. What is the concentration of the iron solution if it takes 45.20 mL of 0.1000 M $Cr_2O_7^{2-}$ solution to titrate 50.00 mL of an acidified iron solution?

   A. 0.5424 M
   B. 0.1000 M
   C. 1.085 M
   D. 0.4520 M
   E. 0.2712 M

5. Tungsten metal may be prepared by reducing WO_3 with H_2 gas. How many grams of tungsten may be prepared from 0.0500 mol of WO_3 with excess hydrogen?

   A. 5.58 g
   B. 0.500 g
   C. 9.19 g
   D. 184 g
   E. 18.4 g

6. Manganese, Mn, forms a number of oxides. A particular oxide is 63.2% Mn. What is the simplest formula for this oxide?

   A. MnO
   B. Mn_2O_3
   C. Mn_3O_4
   D. MnO_2
   E. Mn_2O_7

7. Vanadium forms a number of oxides. In which of the following oxides is the vanadium to oxygen mass ratio 2.39:1.00?

A. VO
B. V_2O_3
C. V_3O_4
D. VO_2
E. V_2O_5

8. How many grams of nitrogen are in 25.0 g of $(NH_4)_2SO_4$?

   A. 5.30 g
   B. 1.30 g
   C. 0.190 g
   D. 2.65 g
   E. 14.0 g

9. Nitrogen forms a number of oxides. Which of the following oxides is 64% nitrogen?

   A. N_2O_5
   B. N_2O_4
   C. N_2O_3
   D. N_2O_2
   E. N_2O

10. Sodium sulfate forms a number of hydrates. A sample of a hydrate is heated until all the water is removed. What is the formula of the original hydrate if it loses 43% of its mass when heated?

    A. $Na_2SO_4.H_2O$
    B. $Na_2SO_4.2H_2O$
    C. $Na_2SO_4.6H_2O$
    D. $Na_2SO_4.8H_2O$
    E. $Na_2SO_4.10H_2O$

11. $3\,Cu(s) + 8\,HNO_3(aq) \rightarrow$

    $3\,Cu(NO_3)_2(aq) + 2\,NO(g) + 4\,H_2O(l)$

    Copper metal reacts with nitric acid according to the above equation. A 0.30-mol sample of copper metal and 10.0 mL of 12 M nitric acid are mixed in a flask. How many moles of NO gas will form?

A. 0.060 mol
B. 0.030 mol
C. 0.010 mol
D. 0.20 mol
E. 0.10 mol

12. Gold(III) oxide, Au_2O_3, can be decomposed to gold metal, Au, plus oxygen gas, O_2. How many moles of oxygen gas will form when 221 g of solid gold(III) oxide is decomposed? The formula weight of gold(III) oxide is 442.

    A. 0.250 mol
    B. 0.500 mol
    C. 1.50 mol
    D. 1.00 mol
    E. 0.750 mol

13. $\_\_ C_4H_{11}N(l) + \_\_ O_2(g)$

    $\rightarrow \_\_ CO_2(g) + \_\_ H_2O(l) + \_\_ N_2(g)$

    When the above equation is balanced, the lowest whole number coefficient for O_2 is:

    A. 4
    B. 16
    C. 22
    D. 27
    E. 2

14. $2\,KMnO_4 + 5\,H_2C_2O_4 + 3\,H_2SO_4$

    $\rightarrow K_2SO_4 + 2\,MnSO_4 + 10\,CO_2 + 8\,H_2O$

    How many moles of $MnSO_4$ are produced when 1.0 mol of $KMnO_4$, 5.0 mol of $H_2C_2O_4$, and 3.0 mol of H_2SO_4 are mixed?

    A. 4.0 mol
    B. 5.0 mol
    C. 2.0 mol
    D. 2.5 mol
    E. 1.0 mol

15. $\_\_ KClO_3 \rightarrow \_\_ KCl + \_\_ O_2$

    After the above equation is balanced, how many moles of O_2 can be produced from 4.0 mol of $KClO_3$?

    A. 2.0 mol
    B. 4.0 mol
    C. 5.0 mol
    D. 6.0 mol
    E. 3.0 mol

16. When the following equation is balanced, it is found that 1.00 mol of C_8H_{18} reacts with how many moles of O_2?

    $\_\_ C_8H_{18} + \_\_ O_2 \rightarrow \_\_ CO_2 + \_\_ H_2O$

    A. 1.00 mol
    B. 10.0 mol
    C. 25.0 mol
    D. 37.5 mol
    E. 12.5 mol

17. $Ca + 2 H_2O \rightarrow Ca(OH)_2 + H_2$

    Calcium reacts with water according to the above reaction. What volume of hydrogen gas, at standard temperature and pressure, is produced from 0.200 mol of calcium?

A. 5.60 L
B. 2.24 L
C. 3.36 L
D. 1.12 L
E. 4.48 L

18. $2 CrO_4^{2-} + 3 SnO_2^{2-} + H_2O$

    $\rightarrow 2 CrO_2^{-} + 3 SnO_3^{2-} + 2 OH^{-}$

    How many moles of OH^- form when 50.0 mL of 0.100 M CrO_4^{2-} is added to a flask containing 50.0 mL of 0.100 M SnO_2^{2-}?

    A. 0.100 mol
    B. 6.66×10^{-3} mol
    C. 3.33×10^{-3} mol
    D. 5.00×10^{-3} mol
    E. 7.50×10^{-3} mol

19. A solution containing 0.20 mol of KBr and 0.20 mol of $MgBr_2$ in 2.0 liters of water is provided. How many moles of $Pb(NO_3)_2$ must be added to precipitate all the bromide as insoluble $PbBr_2$?

    A. 0.10 mol
    B. 0.50 mol
    C. 0.60 mol
    D. 0.30 mol
    E. 0.40 mol

ANSWERS AND EXPLANATIONS

✓ There are multiple "correct" ways to do these calculations. Only one calculation is shown for each answer.

1. D. $50.0 \text{ mL base} \times \dfrac{0.200 \text{ mol base}}{1000 \text{ mL base}} \times \dfrac{1 \text{ mol acid}}{2 \text{ mol base}}$

$\times \dfrac{1000 \text{ mL acid}}{0.100 \text{ mol acid}} = 50.0 \text{ mL}$

2. C. $45.20 \text{ mL base} \times \dfrac{0.1200 \text{ mol base}}{1000 \text{ mL base}} \times \dfrac{1 \text{ mol acid}}{2 \text{ mol base}}$

$$\times \dfrac{1}{20.00 \text{ mL}} \times \dfrac{1000 \text{ mL}}{\text{L}} = 0.1356 \text{ M}$$

3. C. Moles acid = $(50.0 \text{ mL})(0.20 \text{ mol acid}/1000 \text{ mL}) = 0.0100 \text{ mol}$

Moles base = $(50.0 \text{ mL})(0.20 \text{ mol base}/1000 \text{ mL}) = 0.0100 \text{ mol}$

There is sufficient base to react completely with only one of the ionizable hydrogens from the acid. This leaves $H_2AsO_4^-$.

4. A. $\text{Ox} = \text{oxidizing agent} = Cr_2O_7^{2-}$ $\quad$ $\text{Red} = \text{reducing agent} = Fe^{2+}$

$$45.20 \text{ mL Ox} \times \dfrac{0.1000 \text{ mol Ox}}{1000 \text{ mL Ox}} \times \dfrac{6 \text{ mol Red}}{1 \text{ mol Ox}} \times \dfrac{1}{50.00 \text{ mL}}$$

$$\times \dfrac{1000 \text{ mL}}{\text{L}} = 0.5424 \text{ M}$$

5. C. $(0.0500 \text{ mol WO}_3)(1 \text{ mol W}/1 \text{ mol WO}_3)(183.8 \text{ g W}/1 \text{ mol W})$

$$= 9.19 \text{ g W}$$

6. D. $\quad$ 63.2% Mn leaves 36.8% O

$\quad$ $63.2/54.94 = 1.15 \text{ Mn}$ $\quad$ $36.8/16.0 = 2.30 \text{ O}$

Thus, there is 1 Mn / 2 O.

7. C. $\quad$ V: $2.39/50.94 = 0.0469$ $\quad$ O: $1.00/16.0 = 0.0625$

$\quad$ $0.0469/0.0469 = 1$ $\quad\quad$ $0.0625/0.0469 = 1.33$

Multiplying both by three gives: 3 V and 4 O.

8. A. $\quad$ $[25.0 \text{ g}(NH_4)_2SO_4][1 \text{ mol}(NH_4)_2SO_4/132 \text{ g}] \times$

$[2 \text{ mol N}/1 \text{ mol}(NH_4)_2SO_4][14.0 \text{ g N}/1 \text{ mol N}] = 5.30 \text{ g}$

9. E. $\dfrac{(2 \text{ N} \times 14.0 \text{ g}/\text{N})}{44.0 \text{ g N}_2\text{O}} \times 100\% = 64\%$

10. C. $[(6 \text{ H}_2\text{O})(18 \text{ g}/\text{H}_2\text{O})]/(250 \text{ g Na}_2\text{SO}_4 \cdot 6 \text{ H}_2\text{O}) \times 100\% = 43\%$

11. **B.** Calculate the moles of acid:

$$(10.0 \text{ mL})(12 \text{ mol}/1000 \text{ mL}) = 0.12 \text{ mol}$$

The acid is the limiting reactant, and will be used to calculate the moles of NO formed.

$$(0.12 \text{ mol acid})(2 \text{ mol NO}/8 \text{ mol acid}) = 0.030 \text{ mol}$$

12. **E.** The balanced chemical equation is:

$$2 \text{ Au}_2\text{O}_3 \rightarrow 4 \text{ Au} + 3 \text{ O}_2$$
$$(221 \text{ g Au}_2\text{O}_3)(1 \text{ mol Au}_2\text{O}_3/442 \text{ g Au}_2\text{O}_3)(3 \text{ mol O}_2/2 \text{ mol Au}_2\text{O}_3)$$
$$= 0.750 \text{ mol O}_2$$

13. **D.** The balanced equation is:

$$4 \text{ C}_4\text{H}_{11}\text{N}(l) + 27 \text{ O}_2(g) \rightarrow 16 \text{ CO}_2(g) + 22 \text{ H}_2\text{O}(l) + 2 \text{ N}_2(g)$$

14. **E.** The $KMnO_4$ is the limiting reagent. Each mole of $KMnO_4$ will produce a mole of $MnSO_4$.

15. **D.** The balanced equation is:

$$2 \text{ KClO}_3 \rightarrow 2 \text{ KCl} + 3 \text{ O}_2$$
$$(4.0 \text{ mol KClO}_3)(3 \text{ mol O}_2/2 \text{ mol KClO}_3) = 6.0 \text{ mol O}_2$$

16. **E.** The balanced equation is:

$$2 \text{ C}_8\text{H}_{18} + 25 \text{ O}_2 \rightarrow 16 \text{ CO}_2 + 18 \text{ H}_2\text{O}$$
$$(1.00 \text{ mol C}_8\text{H}_{18})(25 \text{ mol O}_2/2 \text{ mol C}_8\text{H}_{18}) = 12.5 \text{ mol O}_2$$

17. **E.** $(0.200 \text{ mol Ca})(1 \text{ mol H}_2/1 \text{ mol Ca})(22.4 \text{ L at STP}/1 \text{ mol H}_2)$

$$= 4.48 \text{ L}$$

18. **C.** There are 5.00×10^{-3} mol of CrO_4^{2-} and an equal number of mol of SnO_2^{2-}. Thus SnO_2^{2-} is the limiting reactant.

$$\left(5.00 \times 10^{-3} \text{ mol SnO}_2^{2-}\right)\left(2 \text{ mol OH}^-/3 \text{ mol SnO}_2^{2-}\right)$$
$$= 3.33 \times 10^{-3} \text{ mol OH}^-$$

19. **D.** The volume of water is irrelevant.

0.20 mol of KBr will require 0.10 mol of $Pb(NO_3)_2$
0.20 mol of $MgBr_2$ will require 0.20 mol of $Pb(NO_3)_2$
Total the two yields.

3 **FREE-RESPONSE QUESTIONS**

Answer the following questions. You have 15 minutes, and you may use a calculator.

A sample of a monoprotic acid was analyzed. The sample contained 40.0% C and 6.71% H. The remainder of the sample was oxygen.

a. Determine the empirical formula of the acid.

b. A 0.2720-g sample of the acid was titrated with standard NaOH solution. Determine the molecular weight of the acid if the sample required 45.00 mL of 0.1000 M NaOH for the titration.

c. A second sample was placed in a flask. The flask was placed in a hot water bath until the sample vaporized. It was found that 1.18 g of vapor occupied 300.0 mL at 100°C and 1.00 atmospheres. Determine the molecular weight of the acid.

d. Using your answer from part **a**, determine the molecular formula for part **b** and for part **c**.

e. Account for any differences in the molecular formulas determined in part **d**.

ANSWERS AND EXPLANATIONS

a. The percent oxygen (53.3%) is determined by subtracting the carbon and the hydrogen from 100%.

For C: $40.0/12.01 = 3.33$	Divide each	C = 1
For H: $6.71/1.008 = 6.66$	of these by	H = 2
For O: $53.3/16.00 = 3.33$	the smallest	O = 1
	(3.33)	

This gives the empirical formula: CH_2O.

You get 1 point for correctly determining any of the elements, and 1 point for getting the complete empirical formula correct.

b. Using HA to represent the monoprotic acid, the balanced equation for the titration reaction is:

$$HA + NaOH \rightarrow NaA + H_2O$$

The moles of acid may then be calculated:

$$(45.00 \text{ mL NaOH})(0.1000 \text{ mol NaOH}/1000 \text{ mL})$$

$$(1 \text{ mol HA}/1 \text{ mol NaOH}) = 4.500 \times 10^{-3} \text{ mol HA}$$

The molecular weight is:

$$0.2720 \text{ g}/4.500 \times 10^{-3} \text{ mol} = 60.44 \text{ g/mol}$$

You get 1 point for the correct number of moles of HA (or NaOH) and 1 point for the correct final answer.

c. This may be done several ways. One way is to use the Ideal Gas Equation. This will be done here. The equation and the value of R are given in the exam booklet.

First find the moles: $n = PV/RT$ Do not forget, you MUST change to Kelvin.

$$n = (1.00 \text{ atm})(300.0 \text{ mL})(1 \text{ L}/1000 \text{ mL})/$$

$$(0.0821 \text{ L atm/mol K})(373 \text{ K})$$

$$n = 9.80 \times 10^{-3} \text{ mol}$$

The molecular weight is: $1.18 \text{ g}/9.80 \times 10^{-3} \text{ mol} = 120 \text{ g/mol}$
    You get 1 point for getting any part of the calculation correct and 1 point for getting the correct final answer.

d. The approximate formula weight from the empirical (CH_2O) formula is: $12 + 2(1) + 16 = 30 \text{ g/mol}$

For part (b): $(60.44 \text{ g/mol}) / (30 \text{ g/mol}) = 2$

Molecular formula $= 2 \times$ Empirical Formula $= C_2H_4O_2$

For part (c): $(120 \text{ g/mol}) / (30 \text{ g/mol}) = 4$

Molecular formula $= 4 \times$ Empirical Formula $= C_4H_8O_4$

You get 1 point for each correct molecular formula. If you got the wrong answer in part **a.**, you can still get credit for one or both of the molecular formulas if you used the part **a.** value correctly.

e. The one formula is double the formula of the other. Thus, the smaller molecule dimerizes to produce the larger molecule.
    You get 1 point if you "combined" two of the smaller molecules.

Total your points. There are 9 points possible.

RAPID REVIEW

- The mole is the amount of substance that contains the same number of particles as exactly 12 g of carbon-12.

- Avogadro's number is the number of particles per mole, 6.022×10^{23} particles.

- A mole is also the formula (atomic, molecular) mass expressed in grams.

- If you have any one of the three—moles, grams, or particles—you can calculate the others.

- The empirical formula indicates what elements are present and the lowest whole-number ratio.

- The molecular formula tells what elements are present and the actual number of each.

- Be able to calculate the empirical formula from percent composition data.

- Stoichiometry is the calculation of the amount of one substance in a chemical equation by using another one.

- <u>Always use the balanced chemical equation</u> in reaction stoichiometry problems.

- Be able to convert from moles of one substance to moles of another, using the stoichiometric ratio derived from the <u>balanced chemical equation.</u>

- In working problems that involve a quantity other than moles, sooner or later it will be necessary to convert to moles.

- The limiting reactant is that reactant that is used up first.

- Be able to calculate the limiting reactant by the use of the mol/coefficient ratio.

- Percent yield is the actual yield (how much was actually formed in the reaction) divided by the theoretical yield (the maximum possible amount of product formed) times 100.

- A solution is a homogeneous mixture composed of a solute (species present in smallest amount) and a solvent (species present in largest amount).

- Concentration describes the relative amount of solute and solvent.

- Molarity is the moles of solute per liter of solution.

- Be able to work reaction stoichiometry problems using molarity.

- <u>Always use the balanced chemical equation</u> in reaction stoichiometry problems.

Chapter 6

Gases

 KEYWORDS AND EQUATIONS

u_{rms} = root mean square speed
r = rate of effusion
STP = 0.000° C and 1.000 atm
$PV = nRT$
$(P + n^2a/V^2)(V - nb) = nRT$
$P_A = P_{total} \times X_A$, where X_A = moles A /total moles
$P_{total} = P_A + P_B + P_C + \cdots$
$P_1V_1/T_1 = P_2V_2/T_2$
$u_{rms} = \sqrt{3kT/m} = \sqrt{3RT/M}$
KE per molecule = $\frac{1}{2} mv^2$
KE per mol = $\frac{3}{2} RTn$
$r_1/r_2 = \sqrt{M_2/M_1}$

1 atm = 760 mm Hg
        = 760 torr

INTRODUCTION

Of the three states of matter—gases, liquids, and solids—gases are probably the best understood and have the best descriptive model. While studying gases in this chapter you will consider four main physical properties—volume, pressure, temperature, and amount—and their interrelationships. These relationships, commonly called gas laws, show up quite often on the AP exam, so you will spend quite a bit of time working problems in this chapter. But before we start looking at the gas laws, let's look at the Kinetic Molecular Theory of Gases, the extremely useful model that scientists use to represent the gaseous state.

KINETIC MOLECULAR THEORY

!

The **Kinetic Molecular Theory** attempts to represent the properties of gases by modeling the gas particles themselves at the microscopic level. There are five main postulates of the Kinetic Molecular Theory:

1. Gases are composed of very small particles, either molecules or individual atoms.
2. The gas particles are tiny in comparison to the distances between them, so we assume that the volume of the gas particles is negligible.
3. These gas particles are in constant motion, moving in straight lines in a random fashion and colliding with each other and the inside walls of the container. The collisions with the inside container walls comprise the pressure of the gas.
4. The gas particles are assumed to neither attract nor repel each other. They may collide with each other, but if they do the collisions are assumed to be elastic. No kinetic energy is lost, only transferred from one gas molecule to another.
5. The *average* kinetic energy of the gas is proportional to the Kelvin temperature.

A gas that obeyed these five postulates would be called an **ideal gas.** However, just as there are no ideal students, there are no ideal gases, only gases that approach ideal behavior. We know that real gas particles do occupy a certain finite volume, and we know that there are interactions between real gas particles. These factors cause real gases to deviate a little from the ideal behavior of the Kinetic Molecular Theory. But a non-polar gas at a low pressure and high temperature would come pretty close to ideal behavior. Later in this chapter, we'll show how to modify our equations to account for non-ideal behavior.

Before we leave the Kinetic Molecular Theory (KMT) and start examining the gas law relationships, let's quantify a couple of the postulates of the KMT. Postulate 3 qualitatively describes the motion of the gas particles. The average velocity of the gas particles is called the **root mean square speed** and is given the symbol u_{rms}. This is a special type of average speed. It is the speed of a gas particle having the average kinetic energy of the gas particles. Mathematically it can be represented as:

$$u_{rms} = \sqrt{3RT/M}$$

where R is the molar gas constant (we'll talk more about it in the section dealing with the ideal gas equation), T is the **Kelvin** temperature and **M** is the molar mass of the gas. These root mean speeds are very high. Hydrogen gas, H_2, at 20° C has a value of approximately 2,000 m/s.

Postulate 5 relates the average kinetic energy of the gas particles to the **Kelvin** temperature. Mathematically we can represent the average kinetic energy per molecule as:

$$KE \text{ per molecule } = 1/2 \ mv^2$$

where m is the mass of the molecule and v is its velocity.

The average kinetic energy per mol of gas is represented by:

$$KE \text{ per mol } = 3/2 \ RT$$

where R again is the ideal gas constant and T is the **Kelvin** temperature. This shows the direct relationship between the average kinetic energy of the gas particles and the **Kelvin** temperature.

GAS LAW RELATIONSHIPS

The gas laws relate the physical properties of volume, pressure, temperature, and amount to each other. First we'll examine the individual laws, and then we'll combine them into one very useful equation. But first, we need to describe a few things concerning pressure.

Pressure

When we use the word **pressure,** we may be referring to the pressure of a gas inside a container or to atmospheric pressure, the pressure due to the weight of the atmosphere above us. These two different types of pressures are measured in slightly different ways. Atmospheric pressure is measured using a **barometer** (Figure 6.1).

An evacuated hollow tube sealed at one end is filled with mercury, and then the open end is immersed in a pool of mercury. Gravity will tend to pull the liquid level inside the tube down, while the weight of the atmospheric gases on the surface of the mercury pool will tend to force the liquid up into the tube. These two opposing forces will quickly balance each other, and the column of mercury inside the tube will stabilize. The height of the column of mercury above the surface of the mercury pool is called the atmospheric pressure. At sea level the column averages 760 mm high. This pressure is also called 1 atmosphere (atm). Commonly, the unit torr is used for pressure, where 1 torr = 1 mm Hg, so that atmospheric pressure at sea level equals 760 torr. The SI unit of pressure is the pascal (Pa), so that 1atm = 760 mm Hg = 760 torr = 101,325 Pa (101.325 kPa). In the United States pounds per square inch (psi) is sometimes used, so that 1 atm = 14.69 psi.

To measure the gas pressure inside a container, a **manometer** (Figure 6.2) is used. As in the barometer, the pressure of the gas is balanced against a column of mercury.

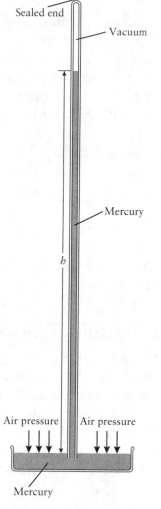

Figure 6.1 The mercury barometer.

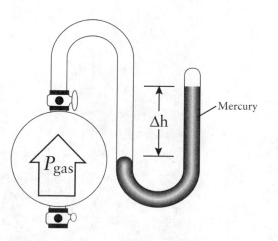

Figure 6.2 The manometer.

Volume–Pressure Relationship: Boyle's Law

 Boyle's law describes the relationship between the volume and pressure of a gas when the temperature and amount are constant. If you have a container like the one shown in Figure 6.3, and you decrease the volume of the container, the pressure of the gas increases because the collisions of gas particles with the container's inside walls increases.

Mathematically this is an inverse relationship, so the product of the pressure and volume is a constant: PV = k.

If you take a gas at an initial volume (V_1) and pressure (P_1) (amount and temperature constant) and change the volume (V_2) and pressure (P_2), you can relate the two sets of conditions to each other by the equation:

$$P_1 V_1 \ = \ P_2 V_2$$

In this mathematical statement of Boyle's law, if you know any three quantities, you can calculate the fourth.

Volume–Temperature Relationship: Charles's Law

 Charles's law describes the volume and temperature relationship of a gas when the pressure and amount are constant. If a sample of gas is heated, the volume must increase for the pressure to remain constant. This is shown in Figure 6.4.

✓ **Remember: In any gas law calculation, you <u>must</u> express the temperature in Kelvin.**

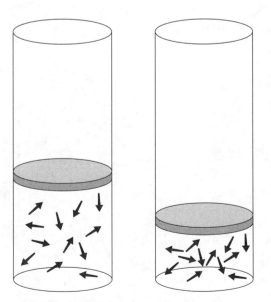

Figure 6.3 Volume-pressure relationship for gases.

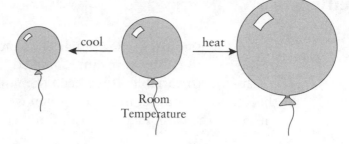

Figure 6.4 Volume-temperature relationship for gases.

There is a direct relationship between the Kelvin temperature and the volume: as one increases, the other also increases. Mathematically, Charles's law can be represented as:

$$V/T = k$$

where k is a constant and the temperature is expressed in Kelvin.

Again, if there is a change from one set of volume–temperature conditions to another, Charles's law can be expressed as:

$$V_1/T_1 = V_2/T_2$$

Pressure–Temperature Relationship: Gay-Lussac's Law

!

Gay-Lussac's law describes the relationship between the pressure of a gas and its Kelvin temperature if the volume and amount are held constant. Figure 6.5 represents the process of heating a given amount of gas at a constant volume.

As the gas is heated the particles move with greater kinetic energy, striking the inside walls of the container more often and with greater force. This causes the pressure of the gas to increase. The relationship between the Kelvin temperature and the pressure is a direct one:

$$P/T = k \quad \text{or} \quad P_1/T_1 = P_2/T_2$$

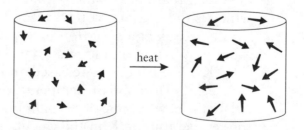

Figure 6.5 Pressure-temperature relationship for gases.

Combined Gas Law

!

In the discussion of Boyle's, Charles's, and Gay-Lussac's laws we held two of the four variables constant, changed the third, and looked at its effect on the fourth variable. If we keep the number of moles of gas constant—that is, no gas can get in or out—then we can combine these three gas laws into one, the **combined gas equation:**

$$(P_1 V_1)/T_1 = (P_2 V_2)/T_2$$

!

Remember: In any gas law calculation, you **must** express the temperature in Kelvin.

In this equation there are six unknowns; given any five, you should be able to solve for the sixth.

Suppose a 5.0-L bottle of gas with a pressure of 2.50 atm at 20° C is heated to 80° C. We can calculate the new pressure using the combined gas law. Before we start working mathematically, however, let's do some reasoning. The volume of the lecture-bottle hasn't changed, and neither has the number of moles of gas inside. Only the temperature and pressure have changed, so this is really a Gay-Lussac's law problem. From Gay-Lussac's law you know that if you increase the temperature, the pressure should increase if the amount and volume are constant. This means that when you calculate the new pressure, it should be greater than 2.50 atm; if it is less, you've made an error. Also, **remember that the temperatures must be expressed in Kelvin.** 20° C = 293 K (K = °C + 273) and 80° C = 353 K.

We will be solving for P_2, so we will take the combined gas law and rearrange for P_2:

$$(T_2 P_1 V_1)/(T_1 V_2) = P_2$$

Substituting in the values:

$$(353 \text{ K})(2.50 \text{ atm})(5.0 \text{ L})/(293 \text{ K})(5.0 \text{ L}) = P_2$$
$$3.0 \text{ atm} = P_2$$

The new pressure is greater than the original pressure, making the answer a reasonable one. Note that all the units canceled except atm, which is the unit that you wanted.

Let's look at a situation in which two conditions change. Suppose a balloon has a volume at sea level of 10.0 L at 760.0 torr and 20° C (293 K). The balloon is released and rises to an altitude where the pressure is 450.0 torr and the temperature is −10° C (263 K). You want to calculate the new volume of the balloon. You know that you have to express the temperature in K in the calculations. It is perfectly fine to leave the pressures in torr. It really doesn't matter what pressure and volume units you use, as long as they are consistent in the problem. The pressure is decreasing, so that should cause the volume to increase (Boyle's law). The temperature is decreasing, so that should cause the volume to decrease (Charles's law). Here you have two competing factors, so it is difficult to predict the end result. You'll simply have to do the calculations and see.

Using the combined gas equation, solve for the new volume (V_2):

$$(P_1V_1)/T_1 = (P_2V_2)/T_2$$

$$(P_1V_1T_2)/(P_2T_1) = V_2$$

Now substitute the known quantities into the equation. (You could substitute the knowns into the combined gas equation first, and then solve for the volume. Do it whichever way is easier for you.)

$$(760.0 \text{ torr})(10.0 \text{ L})(263 \text{ K})/(450.0 \text{ torr})(293 \text{ K}) = V_2$$

$$15.2 \text{ L} = V_2$$

Note that the units canceled, leaving the desired unit of liters. Overall, the volume did increase, so in this case the pressure decrease had a greater effect than the temperature decrease. This seems reasonable looking at the numbers. There is a relatively small change in the Kelvin temperature (293 K versus 263 K) compared to a much larger change in the pressure (760.0 torr versus 450.0 torr).

Volume–Amount Relationship: Avogadro's Law

In all the gas law problems so far, the amount has been constant. But what if the amount changes? That is where Avogadro's law comes into play.

If a container is kept at constant pressure and temperature, and you increase the number of gas particles in that container, the volume will have to increase in order to keep the pressure constant. This means that there is a direct relationship between the volume and the number of moles of gas (n). This is **Avogadro's law** and mathematically it looks like this:

$$V/n = k \quad \text{or} \quad V_1/n_1 = V_2/n_2$$

We could work this into the combined gas law, but more commonly the amount of gas is related to the other physical properties through another relationship that Avogadro developed:

1 mol of any gas occupies 22.4 L at STP

[Standard Temperature and Pressure of 0° C (273 K) and 1 atm]

The combined gas law and Avogadro's relationship can then be combined into the ideal gas equation, which incorporates the pressure, volume, temperature, and amount relationships of a gas.

Ideal Gas Equation

!

The **ideal gas equation** has the mathematical form of PV = nRT, where

P = pressure of the gas in atm, torr, mm Hg, Pa, etc.
V = volume of the gas in L, mL, etc.
n = number of moles of gas
T = Kelvin temperature
R = ideal gas constant: 0.0821 L·atm/K·mol

✓

This is the value for R if the volume is expressed in liters, the pressure in atmospheres, and the temperature in Kelvin (naturally). You could calculate another ideal gas constant based on different units of pressure and volume, but the simplest thing to do is to use the 0.0821 and convert the given volume to liters and the pressure to atm. And remember that you **must express the temperature in Kelvin.**

Let's see how we might use the ideal gas equation. Suppose you want to know what volume 20.0 g of hydrogen gas would occupy at 27° C and 0.950 atm. You have the pressure in atm, you can get the temperature in Kelvin (27° C + 273 = 300 K), but you will need to convert the grams of hydrogen gas to moles of hydrogen gas before you can use the ideal gas equation. Also, remember that hydrogen gas is diatomic, H_2.

First you'll convert the 20.0 g to moles:

$$(20.0 \text{ g}/1) \times (1 \text{ mol } H_2/2.016 \text{ g}) = 9.921 \text{ mol } H_2$$

(We're not worried about significant figures at this point, since this is an intermediate calculation.)

Now you can solve the ideal gas equation for the unknown quantity, the volume.

$$PV = nRT$$

$$V = nRT/P$$

Finally, plug in the numerical values for the different known quantities:

$$V = (9.921 \text{ mol})(0.0821 \text{ L atm}/\text{K mol})(300 \text{ K})/0.950 \text{ atm}$$

$$V = 257 \text{ L}$$

Is the answer reasonable? You have almost 10 mol of gas. It would occupy about 224 L @ STP (10 mol × 22.4 L/mol) by Avogadro's relationship. The pressure is slightly less than standard pressure of 1 atm, which would tend to increase the volume (Boyle's law), and temperature is greater than standard temperature of 0.0° C, which would also increase the volume (Charles's law). So you might expect a volume slightly greater than 224 L, and that is exactly what you found.

✓

Remember, the final thing you do when working any type of chemistry problem is answer the question: Is the answer reasonable?

Dalton's Law of Partial Pressures

! **Dalton's law** says that in a mixture of gases (A+B+C . . .) the total pressure is simply the sum of the partial pressures (the pressures associated with each individual gas). Mathematically, Dalton's law looks like this:

$$P_{Total} = P_A + P_B + P_C + \cdots$$

Commonly Dalton's law is used in calculations involving the collection of a gas over water, as in the displacement of water by oxygen gas. In this situation there is a gas mixture: O_2 and water vapor, $H_2O(g)$. The total pressure in this case is usually atmospheric pressure, and the partial pressure of the water vapor is determined by looking up the vapor pressure of water at the temperature of the water in a reference book. Simple subtraction generates the partial pressure of the oxygen.

If you know how many moles of each gas are in the mixture and the total pressure, you can calculate the partial pressure of each gas by multiplying the total pressure by the mole fraction of each gas:

$$P_A = (P_{Total})(X_A)$$

where X_A = mol fraction of gas A = mol gas A /total mol of gas in the mixture.

Graham's Law of Diffusion and Effusion

! **Graham's law** defines the relationship of the speed of gas diffusion (mixing of gases due to their kinetic energy) or effusion (movement of a gas through a tiny opening) and the gases' molecular weight. In general, the lighter the gas, the faster its rate of effusion. Normally this is set up as the comparison of the effusion rates of two gases, and the specific mathematical relationship is:

$$r_1/r_2 = \sqrt{M_2/M_1}$$

where r_1 and r_2 are the rates of effusion /diffusion of gases 1 and 2 respectively, and M_2 and M_1 are the molecular weights of gases 2 and 1 respectively. **Note that this is an inverse relationship.**

For example, suppose you wanted to calculate the ratio of effusion rates for hydrogen and nitrogen gases. Remember that both are diatomic, so the molecular weight of H_2 is 2.016 g/mol and the molecular weight of N_2 would be 28.02 g/mol. Substituting into the Graham's law equation:

$$r_{H_2}/r_{N_2} = \sqrt{M_{N_2}/M_{H_2}}$$

$$r_{H2}/r_{N2} = (28.02 \text{ g/mol}/2.016 \text{ g/mol})^{1/2} = (13.899)^{1/2} = 3.728$$

Hydrogen gas would effuse through a pinhole 3.728 times as fast as nitrogen gas. The answer is reasonable, since the lower the molecular weight, the faster the gas is moving. Sometimes we measure the effusion rates of a known gas and an unknown gas, and use Graham's law to calculate the molecular weight of the unknown gas.

Gas Stoichiometry

! The gas law relationships can be used in reaction stoichiometry problems. For example, suppose you have a mixture of $KClO_3$ and $NaCl$, and you want to determine how many grams of $KClO_3$ are present. You take the mixture and heat it. The $KClO_3$ decomposes according to the equation:

$$2 \, KClO_3(s) \rightarrow 2 \, KCl(s) + 3 \, O_2(g)$$

The oxygen gas that is formed is collected by displacement of water. It occupies a volume of 542 mL at 27° C. The atmospheric pressure is 755.0 torr.

First you need to determine the pressure of just the oxygen gas. It was collected over water, so the total pressure of 755.0 torr is the sum of the partial pressures of the oxygen and the water vapor:

$$P_{Total} = P_{O_2} + P_{H_2O} \, \text{(Dalton's law)}$$

The partial pressure of water vapor at 27° C is 26.7 torr, so the partial pressure of the oxygen can be calculated by:

$$P_{O_2} = P_{Total} - P_{H_2O} = 755.0 \text{ torr} - 26.7 \text{ torr} = 728.3 \text{ torr}$$

At this point you have 542 mL of oxygen gas at 728.3 torr and 300 K (27° C + 273). From this data you can use the ideal gas equation to calculate the number of moles of oxygen gas produced:

$$PV = nRT$$

$$PV/RT = n$$

You will need to convert the pressure from torr to atm:

$$(728.3 \text{ torr}/1) \times (1 \text{ atm}/760.0 \text{ torr}) = 0.9853 \text{ atm}$$

and express the volume in liters: 542 mL = 0.542 L

Now you can substitute the quantities into the ideal gas equation:

$$(0.9853 \text{ atm})(0.542 \text{ L})/(0.0821 \text{ L} \cdot \text{atm/K} \cdot \text{mol})(300 \text{ K}) = n$$

$$0.02110 \text{ mol } O_2 = n$$

Now you can use the reaction stoichiometry to convert from moles O_2 to moles $KClO_3$ and then to grams $KClO_3$:

$$(0.02110 \text{ mol } O_2/1) \times (2 \text{ mol } KClO_3/3 \text{ mol } O_2)$$

$$\times (122.55 \text{ g } KClO_3/1 \text{ mol } KClO_3) = 1.724 \text{ g } KClO_3$$

Non-Ideal Gases

We have been considering ideal gases, that is, gases that obey the postulates of the Kinetic Molecular Theory. But remember—a couple of those postulates were on shaky ground. The volume of the gas molecules was negligible, and there were no attractive forces between the gas particles. Many times approximations are fine and the ideal gas equation works well. But it would be nice to have a more accurate model for doing extremely precise work or when a polar gas exhibits a relatively large attractive force. In 1873, Johannes van der Waals introduced a modification of the ideal gas equation that attempted to take into account the volume and attractive forces of real gases by introducing two constants—a and b—into the ideal gas equation. van der Waals realized that the actual volume of the gas is less than the ideal gas because gas molecules have a finite volume. He also realized that the more moles of gas present, the greater the ideal and real volume. He compensated for the volume of the gas particles mathematically with:

$$\text{corrected volume} = V - nb$$

where n is the number of moles of gas and b is a different constant for each gas. The larger the gas particle, the more volume it takes up and the larger the b value.

The attraction of the gas particles for each other tends to lessen the pressure of the gas, because the attraction slightly reduces the force of gas particle collisions with the container walls. The amount of attraction depends on the concentration of gas particles and the magnitude of the particles' intermolecular force. The greater the intermolecular forces of the gas, the higher the attraction is, and the less the real pressure. van der Waals compensated for the attractive force with:

$$\text{corrected pressure} = P + an^2/V^2$$

where a is a constant for individual gases. The greater the attractive force between the molecules, the larger the value of a. The n^2/V^2 term corrects for the concentration. Substituting these corrections into the ideal gas equation gives **van der Waals equation:**

$$(P + an^2/V^2)(V - nb) = nRT$$

The larger, more concentrated, and stronger the intermolecular forces of the gas, the more deviation from the ideal gas equation one can expect and the more useful the van der Waals equation becomes.

EXPERIMENTAL

Gas law experiments generally involve pressure, volume, and temperature measurements. In a few cases, other measurements such as mass and time are necessary. You should remember that ΔP, for example, is NOT a measurement; the initial and final pressure measurements are the actual measurements made in the laboratory. Another common error is the application of gas law type information and calculations for non-gaseous materials.

A common consideration is the presence of water vapor, $H_2O(g)$. Water generates a vapor pressure, which varies with the temperature. Dalton's law is used in these cases to adjust the pressure of a gas sample for the presence of water vapor. The total pressure (normally atmospheric pressure) is the pressure of the gas or gases being collected and the water vapor. When the pressure of an individual gas is needed, the vapor pressure of water is subtracted from the total pressure. Finding the vapor pressure of water requires measuring the temperature and using a table showing vapor pressure of water versus temperature.

In Graham's law experiments, time is measured. The amount of time required for a sample to effuse is the measurement. The amount of material effusing divided by the time elapsed is the rate of effusion.

Most gas law experiments use either the combined gas law or the ideal gas equation. Moles of gas are a major factor in many of these experiments. The combined gas law can generate the moles of a gas by adjusting the volume to STP and using Avogadro's relationship of 22.4 L/mol @ STP. The ideal gas equation gives moles from the relationship n = PV/RT.

Two common gas law experiments are "Determination of Molar Mass by Vapor Density" and "Determination of the Molar Volume of a Gas." While it is possible to use the combined gas law (through 22.4 L/mol at STP) for either of these, the ideal gas equation is easier to use. The values for P, V, T, and n must be determined.

The temperature may be determined easily using a thermometer. The temperature measurement is normally in °C. The °C must then be converted to a Kelvin temperature (K = °C + 273).

Pressure is measured using a barometer. If water vapor is present, a correction is needed in the pressure to compensate for its presence. The vapor pressure of water is found in a table of vapor pressure versus temperature. Subtract the value found in this table from the measured pressure (Dalton's law). Values from tables are not considered measurements for an experiment. If you are going to use 0.0821 L atm/mol K for R; convert the pressure to atmospheres.

The value of V may be measured or calculated. A simple measurement of the volume of a container may be made, or a measurement of the volume of displaced water may be required. Calculating the volume requires knowing the number of moles of gas present. No matter how you get the volume, don't forget to convert it to liters.

The values of P, T, and V discussed above may be used, through the use of the ideal gas equation, to determine the number of moles present in a gaseous sample. Stoichiometry is the alternate method of determining the number of moles present. A quantity of a substance is converted to a gas. This conversion may be accomplished in a variety of ways. The most common stoichiometric methods are through volatilization or reaction. The volatilization method is the simplest. A weighed quantity (measure the mass) of a substance is converted to moles by using the molar mass (molecular weight). If a reaction is taking place, the quantity of one of the substances must be determined (normally with the mass and molar mass) and then, through the use of the mole-to-mole ratio, this value is converted to moles.

The values of P, T, and n may be used to determine the volume of a gas. If this volume is to be used with Avogadro's law of 22.4 L/mol, the combined gas law must be employed to adjust the volume to STP. This equation will use the measured values for P and T along with the calculated value of V. These values are combined with STP conditions (0° C and 1.00 atm) to determine the molar volume of a gas.

Combining the value of n with the measured mass of a sample will allow you to calculate the molar mass of the gas.

Do not forget: Values found in tables and conversions from one unit to another are not experimental measurements.

COMMON MISTAKES TO AVOID

1. When using any of the gas laws, be sure you are dealing with gases, not liquids or solids. We've lost track of how many times we've seen people apply gas laws in situations in which no gases were involved.
2. In any of the gas laws, be sure to express the **temperature in Kelvin.** Failure to do so is a quite common mistake.
3. Be sure, especially in stoichiometry problems involving gases, that you are calculating the volume, pressure, etc. of the correct gas. You can avoid this mistake by clearly labeling your quantities (*moles of* O_2 instead of just *moles*).
4. Make sure your **answer is reasonable.** Analyze the problem, don't just write a number down from your calculator.
5. If you have a gas at a certain set of volume/temperature/pressure conditions and the conditions change, you will probably use the combined gas equation. If moles of gas are involved, the ideal gas equation will probably be useful.
6. Make sure your **units cancel.**
7. In using the combined gas equation, make sure you group all initial-condition quantities on one side of the equals sign and all final-condition quantities on the other side.
8. Be sure to use the correct molecular weight for those gases that exist as diatomic molecules—H_2, N_2, O_2, F_2, Cl_2, Br_2, I_2.
9. If the value 22.4 L/mol is to be used, make absolutely sure that it is applied to a **gas** at **STP.**

3 REVIEW QUESTIONS

You have 25 minutes to do the following questions. You may not use a calculator.

1. A sample of argon gas is sealed in a container. The volume of the container is doubled. If the pressure remains constant, what happens to the absolute temperature?

    A. It does not change.
    B. It is halved.
    C. It is doubled.
    D. It is squared.
    E. It cannot be predicted.

2. A sealed rigid container is filled with three ideal gases: A, B, and C. The partial pressure of each gas is known. The temperature and volume of the system are known. What additional information is needed to determine the masses of the gases in the container?

    A. the average distance traveled between molecular collisions
    B. the intermolecular forces
    C. the volume of the gas molecules
    D. the total pressure
    E. the molar masses of the gases

3. Two balloons are at the same temperature and pressure. One contains 14 g of nitrogen and the other contains 20 g of argon. Pick the **false** statement from the following list.

    A. The density of the nitrogen sample is less than the density of the argon sample.
    B. The average speed of the nitrogen molecules is the same as the average speed of the argon molecules.
    C. The average kinetic energy of the nitrogen molecules is the same as the average kinetic energy of the argon molecules.

    D. The volume of the nitrogen container is the same as the volume of the argon container.
    E. The number of molecules in the nitrogen container is the same as the number of atoms in the argon container.

4. An experiment to determine the molecular weight of a gas begins by heating a solid to produce a gaseous product. The gas passes through a tube and displaces water in an inverted water-filled bottle. Which of the following necessary items may be determined after the experiment is completed?

    A. vapor pressure of water
    B. temperature of the displaced water
    C. barometric pressure in the room
    D. mass of the solid used
    E. volume of the displaced water

5. The true volume of a real gas is larger than that calculated from the ideal gas equation. This occurs because the ideal gas equation does NOT correct for:

    A. the attraction between the molecules
    B. the shape of the molecules
    C. the volume of the molecules
    D. the mass of the molecules
    E. the speed the molecules are moving

6. Aluminum metal reacts with HCl to produce aluminum chloride and hydrogen gas. How many grams of aluminum metal must be added to an excess of HCl to produce 33.6 L of hydrogen gas, if the gas is at STP?

A. 18.0 g
B. 35.0 g
C. 27.0 g
D. 4.50 g
E. 9.00 g

7. A reaction produces a gaseous mixture of carbon dioxide, carbon monoxide, and water vapor. After one reaction the mixture was analyzed and found to contain 0.60 mol of carbon dioxide, 0.30 mol of carbon monoxide, and 0.10 mol of water vapor. If the total pressure of the mixture was 0.80 atm, what was the partial pressure of the carbon monoxide?

A. 0.080 atm
B. 0.34 atm
C. 0.13 atm
D. 0.24 atm
E. 0.48 atm

8. A sample of methane gas was collected over water at 35° C. The sample was found to have a total pressure of 756 mm Hg. Determine the partial pressure of the methane gas in the sample (vapor of water at 35° C is 41 mm Hg).

A. 760 mm Hg
B. 41 mm Hg
C. 715 mm Hg
D. 797 mm Hg
E. 756 mm Hg

9. A sample of oxygen gas with a volume of 8.00 L at 127° C and 775 mm Hg is heated until it expands to a volume of 20.00 L. Determine the final temperature of the oxygen gas, if the pressure remains constant.

A. 727° C
B. 318° C
C. 1000° C
D. 160° C
E. 45° C

10. The average kinetic energy of nitrogen molecules changes by what factor when the temperature is increased from 30° C to 60° C?

A. (333 – 303)
B. 2
C. ½
D. square root (303 – 333)
E. 28

11. A 1.15-mol sample of carbon monoxide gas has a temperature of 27° C and a pressure of 0.327 atm. If the temperature is lowered to 17° C, at constant volume, what would be the new pressure?

A. 0.316 atm
B. 0.519 atm
C. 0.206 atm
D. 0.338 atm
E. 0.363 atm

12. An ideal gas sample weighing 1.28 grams at 121° C and 1.03 atm has a volume of 0.250 L. Determine the molar mass of the gas.

A. 322 g/mol
B. 161 g/mol
C. 0.00621 g/mol
D. 80.5 g/mol
E. 49.4 g/mol

13. Increasing the temperature of an ideal gas from 50° C to 75° C at constant volume will cause which of the following to increase for the gas?

I. the average distance between the molecules
II. the average speed of the molecules
III. the average molecular mass of the gas

A. III only
B. I only
C. II only
D. II and III
E. I and II

14. If a sample of CH_4 effuses at a rate of 9.0 mol per hour at 35° C, which of the gases below will effuse at approximately twice the rate under the same conditions?

   A. CO
   B. He
   C. O_2
   D. F_2
   E. SiH_4

15. A steel tank containing argon gas has additional argon gas pumped into it at constant temperature. Which of the following is true for the gas in the tank?

   A. There is no change in the number of gas atoms.
   B. There is an increase in the volume of the gas.
   C. There is a decrease in the pressure exerted by the gas.
   D. The gas atoms travel with the same average speed.
   E. The gas atoms are separated by a greater average distance.

16. $2 N_2O_5(s) \rightarrow 4NO_2(g) + O_2(g)$

   A 2 L evacuated flask has a 0.2 mol sample of $N_2O_5(s)$ sealed inside it. The flask is heated to decompose the solid and cooled to 300 K. The $N_2O_5(s)$ is completely decomposed according to the balanced equation above. What is the nearest value to the final total pressure of the gases in the flask? (The value of the gas constant, R, is 0.082 L atm $mol^{-1}K^{-1}$).

   A. 0.6 atm
   B. 6 atm
   C. 0.05 atm
   D. 1.2 atm
   E. 3 atm

17. A glass container is filled, at room temperature, with an equal numbers of moles of $H_2(g)$, $O_2(g)$, and $NO_2(g)$. The gases slowly leak out through a pinhole. After some of the gas has effused, which of the following is true of the relative values for the partial pressures of the gases remaining in the container?

   A. $H_2 < NO_2 < O_2$
   B. $NO_2 < H_2 < O_2$
   C. $H_2 = NO_2 = O_2$
   D. $O_2 < NO_2 < H_2$
   E. $H_2 < O_2 < NO_2$

18. Choose the gas that probably shows the greatest deviation from ideal gas behavior.

   A. He
   B. O_2
   C. SF_4
   D. SiH_4
   E. Ar

19. Determine the formula for a gaseous silane (Si_nH_{2n+2}) if it has a density of 5.47 g per L at 0° C and 1.00 atm.

   A. SiH_4
   B. Si_2H_6
   C. Si_3H_8
   D. Si_4H_{10}
   E. Si_5H_{12}

20. Which of the following best explains why a hot air balloon rises?

   A. The heating of the air causes the pressure inside the balloon to increase.
   B. The cool outside air pushes the balloon higher.
   C. The temperature difference between the inside and outside air causes convection currents.
   D. Hot air has a lower density than cold air.
   E. Cooler air diffuses more slowly than the warmer air.

ANSWERS AND EXPLANATIONS

✓

1. **C.** This question relates to the combined gas law: $P_1V_1/T_1 = P_2V_2/T_2$. Since the pressure remains constant, the pressures may be removed from the combined gas law to produce Charles's law: $V_1/T_1 = V_2/T_2$. This equation may be rearranged to: $T_2 = V_2T_1/V_1$. The doubling of the volume means $V_2 = 2 V_1$. On substituting: $T_2 = 2V_1T_1/V_1$; giving $T_2 = 2 T_1$. The identity of the gas is irrelevant in this problem.

2. **E.** This problem depends on the ideal gas equation: $PV = nRT$. R, V, and T are known, and by using the partial pressure for a gas the number of moles of that gas may be determined. To convert from moles to mass, the molar mass of the gas is needed.

3. **B.** Since T and P are known, and since the moles (n) can be determined from the masses given, this question could use the ideal gas equation. The number of moles of each gas is 0.50. Equal moles of gases, at the same T and P, have equal volumes. Equal volume eliminates answer choice D. Equal volume also means that the greater mass has the greater density, eliminating choice A. Equal moles means that the numbers of molecules and atoms are equal, eliminating choice E. The average kinetic energy of a gas depends on the temperature. If the temperatures are the same, then the average kinetic energy is the same, eliminating C. Finally, at the same temperature, heavier gases travel slower than lighter gases. Nitrogen is lighter than argon, so it travels at a faster average speed, making B the correct answer.

4. **A.** This experiment requires the ideal gas equation. The mass of the solid is needed (to convert to moles); this eliminates answer choice D. The volume, temperature, and pressure must also be measured during the experiment, eliminating choices B, C, and E. The measured pressure is the total pressure. Eventually the total pressure must be converted to the partial pressure of the gas using Dalton's law. The total pressure is the sum of the pressure of the gas plus the vapor pressure of water. The vapor pressure of water can be looked up in a table when the calculations are performed (only the temperature is needed to find the vapor pressure in a table). Answer A is correct.

5. **C.** Real gases are different from ideal gases because of two basic factors (see the van der Waals equation): molecules have a volume, and molecules attract each other. The molecules' volume is subtracted from the observed volume for a real gas (giving a smaller volume), and the pressure has a term added to compensate for the attraction of the molecules (correcting for a smaller pressure). Since these are the only two directly related factors, answers B, D, and E are eliminated. The question is asking about volume; thus, the answer is C. You should be careful of "NOT" questions such as this one.

6. **C.** A balanced chemical equation is needed:

$$2 \text{ Al} + 6 \text{ HCl} \rightarrow 2 \text{ AlCl}_3 + 3 \text{ H}_2$$

The reaction produced 33.6L/22.4 L or 1.50 mol at STP. To produce this quantity of hydrogen, (2 mol Al/3 mol H_2) × 1.50 moles H_2 = 1.00 mol of Al. The atomic weight of Al is 27.0; thus, 27.0 g of Al are required.

7. **D.** The partial pressure of any gas is equal to its mole fraction times the total pressure. The mole fraction of carbon monoxide is [0.30/(0.60 + 0.30 + 0.10)] = 0.30, and the partial pressure of CO is 0.30 × 0.80 atm = 0.24 atm.

8. **C.** Using Dalton's law ($P_{Total} = P_A + P_B + \ldots$), the partial pressure may be found by: 756 mm Hg – 41 mm Hg = 715 mm Hg.

9. **A.** The answer may be found using the combined gas law. Removing the constant pressure leaves Charles's law: $V_1/T_1 = V_2/T_2$. This is rearranged to: $T_2 = V_2 T_1/V_1 = (20.00 \text{ L} \times 400 \text{ K})/(8.00 \text{ L}) = 1000$ K (= 727° C). The other answers result from common errors in this problem.

10. **A.** The average kinetic energy of the molecules depends on the temperature. The correct answer involves a temperature difference (333 K – 303 K). Do not forget that ALL gas law calculations require Kelvin temperatures.

11. **A.** You can begin by removing the volume (constant) from the combined gas law to produce Gay-Lussac's law = $P_1/T_1 = P_2/T_2$. This equation may be rearranged to: $P_2 = P_1 T_2/T_1 = (0.327 \text{ atm} \times 290 \text{ K})/(300 \text{ K}) = 0.316$ atm. The moles are not important since they do not change. Some of the other answers result from common errors.

12. **B.** The molar mass may be obtained by dividing the grams by the number of moles (calculated from the ideal gas equation). Do not forget to convert the temperature to Kelvins.

13. **C.** Choice I requires an increase in volume. Choice II requires an increase in temperature. Choice III requires a change in the composition of the gas.

14. **B.** Lighter gases effuse faster. The only gas among the choices that is lighter than methane is helium. To calculate the molar mass, you would begin with the molar mass of methane and divide by the rate difference squared: $M_A = M_B (½)^2$.

15. **D.** A steel tank will have a constant volume, and the problem states that the temperature is constant. Adding gas to the tank will increase the moles (molecules) of the gas and the pressure (forcing the molecules closer together). A constant temperature means there will be a constant average speed.

16. **B.** The pressure is calculated using the ideal gas equation. A common mistake is forgetting that 5 mol of gas are produced for every 2 mol of solid reactant. The ideal gas equation is rearranged to $P = nRT/V$ = ($\frac{5}{2}$)(0.2 mol)(0.082 L atm mol^{-1} K^{-1}). (300 K)/(2 L) = 6 atm.

17. **E.** The lighter the gas, the faster it effuses (escapes). Equal moles of gases in the same container would give equal initial partial pressures. The partial pressures would be reduced relative to the masses of the molecules, with the lightest gas being reduced the most.

18. **C.** Deviations from ideal behavior depend on the size and the intermolecular forces between the molecules. The greatest deviation would be for a large polar molecule. Sulfur tetrafluoride is the largest molecule, and it is the only polar molecule listed.

19. **D.** The molar mass of gas must be determined. The simplest method to find the molar mass is: (5.47 g/L) × (22.4 L/mol) = 123 g/mol (simple factor label). The molar mass may also be determined by dividing the mass of the gas by the moles (using 22.4 L/mol for a gas at STP and using 1 L). If you did not recognize the conditions as STP, you could find the moles from the ideal gas equation. The correct answer is the gas with the molar mass closest to 123 g/mol.

20. **D.** The hot air balloon rises because it has a lower density than air. "Lighter" objects will float on "heavy" objects.

FREE-RESPONSE QUESTIONS

You have 20 minutes to do the following questions. You may use a calculator.

A hydrogen gas sample is collected over water. The volume of the sample was 190.0 mL at 26° C, and the pressure in the room was 754 mm Hg. The vapor pressure of water at 26° C is 25.2 mm Hg.

a. Calculate the number of moles of hydrogen in the sample.

b. Calculate how many molecules of water vapor are present in the sample.

c. Determine the density (in g/L) of the gas mixture.

d. Determine the mole fraction of water.

ANSWERS AND EXPLANATIONS

✓

a. $P_{total} = 754$ mm Hg $\qquad$ $P_{hydrogen} = 754 - 25.2 = 729$ mm Hg
$P = 729/760 = 0.959$ atm
$V = 190.0$ mL $= 0.1900$ L $\qquad$ $T = 26°$ C $= 299$ K
$R = 0.0821$ L atm mol^{-1} K^{-1}

$n = PV/RT$

$\quad = (0.959$ atm $\times 0.1900$ L$)/(0.0821$ L atm mol^{-1} $K^{-1} \times 299$ K$)$

$\quad = 0.00742$ mol H_2

Give yourself 1 point for the correct answer (no deduction for rounding differently). You must include *all* parts of the calculation (including "=").
Give yourself 1 point for the correct equation, or for any other correct calculation.
Do not give yourself more than 2 points total for this part.

b. $P_{water} = 25.2 / 760 = 0.0332$ tm T and V are the same as in part a.
Avogadro's number $= 6.022 \times 10^{23}$ molecules $mol^{-1} = N$

$n = PV/RT$

$\quad = (0.0332$ atm $\times 0.1900$ L$)/(0.0821$ L atm mol^{-1} $K^{-1} \times 299$ K$)$

$\quad = 2.57 \times 10^{-4}$ mol H_2O

molecules $= (2.57 \times 10^{-4}$ mol$) \times (6.022 \times 10^{23}$ molecules $mol^{-1})$

$\qquad\qquad = 1.35 \times 10^{20}$ molecules

Give yourself 1 point for the correct answer (no deduction for rounding differently). You must include *all* parts of the calculation (including "=").
Give yourself 1 point for the correct equation, or for any other correct calculation.
Do not give yourself more than 2 points total for this part.

c. $(0.00742$ mol $H_2) \times (2.016$ g $H_2/$mol $H_2) = 0.0150$ g H_2

$(2.57 \times 10^{-4}$ mol $H_2O) \times (18.02$ g $H_2O/$mol $H_2O) = 0.00463$ g H_2O

total mass $= 0.0150$ g $H_2 + 0.00463$ g $H_2O = 0.0196$ g

density $= 0.0196$ g$/0.1900$ L $= 0.103$ g$/$L

Give yourself 1 point for the correct answer (no deduction for rounding differently). You must include *all* parts of the calculation (including "=").

Give yourself 1 point for the correct equation, or for any other correct calculation.

Do not give yourself more than 2 points total for this part.

d. 0.00742 mol H_2 and 2.57×10^{-4} mol H_2O

total moles $= (0.00742 + 2.57 \times 10^{-4}) = 0.00768$ mol

Mole fraction $H_2O = (2.57 \times 10^{-4}$ mol $H_2O)/(0.00768$ mol$)$

$= 0.0335$

Give yourself 1 point for the correct answer (no deduction for rounding differently). You must include *all* parts of the calculation (including "=").

Give yourself 1 point for the correct equation, or for any other correct calculation.

Do not give yourself more than 2 points total for this part.

Total score = sum of parts a–d.

RAPID REVIEW

- Kinetic Molecular Theory—Gases are small particles of negligible volume moving in a random straight-line motion, colliding with the container walls (that is the gas pressure) and with each other. During these collisions no energy is lost, but energy may be transferred from one particle to another; the Kelvin temperature is proportional to the average kinetic energy. There is assumed to be no attraction between the particles.

- Pressure—Know how a barometer operates and the different units used in atmospheric pressure.

- Boyle's law—The volume and pressure of a gas are inversely proportional if the temperature and amount are constant.

- Charles's law—The volume and temperature of a gas are directly proportional if the amount and pressure are constant.

- Gay-Lussac's law—The pressure and temperature of a gas are directly proportional if the amount and volume are constant.

- Combined gas law—Know how to use the combined gas equation $P_1V_1/T_1 = P_2V_2/T_2$.

- Avogadro's law—The number of moles and volume of a gas are directly proportional if the pressure and temperature are constant. Remember that 1 mol of an ideal gas @ STP (1 atm & 0° C) occupies a volume of 22.4 L.

- Ideal gas equation—Know how to use the ideal gas equation $PV = nRT$

- Dalton's law—The sum of the partial pressures of the individual gases in a gas mixture is equal to the total pressure: $P_{Total} = P_A + P_B + P_c + \ldots$

- Graham's law—The lower the molecular weight of a gas, the faster it will effuse/diffuse. Know how to use Graham's Law: $r_1/r_2 = (M_2/M_1)^{1/2}$

- Gas stoichiometry—Know how to apply the gas laws to reaction stoichiometry problems.

- Non-ideal gases—Know how the van der Waals equation accounts for the non-ideal behavior of real gases.

- Tips—Make sure the **temperature is in Kelvin;** gas laws are being applied to gases only; the **units cancel;** and the **answer is reasonable.**

Chapter 7

Thermodynamics

KEYWORDS AND EQUATIONS

✓ $S°$ = standard entropy $H°$ = standard enthalpy
$G°$ = standard free energy q = heat
c = specific heat capacity C_p = molar heat capacity at constant pressure

$\Delta S° = \Sigma\ S°$ products $- \Sigma\ S°$ reactants
$\Delta H° = \Sigma\ \Delta H_f°$ products $- \Sigma\ \Delta H_f°$ reactants
$\Delta G° = \Sigma\ \Delta G_f°$ products $- \Sigma\ \Delta G_f°$ reactants
$\Delta G° = \Delta H° - T\Delta S°$
$\quad = -RT \ln K = -2.303\ RT \log K$
$\quad = -n\ F\ E°$
$\Delta G = \Delta G° + RT \ln Q = \Delta G° + 2.303\ RT \log Q$
$q = mc\Delta T$
$C_p = \Delta H/\Delta T$

INTRODUCTION

Thermodynamics is the study of heat and its transformations. **Thermochemistry** is the part of thermodynamics that deals with changes in heat that take place during chemical reactions. We will be describing energy changes in this chapter. Energy can be of two types: kinetic or potential. **Kinetic energy** is energy of motion, while **potential energy** is stored energy. Energy can be converted from one form to another but, unless a nuclear reaction occurs, energy cannot be created or destroyed (Law of Conservation of Energy). We will discuss energy exchanges between a system and surroundings. The **system** is that part of the universe that we are studying. It may be a beaker or it may be Earth. The **surroundings** are the rest of the universe that is being affected by the change.

The most common units of energy are used in the study of thermo-dynamics are the joule and the calorie. The **joule (J)** is defined as:

$$1\ J = 1\ kg\ m^2/s^2$$

The **calorie** was originally defined as the amount of energy needed to raise the temperature of 1 g of water 1° C. Now it is defined in terms of its relationship to the joule:

$$1\ cal = 4.184\ J$$

! It is important to realize that this is not the same calorie that is commonly associated with food and diets. That is the nutritional Calorie, which is really a kilocalorie (1 C = 1000 cal).

CALORIMETRY

Calorimetry is the laboratory technique used to measure the heat released or absorbed during a chemical or physical change. The quantity of heat absorbed or released during a chemical or physical change is represented as q and is proportional to the change in temperature of the system being studied. This system has what is called a **heat capacity,** which is the quantity of heat needed to change the temperature 1 K. It has the form:

$$\text{heat capacity} = q/\Delta T$$

Heat capacity most commonly has units of J/K. The **specific heat capacity (or specific heat) (c)** is the quantity of heat needed to raise the temperature of 1 g of a substance 1 K:

$$c = q/\text{mass} \times \Delta T \text{ or } q = c \times \text{mass} \times \Delta T$$

The specific heat capacity commonly has units of J/g·K. Because of the original definition of the calorie, the specific heat capacity of water is 4.184 J/g·K. If the specific heat capacity, the mass, and the change of temperature are all known, the amount of energy absorbed can easily be calculated.

Another related quantity is the **molar heat capacity (C),** the amount of heat needed to change the temperature of 1 mol of a substance 1 K.

Calorimetry involves the use of a laboratory instrument called a calorimeter. Two types of calorimeters, a simple coffee-cup calorimeter and a more sophisticated bomb calorimeter, are shown in Figure 7.1. In both, a reaction is carried out with known amounts of reactants and the change in temperature is measured.

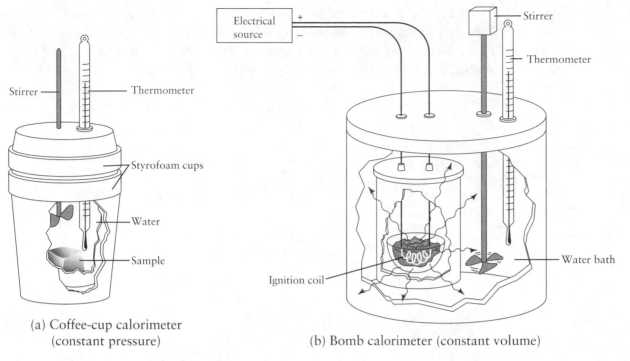

(a) Coffee-cup calorimeter
(constant pressure)

(b) Bomb calorimeter (constant volume)

Figure 7.1 Two types of calorimeters.

The coffee-cup calorimeter can be used to measure the heat changes in reactions that are open to the atmosphere: q_p, constant pressure reactions. These might be reactions that occur in open beakers and the like. This type of calorimeter is commonly used to measure the specific heats of solids. A known mass of solid is heated to a certain temperature and then is added to the calorimeter containing a known mass of water at a known temperature. The final temperature is then measured. We know that the heat lost by the solid (the system) is equal to the heat gained by the surroundings (the water and calorimeter, although for simple coffee-cup calorimetry the heat gained by the calorimeter is small and is ignored):

$$-q_{solid} = q_{water}$$

Substituting the mathematical relationship for q gives:

$$-(c_{solid} \times mass_{solid} \times \Delta T_{solid}) = c_{water} \times mass_{water} \times \Delta T_{water}$$

This equation can then be solved for the specific heat capacity of the solid.

The constant-volume bomb calorimeter is used to measure the energy changes that occur during combustion reactions. A weighed sample of the substance being investigated is placed in the calorimeter, and compressed oxygen is added. The sample is ignited by a hot wire, and the temperature change of the calorimeter and a known mass of water is measured. The heat capacity of the calorimeter/water system is commonly known.

A 1.5886 g sample of glucose ($C_6H_{12}O_6$) was ignited in a bomb calorimeter. The temperature increased by 3.682°C. The heat capacity of the calorimeter was 3.562kJ/°C, and the calorimeter contained 1.000 kg of water. Find the molar heat of reaction (i.e., J/mole) for:

$$C_6H_{12}O_6(s) + 6\,O_2(g) \rightarrow 6\,CO_2(g) + 6\,H_2O(l)$$

Answer:

$$\frac{(3.562\ kJ)}{(°C)}(3.682°\ C) = 13.12\ kJ$$

$$(1.000\ kg)\frac{(1000\ g)(4.184\ J)(1\ kJ)}{(1\ kg)(g\ °C)(1000\ J)}(3.682°\ C) = 15.40\ kJ$$

total heat = 28.52 kJ

Note: The temperature increased so the reaction was exothermic (−)

$$\rightarrow -28.52\ kJ$$

This is not molar (yet)

$$(1.5886\ g)\frac{(1\ mol)}{(180.16\ g)} = 8.8177 \times 10^{-3}\ mol$$

Thus:

$$\frac{-28.52\ kJ}{8.8177 \times 10^{-3}\ mol} = -3234\ kJ/mol$$

LAWS OF THERMODYNAMICS

The **First Law of Thermodynamics** states that the total energy of the universe is constant. This is simply the Law of Conservation of Energy. This can be mathematically stated as:

$$\Delta E_{universe} = \Delta E_{system} + \Delta E_{surroundings} = 0$$

The Second Law of Thermodynamics involves a term called entropy. **Entropy (S)** is related to the disorder of a system. The **Second Law of Thermodynamics** states that all processes that occur spontaneously move in the direction of an increase in entropy of the universe (system + surroundings). Mathematically, this can be stated as:

$$\Delta S_{universe} = \Delta S_{system} + \Delta S_{surroundings} > 0 \quad \text{for a spontaneous process}$$

For a reversible process, a system at equilibrium, $\Delta S_{universe} = 0$. The qualitative entropy change (increase or decrease of entropy) for a system can sometimes be determined using a few simple rules:

1. Entropy increases when the number of molecules increases during a reaction.
2. Entropy increases with an increase in temperature.
3. Entropy increases when a gas is formed from a liquid or solid.
4. Entropy increases when a liquid is formed from a solid.

Let us now look at some applications of these first two laws of thermodynamics.

PRODUCTS MINUS REACTANTS

Enthalpies

Many of the reactions which chemists study are reactions that occur at constant pressure. During the discussion of the coffee-cup calorimeter, the heat change at constant temperature was defined as q_p. Because this constant pressure situation is so common in chemistry, a special thermodynamic term is used to describe this energy, enthalpy. The **enthalpy change, ΔH,** is equal to the heat gained or lost by the system during constant pressure conditions. The following sign conventions apply:

If $\Delta H > 0$ the reaction is endothermic

If $\Delta H < 0$ the reaction is exothermic

The ΔH is sometimes called the $\Delta H_{reaction}$. The ΔH often is given in association with a particular reaction. For example, the enthalpy change associated with the formation of water from hydrogen and oxygen gases can be shown in this fashion:

$$2\,H_2(g) + O_2(g) \rightarrow 2\,H_2O(g) \qquad \Delta H = -483.6\ kJ$$

The negative sign indicates that this reaction is exothermic. This value of ΔH is for the production of 2 mol of water. If 4 mol were produced, the ΔH would be twice -483.6 kJ. The techniques developed in working reaction stoichiometry problems (Chapter 5) apply here also.

If the reaction above for the formation of water were reversed, the sign of the ΔH would be reversed. That would indicate that it would take 483.6 kJ of energy to decompose 2 mol of water. This would now become an endothermic process.

The ΔH is dependent upon the state of matter. The enthalpy change would be different for the formation of liquid water instead of gaseous water.

The ΔH can also indicate whether a reaction will be spontaneous. A negative (exothermic) value of the ΔH is associated with a spontaneous reaction. However, in many reactions this is not the case. There are other factors to consider in predicting a reaction's spontaneity. We will cover these other factors a little later in this chapter.

Enthalpies of reaction can be measured using a calorimeter. However, they can also be calculated in a couple of ways. **Hess's law** states that if a reaction occurs in a series of steps, then the enthalpy change for the overall reaction is simply the sum of the enthalpy changes of the individual steps. If, in adding the equations of the steps together, it is necessary to reverse one of the given reactions, then the sign of the ΔH must be reversed. Also, particular attention must be used if the reaction stoichiometry has to be adjusted. The value of an individual ΔH may need to be adjusted.

It doesn't matter whether the steps used are the actual steps in the mechanism of the reaction, because $\Delta H_{reaction}$ (ΔH_{rxn}) is a **state function**, a function that doesn't depend on the pathway, only the initial and final states.

Given the following information:

$$C(s) + O_2(g) \rightarrow CO_2(g) \qquad\qquad \Delta H = -393.5 \text{ kJ}$$

$$H_2(g) + (1/2)O_2(g) \rightarrow H_2O(l) \qquad\qquad \Delta H = -285.8 \text{ kJ}$$

$$C_2H_2(g) + (5/2)O_2(g) \rightarrow 2\,CO_2(g) + H_2O(l) \qquad \Delta H = -1299.8 \text{ kJ}$$

Find the enthalpy change for:

$$2\,C(s) + H_2(g) \rightarrow C_2H_2(g)$$

Answer:

$$2[C(s) + O_2(g) \rightarrow CO_2(g)] \qquad\qquad 2\,(-393.5 \text{ kJ})$$

$$H_2(g) + (1/2)\,O_2(g) \rightarrow H_2O(l) \qquad\qquad -285.8 \text{ kJ}$$

$$2\,CO_2(g) + H_2O(l) \rightarrow C_2H_2(g) + (5/2)\,O_2(g) \qquad -(-1299.8 \text{ kJ})$$

$$2\,C(s) + H_2(g) \rightarrow C_2H_2(g) \qquad\qquad 227.0 \text{ kJ}$$

Enthalpies of reaction can also be calculated from individual enthalpies of formation (or heats of formation), ΔH_f, for the reactants and products. Because the temperature and pressure and state of the substance will cause these enthalpies to vary, it is common to use a standard state convention. For gases, the standard state is 1 atm pressure. For a substance in an aqueous solution, the standard state is 1 molar concentration. And for a pure substance (compound or element) the standard state is the most stable form at 1 atm pressure and 25° C. A superscript zero to the right of the H indicates a standard state, $\Delta H°$. The **standard enthalpy of formation** of a compound ($\Delta H_f°$) is the change in enthalpy when 1 mol of the compound is formed from its elements when all substances are in their standard states. These values are then tabulated and can be used determining the $\Delta H°_{rxn}$.

The $\Delta H_f°$ of an element in its standard state is zero.

The $\Delta H_f°_{rxn}$ can be determined from the tabulated $\Delta H_f°$ of the individual reactants and products. It is the sum of the $\Delta H_f°$ of the products minus the sum of the $\Delta H_f°$ of the reactants:

$$\Delta H°_{rxn} = \sum \Delta H_f° \text{ products} - \sum \Delta H_f° \text{ reactants}$$

In using this equation be sure to consider the number of moles of each, because the $\Delta H_f°$ for the individual compounds refer to the formation of 1 mol.

Calculate ΔH_{rxn} for:

$$6\,H_2O(g) + 4\,NO(g) \rightarrow 5\,O_2(g) + 4\,NH_3(g)$$

$$\Delta H_{rxn} = \left\{ 5[\Delta H°_f\ O_2(g)] + 4[\Delta H°_f\ NH_3(g)] \right\}$$

$$- \left\{ [6\Delta H°_f\ H_2O(g)] + 4[\Delta H°_f\ NO_3(g)] \right\}$$

$$= [5(0.00\text{ kJ}) + 4(-46.19\text{ kJ})] - [6(-241.85\text{ kJ}) + 4(90.37)]$$

$$= 904.68\text{ kJ}$$

People commonly forget to subtract *all* the reactants from the products. The values of the $\Delta H°_f$ will be given to you on the AP exam, or you will be asked to stop before putting the numbers into the problem.

An alternative means of estimating the heat of reaction is to take the sum of the average bond energies of the reactant molecules and subtract the sum of the average bond energies of the product molecules.

Entropies

In much the same way the $\Delta H°$ was calculated, the **standard molar entropies (S°)** of elements and compounds can be tabulated. This is the entropy associated with 1 mol of a substance in its standard state. Entropies are also tabulated, but unlike enthalpies, the entropies of elements are not zero. For a reaction, the standard entropy change is calculated the same way as the enthalpies of reaction:

$$\Delta S° = \sum S° \text{ products} - \sum S° \text{ reactants}$$

Calculate $\Delta S°$ for the following. If you do not have a table of $S°$ values, just set up the problems.

Note: These are thermochemical equations, so fractions are allowed.

a. $H_2(g) + \frac{1}{2} O_2(g) \rightarrow H_2O(g)$
b. $H_2(g) + \frac{1}{2} O_2(g) \rightarrow H_2O(l)$
c. $CaCO_3(s) + H_2SO_4(l) \rightarrow CaSO_4(s) + H_2O(g) + CO_2(g)$

Answers:

a. H_2O H_2 O_2

188.7 J/mol K – [131.0 + 1/2(205.0)]J/mol K

= –44.8 J/mol K

b. H_2O H_2 O_2

69.9 J/mol K – [131.0 + 1/2(205.0)]J/mol K

= –163.6 J/mol K

c. $CaSO_4$ H_2O CO_2 $CaCO_3$ H_2SO_4

107 + 188.7 + 213.6 – [92.9 + 157] J/mol K

= 259 J/mol K

One of the goals of chemists is to be able to predict whether a reaction will be spontaneous. Some general guidelines for a spontaneous reaction have already been presented (negative ΔH and positive ΔS), but neither is a reliable predictor by itself. Temperature plays a part also. A thermodynamic factor that takes into account the entropy, enthalpy, and temperature of the reaction should be the best indicator of spontaneity. This factor is called the Gibbs free energy.

Gibbs Free Energy

The **Gibbs free energy (G)** is a thermodynamic function that combines the enthalpy, entropy, and temperature:

$$G = H - TS \text{ where T is the Kelvin temperature}$$

Like most thermodynamic functions, only the change in Gibbs free energy can be measured, so the relationship becomes:

$$\Delta G = \Delta H - T \Delta S$$

ΔG is the best indicator chemists have as to whether or not a reaction is spontaneous:

!

- If $\Delta G > 0$, the reaction is not spontaneous; energy must be supplied to cause the reaction to occur.
- If $\Delta G < 0$, the reaction is spontaneous.
- If $\Delta G = 0$, the reaction is at equilibrium.

If there is a ΔG associated with a reaction and that reaction is then reversed, the sign of the ΔG changes.

Just like with the enthalpy and entropy, the standard Gibbs free energy change, ($\Delta G°$), is calculated:

$$\Delta G° = \sum \Delta G_f° \text{ products} - \sum \Delta G_f° \text{ reactants}$$

The $\Delta G_f°$ of an element in its standard state is zero.

$\Delta G°$ for a reaction may also be calculated by using the standard enthalpy and standard entropy of reaction:

$$\Delta G° = \Delta H°_{rxn} - T \Delta S°_{rxn}$$

Calculate $\Delta G°$ for:

(If you do not have a table of $\Delta G°$ values, just set up the problems.)

a. $2 NH_4Cl(s) + CaO(s) \rightarrow CaCl_2(s) + H_2O(l) + 2 NH_3(g)$
b. $C_2H_4(g) + H_2O(g) \rightarrow C_2H_5OH(l)$
c. $Ca(s) + 2 H_2SO_4(l) \rightarrow CaSO_4(s) + SO_2(g) + 2 H_2O(l)$

Answers:

a.

$CaCl_2(s)$	$H_2O(l)$	$NH_3(g)$	$NH_4Cl(s)$	$CaO(s)$
–750.2	–237.2	–16.6	–203.9	–604.2 kJ/mol

$[–750.2 + (–237.2) + 2(–16.6)] – [2(–203.9) + (–604.2)]$
$= –8.6$ kJ/mole

b.

$C_2H_5OH(l)$	$C_2H_4(g)$	$H_2O(g)$
–174.18	68.12	–228.6

$–174.18 – [68.12 + (–228.6)] = –13.7$ kJ/mol

c.

$CaSO_4(s)$	$SO_2(g)$	$H_2O(l)$	$Ca(s)$	$H_2SO_4(l)$
–1320.3	–300.4	–237.2	0.0	–689.9 kJ/mol

$[(–1320.3) + (–300.4) + 2(–237.2)] – [(0.0) + 2(–689.9)]$
$= –715.3$ kJ/mol

THERMODYNAMICS AND EQUILIBRIUM

Thus far, we have considered only situations at standard conditions. But how do we cope with nonstandard conditions? The change in Gibbs free energy at nonstandard conditions is:

$$\Delta G = \Delta G° + RT \ln Q = \Delta G° + 2.303 \log Q$$

Q is the activity quotient, products over reactants. This equation allows the calculation of the ΔG under those situations in which the concentrations or pressures are not 1.

Calculate ΔG for the following at 500 K:

$$2 \text{ NO(g)} + O_2(g) \rightarrow 2 \text{ NO}_2(g)$$

2.00 M   0.500 M   1.00 M

(Assume $\Delta G°_f = \Delta G^{500}_f$)

$\Delta G°_f$ (86.71   0.000   51.84) kJ/mol

$\Delta G_{rxn} = 2(51.84) - [2(86.71) + 0.000] = -69.74$ kJ/mol

$\Delta G^{500} = \Delta G_{rxn} + RT \ln Q$

$$Q = \frac{[NO_2]^2}{[NO]^2[O_2]}$$

$$= (-69.74 \text{ kJ})(1000 \text{ J/kJ}) + (8.314)(500) \ln \frac{(1.00)^2}{(2.00)^2(0.500)}$$

$$= -7.262 \times 10^4 \text{ J/mol}$$

Note that Q, when at equilibrium, becomes K. This equation gives us a way to calculate the equilibrium constant, K, from a knowledge of the standard Gibbs free energy of the reaction and the temperature.

If the system is at equilibrium, then $\Delta G = 0$ and the equation above becomes:

$$\Delta G° = -RT \ln K = -2.303 \text{ RT} \log K$$

Calculate $\Delta G°$ for:

$$2 O_3(g) \rightleftharpoons 3 O_2(g) \qquad K_p = 4.17 \times 10^{14}$$

Answer:

Note: ° = 298 K

$$\Delta G^\circ = -RT \ln K$$

$$= \frac{-(8.314\ \text{J})}{(\text{mol K})}(298\ \text{K}) \ln 4.17 \times 10^{14}$$

$$= -8.34 \times 10^4\ \text{J/mol}$$

EXPERIMENTAL

The most common thermodynamic experiment is a calorimetry experiment. In this experiment the heat of transition or heat of reaction is determined.

The experiment will require a balance to determine the mass of a sample and possibly a pipette to measure a volume, from which a mass may be calculated using the density. A calorimeter, usually a polystyrene (Styrofoam) cup, is needed to contain the reaction. Finally, a thermometer is required. Tables of heat capacities or specific heats may be provided.

Mass, and possible volume, measurements along with the initial and final temperatures are needed. Remember: you *measure* the initial and final temperature so you can *calculate* the change in temperature.

After the temperature change is calculated, there are several ways to proceed. If the calorimeter contains water, the heat may be calculated by multiplying the specific heat of water by the mass of water by the temperature change. The heat capacity of the calorimeter may be calculated by dividing the heat by the temperature change. If a reaction is carried out in the same calorimeter, the heat from that reaction is the difference between the heat with and without a reaction.

Do not forget, if the temperature increases, the process is exothermic and the heat has a negative sign. The opposite is true if the temperature drops.

COMMON MISTAKES TO AVOID

1. Be sure your units cancel giving you the unit desired in the final answer.
2. Check your significant figures.
3. Don't mix energy units J and cal.
4. Don't confuse the heat capacity, specific heat, and the molar heat capacity.
5. Watch your signs in all the thermodynamic calculations. They are extremely important.
6. Don't confuse enthalpy, ΔH, and entropy, ΔS.
7. Pay close attention to the state of matter for your reactants and products, and choose the corresponding value in your tabulated entropies and enthalpies.
8. Remember: **products minus reactants.**

9. ΔH_f and ΔG_f are for 1 mol of substance. Use appropriate multipliers if needed.
10. ΔH_f for an element in its standard state is zero.
11. All temperatures are in Kelvin.
12. When using $\Delta G° = \Delta H°_{rxn} - T \Delta S°_{rxn}$, pay particular attention to your enthalpy and entropy units. Commonly enthalpies will use kJ and entropies J.

3 REVIEW QUESTIONS

Answer the following questions. You have 20 minutes. You may not use a calculator.

Choose the type of energy that best relates to questions 1–4.

A. free energy
B. lattice energy
C. kinetic energy
D. activation energy
E. ionization energy

1. The minimum energy required to initiate a reaction

2. The minimum energy required for a non-spontaneous reaction

3. The average _____ is the same for any ideal gas at a given temperature.

4. The energy released when the gaseous ions combine to form an ionic solid

5. Given the following information:

$C(s) + O_2(g)$ $\Delta H = -393.5$ kJ
$\rightarrow CO_2(g)$

$H_2(g) + (1/2) O_2(g)$ $\Delta H = -285.8$ kJ
$\rightarrow H_2O(l)$

$C_2H_2(g) + (5/2) O_2(g)$
$\rightarrow 2 CO_2(g) + H_2O(l)$ $\Delta H = -1299.8$ kJ

Find the enthalpy change for:
$2 C(s) + H_2(g) \rightarrow C_2H_2(g)$

A. 454.0 kJ
B. −227.0 kJ

C. 0.0 kJ
D. 227.0 kJ
E. −454.0 kJ

6. A sample of gallium metal is sealed inside a well-insulated rigid container. The temperature inside the container is at the melting point of gallium metal. What can be said about the energy and the entropy of the system after equilibrium has been established? Assume the insulation prevents any energy change with the surroundings.

A. The total energy increases.
   The total entropy will increase.
B. The total energy is constant.
   The total entropy is constant.
C. The total energy is constant.
   The total entropy will decrease.
D. The total energy is constant.
   The total entropy will increase.
E. The total energy decreases.
   The total entropy will decrease.

7. When ammonium chloride dissolves in water, the temperature drops. Which of the following conclusions may be related to this?

A. The hydration energies of the ions are very high.
B. Ammonium chloride produces an ideal solution in water.
C. The heat of solution for ammonium chloride is exothermic.

D. Ammonium chloride has a low lattice energy.
E. Ammonium chloride is more soluble in hot water.

8. Choose the reaction expected to have the greatest increase in entropy.

A. $H_2O(g) \rightarrow H_2O(l)$
B. $C(s) + O_2(g) \rightarrow CO_2(g)$
C. $Ca(s) + H_2(g) \rightarrow CaH_2(s)$
D. $N_2(g) + 3\ H_2(g) \rightarrow 2\ NH_3(g)$
E. $2\ KClO_3(s) \rightarrow 2\ KCl(s) + 3\ O_2(g)$

9. Under standard conditions calcium metal reacts readily with chlorine gas. What conclusions may be drawn from the fact?

A. $K_{eq} < 1$ and $\Delta G° > 0$
B. $K_{eq} > 1$ and $\Delta G° = 0$
C. $K_{eq} < 1$ and $\Delta G° < 0$
D. $K_{eq} > 1$ and $\Delta G° < 0$
E. $K_{eq} > 1$ and $\Delta G° > 0$

10. Which of the following combinations is true when sodium chloride melts?

A. $\Delta H > 0$ and $\Delta S > 0$
B. $\Delta H = 0$ and $\Delta S > 0$
C. $\Delta H > 0$ and $\Delta S < 0$
D. $\Delta H < 0$ and $\Delta S < 0$
E. $\Delta H < 0$ and $\Delta S > 0$

11. Which of the following reactions have a negative entropy change?

I. $2\ H_2(g) + O_2(g) \rightarrow 2\ H_2O(l)$
II. $2\ NH_3(g) \rightarrow N_2(g) + 3\ H_2(g)$
III. $Ca(s) + Cl_2(g) \rightarrow CaCl_2(s)$

A. II only
B. I only
C. I, II, and III
D. III only
E. I and III

12. A certain reaction is non-spontaneous under standard conditions, but becomes spontaneous at higher temper-

atures. What conclusions may be drawn under standard conditions?

A. $\Delta H < 0$, $\Delta S > 0$, and $\Delta G > 0$
B. $\Delta H > 0$, $\Delta S < 0$, and $\Delta G > 0$
C. $\Delta H > 0$, $\Delta S > 0$, and $\Delta G > 0$
D. $\Delta H < 0$, $\Delta S < 0$, and $\Delta G > 0$
E. $\Delta H > 0$, $\Delta S > 0$, and $\Delta G = 0$

13. $2\ H_2(g) + O_2(g) \rightarrow 2\ H_2O(g)$

From the table below, determine the enthalpy change for the above reaction.

Bond	Average Bond Energy (kJ/mol)
H–H	436
O=O	499
H–O	464

A. 0 kJ
B. 485 kJ
C. –485 kJ
D. 464 kJ
E. 443 kJ

14. What is the energy required to convert a gaseous atom, in the ground state, to a gaseous cation?

A. ionization energy
B. kinetic energy
C. activation energy
D. lattice energy
E. free energy

15. Which of the following reactions would be accompanied by the greatest decrease in entropy?

A. $N_2(g) + 3\ H_2(g) \rightarrow 2\ NH_3(g)$
B. $C(s) + O_2(g) \rightarrow CO_2(g)$
C. $2\ H_2(g) + O_2(g) \rightarrow 2\ H_2O(g)$
D. $2\ Na(s) + Cl_2(g) \rightarrow 2\ NaCl(s)$
E. $2\ KClO_3(s) \rightarrow 2\ KCl(s) + 3\ O_2(g)$

16. $CO(g) + 2\ H_2(g) \rightarrow CH_3OH(g)\ \Delta H = -91$ kJ

Determine ΔH for the above reaction if $CH_3OH(l)$ were formed in the above reaction instead of $CH_3OH(g)$. The

ΔH of vaporization for CH_3OH is 37 kJ/mol.

A. -128 kJ
B. -54 kJ
C. $+128$ kJ
D. $+54$ kJ
E. -37 kJ

17. A solution is prepared by dissolving solid ammonium nitrate, NH_4NO_3, in water. The initial temperature of the water was 25° C, but after the solid had dissolved, the temperature had fallen to 20° C. What conclusions may be made about ΔH and ΔS?

A. $\Delta H < 0$ $\Delta S > 0$
B. $\Delta H > 0$ $\Delta S > 0$
C. $\Delta H > 0$ $\Delta S < 0$
D. $\Delta H < 0$ $\Delta S < 0$
E. $\Delta H = 0$ $\Delta S > 0$

ANSWERS AND EXPLANATIONS

1. **D.** You may wish to see Kinetics (Chapter 12) if you have forgotten what the activation energy is.

2. **A.** The free energy is the minimum energy required for a non-spontaneous reaction and the maximum energy available for a spontaneous reaction.

3. **C.** This is a basic postulate of kinetic molecular theory.

4. **B.** This is the reverse of the lattice energy definition.

5. **D.**

$2[C(s) + O_2(g) \rightarrow CO_2(g)]$	$2(-393.5$ kJ$)$
$H_2(g) + (1/2) O_2(g) \rightarrow H_2O(l)$	-285.8 kJ
$2 CO_2(g) + H_2O(l) \rightarrow C_2H_2(g) + (5/2) O_2(g)$	$-(-1299.8$ kJ$)$
$2 C(s) + H_2(g) \rightarrow C_2H_2(g)$	227.0 kJ

6. **D.** The system is insulated and no work can be done on or by the system (rigid container); thus, the energy is constant. At the melting point, some of the gallium will spontaneously melt; spontaneous processes increase entropy.

7. **E.** The process is endothermic (the ammonium chloride is absorbing heat to cool the water). Endothermic processes are "helped" by higher temperatures. Answers A and C, and possibly D would give an increase in temperature. There is insufficient information about answer B.

8. **E.** The reaction showing the greatest increase in the number of moles of gas will show the greatest entropy increase. If no gases are present, then the greatest increase in the number of moles of liquid would yield the greatest increase.

9. **D.** If the reaction occurs readily, it must be spontaneous. Spontaneous reactions require $\Delta G° < 0$. A negative free energy leads to a large K (> 1).

10. **A.** Heat is required to melt something ($\Delta H > 0$). A transformation from a solid to a liquid gives an increase in entropy.

11. **E.** Equations I and III both have an overall decrease in the amount of gas (high entropy) present. Equation II produce more gas (increases entropy).

12. **C.** Nonspontaneous $\rightarrow \Delta G > 0$

    Since the reaction becomes spontaneous, the sign must change. Recalling: $\Delta G = \Delta H - T\Delta S$ The sign change at higher temperature means that the entropy term (with $\Delta S > 0$) must become more negative than the enthalpy term ($\Delta H > 0$).

13. **C.** $[2(436 \text{ kJ}) + 499 \text{ kJ}] - \{2[2(464 \text{ kJ})]\} = -485 \text{ kJ}$

14. **A.** This is the definition of ionization energy.

15. **A.** The reaction that produces the most gas will have the greatest increase in entropy; the one losing the most gas would have the greatest decrease.

16. **A.** $CO(g) + 2 H_2(g) \rightarrow CH_3OH(g) \qquad \Delta H = -91 \text{ kJ}$

    $CH_3OH(g) \rightarrow CH_3OH(l) \qquad \Delta H = -37 \text{ kJ}$

    $CO(g) + 2 H_2(g) \rightarrow CH_3OH(l) \qquad \Delta H = -128 \text{ kJ}$

17. **B.** Dissolving always has: $\Delta S > 0$. A decrease in temperature means the process has: $\Delta H > 0$.

FREE-RESPONSE QUESTIONS

Answer the following questions. You have 10 minutes, and you may not use a calculator.

$$Xe(g) + 3 F_2(g) \Leftrightarrow XeF_6(g)$$

Under standard conditions, the enthalpy change for the reaction going from left to right (forward reaction) is: $\Delta H° = -294 \text{ kJ}$.

a. Is the value of $\Delta S°$, for the above reaction, positive or negative? Justify your conclusion.

b. The above reaction is spontaneous under standard conditions. Predict what will happen to ΔG for this reaction as the temperature is increased. Justify your prediction.

c. Will the value of K remain the same, increase, or decrease as the temperature increases? Justify your prediction.

d. Show how the temperature at which the reaction changes from spontaneous to nonspontaneous can be predicted. What additional information is needed?

ANSWERS AND EXPLANATIONS

a. The value is negative. Give yourself 1 point if you predicted this.

The decrease in the number of moles of gas, during the reaction, means there is a decrease in entropy. Give yourself 1 point for discussing the number of moles of gas. You may get this point even if you did not get the first point.

b. Recalling: $\Delta G = \Delta H - T\Delta S$

The value of ΔG will increase (become less negative). Give yourself 1 point for this answer if it is obvious that increasing means less negative.

In general, both ΔH and ΔS are relatively constant. As the temperature increases, the value of the entropy term, $T\Delta S$, becomes more negative. The negative sign in front or this term leads to a positive contribution. The value of ΔG will first become less negative (more positive), and eventually the value will be positive (no longer spontaneous). Give yourself 1 point for the $\Delta G = \Delta H - T\Delta S$ argument even if you did not get the first point.

c. Recalling: $\Delta G = -RT \ln K$

The value of K will decrease. You get 1 point for this answer.

As the value of ΔG increases (see part b) the value of K will decrease. You get 1 point for using $\Delta G = -RT \ln K$ in your discussion. If you got the justification for part b wrong, and you used the same argument here, you will not be penalized twice. You still get your point.

d. Recalling: $\Delta G = \Delta H - T\Delta S$

Rearranging this equation to: $T = (\Delta G - \Delta H)/\Delta S$ will allow the temperature to be estimated. This is worth 1 point.

To do the calculation, the value of ΔS is needed. Give yourself 1 point for this.

There are a total of 8 points possible. All of the mathematical relations presented in the answers are provided in the exam booklet.

RAPID REVIEW

- Thermodynamics is the study of heat and its transformations.
- Kinetic energy is energy of motion, while potential energy is stored energy.
- The common units of energy are the joule, J, and the calorie, cal.

- A calorimeter is used to measure the heat released or absorbed during a chemical or physical change. Know how a calorimeter works.

- The specific heat capacity is the amount of heat needed to change the temperature of 1 gram of a substance 1 K, while the molar heat capacity is the heat capacity per mole.

- The heat lost by the system in calorimetry is equal to the heat gained by the surroundings.

- The specific heat (c) of a solid can be calculated by: $-(c_{solid} \times mass_{solid} \times \Delta T_{solid}) = c_{water} \times mass_{water} \times \Delta T_{water}$

- The First law of Thermodynamics states that the total energy of the universe is constant. (Energy is neither created nor destroyed.)

- The Second Law of Thermodynamics states that all spontaneous processes move in a way that increases the entropy (disorder) of the universe.

- The enthalpy change, ΔH, is equal to the heat lost or gained by the system under constant pressure conditions.

- ΔHs are associated with a specific reaction. If that reaction is reversed, the sign of ΔH changes. If one has to use a multiplier on the reaction, it must also be applied to the ΔH value.

- The standard enthalpy of formation of a compound, ΔH_f°, is the enthalpy change when 1 mol of the substance is formed from its elements and all substances are in their standard states.

- The standard enthalpy of formation of an element in its standard state is zero.

- $\Delta H^\circ_{rxn} = \Sigma \, \Delta H_f^\circ$ products $- \, \Sigma \, \Delta H_f^\circ$ reactants. Know how to apply this equation.

- ΔH°_{rxn} is usually negative for a spontaneous reaction.

- $\Delta S^\circ = \Sigma \, S^\circ$ products $- \, \Sigma \, S^\circ$ reactants. Know how to apply this equation.

- ΔS° is usually positive for a spontaneous reaction.

- The Gibbs free energy is a thermodynamic quantity that relates the enthalpy and entropy and is the best indicator for whether or not a reaction is spontaneous.

- If $\Delta G^\circ > 0$ the reaction is not spontaneous; if $\Delta G^\circ < 0$, the reaction is spontaneous; and if $\Delta G^\circ = 0$, the reaction is at equilibrium.

- $\Delta G^\circ = \Sigma \, \Delta G_f^\circ$ products $- \, \Sigma \, \Delta G_f^\circ$ reactants. Know how to apply this equation.

- $\Delta G^\circ = \Delta H^\circ_{rxn} - T \, \Delta S^\circ_{rxn}$. Know how to apply this equation.

- For a system not at equilibrium: $\Delta G = \Delta G^\circ + RT \ln Q = \Delta G^\circ + 2.303 \, RT \log Q$. Know how to apply this equation.

- For a system at equilibrium: $\Delta G^\circ = -RT \ln K = -2.303 \, RT \log K$. Know how to apply this equation to calculate equilibrium constants.

Chapter 8

Spectroscopy, Light, and Electrons

 2 KEYWORDS AND EQUATIONS

$\checkmark$

E = energy ν = frequency λ = wavelength
p = momentum   v = velocity   n = principal quantum number
m = mass $\Delta E = h\nu$ or $E = h\nu$ $c = \lambda\nu$ $\lambda = h/mv$ $p = mv$
$E_n = (-2.178 \times 10^{-18}/n^2)$ J

INTRODUCTION

 In developing the model of the atom it was thought initially that all sub-atomic particles obeyed the laws of classical physics—that is, they were tiny bits of matter. Later, however, it was discovered that this particle view of the atom could not explain many of the observations being made. About this time the dual particle/wave model of matter began to gain favor. It was discovered that in many cases, especially when dealing with the behavior of electrons, describing some of their behavior in terms of waves explained the observations much better. Thus, the quantum mechanical model of the atom was born.

THE NATURE OF LIGHT

Light is a part of the **electromagnetic spectrum**—radiant energy composed of gamma rays, x-rays, ultraviolet light, visible light, etc. Figure 8.1 shows the electromagnetic spectrum.

The energy of the electromagnetic spectrum moves through space as waves that have three associated variables—frequency, wavelength, and amplitude. The **frequency,** ν, is the number of waves that pass a point per

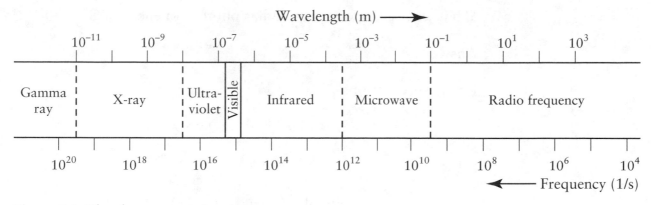

Figure 8.1 The electromagnetic spectrum.

second. **Wavelength,** λ, is the distance between two identical points on a wave. **Amplitude** is the height of the wave and is related to the intensity (or brightness, for visible light) of the wave. Figure 8.2 shows the wavelength and amplitude of a wave.

The energy associated with a certain frequency of light is related by the equation:

$$E = h\nu \qquad \text{where h is Planck's constant} = 6.63 \times 10^{-34} \text{ Js}$$

In developing the quantum mechanical model of the atom, it was found that an atom can have only certain distinct quantities of energy associated with it, and that in order to change its energy it has to absorb or emit a certain amount of energy. The energy that is emitted or absorbed is really the difference in the two energy states and can be calculated by:

$$\Delta E = h\nu$$

All electromagnetic radiation travels at about the same speed in a vacuum, 3.00×10^8 m/s. This constant is called the **speed of light (c).** The product of the frequency and the wavelength is the speed of light:

$$c = \nu \times \lambda$$

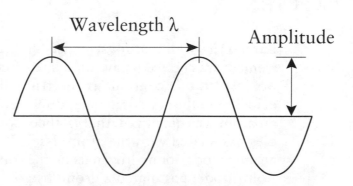

Figure 8.2 Wavelength and amplitude of a wave.

What wavelength of radiation has photons of energy 7.83×10^{-19} J?

Answer:

Using the equations

$$\Delta E = h\nu \quad \text{and} \quad c = \nu \times \lambda$$

we get

$$\nu = \Delta E / h \quad \text{and} \quad \lambda = c / \nu$$

Plugging in the appropriate values:

$$\nu = \Delta E/h = 7.83 \times 10^{-19} \text{ J}/6.63 \times 10^{-34} \text{ Js} = 1.18 \times 10^{15} \text{ s}^{-1}$$

Then:

$$\lambda = c/\nu = (3.00 \times 10^{8} \text{ m/s})/(1.18 \times 10^{15} \text{ s}^{-1}) = 2.54 \times 10^{-7} \text{ m}$$

This answer could have been calculated more quickly by combining the original two equations to give:

$$\lambda = hc/\Delta E$$

WAVE PROPERTIES OF MATTER

The concept that matter possesses both particle and wave properties was first postulated by de Broglie in 1925. He introduced the equation $\lambda = h/mv$, which indicates a mass (m) moving with a certain velocity (v) would have a specific wavelength (λ) associated with it. If the mass is very large (a locomotive), the associated wavelength is insignificant. However, if the mass is very small (an electron), the wavelength is measurable. The denominator may be replaced with the momentum of the particle ($p = mv$).

ATOMIC SPECTRA

Late in the 19th century scientists discovered that when the vapor of an element was heated it gave off a **line spectrum,** a series of fine lines of colors instead of a **continuous spectrum** like a rainbow. This was used as evidence in the developing quantum mechanical model that the energy in an atom was **quantized,** that is, there could only be certain distinct energies associated with the atom. Niels Bohr developed the first modern atomic model for hydrogen using the concepts of quantized energies. The Bohr model postulated a **ground state** for the atom, an energy state of lowest energy, and an **excited state,** an energy state of higher energy. In order for an atom to go from its ground state to an excited state, it must absorb a certain amount of energy. If the atom dropped back from that excited state to its ground state, that same amount of energy would be emitted. Bohr's model also allowed scientists to develop a method of calculating the energy associated with a particular energy level for the electron in the hydrogen atom:

$$E = -2.178 \times 10^{-18} \, J \, (Z^2/n^2)$$

where Z is the charge on the nucleus and n is the energy state. This equation can then be modified to calculate the energy difference between any two energy levels:

$$\Delta E = -2.18 \times 10^{-18} \, J \left(\frac{1}{n^2_{final}} - \frac{1}{n^2_{initial}} \right)$$

ATOMIC ORBITALS

Bohr's model worked well for hydrogen, the simplest atom, but didn't work very well for any others. In the early 1900s Schrödinger developed a more involved model and set of equations that better described atoms by using quantum mechanical concepts. His model introduced a mathematical description of the electron's motion called a **wave function** or **atomic orbital.** Squaring the wave function (orbital) gives the volume of space in which the probability of finding the electron is high. This is commonly referred to as the **electron cloud (electron density).**

Schrödinger's equation required the use of three **quantum numbers** to describe each electron within an atom corresponding to the orbital size, shape, and orientation in space. It was also found that a quantum number concerning the spin of the electron was needed.

The first quantum number is the **principal quantum number (n)** that describes the size of the orbital and relative distance from the nucleus. The allowed (by the mathematics of the Schrödinger equation) values are positive integers (1, 2, 3, 4, etc.). The smaller the value of n, the closer the orbital is to the nucleus. This is sometimes called the atom's **shell.**

The second quantum number is the **angular momentum quantum number (l)** that describes the shape of the orbital. Its value is related to the principal quantum number and has allowed values of 0 to (n − 1). For example, if n = 3, then the possible values of l would be 0, 1, and 2 (3 − 1). This value of l defines the shape of the orbital:

- If l = 0, the orbital is called an s orbital and has a spherical shape with the nucleus at the center of the sphere. The greater the value of n, the larger the sphere.
- If l = 1, the orbital is called a p orbital with two lobes of high electron density on either side of the nucleus. This makes for an hourglass or dumbbell shape.

- If $l = 2$, the orbital is a d orbital with a variety of shapes.
- If $l = 3$, the orbital is an f orbital with more complex shapes.
- If $l = 4$, the orbital is a g orbital, with even more complex shapes.

Figure 8.3 shows the shapes of the s, p, and d orbitals. These are sometimes called **sublevels** or **subshells**.

The third quantum number is the **magnetic quantum number** ($\mathbf{m}_l$). It describes the orientation of the orbital around the nucleus. The possible

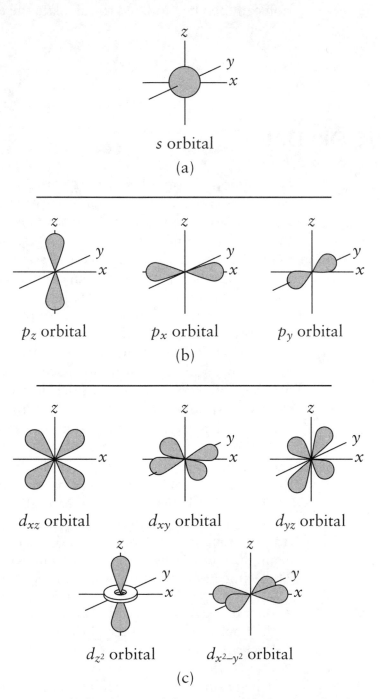

Figure 8.3 The shapes of the s, p, and d atomic orbitals.

values of m_l depend on the value of the angular momentum quantum number, l. The allowed values for m_l are $-l$ through zero to $+l$. For example, for $l = 2$, the possible values of m_l would be $-2, -1, 0, +1, +2$. This is why, for example, if $l = 1$ (a p orbital), then there are three p orbitals corresponding to m_l values of $-1, 0, +1$. This is also shown in Figure 8.3.

The fourth quantum number, the **spin quantum number (m_s),** indicates the direction the electron is spinning. There are only two possible values for m_s, $+\frac{1}{2}$ and $-\frac{1}{2}$.

The quantum numbers for the six electrons in carbon would be:

Quantum number	First electron	Second electron	Third electron	Fourth electron	Fifth electron	Sixth electron
n	1	1	2	2	2	2
l	0	0	0	0	1	1
m_l	0	0	0	0	-1	0
m_s	$+\frac{1}{2}$	$-\frac{1}{2}$	$+\frac{1}{2}$	$-\frac{1}{2}$	$+\frac{1}{2}$	$-\frac{1}{2}$

EXPERIMENTAL

No experimental questions related to this chapter have appeared on the AP exam in recent years.

COMMON MISTAKES TO AVOID

1. Be sure not to confuse wavelength and frequency.
2. The speed of light is 3.00×10^8 m/s. The exponent is positive.
3. To calculate the difference in energy between two energy levels, $\Delta E = -2.18 \times 10^{-18}$ J $(1/n^2_{final} - 1/n^2_{initial})$.
4. The values of m_l include zero.
5. Do not confuse velocity (v) and frequency (ν).

REVIEW QUESTIONS

You have 15 minutes. You may not use a calculator.

Questions 1–4 refer to the following orbital diagrams.

A. 1s ↑ 2s ↑↓
B. 1s ↑↓ 2s ↑
C. [Kr] 5s ↑↓ 4d ↑ ↑ ___ ___
D. [Ne] 3s ↑↓ 3p ↑ ↑ ↑
E. 1s ↑↓ 2s ↑↓ 2p ↑↓ ↑↓ ↑↓

1. The least reactive element is represented by:

2. The transition element is represented by:

3. The most chemically reactive element is represented by:

4. The element in an excited state is represented by:

5. The ground-state configuration of Fe^{2+} is which of the following?

   A. $1s^2 2s^2 2p^6 3s^2 3p^6 3d^5 4s^1$
   B. $1s^2 2s^2 2p^6 3s^2 3p^6 3d^6$
   C. $1s^2 2s^2 2p^6 3s^2 3p^6 3d^6 4s^2$
   D. $1s^2 2s^2 2p^6 3s^2 3p^6 3d^8 4s^2$
   E. $1s^2 2s^2 2p^6 3s^2 3p^6 3d^4 4s^2$

6. Which of the following only contains atoms that are diamagnetic in their ground state?

   A. Kr, Ca, and P
   B. Cl, Mg, and Cd
   C. Ar, K, and Ba
   D. He, Sr, and C
   E. Ne, Be, and Zn

7. A valence electron from an arsenic atom might have an electron with the following set of quantum numbers in the ground state.

   A. $n = 4$; $l = 1$; $m_l = 0$; $m_s = +\frac{1}{2}$
   B. $n = 4$; $l = 1$; $m_l = 2$; $m_s = -\frac{1}{2}$
   C. $n = 3$; $l = 1$; $m_l = 0$; $m_s = +\frac{1}{2}$
   D. $n = 5$; $l = 1$; $m_l = -1$; $m_s = -\frac{1}{2}$
   E. $n = 4$; $l = 2$; $m_l = +1$; $m_s = +\frac{1}{2}$

Use the following ground-state electron configurations for questions 8–11:

   A. $1s^2 1p^6 2s^2 2p^3$
   B. $1s^2 2s^2 2p^6 3s^2 3p^6 4s^2 3d^{10} 4p^6 5s^2 4d^1$
   C. $1s^2 2s^2 2p^6 3s^2 3p^6 3d^3$
   D. $1s^2 2s^2 2p^5$
   E. $1s^2 2s^2 2p^6 3s^2 3p^6 4s^2 3d^{10} 4p^6$

8. The electron configuration of a halogen is:

9. This is a possible configuration for a transition metal atom.

10. This electron configuration is not possible.

11. This is a possible configuration of a transition metal ion.

The following answers are to be used for questions 12–15:

   A. Pauli exclusion principle
   B. electron shielding
   C. the wave properties of matter
   D. Heisenberg uncertainty principle
   E. Hund's rule

12. The exact position of an electron is not known.

13. Oxygen atoms, in their ground state, are paramagnetic.

14. An atomic orbital can hold no more than two electrons.

15. The reason the 4s orbital fills before the 3d:

16. In the ground state the highest energy electron of a rubidium atom might have which of the following sets of quantum numbers?

   A. $n = 5$; $l = 0$; $m_l = 1$; $m_s = +\frac{1}{2}$
   B. $n = 5$; $l = 1$; $m_l = 1$; $m_s = +\frac{1}{2}$
   C. $n = 4$; $l = 0$; $m_l = 0$; $m_s = +\frac{1}{2}$
   D. $n = 5$; $l = 0$; $m_l = 0$; $m_s = +\frac{1}{2}$
   E. $n = 6$; $l = 0$; $m_l = 0$; $m_s = +\frac{1}{2}$

17. Calcium reacts with element X to form an ionic compound. If the ground-state electron configuration of X is $1s^2 2s^2 2p^4$, what is the simplest formula for this compound?

   A. CaX
   B. CaX_2
   C. Ca_4X_2
   D. Ca_2X_2
   E. Ca_2X_3

ANSWERS AND EXPLANATIONS

✓

1. **E.** This configuration represents a noble gas (neon). The outer s and p orbitals are filled.

2. **C.** Transition elements have partially filled d orbitals. This configuration is for the metal titanium.

3. **B.** The single electron in the s orbital indicates that this is a very reactive alkali metal (Li).

4. **A.** The 1s orbital is not filled. One indication of excited states is to have one or more inner orbitals unfilled.

5. **B.** The electron configuration for iron is $1s^2 2s^2 2p^6 3s^2 3p^6 3d^6 4s^2$. To produce an iron(II) ion the two 4s electrons are removed first.

6. **E.** The elements that are normally diamagnetic are those in the same columns of the periodic table as Be, Zn, and He. All others are normally paramagnetic.

7. **A.** The electron configuration for arsenic is $1s^2 2s^2 2p^6 3s^2 3p^6 4s^2 3d^{10} 4p^3$. The valence shell is the outer shell (largest n). In this case the outer shell electrons are $4s^2 4p^3$. This means that n = 4, and that $l = 0$ or 1. If $l = 0$, then $m_l = 0$; and if $l = 1$, then $m_l = -1, 0,$ or $+1$. Finally, m_s must be either $+\frac{1}{2}$ or $-\frac{1}{2}$.

8. **D.** Halogens have a valence shell with $s^2 p^5$.

9. **B.** Transition metals have partially filled d orbitals (d^{1-10}), along with an s^1 or s^2.

10. **A.** There is no such thing as a 1p.

11. **C.** The outer s electrons are not present in most transition metal ions.

12. **D.** This is part of the Heisenberg uncertainty principle.

13. **E.** The four electrons in the oxygen 2p orbitals are arranged with one pair and two unpaired electrons with spins parallel. This makes the oxygen atom paramagnetic. This arrangement is due to Hund's rule.

14. **A.** The Pauli exclusion principle restricts the number of electrons that can occupy a single orbital.

15. **B.** The d orbitals are shielded more efficiently than the s orbitals. Thus, the less shielded d orbitals do not fill as readily as s orbitals with similar energy.

16. **D.** The electron configuration of rubidium is $1s^2 2s^2 2p^6 3s^2 3p^6 4s^2 3d^{10} 4p^6 5s^1$. This gives n = 5 and $l = 0$ for the last electron. If $l = 0$ then m_l must equal 0. The value of m_s may be either $+\frac{1}{2}$ or $-\frac{1}{2}$.

17. **A.** Calcium will for a +2 ion (Ca^{2+}), and X will need to gain two electrons to fill its outer shell and become a −2 ion (X^{2-}). The simplest formula for a compound containing a +2 ion and a −2 ion would be

CaX. The other answers involve different charges or a formula that has not been simplified.

FREE-RESPONSE QUESTIONS

 Answer the following questions. You have 15 minutes, and you may use a calculator.

a. The bond energy of fluorine is 159 kJ/mol.
   i. Determine the energy, in J, of a photon of light needed to break a F-F bond.
   ii. Determine the frequency of this photon, in s^{-1}.
   iii. Determine the wavelength of this photon in nanometers.

b. Determine the wavelength, in m, of an alpha particle traveling at 5.2×10^7 m/s. An alpha particle has a mass of 6.6×10^{-24} g.

c. Barium imparts a characteristic green color to a flame. The wavelength of this light is 551 nm. Determine the energy involved in kJ/mol.

ANSWERS AND EXPLANATIONS

a. Several of the equations given at the beginning of the exam are needed. In addition, the values of Planck's constant, Avogadro's number, and the speed of light are needed. These constants are also given on the exam.

   i. This is a simple conversion problem:

$$\frac{159 \text{ kJ (1 mol) 1000 J}}{\text{mol} \, (6.022 \times 10^{23}) \, 1 \text{ kJ}} = 2.64 \times 10^{-19} \text{ J}$$

   Give yourself 1 point if you got this answer.

   ii. This part requires the equation $\Delta E = h\nu$:

$$\nu = \frac{\Delta E}{h} = \frac{2.64 \times 10^{-19} \text{ J}}{6.63 \times 10^{-34} \text{ Js}} = 3.98 \times 10^{14} \text{ s}^{-1}$$

Give yourself 1 point for this answer. If you got the wrong answer in the preceding part, but used it correctly here (in place of the 2.64×10^{-19} J), you still get 1 point.

iii. The equation $c = \lambda v$ is needed.

$$\lambda = \frac{c}{v} = \frac{(3.0 \times 10^8 \text{ m/s})(10^9 \text{nm})}{(3.98 \times 10^{14} \text{s}^{-1})(1 \text{ m})} = 7.5 \times 10^2 \text{nm}$$

Again, give yourself 1 point for the correct answer. If you correctly used a wrong answer from the preceding part, you still get 1 point.

b. This equation requires the de Broglie relationship (also given in the AP exam booklet). Do not mistake a v for a v. You will also need to know $J = \text{kgm}^2/\text{s}^2$.

$$\lambda = \frac{h}{mv} = \frac{(6.63 \times 10^{-34} \text{ Js})(\text{kg m}^2/\text{s}^2)(1000 \text{ g})}{(6.6 \times 10^{-24} \text{g})(5.2 \times 10^7 \text{ m/s})(\text{J})(\text{kg})} = 1.9 \times 10^{-15} \text{ m}$$

This answer is worth 1 point.

c. This can be done as a one-step or a two-step problem. The AP text booklet gives you the equations to solve this directly as a two-step problem. This method will be done here. The two equations may be combined to produce an equation that will allow you to do the problem in one step.

Using $c = \lambda v$:

$$v = c/\lambda = \frac{(3.0 \times 10^8 \text{ m/s})(10^9 \text{nm})}{(551 \text{ nm})(1 \text{ m})} = 5.4 \times 10^{14} \text{ s}^{-1}$$

Using $\Delta E = hv$:

$$\Delta E = (6.63 \times 10^{-34} \text{ Js})(5.4 \times 10^{14} \text{s}^{-1})(1 \text{ kJ}/1000 \text{ J})(6.022 \times 10^{23}/\text{mol})$$
$$= 2.2 \times 10^2 \text{ kJ/mol}$$

Give yourself 1 point for each of these answers. If you did the problem as a one-step problem, give yourself 2 points if you got the final answer correct, or 1 point if you left out any of the conversions. The total for this question is 6 points.

RAPID REVIEW

- Know the parts of the electromagnetic spectrum.
- The frequency, ν, is defined as the number of waves that pass a point per second.
- The wavelength, λ, is the distance between two identical points on a wave.
- Amplitude is the height of the wave and is related to the intensity (or brightness for visible light) of the wave.
- The energy of light is related to the frequency by $E = h\nu$.
- The product of the frequency and wavelength of light is the speed of light: $c = \nu \times \lambda$.
- An orbital or wave function is a quantum mechanical mathematical description of the electron.
- The ground state of an atom is its lowest energy state.
- An excited state of an atom is of higher energy than the ground state.
- The energy of an atom is quantized, existing in only certain distinct energy states.
- Quantum numbers are numbers used in Schrödinger's equation to describe the orbital size, shape, and orientation in space and spin.
- The principal quantum number, n, describes the size of the orbital. It must be a positive integer. It is sometimes referred to as the atom's shell.
- The angular momentum quantum number, l, defines the shape of the electron cloud. If $l = 0$, it is an s orbital; if $l = 1$, it is a p orbital; if $l = 2$, it is a d orbital; if $l = 3$, it is an f orbital, etc.
- The magnetic quantum number, m_l, describes the orientation of the orbital around the nucleus. It can be integer values ranging from $-l$ through 0 to $+l$.
- The spin quantum number, m_s, describes the spin of the electron and can only have values of $+\frac{1}{2}$ and $-\frac{1}{2}$.
- Be able to write the quantum numbers associated with the first 20 electrons.

Chapter 9

Bonding

KEYWORDS AND EQUATIONS

✓ There are no keywords or equations on the AP exam specific to this chapter.

INTRODUCTION

The difference between elements and compounds was discussed in Chapter 3, and chemical reactions were discussed in Chapter 4. But what are the forces holding together a compound? What is the difference in bonding between table salt and sugar? What do these compounds look like in three-dimensional space?

Compounds have a certain fixed proportion of elements. The periodic table often can be used to predict the type of bonding that might exist between elements. The following general guidelines apply:

metals + nonmetals → ionic bonds
nonmetal + nonmetal → covalent bonds
metal + metal → metallic bonding

We will discuss the first two types of bonding, ionic and covalent, in some depth. Metallic bonding is a topic that is very rarely encountered on the AP exam. Suffice it to say that metallic bonding is a bonding situation between metals in which the valence electrons are donated to a vast electron pool (sometimes called a "sea of electrons"), so that the valence electrons are free to move throughout the entire metallic solid.

The basic concept that drives bonding is the stability of the noble gas family (the group VIIIA or group 18 elements). Their extreme stability (lower energy state) is related to the fact that they have a filled valence shell, a full complement of eight valence electrons. This is called the **octet rule**. During chemical reactions, atoms lose, gain, or share electrons in order to achieve a filled valence shell, to complete their octet. By completing their valence shell in this fashion they become **isoelectronic**, having the same number and arrangement of electrons, as the closest noble gas. There are numerous exceptions to the octet rule, for example, some atoms will have more than an octet.

LEWIS ELECTRON-DOT STRUCTURES

The **Lewis electron-dot symbol** is a way of representing the element and its valence electrons. The chemical symbol is written, which represents the atom's nucleus and all inner shell electrons. The valence, or outer shell, electrons are represented as dots surrounding the atom's symbol. Take the valence electrons, distribute them as dots one at a time around the four sides of the symbol and then pair them up until all the valence electrons are distributed. Figure 9.1 shows the Lewis symbol for several different elements.

The Lewis symbols will be used in the discussion of bonding, especially covalent bonding, and will form the basis of the discussion of molecular geometry.

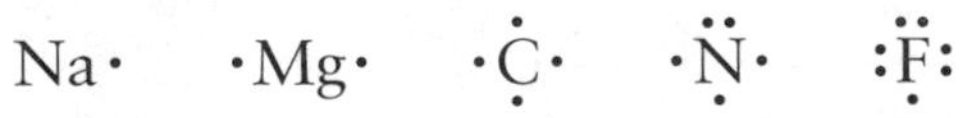

$$\text{Na}\cdot \qquad \cdot\text{Mg}\cdot \qquad \cdot\overset{\cdot}{\text{C}}\cdot \qquad \cdot\overset{\cdot\cdot}{\text{N}}\cdot \qquad :\overset{\cdot\cdot}{\text{F}}:$$

Figure 9.1 Lewis electron-dot symbols for selected elements.

IONIC AND COVALENT BONDING

Ionic Bonding

Ionic bonding involves the transfer of electrons from a metal to a nonmetal with the formation of **cations** (positively charged ions) and **anions** (negatively charged ions). The attraction of the opposite charges forms the ionic solid. The metal loses electrons to form a cation (the positive charge results from having more protons than electrons), and the nonmetal becomes the anion by gaining electrons (it now has more electrons than protons). This is shown in Figure 9.2 for the reaction of sodium and chlorine to form sodium chloride.

The number of electrons lost by the metal and gained by the nonmetal is determined by the number of electrons lost or gained by the atom to achieve a full octet. There is a rule of thumb that an atom can gain or lose one or two and, in rare occasions, three electrons, but not more than that. Sodium has one valence electron in energy level 3. If it lost that one, the valence shell, now energy level 2, would be full (a more common way of showing this is with zero electrons). Chlorine, having seven valence elec-

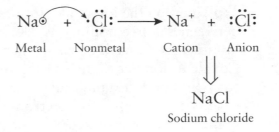

Figure 9.2 Formation of sodium chloride.

trons, needs to gain one more in order to fill its octet. So an electron is transferred from sodium to chlorine, completing the octet for both.

If magnesium, with two valence electrons to be lost, reacts with chlorine (which needs one additional electron), then magnesium will donate one valence electron to each of *two* chlorine atoms, forming the ionic compound $MgCl_2$. Make sure the formula has the lowest whole number ratio of elements.

If aluminum, with three valence electrons to be lost, reacts with oxygen, which needs two additional electrons to complete its octet, then the lowest common factor between 3 and 2 must be found—6. Two aluminum atoms would each lose 3 electrons (total of 6 electrons lost) to three oxygen atoms, which would each gain two electrons (total 6 electrons gained). The total number of electrons lost must equal the total number of electrons gained.

Another way of deriving the formula of the ionic compound is the **crisscross rule.** In this technique the cation and anion are written side by side. The numerical value of the superscript charge on the cation (without the sign) becomes the subscript on the nonmetal in the compound, and the superscript charge on the anion becomes the subscript on the metal in the compound. Figure 9.3 illustrates the crisscross rule for the reaction between aluminum and oxygen.

If magnesium reacts with oxygen, then automatic application of the crisscross rule would lead to the formula Mg_2O_2, which is incorrect because the subscripts are not in the lowest whole number ratio. For the same reason, lead (IV) oxide would have the formula PbO_2 and not Pb_2O_4.

$$Al^{3+} \diagdown\!\!\!\!\diagup O^{2-} \implies Al_2O_3$$

Figure 9.3 Using the crisscross rule.

Covalent Bonding

Consider two hydrogen atoms approaching each other. Both have only one electron, and each requires an additional electron to become isoelectronic with the nearest noble gas, He. One hydrogen atom could lose an electron; the other could gain that electron. One atom would have achieved its noble gas arrangement; but the other, the atom that lost its electron, has moved farther away from stability. The formation of the very stable H_2 cannot be explained by the loss and gain of electrons. In this situation, like that between any two nonmetals, electrons are shared, not lost and gained. No ions are formed. It is a covalent bond that holds the atoms together. **Covalent bonding** is the sharing of one or more *pairs* of electrons. The covalent bonds in a **molecule** often are represented by a dash, which represents a shared *pair* of electrons. These covalent bonds may be single bonds, one pair of shared electrons as in H-H; double bonds, two shared pairs of electrons $H_2C=CH_2$; or triple bonds, three shared pairs of electrons, $N \equiv N$. The same driving force forms a covalent bond as an ionic bond—establishing a stable (lower energy) electron arrangement. In the case of the covalent bond, it is accomplished through sharing electrons.

In the hydrogen molecule the electrons are shared equally. Each hydrogen nucleus has one proton equally attracting the bonding pair of electrons. A bond like this is called a **nonpolar covalent bond.** In cases where the two atoms involved in the covalent bond are not the same, the attraction is not equal, and the bonding electrons are pulled toward the atom with the greater attraction. The bond becomes a **polar covalent bond,** with the atom that has the greater attraction taking on a partial negative charge and the other atom a partial positive charge. Consider for example, HF(g). The fluorine has a greater attraction for the bonding pair of electrons and so takes on a partial negative charge. Many times, instead of using a single line to indicate the covalent bond, an arrow is used with the arrow head pointing toward the atom that has the greater attraction for the electron pair:

$$^{\delta+}H - F^{\delta-}$$
$$\rightarrow$$

The **electronegativity (EN)** is a measure of the attractive force that an atom exerts on a bonding pair of electrons. Electronegativity values are tabulated. In general, electronegativities increase from left to right on the periodic table, except for the noble gases, and decrease going from top to bottom. This means that fluorine has the highest electronegativity of any element. If the difference in the electronegativities of the two elements involved in the bond is great (>1.7), the bond is considered to be mostly ionic in nature. If the difference is slight (<0.4), it is mostly covalent. Anything in between is polar covalent.

Many times the Lewis structure will be used to indicate the bonding pattern in a covalent compound. In Lewis formulas the valence electrons that are not involved in bonding are shown as dots surrounding the element symbols, while a bonding pair of electrons is represented as a dash. There are several ways of deriving the Lewis structure, but here is one that works well for those compounds that obey the octet rule.

Draw the Lewis structural formula for CH_4O.

First, write a general framework for the molecule. In this case the carbon must be bonded to the oxygen, because hydrogen can only form one bond. Remember: **Carbon forms four bonds.**

$$H$$
$$H \quad C \quad O \quad H$$
$$H$$

To determine where all the electrons are to be placed, apply the N – A = S rule where:

N = sum of valence electrons needed for each atom. The two allowed values are two for hydrogen and eight for all other elements.
A = sum of all available valence electrons
S = # of electrons shared and S/2 = # bonds

For CH_4O, we would have:

	1 C		**4 H**		**1 O**	
N	8	+	4 (2) = 8	+	8	= 24
A	4	+	4 (1) = 4	+	6	= 14

$$S = N - A = 24 - 14 = 10 \qquad \text{bonds} = S/2 = 10/2 = 5$$

Place the electron pairs, as dashes, between the adjacent atoms in the framework and then distribute the remaining available electrons so that each atom has its full octet, eight electrons—bonding or nonbonding, shared or not, for every atom except hydrogen, which gets two. Figure 9.4 shows the Lewis structural formula of CH_4O.

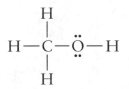

Figure 9.4 Lewis structure of CH_4O.

Lewis structures may also be written for polyatomic anion or cations. The N–A=S rule can be used, but if the ion is an anion, extra electrons equal to the magnitude of the negative charge must be added to the electrons available. If the ion is a cation, electrons must be subtracted.

As we have mentioned previously, there are many exceptions to the octet rule. In these cases, the N–A=S rule does not apply, as illustrated by the following example.

Draw the Lewis structure for XeF_4.

Answer:

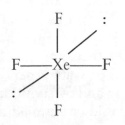

Each of the fluorines will have an additional three pairs of electrons. Only the four fluorine atoms have their octets.

MOLECULAR GEOMETRY—VSEPR

The shape of a molecule has quite a bit to do with its reactivity. This is especially true in biochemical processes, where slight changes in shape in three-dimensional space might make a certain molecule inactive or cause an adverse side effect. One way to predict the shape of molecules is the **valence-shell electron pair repulsion (VSEPR) theory.** The basic idea behind this theory is that the valence electron pairs surrounding a central atom, whether involved in bonding or not, will try to move as far away from each other as possible to minimize the repulsion between the like charges. Two geometries can be determined; the *electron-group geometry,* in which all electron pairs surrounding a nucleus are considered, and *molecular geometry,* in which the nonbonding electrons become "invisible" and only the geometry of the atomic nuclei are considered. For the purposes of geometry, double and triple bonds count the same as single bonds. To determine the geometry:

1. Write the Lewis electron-dot formula of the compound.
2. Determine the number of electron pair groups surrounding the central atom(s). Remember that double and triple bonds count the same as a single bond.
3. Determine the geometric shape that maximizes the distance between the electron groups. This is the geometry of the electron groups.
4. Mentally allow the nonbonding electrons to become invisible. They are still there and are still repelling the other electron pairs, but we don't "see" them. The molecular geometry is determined by the remaining arrangement of atoms (as determined by the bonding electron groups) around the central atom.

Figure 9.5 shows the electron-group and molecular geometry for two to six electron pairs.

For example, let's determine the electron-group and molecular geometry of carbon dioxide, CO_2, and water, H_2O. At first glance, one might imagine that the geometry of these two compounds would be similar since both have a central atom with two groups attached. Let's see if that is true.

First, write the Lewis structure of each. Figure 9.6 shows the Lewis structures of these compounds.

Next, determine the electron group geometry of each. For carbon dioxide, there are two electron groups around the carbon, so it would be linear. For water, there are four electron pairs around the oxygen—two bonding and two nonbonding electron pairs—so the electron-group geometry would be tetrahedral.

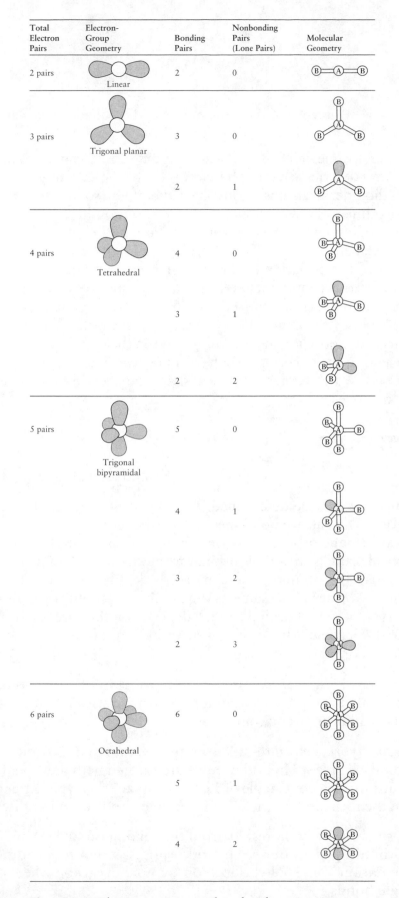

Total Electron Pairs	Electron-Group Geometry	Bonding Pairs	Nonbonding Pairs (Lone Pairs)	Molecular Geometry
2 pairs	Linear	2	0	
3 pairs	Trigonal planar	3	0	
		2	1	
4 pairs	Tetrahedral	4	0	
		3	1	
		2	2	
5 pairs	Trigonal bipyramidal	5	0	
		4	1	
		3	2	
		2	3	
6 pairs	Octahedral	6	0	
		5	1	
		4	2	

Figure 9.5 Electron-group and molecular geometry.

$$\ddot{O}\!=\!C\!=\!\ddot{O}$$

Carbon Dioxide

$$\overset{\displaystyle H}{\underset{\displaystyle :\ddot{O}\!-\!H}{|}}$$

Water

Figure 9.6 Lewis structures of carbon dioxide and water.

Finally, mentally allow the nonbonding electron pairs to become invisible and describe what is left in terms of the molecular geometry. For carbon dioxide, all groups are involved in bonding so the molecular geometry is also linear. However, water has two nonbonding pairs of electrons so the remaining bonding electron pairs (and hydrogen nuclei) are in a bent arrangement.

This determination of the molecular geometry of carbon dioxide and water also accounts for the fact that carbon dioxide does not possess a dipole and water has one, even though both are composed of polar covalent bonds. Carbon dioxide, because of its linear shape, has partial negative charges at both ends and a partial charge in the middle. To possess a dipole, one end of the molecule must have a positive charge and the other a negative end. Water, because of its bent shape, satisfies this requirement. Carbon dioxide does not.

VALENCE BOND THEORY

The VSEPR theory is only one way in which the molecular geometry of molecules may be determined. Another way involves the valence bond theory. The **valence bond theory** describes covalent bonding as the mixing of atomic orbitals to form a new kind of orbital, a hybrid orbital. **Hybrid orbitals** are atomic orbitals formed as a result of mixing the atomic orbitals of the atoms involved in the covalent bond. The number of hybrid orbitals formed is the same as the number of atomic orbitals mixed, and the type of hybrid orbital formed depends on the types of atomic orbitals mixed. Figure 9.7 shows the hybrid orbitals resulting from the mixing of s, p, and d orbitals.

sp hybridization results from the overlap of an s orbital with one p orbital. Two sp hybrid orbitals are formed with a bond angle of $180°$. This is a linear orientation.

sp^2 hybridization results from the overlap of an s orbital with two p orbitals. Three sp^2 hybrid orbitals are formed with a trigonal planar orientation and a bond angle of $120°$. One place this type of bonding occurs is in the formation of the C- to C- double bond, as will be discussed later.

sp^3 hybridization results from the mixing on one s orbital and three p orbitals, giving four sp^3 hybrid orbitals with a tetrahedral geometric orientation. This sp^3 hybridization is found in carbon when it forms four single bonds.

sp^3d hybridization from the blending of an s orbital, three p orbitals, and one d orbital. The result is five sp^3d orbitals with a trigonal bipyra-

	Linear	Trigonal planar	Tetrahedral	Trigonal bipyramidal	Octahedral
Atomic orbitals mixed	one s one p	one s two p	one s three p	one s three p one d	one s three p two d
Hybrid orbitals formed	two sp	three sp^2	four sp^3	five sp^2d	six sp^3d^2
Unhybridized orbitals remaining	two p	one p	none	four d	three d
Orientation					

Figure 9.7 Hybridization of s, p, and d orbitals.

midal orientation. This type of bonding occurs in compounds like PCl_5. Note that this compound is an exception to the octet rule.

sp^3d^2 hybridization occurs when one s, three p, and two d orbitals are mixed, giving an octahedral arrangement. SF_6 is an example. Again, this is an exception to the octet rule. If one starts with this structure and one of the bonding pairs becomes a lone pair, then a square pyramidal shape results, while two lone pairs gives a square planar shape.

Figure 9.8 shows the hybridization that occurs in ethylene, $H_2C=CH_2$. Each carbon has undergone sp² hybridization. On each carbon, two of the hybrid orbitals have overlapped with an s orbital on a hydrogen atom, to form a carbon-to-hydrogen covalent bond. The third sp² hybrid orbital has overlapped with the sp² hybrid on the other carbon to form a carbon-to-carbon covalent bond. Note that the remaining p orbital on each carbon that has not undergone hybridization is also overlapping above and below a line joining the carbons. In ethylene there are two types of bonds. In **sigma (σ) bonds** the overlap of the orbitals occurs on a line between the two atoms involved in the covalent bond. In ethylene, the C–H bonds and one of the C–C bonds are sigma bonds. In **pi (π) bonds** the overlap of orbitals occurs above and below a line through the two nuclei of the atoms involved in the bond. A double bond always is composed of one sigma and one pi bond. A carbon-to-carbon triple bond results from the overlap of an sp hybrid orbital and two p orbitals on one carbon, with the same on the other carbon. In this situation there will be one sigma bond (overlap of the sp hybrid orbitals) and two pi bonds (overlap of two sets of p orbitals).

MOLECULAR ORBITAL THEORY

Still another model to represent the bonding that takes place in covalent compounds is the molecular orbital theory. In the **molecular orbital (MO) theory** of covalent bonding, atomic orbitals (AOs) on the individual atoms combine to form orbitals that encompass the entire molecule. These are

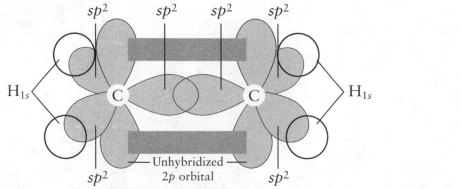

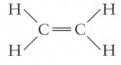

Figure 9.8 Hybridization in ethylene, $H_2C=CH_2$.

called molecular orbitals (MOs). These molecular orbitals have definite shapes and energies associated with them. When two atomic orbitals are added, two molecular orbitals are formed, one bonding and one anti-bonding. The bonding MO is of lower energy than the antibonding MO. In the molecular orbital mode the atomic orbitals are added together to form the molecular orbitals. Then the electrons are added to the molecular orbitals following the rules used previously filling orbitals: lowest energy orbitals get filled first, maximum of two electrons per orbital, and half-fill orbitals of equal energy before pairing electrons (see Chapter 3). When s atomic orbitals are added, one sigma bonding (σ) and one sigma antibonding (σ^*) molecular orbital are formed. Figure 9.9 shows the molecular orbital diagram for H_2.

Note that the two electrons (one from each hydrogen) have both gone into the sigma bonding MO. The bonding situation can be calculated in the molecular orbital theory by calculating the MO bond order. The MO

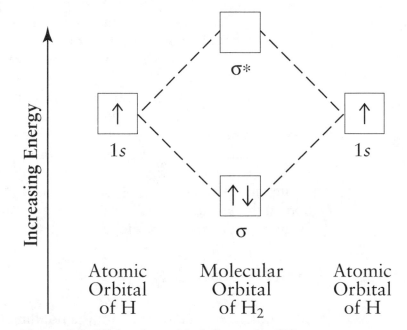

Figure 9.9 Molecular orbital diagram of H_2.

bond order is the number of electrons in bonding MOs minus the number of electrons in antibonding MOs, divided by 2. For H_2 in Figure 9.9, the bond order would be $(2-0)/2 = 1$. A stable bonding situation exists between two atoms when the bond order is greater than zero. The larger the bond order, the stronger the bond.

When 2 sets of p orbitals combine, one sigma bonding and one sigma antibonding MO are formed, along with two bonding pi MOs and two pi antibonding (π^*) MOs. Figure 9.10 shows the MO diagram for O_2.

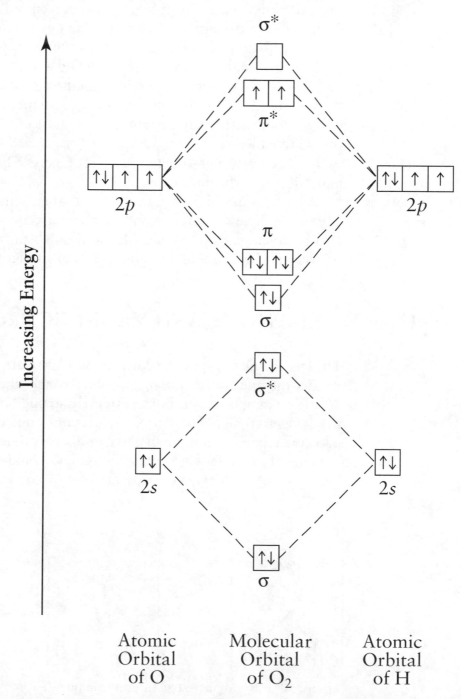

Figure 9.10 Molecular orbital diagram of valence shell electrons of O_2.

For the sake of simplicity, the 1s orbitals of each oxygen and the MOs for these elections are not shown, just the valence electron orbitals.

The bond order for O_2 would be $(10-6)/2 = 2$. (Don't forget to count the bonding and antibonding electrons at energy level 1.)

RESONANCE

Sometimes when writing the Lewis structure of a compound, more than one possible structure is generated for a given molecule. The nitrate ion, NO_3^-, is a good example. Three possible Lewis structures can be written for this polyatomic anion, differing in which oxygen is double bonded to the nitrogen. None truly represents the actual structure of the nitrate ion; that would require an average of all three Lewis structures. Resonance theory is used to describe this situation. **Resonance** occurs when more than one Lewis structure can be written for a molecule. The individual structures are called resonance structures (or forms) and are written with a two-headed arrow ($\leftrightarrow$) between them. Figure 9.11 shows the three resonance forms of the nitrate ion.

Again, let us emphasize that the actual structure of the nitrate is not any of the three shown. It is not flipping back and forth among the three. It is an average of all three. All the bonds are the same, intermediate between single bonds and double bonds in strength and length.

BOND LENGTH, STRENGTH, AND MAGNETIC PROPERTIES

The length and strength of a covalent bond is related to its bond order. The greater the bond order, the shorter and stronger the bond. Diatomic nitrogen, for example, has a short, extremely strong bond due to its nitrogen-to-nitrogen triple bond. A triple bond is not quite three times the strength of a single bond, but more like two and a half times.

One of the advantages of the molecular orbital model is that it can predict some of the magnetic properties of molecules. If molecules are placed

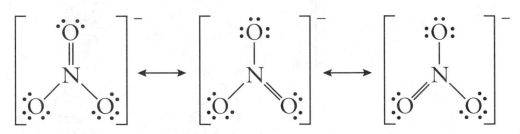

Figure 9.11 Resonance structures of the nitrate ion, NO_3^-.

in a strong magnetic field, they exhibit one of two magnetic behaviors: **para-magnetism,** the attraction to a magnetic field, or **diamagnetism,** the repulsion from the magnetic field. Paramagnetism is associated with the presence of unpaired electrons, while diamagnetism is associated with paired electrons. Look at Figure 9.10, the MO diagram for diatomic oxygen. Note that it does have two unpaired electrons in the π^*_{2p} antibonding orbital. Thus, one would predict based on the MO model, that oxygen should be paramagnetic, and that is exactly what is observed in the laboratory.

EXPERIMENTAL

There have been no experimental questions concerning this material on recent AP Chemistry exams.

COMMON MISTAKES TO AVOID

1. Remember that metals + nonmetals form ionic bonds, while the reaction of two nonmetals forms a covalent bond.
2. The octet rule does not always work, but for the representative elements it works a vast majority of the time.
3. Atoms that lose electrons form cations; atoms that gain electron form anions.
4. In writing the formulas of ionic compounds, make sure the subscripts are in the lowest ratio of whole numbers.
5. When using the crisscross rule be sure the subscripts are reduced to the lowest whole number ratio.
6. When using the N – A = S rule in writing Lewis structures, be sure you add electrons to the A term for a polyatomic anion, and subtract electrons for a polyatomic cation.
7. In the N – A = S rule, only the *valence* electrons are counted.
8. In using the VSEPR theory, when going from the electron-group geometry to the molecular geometry, start with the electron-group geometry; make the nonbonding electrons mentally invisible; and then describe what is left.
9. When adding electrons to the molecular orbitals, remember: lowest energy first. On orbitals with equal energies, half fill and then pair up.
10. When writing Lewis structures of polyatomic ions, don't forget to show the charge.
11. When you draw resonance structures, you can only move electrons (bonds). Never move the atoms.
12. When answering questions, the stability of the noble gas configurations is a result, not an explanation. Your answers will require an explanation, i.e., lower energy state.

3 REVIEW QUESTIONS

Answer the following questions. You have 25 minutes, and you may not use a calculator.

1. VSEPR predicts a SbF$_5$ molecule will be which of the following shapes?

   A. tetrahedral
   B. trigonal bipyramidal
   C. square pyramid
   D. trigonal planar
   E. square planar

2. The shortest bond would be present in which of the following substances?

   A. I$_2$
   B. CO
   C. CCl$_4$
   D. O$_2{}^{2-}$
   E. SCl$_2$

3. Which of the following does not have one or more π bonds?

   A. H$_2$O
   B. HNO$_3$
   C. O$_2$
   D. N$_2$
   E. NO$_2{}^-$

4. Which of the following is polar?

   A. SF$_4$
   B. XeF$_4$
   C. CF$_4$
   D. SbF$_5$
   E. BF$_3$

5. Resonance structures are needed to describe the bonding in which of the following?

   A. H$_2$O
   B. ClF$_3$
   C. HNO$_3$
   D. CH$_4$
   E. NH$_3$

For questions 6 and 7, pick the best choice from the following:

   A. ionic bonds
   B. hybrid orbitals
   C. resonance structures
   D. hydrogen bonding
   E. van der Waals attractions

6. An explanation of the equivalent bond lengths of the nitrite ion is:

7. Most organic substances have low melting points. This may be because, in most cases, the intermolecular forces are:

8. Which of the following has more than one unshared pair of valence electrons on the central atom?

   A. BrF$_5$
   B. NF$_3$
   C. IF$_7$
   D. ClF$_3$
   E. CF$_4$

9. What is the expected hybridization of the central atom in a molecule of TiCl$_4$? This molecule is tetrahedral.

   A. sp^{3}d^2
   B. sp^{3}d
   C. sp
   D. sp^2
   E. sp^3

10. The species in the following set do not include which of the following geometries?

   SiCl$_4$, BrF$_4{}^-$, C$_2$H$_2$, TeF$_6$, NO$_3{}^-$

   A. square planar
   B. tetrahedral
   C. octahedral

D. trigonal pyramidal
E. linear

11. The only substance listed below that contains ionic, σ, and π bonds is:

    A. Na_2CO_3
    B. $HClO_2$
    C. H_2O
    D. CO_2
    E. $NaCl$

For problems, 12–14 choose a molecule from the following list:

    A. C_2
    B. F_2
    C. B_2
    D. O_2
    E. Ne_2

12. The paramagnetic molecule with a bond order of two.

13. The diamagnetic molecule with no antibonding electrons.

14. The paramagnetic molecule with antibonding electrons.

15. The electron pairs point toward the corner of which geometrical shape for a molecule with sp^2 hybrid orbitals?

    A. trigonal planar
    B. octahedron
    C. trigonal bipyramid
    D. trigonal pyramid
    E. tetrahedron

16. Regular tetrahedral molecules or ions include which of the following?

    I. CH_4
    II. SF_4
    III. NH_4^+

       A. I, II, and III
       B. I and III only
       C. I only
       D. I and II only
       E. II only

17. Which molecule or ion in the following list has the greatest number of unshared electrons around the central atom?

    A. CF_4
    B. ClF_3
    C. BF_3
    D. NH_4^+
    E. IF_5

18. Which of the following molecules is the least polar?

    A. PH_3
    B. CH_4
    C. H_2O
    D. NO_2
    E. HCl

19. What types of hybridization of carbon are in the compound 1,4-butadiene, $CH_2CHCHCH_2$?

    I. sp^3
    II. sp^2
    III. sp

       A. I and II
       B. I, II, and III
       C. I and III
       D. I only
       E. II only

20. Which of the following molecules is the most polar?

    A. C_2H_2
    B. N_2
    C. CH_3I
    D. BF_3
    E. NH_3

21. Which of the following processes involves breaking an ionic bond?

    A. $H_2(g) + Cl_2(g) \rightarrow 2\ HCl(g)$
    B. $I_2(g) \rightarrow 2\ I(g)$
    C. $Na(s) \rightarrow Na(g)$
    D. $2\ C_2H_6(g) + 7\ O_2(g) \rightarrow 4\ CO_2(g)$
       $+ 6\ H_2O(g)$
    E. $2\ KBr(s) \rightarrow 2\ K(g) + Br_2(g)$

ANSWERS AND EXPLANATIONS

✓

1. **B.** The Lewis (electron dot) structure has five bonding pairs around the central Sb and no lone pairs. VSEPR predicts this number of pairs to give a trigonal bipyramidal structure.

2. **B.** All the bonds except in CO are single bonds. The CO bond is a triple bond. Triple bonds are shorter than double bonds, which are shorter than single bonds. Drawing Lewis structures might help you answer this question.

3. **A.** Answers B–E contain molecules or ions with double or triple bonds. Double and triple bonds contain π bonds. Water only has single (σ) bonds. If any are not obvious, draw a Lewis structure.

4. **A.** The VSEPR model predicts all the other molecules to be nonpolar.

5. **C.** All the other answers involve species containing only single bonds. Substances without double or triple bonds seldom need resonance structures.

6. **C.** Resonance causes bonds to have the same average length.

7. **E.** Many organic molecules are nonpolar. Nonpolar substances are held together by weak van der Waals attractions.

8. **D.** Lewis structures are required. You do not need to draw all of them. A and B have one unshared pair, while C and E have no unshared pairs. D has two unshared pairs of electrons.

9. **E.** Tetrahedral molecules are normally sp^3 hybridized.

10. **D.** $SiCl_4$ is tetrahedral. BrF_4^- is square planar. C_2H_2 is linear. TeF_6 is octahedral. NO_3^- is trigonal planar. If you are uncertain about any of these Lewis structures and VSEPR are needed.

11. **A.** Only A and E are ionic. The chloride ion has no internal bonds, so σ, and π bonds are not possible.

12–14. Sketch a molecular orbital energy level diagram. Use the same diagram to save time, unless it becomes too messy.

12. **D.**

13. **A.**

14. **D.**

15. **A.** This hybridization requires a geometrical shape with three corners.

16. **B.** One or more Lewis structures may help you. I and III are tetrahedral, and II is an irregular tetrahedron (see-saw).

17. **B.** A has 0. B has 2. C and D have 0. E has 1. You may need to draw one or more Lewis structures.

18. **B.** All the molecules are polar except B.

19. **E.** The structure is: H—C=C—C=C—H

    | | | |

    H H H H

All the carbon atoms have one double and two single bonds. This combination is sp^2.

20. **E.** Drawing one or more Lewis structures may help you. Only C and E are polar. Only the ammonia has hydrogen bonding which is very very polar.

21. **E.** C is metallic bonding. All the others involve covalently bonded molecules.

FREE-RESPONSE QUESTIONS

Answer the following questions. You have 15 minutes, and you may not use a calculator.

Answer each of the following with respect to chemical bonding and structure.

a. The nitrite ion, NO_2^-, and the nitrate ion, NO_3^-, both play a role in nitrogen chemistry.

   i. Draw the Lewis (electron dot) structure for the nitrite ion and the nitrate ion.

   ii. Predict which ion will have the shorter bond length and justify your prediction.

b. Using Lewis (electron dot) structures, explain why the ClF_3 molecule is polar and the BF_3 molecule is not polar.

c. Consider the following substances and their melting points:

Substance	Melting point (°C)
SrS	>2000
KCl	770
H_2O	0.00
H_2S	−85.5
CH_4	−182

Explain the relative values of the melting points of these substances.

ANSWERS AND EXPLANATIONS

✓

a.

i. Nitrite ion: [:Ö::N:Ö:]⁻   Nitrate ion: [:Ö::N:Ö:]⁻
                                                    :Ö:

Give yourself 1 point for each structure that is correct. The double bonds could be between the nitrogen and any of the oxygens, not just the ones shown. Only one double bond per structure is allowed.

ii. If you predicted the nitrite ion has the shorter bond length, you have earned 1 point.

The explanation must invoke resonance. You do not need to show all the resonance structures. You need to mention that the double bond "moves" from one oxygen to another. In the nitrite ion, each N-O bond is a double bond half the time and a single bond the other half. This gives an average of 1.5 bonds between the nitrogen and each of the oxygens. Similarly, for the nitrate ion, each N-O bond spends one-third of the time as a double bond, and two-thirds of the time as a single bond. The average N-O bond is 1.33. The larger the average number of bonds, the shorter the bond is. This explanation will get you 1 point.

b. Give yourself 1 point for each correct Lewis structure.

BF₃   ClF₃

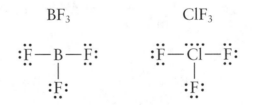

The BF₃, with three bonding pairs and zero nonbonding pairs on the central atom, is polar. The ClF₃, with five pairs about the central atom, is polar because of the two lone pairs. Give yourself 1 point for this explanation.

c. You get 1 point for saying that the two compounds with the highest melting points are ionic and the other compounds are molecular.

You get 1 point if you say that SrS is higher than KCl because the charges on the ions in SrS are higher.

You get 1 point if you say H_2O is higher than the lowest two because of hydrogen bonding.

You get 1 point if you say H_2S is higher than CH_4 because H_2S is polar and CH_4 is nonpolar.

There are a maximum of 11 points.

RAPID REVIEW

- Compounds are pure substances that have a fixed proportion of elements.

- Metals react with nonmetals to form ionic bonds, and nonmetals react with other nonmetals to form covalent bonds.

- The Lewis electron-dot structure is a way of representing the element and its valence electrons.

- Atoms lose, gain, or share electrons to achieve the same electronic configuration (become isoelectronic) as the nearest noble gas.

- Atoms are generally most stable when they have a complete octet (eight electrons).

- Ionic bonds result when a metal loses electrons to form cations and a nonmetal gains those electrons to form an anion.

- The attraction of the opposite charges (anions and cations) forms the ionic bond.

- The crisscross rule can help determine the formula of an ionic compound.

- In covalent bonding two atoms share one or more electron pairs.

- If the electrons are shared equally, the bond is a nonpolar covalent bond, but unequal sharing results in a polar covalent bond.

- The element that will have the greatest attraction for a bonding pair of electrons is related to its electronegativity.

- Electronegativity values increase from left to right on the periodic table and decrease from top to bottom.

- The $N - A = S$ rule can be used to help draw the Lewis structure of a molecule.

- Molecular geometry, the arrangement of atoms in three-dimensional space, can be predicted using the VSEPR theory. This theory says the electron pairs around a central atom will try to get as far as possible from each other to minimize the repulsive forces.

- In using the VSEPR theory, first determine the electron-group geometry, then the molecular geometry.

- The valence bond theory describes covalent bonding as the overlap of atomic orbitals to form a new kind of orbital, a hybrid orbital.

- The number of hybrid orbitals is the same as the number of atomic orbitals that were mixed together.

- There are a number of different types of hybrid orbitals, such as sp, sp^2, and sp^3.

- In the valence bond theory, sigma bonds overlap on a line drawn between the two nuclei, while pi bonds result from the overlap of atomic orbitals above and below a line connecting the two atomic nuclei.

- A double or triple bond is always composed of one sigma bond and the rest pi.

- In the molecular orbital (MO) theory of covalent bonding, atomic orbitals form molecular orbitals that encompass the entire molecule.

- The MO theory uses bonding and antibonding orbitals.

- The bond order is (# electrons in bonding MOs – # electrons in antibonding MOs)/2.

- Resonance occurs when more than one Lewis structure can be written for a molecule. The actual structure of the molecule is an average of the Lewis resonance structures.

- The higher the bond order, the shorter and stronger the bond.

- Paramagnetism, the attraction of a molecule to a magnetic field, is due to the presence of unpaired electrons. Diamagnetism, the repulsion of a molecule from a magnetic field, is due to the presence of paired electrons.

Chapter 10

Solids, Liquids, and Intermolecular Forces

 KEYWORDS AND EQUATIONS

✓ No specific keywords or equations are listed on the AP exam for this topic.

INTRODUCTION

 In Chapter 6 we discussed the gaseous state. In this chapter we will discuss the liquid and solid states and the forces that exist between the particles—the intermolecular forces. A substance's state of matter depends on two factors: the kinetic energy of the particles, and the intermolecular forces between the particles. The kinetic energy tends to move the particles away from each other. The temperature of the substance is a measure of the average kinetic energy of the molecules. As the temperature increases, the average kinetic energy increases and the particles tend to move farther apart. This is consistent with our experience of heating ice, for example, and watching it move from the solid state to the liquid state and finally to the gaseous state. For this to happen, the kinetic energy overcomes the forces between the particles, the intermolecular forces.

In the solid state the kinetic energy of the particles cannot overcome the intermolecular forces; the particles are held close together due to the intermolecular forces. As the temperature increases, the kinetic energy increases and begins to overcome the attractive intermolecular forces. The substance might melt, going from the solid to the liquid state. As this melting takes place, the temperature remains constant even though energy is being added. The temperature at which the solid converts into the liquid state is called the **melting point (m.p.)** of the solid.

After all the solid has been converted into a liquid, the temperature again starts to rise as energy is added. The particles are still relatively close together, but possess enough kinetic energy to move easily with respect to each other. Finally, if enough energy is added, the particles start to break free of the intermolecular forces keeping them relatively close together and escape the liquid as essentially independent gas particles. This process of going from the liquid state to the gaseous state is called **boiling,** and the temperature at which this occurs is called the **boiling point (b.p.)** of the liquid. Sometimes, however, a solid can go directly from the solid state to the gaseous state without ever having become a liquid. This process is called **sublimation.** Dry ice, solid carbon dioxide, readily sublimes.

These changes of state, called **phase changes,** are related to temperature, but sometimes pressure can influence these changes. We will see how these relationships can be diagrammed later in this chapter.

STRUCTURES AND INTERMOLECULAR FORCES

Intermolecular forces are attractive or repulsive forces between molecules caused by partial charges. The attractive forces are the ones that work to overcome the randomizing forces of kinetic energy. The structure and type of bonding of a particular substance has quite a bit to do with the type of interaction and the strength of interaction. Before we start examining the different types of intermolecular forces, recall from Chapter 9 on bonding that those molecules that have polar covalent bonding (unequal sharing of the bonding electron pair) may become dipoles (molecules with a positive and negative end due to charge separation within the molecule). Dipoles are often involved in the intermolecular forces.

Ion–Dipole Intermolecular Forces

These forces are due to the attraction of an ion and one end of a polar molecule (dipole). This type of attraction is especially important in aqueous salt solutions, where the ion attracts water molecules and may form a hydrated ion, such as $Al(H_2O)_6^{3+}$. This is the strongest of the intermolecular forces.

It is also important to realize that this intermolecular force is unique in requiring two different species—an ion and a polar molecule.

Dipole–Dipole Intermolecular Forces

These forces result from the attraction of the positive end of one dipole to the negative end of another dipole. For example, in gaseous hydrogen chloride, HCl(g), the hydrogen end has a partial positive charge and the chlorine end has a partial negative charge, due to its higher electronegativity. Dipole–dipole attractions are especially important in polar liquids. They tend to be a rather strong force, although not nearly as strong as ion–dipole attraction.

Hydrogen Bond Intermolecular Forces

Hydrogen bonding is a specific type of dipole–dipole attraction in which a hydrogen atom is polar-covalently bonded to one of the following extremely electronegative elements: N, O, or F. These are extremely polar bonds in nature, so there is a great degree of charge separation within the molecule. Therefore, the attraction of the positively charged hydrogen of one molecule and the negatively charged N, O, or F of another molecule is extremely strong. These hydrogen bonds may, in many cases, be stronger than the typical dipole–dipole interaction.

Hydrogen bonding explains why HF(aq) is a weak acid, while HCl(aq), HBr(aq), etc. are strong acids. The hydrogen bond between the hydrogen of one HF molecule and the fluorine of another "traps" the hydrogen, so it is much harder to break its bonds and free the hydrogen to be donated as an H^+. Hydrogen bonding also explains why water has such unusual properties, for example, its unusually high boiling point and the fact that its solid phase is less dense than its liquid phase. The hydrogen bonds tend to stabilize the water molecules and keep them from readily escaping into the gas phase. When water freezes, the hydrogen bonds are stabilized and lock the water molecules into a framework with a lot of open space. Therefore, ice floats in liquid water. Hydrogen bonding also holds the strands of DNA together.

Ion-Induced Dipole and Dipole-Induced Dipole Intermolecular Forces

These types of attraction occur when the charge on an ion or a dipole distorts the electron cloud of a nonpolar molecule and induces a temporary dipole in the nonpolar molecule. These are fairly weak interactions.

London (Dispersion) Intermolecular Force

This intermolecular attraction occurs in nonpolar substances. It arises from the momentary distortion of the electron cloud with the creation of a very weak dipole. The weak dipole induces a dipole in another nonpolar molecule. This is an extremely weak interaction, but it is strong enough to allow us to liquefy nonpolar gas such as hydrogen, H_2, and nitrogen, N_2. If there were no intermolecular forces attracting these molecules, it would be impossible to liquefy them.

THE LIQUID STATE

At the microscopic level, liquid particles are in constant flux. They may exhibit short-range areas of order, but these do not last very long. Clumps of particles may form and then break apart. At the macroscopic level, a liquid has a specific volume but no fixed shape. Three other macroscopic properties deserve discussion: surface tension, viscosity, and capillary action. In the body of a liquid the molecules are pulled in all different ways by the intermolecular forces between them. At the surface of the liquid, the molecules are only being pulled into the body of the liquid from the sides and below, not above. The effect of this unequal attraction is that the liquid tries to minimize its surface area by forming a sphere. In a large pool of liquid where this is not possible, the surface behaves as if it had a thin "skin" over it. It requires force to break the attractive forces at the surface. The amount of force required to break through this molecular layer at the surface is called the liquid's **surface tension.** The greater the intermolecular forces, the greater the surface tension. Polar liquids, especially those that may undergo hydrogen bonding, have a much higher surface tension than nonpolar liquids.

Viscosity, the resistance of liquids to flow, is affected by intermolecular forces, temperature, and molecular shape. Liquids with strong intermolecular forces tend to have a higher viscosity than those with weak intermolecular forces. Again, polar liquids tend to have a higher viscosity than nonpolar liquids. As the temperature increases, the kinetic energy of the particles becomes greater, overcoming the intermolecular attractive forces. This causes a lower viscosity. Finally, the longer and more complex the molecules, the more contact the particles will have as they slip by each other, increasing the viscosity.

Capillary action is the spontaneous rising of a liquid through a narrow tube against the force of gravity. It is caused by competition between the intermolecular forces in the liquid and those attractive forces between the liquid and the tube wall. The stronger the attraction between the liquid and the tube, the higher the level will be. Liquids that have weak attractions to the walls, like mercury in a glass tube, have a low capillary action. Liquids like water in a glass tube have strong attractions to the walls and will have a high capillary action.

As we have noted before, water, because of its stronger intermolecular forces (hydrogen bonding) has some very unusual properties. It will dissolve a great number of substances, both ionic and polar covalent, because of its polarity and ability to form hydrogen bonds. It is sometimes called the "universal solvent." It has a high **heat capacity,** the heat absorbed to cause the temperature to rise, and a high **heat of vaporization,** the heat needed to transform the liquid into a gas. Both of these thermal properties are due to the strong hydrogen bonding between the water molecules. Water has a high surface tension for the same reason. The fact that the solid form of water (ice) is less dense than liquid water is because water molecules in ice are held in a rigid, open crystalline framework by the hydrogen bonds. As the ice starts melting, the crystal structure breaks and water molecules fill the holes in the structure, increasing the density. The density reaches a maximum at around 4° C; then the increasing kinetic energy of the particles causes the density to begin to decrease.

THE SOLID STATE

At the macroscopic level a **solid** is defined as a substance that has both a definite volume and a definite shape. At the microscopic level, solids may be one of two types—amorphous or crystalline. **Amorphous solids** lack extensive ordering of the particles. There is a lack of regularity of the structure. There may be small regions of order separated by large areas of disordered particles. They resemble liquids more than solids in this characteristic. Amorphous solids have no distinct melting point. They simply get softer and softer as the temperature rises. Glass, rubber, and charcoal are examples of amorphous solids.

Crystalline solids display a very regular ordering of the particles in a three-dimensional structure called the **crystal lattice.** In this crystal lattice there are repeating units called **unit cells.** Figure 10.1 shows the relationship of the unit cell to the crystal lattice.

Several types of unit cells are found in solids. The cubic system is the type most commonly appearing on the AP exam. Three types of unit cells are found in the cubic system:

1. The **simple cubic unit cell** has particles located at the corners of a simple cube.
2. The **body-centered unit cell** has particles located at the corners of the cube and in the middle of the cube.
3. The **face-centered unit cell** has particles at the corners and one in the middle of each face of the cube, but not in the center.

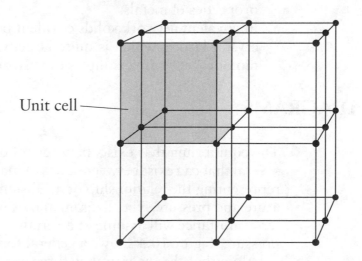

Unit cell

Figure 10.1 The crystal lattice for a simple cubic unit cell.

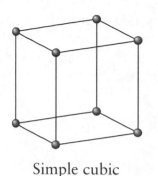
Simple cubic

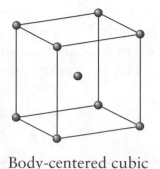
Body-centered cubic

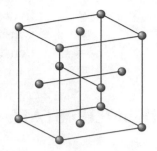
Face-centered cubic

Figure 10.2 The three types of unit cells of the cubic lattice.

Figure 10.2 shows three types of cubic unit cells.

Five types of crystalline solids are found in nature:

1. In **atomic solids** individual atoms are held in place by London forces. The noble gases are the only atomic solids known.
2. In **molecular solids** lattices composed of molecules are held in place by London forces, dipole–dipole forces, and hydrogen bonding. Solid methane and water are examples of molecular solids.
3. In **ionic solids** lattices composed of ions are held together by the attraction of opposite charges of the ions. These crystalline solids tend to be strong with high melting points because of the strength of the intermolecular forces. NaCl and other salts are examples of ionic solids. Figure 10.3 shows the lattice structure of NaCl. Each sodium cation is surrounded by six chloride anions, and each chloride anion is surrounded by six sodium cations.
4. In **metallic solids** metal atoms occupying the crystal lattice are held together by metallic bonding. In **metallic bonding** the electrons of the atoms are delocalized and are free to move throughout the entire solid. This explains electrical and thermal conductivity as well as many other properties of metals.
5. In **covalent network solids** covalent bonds join atoms together in the crystal lattice, which is quite large. Graphite, diamond, and silicon dioxide (SiO_2) are examples of network solids.

PHASE DIAGRAMS

The equilibrium that exists between a liquid and its vapor is just one of several that can exist between states of matter. A **phase diagram** is a graph representing the relationship of a substance's states of matter to temperature and pressure. The diagram allows us to predict which state of matter a substance will assume at a certain combination of temperature and pressure. Figure 10.4 shows a general form of the phase diagram.

Note that the diagram has three general areas corresponding to the three states of matter—solid, liquid, and gas. The line from A to C represents the solid's change in vapor pressure with changing temperature,

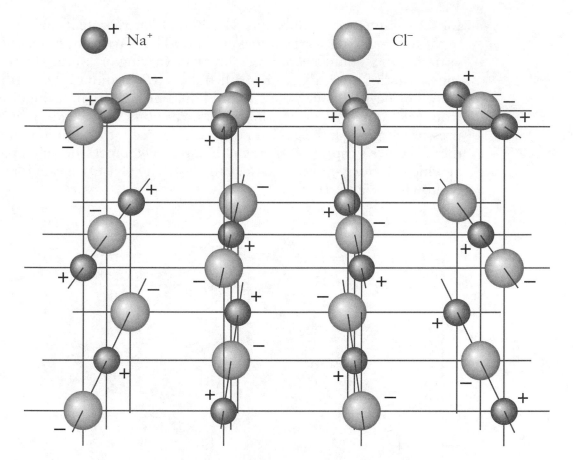

Figure 10.3 Sodium chloride crystal lattice.

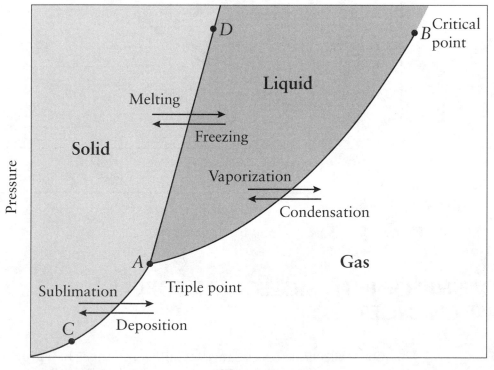

Figure 10.4 A phase diagram.

for the sublimation equilibrium. The A-to-D line represents the variation in the melting point with varying pressure. The A-to-B line represents the variation of a liquid's vapor pressure with varying pressure. The B point shown on this phase diagram is called the **critical point** of the substance, the point beyond which the gas and liquid phases are indistinguishable from each other. At or beyond this critical point, no matter how much pressure is applied, the gas cannot be condensed into a liquid. Point A is the substance's **triple point,** the combination of temperature and pressure at which all three states of matter can exist. The phase diagram for water is shown in Figure 10.5.

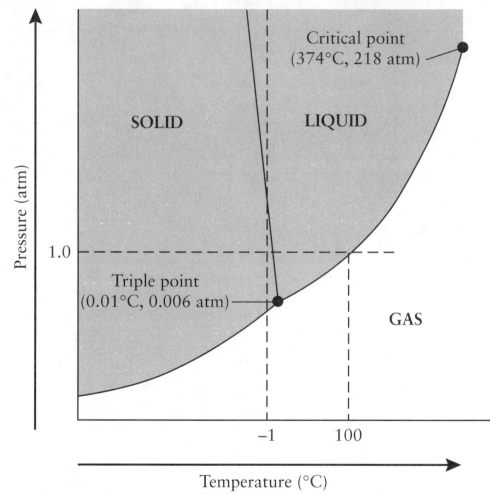

Figure 10.5 Phase diagram for H_2O.

RELATIONSHIP OF INTERMOLECULAR FORCES TO PHASE CHANGES

The intermolecular forces can affect phase changes to a great degree. The stronger the intermolecular forces present in a liquid, the more kinetic energy must be added to convert it into a gas. Conversely, the stronger the intermolecular forces between the gas particles, the easier it will be to condense the gas into a liquid. In general, the lower the intermolecular forces, the higher the vapor pressure. The same type of reasoning can be used about the other phase equilibria.

Example: Based on intermolecular forces, predict which will have the higher vapor pressure and higher boiling point, water or dimethyl ether, CH_3-O-CH_3.

Answer: Dimethyl ether will have the higher vapor pressure and the lower boiling point.

Explanation: Water is a polar substance with strong intermolecular hydrogen bonds. Dimethyl ether is a polar material with weaker intermolecular forces (dipole–dipole). It will take much more energy to vaporize water, thus, water has a lower vapor pressure and higher boiling point.

EXPERIMENTAL

There have been no experimental questions about this material on recent AP exams.

COMMON MISTAKES TO AVOID

1. Don't confuse the various types of intermolecular forces.
2. The melting point and the freezing point are identical.
3. Hydrogen bonding can only occur when a hydrogen atom is bonded to an N, O, or F.
4. When moving from point to point in a phase diagram, pay attention to what phases the substances passes through.
5. In looking at crystal lattice diagrams, be sure to count all the particles in all three dimensions that surround another particle.

REVIEW QUESTIONS

Answer the following questions. You have 20 minutes, and you may not use a calculator.

Choose from the following descriptions of solids for questions 1–4.

A. composed of macromolecules held together by strong bonds
B. composed of atoms held together by delocalized electrons
C. composed of positive and negative ions held together by electrostatic attractions
D. composed of molecules held together by intermolecular dipole–dipole interactions
E. composed of molecules held together by intermolecular London forces

1. Fe(s)

2. $KNO_3(s)$

3. $SiO_2(s)$

4. $HCl(s)$

For questions 5 and 6 choose from the following.

    A. an ionic solid

    B. a metallic solid

    C. a molecular solid containing nonpolar molecules

    D. a covalent network solid

    E. a molecular solid containing polar molecules

5. Diamond, $C(s)$

6. Solid sulfur dioxide, $SO_2(s)$

7. The approximate boiling points for hydrogen compounds of some elements in the nitrogen family are: (SbH_3 15° C), (AsH_3 −62° C), (PH_3 −87° C), and (NH_3 −33° C). The best explanation for the fact that NH_3 does not follow the trend of the other hydrogen compounds is

    A. NH_3 is the only one to exhibit hydrogen bonding

    B. NH_3 is the only one that is water soluble

    C. NH_3 is the only one that is nearly ideal in the gas phase

    D. NH_3 is the only one that is a base

    E. NH_3 is the only one that is nonpolar

8. The critical point is

    A. the highest temperature and pressure where the substance may exist as discrete liquid and gas phases

    B. the temperature and pressure where the substance exists in equilibrium as solid, liquid, and gas phases

    C. the highest temperature and pressure where a substance can sublime

    D. the highest temperature and pressure where the substance may exist as discrete liquid and solid phases

    E. the highest temperature and pressure where the substance may exist as discrete solid and gas phases

9. For all one-component phase diagrams, choose the correct statement from the following list.

    A. The line separating the gas from the liquid phase may have a positive or negative slope.

    B. The line separating the solid from the liquid phase may have a positive or negative slope.

    C. The line separating the solid from the liquid phase has a positive slope.

    D. The temperature at the triple point is the same as at the freezing point.

    E. The triple point is at a pressure above 1 atm.

Choose the appropriate answer from the following list for questions 10 and 11.

    A. London dispersion forces

    B. covalent bonding

    C. hydrogen bonding

    D. metallic bonding

    E. ionic bonding

10. This is the reason why argon may be solidified at a sufficiently low temperature.

11. This is the reason why diamond is so hard.

12. The triple point

    A. represents the highest pressure at which the liquid can exist

    B. is the lowest pressure at which the liquid can exist

    C. represents the lowest temperature at which the vapor can exist

    D. is 0.15 K higher than the melting point of the solid

    E. is at a pressure of 1 atm

13. A sample of a pure liquid is placed in an open container and heated to the boiling point. Which of the following may increase the boiling point of the liquid?

 I. The size of the container is increased.
 II. The container is sealed.
 III. A vacuum is created over the liquid.

   A. II and III
   B. I and III
   C. III only
   D. II only
   E. I only

14. Which of the following best explains why 1-butanol, $CH_3CH_2CH_2CH_2OH$, has a higher surface tension than its isomer, diethyl ether, $CH_3CH_2OCH_2CH_3$?

   A. the higher density of 1-butanol
   B. the lower specific heat of 1-butanol
   C. the lack of hydrogen bonding in 1-butanol
   D. the higher molecular mass of 1-butanol
   E. the presence of hydrogen bonding in 1-butanol

15. Pick the answer that most likely represents the substances' relative solubilities in water.

   A. $CH_3CH_2CH_2CH_3 <$ $CH_3CH_2CH_2OH < HOCH_2CH_2OH$
   B. $CH_3CH_2CH_2OH <$ $CH_3CH_2CH_2CH_3 <$ $HOCH_2CH_2OH$
   C. $CH_3CH_2CH_2CH_3 <$ $HOCH_2CH_2OH < CH_3CH_2CH_2OH$
   D. $HOCH_2CH_2OH < CH_3CH_2CH_2OH$ $< CH_3CH_2CH_2CH_3$
   E. $CH_3CH_2CH_2OH < HOCH_2CH_2OH$ $< CH_3CH_2CH_2CH_3$

16. What is the energy change that accompanies the conversion of molecules in the gas phase to a liquid?

   A. condensation energy
   B. deposition energy
   C. sublimation energy
   D. lattice energy
   E. vaporization energy

17. Which of the following explains why the melting point of sodium chloride (NaCl 801° C) is lower than the melting point of calcium fluoride (CaF_2 1423° C)?

 I. The chloride ion is smaller than the fluoride ion.
 II. The ratio of anions to cations is lower in sodium chloride.
 III. The charge on a sodium ion is less than the charge on a calcium ion.

   A. I and II
   B. I, II, and III
   C. III only
   D. II only
   E. I only

18. Which point on the diagram below might represent the normal melting point?

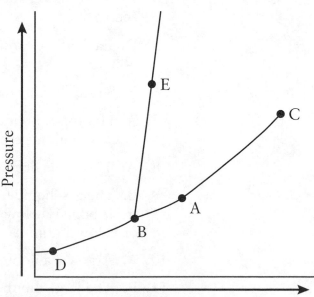

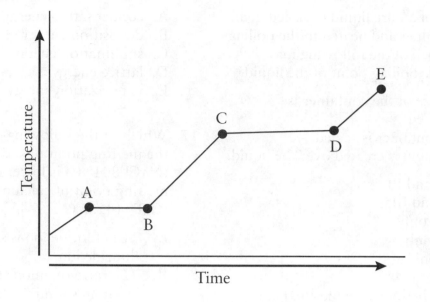

19. The above diagram represents the heating curve for a pure crystalline substance. The solid is the only phase present up to point

A. C
B. B
C. E
D. A
E. D

ANSWERS AND EXPLANATIONS

✓

1. **B.** This answer describes a metallic solid.

2. **C.** This answer describes an ionic solid.

3. **A.** This answer describes a covalent network solid.

4. **D.** This answers describes a solid consisting of discrete polar molecules.

5. **D.** Each of the carbon atoms is covalently bonded to four other carbon atoms.

6. **E.** Sulfur dioxide molecules are polar.

7. **A.** Hydrogen bonding occurs when hydrogen is directly bonded to F, O, and in this case N.

8. **A.** This is the definition of the critical point.

9. **B.** The gas–liquid line always has a positive slope. B negates C. The triple point is below the freezing point. The triple point may be above or below 1 atm.

10. **A.** Argon is a noble gas; none of the bonding choices are options.

11. **B.** The large number (four) of strong covalent bonds between the carbon atoms.

12. **B.** The bottom of the liquid region on the phase diagram is the triple point.

13. **D.** The size of the container is irrelevant. Sealing the container will cause an increase in pressure that will increase the boiling point. A decrease in pressure will lower the boiling point.

14. **E.** The compound with the higher surface tension is the one with the stronger intermolecular force. The hydrogen bonding in 1-butanol is stronger than the dipole–dipole attractions in diethyl ether.

15. **A.** The sequence for these similar molecules is nonpolar, then one hydrogen bond, then two hydrogen bonds.

16. **A.** This change is condensation, so the energy is the condensation energy.

17. **C.** The only applicable factor listed is the charge difference. The chloride ion is larger than the fluoride ion. The ion ratio is not important.

18. **E.** The point must be on the line separating the solid from the liquid phase.

19. **D.** The solid begins to melt at A, and finishes melting at B.

FREE-RESPONSE QUESTIONS

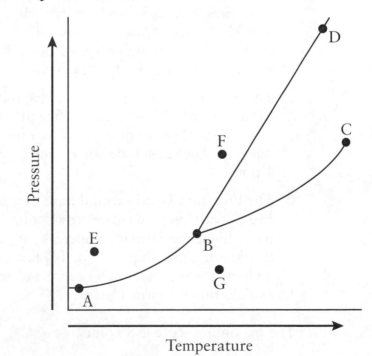

The above figure shows a typical phase diagram for a one-component system. Use this diagram to answer the following questions.

a. What is point C called? List the characteristics of this point.

b. What happens to a substance at point E if the temperature is increased at constant pressure?

c. Assume point F is at 0° C and 1 atm. Describe the changes that would occur when moving directly from point F to point G (still at 0° C).

d. Solid bismuth is less dense than liquid bismuth. How would this change the appearance of the diagram? Explain.

ANSWERS AND EXPLANATIONS

a. Point C is the critical point. Give yourself 1 point if you gave this answer. This is the highest temperature and pressure where the liquid and gas phases can be distinguished. This answer is worth 1 point.

b. At point E the substance is a solid. Increasing the temperature, at constant pressure, will cause a horizontal movement to the right. When line AB is reached, the solid will sublime. After line AB is passed, only the vapor is present. You get 1 point for noting a movement to the right. You get 1 point for discussing the change from solid to gas.

c. The substance is a solid at point F, and it will remain a solid until line BD is reached. When it reaches line BD, it melts. This is worth 1 point. The substance then passes through the liquid phase until line BC is reached. The substance boils when it reaches line BC. This is worth 1 point.

d. The line from B to D would have a negative slope instead of a positive slope. This answer is worth 1 point. The denser phase is more stable at higher pressures. An increase in pressure will cause a change to the denser phase (liquid). The BD line must "lean" to the left so that an increase in pressure will cause a change from solid to liquid. This explanation is worth 1 point.

The maximum score is 8 points.

RAPID REVIEW

• The state of matter in which a substance exists depends on the competition between the kinetic energy of the particles (temperature) and the strength of the intermolecular forces between the particles.

- The melting point is the temperature at which a substance goes from the solid to the liquid state.

- The boiling point is the temperature at which a substance goes from the liquid to the gaseous state.

- Sublimation is the conversion of a solid to a gas without ever having become a liquid.

- Intermolecular forces are the attractive or repulsive forces between atoms, molecules, or ions due to full or partial charges.

- Phase changes are changes of state.

- Ion–dipole intermolecular forces occur between ions and polar molecules.

- Dipole–dipole intermolecular forces occur between polar molecules.

- Hydrogen bonds are intermolecular forces between dipoles in which there is a hydrogen atom attached to an N, O, or F atom.

- Ion-induced dipole intermolecular forces occur between an ion and a nonpolar molecule.

- London (dispersion) forces are intermolecular forces between non-polar molecules.

- Liquids possess surface tension (liquids behaving as if they had a thin "skin" on their surface due to unequal attraction of molecules at the surface of the liquid), viscosity (resistance to flow), and capillary action (flow up a small tube).

- Amorphous solids have very little structure in the solid state.

- Crystalline solids have a great deal of structure in the solid.

- The crystal lattice of a crystalline solid is the regular ordering of the unit cells.

- Cubic unit cells include the simple cubic, body centered, and face centered.

- Know the five types of crystalline solids: atomic, molecular, ionic, metallic, and network.

- A phase diagram is a graph displaying the relationship of a substance's states of matter to temperature and pressure.

- The critical point on a phase diagram is that point beyond which the gaseous and liquid states merge. No matter how much pressure is applied, the substance cannot be condensed into a liquid.

- The triple point is the combination of temperature and pressure on a phase diagram where all three states of matter can exist.

- Phase changes can be related to the strength of intermolecular forces.

Chapter 11

Solutions and Colligative Properties

KEYWORDS AND EQUATIONS

Π = osmotic pressure

i = van't Hoff factor

K_f = molal freezing-point depression constant

K_b = molal boiling-point elevation constant

K_f for water = 1.86 K kg mol^{-1}

K_b for water = 0.512 K kg mol^{-1}

$\Delta T_f = iK_f \times$ molality

$\Delta T_b = iK_b \times$ molality

$\Pi = (nRT/V)\, i$

$\pi = MRT$

INTRODUCTION

A **solution** is a homogeneous mixture composed of solvent and one or more solutes. The **solvent** is normally the substance present in the greatest amount. Commonly the solvent is a liquid, but it doesn't have to be. Our atmosphere is a solution with nitrogen as the solvent; it is the gas present in the largest amount (79%). Many times you will be dealing with a solution in which water is the solvent, an **aqueous solution**. The **solute** is the substance that is present in the solution in the smaller amount. You may have more than one solute in a solution. For example, if you dissolved table salt (sodium chloride) and table sugar (sucrose) in water, you would have one solvent (water) and two solutes (sodium chloride and sucrose).

Some substances will dissolve in a particular solvent and others will not. There is a general rule in chemistry that states that "*like dissolves like.*" This simply means that polar substances (salts, alcohols, etc.) will dissolve in polar solvents such as water, and nonpolar solutes, such as naphthalene, will dissolve in nonpolar solvents such as benzene. The solubility of a particular solute is normally expressed in terms of grams solute per 100 mL of solvent (g/mL) at a specified temperature. The temperature must be specified because the solubility of a particular substance will vary with the temperature. Normally, the solubility of solids dissolving in liquids increases with increasing temperature, while the reverse is true for gases dissolving in liquids.

A solution in which one has dissolved the maximum amount of solute per given amount of solvent at a given temperature is called a **saturated solution.** An **unsaturated solution** has less than the maximum amount of solute dissolved. Sometimes, if the temperature, purity of the solute and solvent, and other factors are just right, you might be able to dissolve more than the maximum amount of solute, resulting in a **supersaturated solution.** Supersaturated solutions are unstable, and sooner or later separation of the excess solute will occur, until a saturated solution is formed.

The formation of a solution depends on many factors, such as the nature of the solvent, the nature of the solute, the temperature, and the pressure. Some of these factors were addressed in Chapter 4. In general, the solubility of a solid or liquid will increase with temperature and be unaffected by pressure changes. The solubility of a gas will decrease with increasing temperature and will increase with increasing partial pressure of the gas (**Henry's Law**).

CONCENTRATION UNITS

There are many ways of expressing the relative amounts of solute(s) and solvent in a solution. The terms saturated, unsaturated, and supersaturated give a qualitative measure, as do the terms dilute and concentrated. The term **dilute** refers to a solution that has a relatively small amount of solute in comparison to the amount of solvent. **Concentrated,** on the other hand, refers to a solution that has a relatively large amount of solute in comparison to the solvent. However, these terms are very subjective. If you dissolve 0.1 g of sucrose per liter of water, that solution would probably be considered dilute; 100 g of sucrose per liter would probably be considered concentrated. But what about 25 g per liter—dilute or concentrated? In order to communicate effectively, chemists use quantitative ways of expressing the concentration of solutions. Several concentration units are useful, including percentage, molarity, and molality.

Percentage

One common way of expressing the relative amount of solute and solvent is through percentage, amount-per-hundred. Percentage can be expressed in three ways:

mass percent
mass/volume percent
volume/volume percent

Mass (Sometimes Called Weight) Percentage

The mass percentage of a solution is the mass of the solute divided by the mass of the solution, multiplied by 100% to get percentage. The mass is commonly measured in grams.

$$\text{mass \%} = (\text{grams of solute/grams solution}) \times 100\%$$

A solution is prepared by dissolving 25.2 g of sodium chloride in 250.0 g of water. Calculate the mass percent of the solution.

Answer:

$$\text{mass \%} = \frac{(25.2 \text{ g solute})}{(25.2 + 250.0) \text{ g solution}} \times 100\% = 9.16\%$$

A common error is forgetting to add the solute and solvent masses together in the denominator.

When solutions of this type are prepared, the solute and solvent are weighed out separately and then mixed together to form a solution. The final volume of the solution is unknown.

Mass/Volume Percentage

The mass/volume percent of a solution is the mass of the solute divided by the volume of the solution, multiplied by 100% to yield percentage. The volume of the solution is generally expressed in milliliters.

$$\text{mass/volume \%} = (\text{grams solute/volume of solution}) \times 100\%$$

When mass/volume solutions are prepared, the grams of the solute are weighed out and dissolved and diluted to the required volume.

A solution is prepared by mixing 125.0 g of benzene with 250.0 g of toluene. The density of benzene is 0.8765 g/mL, and the density of toluene is 0.8669 g/mL. Determine the mass/volume percentage of the solution.

Answer:

First, determine the volume of the solution.

$$\begin{aligned} \text{solution volume} &= (125.0 \text{ g benzene})(\text{mL} / 0.8765 \text{ g benzene}) \\ &\quad + (250.0 \text{ g toluene})(\text{mL} / 0.8669 \text{ g toluene}) \\ &= 431.0 \text{ mL} \end{aligned}$$

Then

$$\text{mass volume \%} = \frac{(125.0 \text{ bezene})}{431.0 \text{ mL solution}} \times 100\% = 28.99\%$$

Notice that it is not necessary to know the chemical formula of either constituent. A common error is forgetting to add the solute and solvent volumes together.

Volume/Volume Percentage

The third case is one in which both the solute and solvent are liquids. The volume percent of the solution is the volume of the solute divided by the volume of the solution, multiplied by 100% to generate the percentage.

$$\text{volume \%} = (\text{volume solute/volume solution}) \times 100\%$$

When volume percent solutions are prepared, the mL of the solute is diluted with solvent to the required volume.

Determine the volume percentage of carbon tetrachloride in a solution prepared by dissolving 100.0 mL of carbon tetrachloride and 100.0 mL of methylene chloride in 750.0 mL of chloroform. Assume the volumes are additive.

Answer:

$$\text{volume \%} = \frac{(100.0 \text{ mL carbon tetrachloride})}{(100.0 + 100.0 + 750.0) \text{ mL solution}} \times 100\% = 10.53\%$$

A common error is not to add all the volumes together to get the volume of the solution.

If the solute is ethyl alcohol and the solvent is water, then another concentration term is used, proof. The **proof** of an aqueous ethyl alcohol solution is twice the volume percent. A 45.0 volume % ethyl alcohol solution would be 90.0 proof.

Molarity

Percentage concentration is common in everyday life (3% hydrogen peroxide, 5% acetic acid vinegar, etc.). The concentration unit most commonly used by chemists is molarity. **Molarity (M)** is the number of moles of solute per liter of solution.

$$M = \text{moles solute/Liter solution}$$

In preparing a molar solution, the correct number of moles of solute (commonly converted to grams using the molar mass) is dissolved and diluted to the required volume.

Determine the molarity of sodium sulfate in a solution produced by dissolving 15.2 g of Na_2SO_4 in sufficient water to produce 750.0 mL of solution.

$$\text{molarity} = \frac{15.2 \text{ g } Na_2SO_4}{750.0 \text{ mL}} \times \frac{1 \text{ mol } Na_2SO_4}{142 \text{ g } Na_2SO_4} \times \frac{1000 \text{ mL}}{1 \text{ L}} = 0.143 \text{ M}$$

The most common error is not being careful with the units. Grams must be converted to moles, and milliliters must be converted to liters.

Another way to prepare a molar solution is by dilution of a more concentrated solution to a more dilute one by adding solvent. The following equation can be used:

$$(M_{\text{before dillution}})(V_{\text{before dillution}}) = (M_{\text{after dillution}})(V_{\text{after dillution}})$$

Determine the final concentration when 500.0 mL of water is added to 400.0 mL of a 0.1111 M solution of HCl. Assume the volumes are additive.

$$M_{\text{before}} = 0.1111\,M \qquad M_{\text{after}} = ?$$
$$V_{\text{before}} = 400.0\,\text{mL} \qquad V_{\text{before}} = (400.0 + 500.0)\,\text{mL}$$

$$M_{\text{after}} = (M_{\text{before}})(V_{\text{before}})/(V_{\text{after}}) = (0.1111\,M)\,(400.0\,\text{mL})/(900.0\,\text{mL})$$
$$= 0.04938\,M$$

The most common error is forgetting to add the two volumes.

Molality

Sometimes the varying volumes of a solution's liquid component(s) due to changes in temperature presents a problem. Many times volumes are not additive, but mass is additive. The chemist then resorts to defining concentration in terms of the molality. **Molality (m)** is defined as the moles of solute per kilogram of solvent.

m = moles solute/kilograms solution

Notice that this equation uses kilograms of solvent, not solution. The other concentration units use mass or volume of the solution. Molal solutions use the mass of the *solvent*. For dilute aqueous solutions, the molarity and the molality will be close to the same numerical value.

Ethylene glycol ($C_2H_6O_2$) is used in antifreeze. Determine the molality of ethylene glycol in a solution prepared by adding 62.1 g of ethylene glycol to 100.0 g of water.

$$\text{molality} = \frac{62.1\,\text{g}\,C_2H_6O_2}{100.0\,\text{g}\,H_2O} \times \frac{1000\,\text{g}}{1\,\text{kg}} \times \frac{1\,\text{mol}\,C_2H_6O_2}{62.1\,\text{g}\,C_2H_6O_2} = 10.0\,\text{m}\,C_2H_6O_2$$

The most common error is to use the total grams in the denominator instead of just the grams of solvent.

ELECTROLYTES AND NONELECTROLYTES

An **electrolyte** is a substance that, when dissolved in water or melted, conducts an electrical current. A **nonelectrolyte** does not conduct a current when dissolved in water or melted. The conduction of the electrical current is usually determined using a light bulb connected to a power source and two electrodes. The electrodes are placed in the aqueous solution or melt, and if a conducting medium is present, such as ions, the light bulb will light, indicating the substance is an electrolyte.

The ions that conduct the electrical current can result from a couple of sources. They may result from the dissociation of an ionically bonded substance (a salt). If sodium chloride (NaCl) is dissolved in water, it dissociates into the sodium cation (Na^+) and the chloride anion (Cl^-). But certain covalently bonded substances may also produce ions if dissolved in water, a process called ionization. For example, acids, both inorganic and organic, will produce ions when dissolved in water. Some acids, such as hydrochloric acid (HCl), will essentially completely ionize. Others, such as acetic acid (CH_3COOH), will only partially ionize. They establish an equilibrium with the ions and the unionized species (see Chapter 13 for more on chemical equilibrium).

$$HCl(aq) \rightarrow H^+ + Cl^- \qquad 100\% \text{ ionization}$$

$$CH_3COOH(aq) \rightleftharpoons H^+ + CH_3COO^- \qquad \text{partial ionizaiton}$$

Species such as HCl that completely ionize in water are called **strong electrolytes,** and those that only partially ionize are called **weak electrolytes.** Salts also fall into the strong electrolyte category.

COLLIGATIVE PROPERTIES

!

Some of the properties of solutions depend on the chemical and physical nature of the individual solute. The blue color of a copper(II) sulfate solution and the sweetness of a sucrose solution are related to the properties of those solutes. However, some solution properties simply depend on the *number* of solute particles, not the type of solute. These properties are called **colligative properties** and include:

- vapor pressure lowering
- freezing point depression
- boiling point elevation
- osmotic pressure

Vapor Pressure Lowering

If a liquid is placed in a sealed container, molecules will evaporate from the surface of the liquid and eventually establish a gas phase over the liquid that is in equilibrium with the liquid phase. This is called the **vapor pressure** of the liquid. Vapor pressure is temperature dependent; the higher the temperature, the higher the vapor pressure. If the liquid is made a solvent by adding a nonvolatile solute, the vapor pressure of the resulting solution is always less than that of the pure liquid. The vapor pressure has been lowered by the addition of the solute; the amount of lowering is proportional to the number of solute particles added and is thus a colligative property.

Solute particles are evenly distributed throughout a solution, even at the surface. Thus, there are fewer solvent particles at the gas–liquid interface where evaporation takes place. Fewer solvent particles escape into the gas phase, and so the vapor pressure is lower. The higher the concentration of solute particles, the less solvent is at the interface and the lower the vapor pressure.

Freezing Point Depression

The freezing point of a solution of a nonvolatile solute is always lower than the pure solvent and is independent of the type of solute. It is the number of solute particles that determines the amount of the lowering of the freezing point. The amount of lowering of the freezing point is proportional to the molality of the solute and is given by the equation

$$\Delta T_f = iK_f \times \text{molality}$$

where ΔT_f is the number of degrees that the freezing point has been lowered (the difference in the freezing point of the pure solvent and the solution); K_f is the freezing point depression constant (a constant of the individual solvent); the **molality** is the molality of the solute; and i is the van't Hoff factor—the ratio of the number of moles of particles released into solution per mole of solute dissolved. For a nonelectrolyte, such as sucrose, the van't Hoff factor would be 1. For an electrolyte, such as sodium chloride, you must take into consideration that if 1 mol of NaCl dissolves, 2 mol of particles would result (1 mol Na^+, 1 mol Cl^-). Therefore, the van't Hoff factor should be 2. However, because sometimes there is a pairing of ions in solution, the observed van't Hoff factor is slightly less (1.9 for a 0.05 m NaCl solution). The more dilute the solution, the closer the observed van't Hoff factor should be to the expected factor. If you can calculate the molality of the solution, you can also calculate the freezing point of the solution.

Determine the freezing point of an aqueous solution containing 10.50 g of magnesium bromide in 200.0 g of water.

$$\Delta T = iK_f m = 3(1.86 \text{ K kg mol}^{-1}) \left[\frac{(10.50 \text{ g MgBr}_2)}{(1 \text{ mol MgBr}_2/184.113 \text{ g MgBr}_2)} \middle/ \frac{}{(200.0 \text{ g})/(1 \text{ kg}/1000 \text{ g})} \right]$$

$$= 1.59 \text{ K}$$

$$T_{fp} = (273.15 - 1.59) \text{ K} = 271.56 \text{ K} (= -1.59° \text{ C})$$

The most common mistake is to forget to subtract the ΔT value from the normal freezing point.

The freezing point depression technique is also commonly used to calculate the molar mass of a solute.

A solution is prepared by dissolving 0.490 g of an unknown compound in 50.00 mL of water. The freezing point of the solution is −0.201° C. Assuming the compound is a nonelectrolyte, what is the molecular weight of the compound? Use 1.00 g/mL as the density of water.

$$m = \Delta T / K_f = 0.201 \text{ K} / (1.86 \text{ K kg mol}^{-1}) = 0.108 \text{ mol} / \text{kg}$$

$$50.00 \text{ mL} (1.00 \text{ g} / \text{mL}) (1 \text{ kg} / 1000 \text{ g}) = 0.0500 \text{ kg}$$

$$(0.108 \text{ mol} / \text{kg}) (0.0500 \text{ kg}) = 0.00540 \text{ mol}$$

$$0.490 \text{ g} / 0.00540 \text{ mol} = 90.7 \text{ g} / \text{mol}$$

Many students make the mistake of stopping before they complete this problem.

Boiling Point Elevation

!

Just as the freezing point of a solution of a nonvolatile solute is always lower than that of the pure solvent, the boiling point of a solution is always higher than the solvent's. Again, only the number of solute particles affects the boiling point. The mathematical relationship is similar to the one for the freezing point depression above and is

$$\Delta T_b = iK_b \times \text{molality}$$

where ΔT_b is the number of degrees the boiling point has been elevated (the difference between the boiling point of the pure solvent and the solution); K_b is the boiling point elevation constant; the **molality** is the molality of the solute; and **i** is the van't Hoff factor. You can calculate a solution's boiling point if you know the molality of the solution. If you know the amount of the boiling point elevation and the molality of the solution, you can calculate the value of the van't Hoff factor, i.

Determine the boiling point of a solution prepared by adding 15.00 g of NaCl to 250.0 g water. ($K_b = 0.512 \text{ K kg mol}^{-1}$)

$$\Delta T = iK_b m = 2(0.512 \text{ K kg mol}^{-1}) \left[\frac{(15.00 \text{ g NaCl})(1 \text{ mol NaCl}/58.44 \text{ g NaCl})}{(250.0 \text{ g})/(1 \text{ kg}/1000 \text{ g})} \right]$$

$$= 1.05 \text{ K}$$

$$T_{bp} = (373.15 + 1.05) \text{ K} = 374.20 \text{ K} (= 101.05° \text{ C})$$

A 1.00 molal aqueous solution of trichloroacetic acid (CCl_3COOH) is heated to the boiling point. The solution has a boiling point of 100.18° C.

Determine the van't Hoff factor for trichloroacetic acid (K_b for water = 0.512 K kg mol^{-1}).

$$\Delta T = (101.18 - 100.00) = 0.18°\,C = 0.18\ K$$

$$i = \Delta T/K_b m = 0.18\ K/(0.512\ K\ kg\ mol^{-1})(1.00\ mol\ kg^{-1}) = 0.35$$

A common mistake is the assumption that the van't Hoff factor must be a whole number. This is only true for strong electrolytes at very low concentrations.

Osmotic Pressure

If you were to place a solution and a pure solvent in the same container but separate them by a **semipermeable membrane** (which allows the passage of solvent molecules but not solute particles) you would observe that the level of the solvent side would decrease while the solution side would increase. This indicates that the solvent molecules are passing through the semipermeable membrane, a process called **osmosis.** Eventually the system would reach equilibrium, and the difference in levels would remain constant. The difference in the two levels is related to the **osmotic pressure.** In fact, one could exert a pressure on the solution side exceeding the osmotic pressure, and solvent molecules could be forced back through the semipermeable membrane into the solvent side. This process is called **reverse osmosis** and is the basis of the desalination of seawater for drinking purposes. These processes are shown in Figure 11.1.

The osmotic pressure is a colligative property and mathematically can be represented as

$$\Pi = (nRT/V)\,i$$

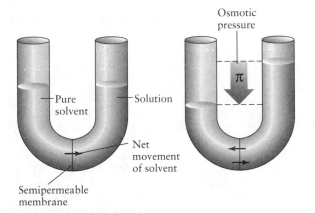

Figure 11.1 Osmotic pressure.

where **Π** is the osmotic pressure in atmospheres; **n** is the number of moles of solute; **R** is the ideal gas constant 0.08206 L·atm/K·mol; **T** is the Kelvin temperature; **V** is the volume of the solution; and **i** is the van't Hoff factor. Measurements of the osmotic pressure can be used to calculate the molar mass of a solute. This is especially useful in determining the molar mass of large molecules such as proteins.

A solution prepared by dissolving 8.95 mg of a gene fragment in 35.0 mL of water has an osmotic pressure of 0.335 torr at 25.0° C. Assuming the fragment is a nonelectrolyte, determine the molar mass of the gene fragment.

Rearrange $\Pi = (nRT/V)$ i to n = Π V/RT (i = 1 for a nonelectrolyte)

$$\frac{(0.335 \text{ torr})(35.0 \text{ mL})(1 \text{ atm})(1 \text{ L})}{(0.08206 \text{ L atm/mol K})(298.2 \text{ K})(760 \text{ torr})(1000 \text{ mL})} = 6.30 \times 10^{-7} \text{ mol}$$

$$\frac{(8.95 \text{ mg})(0.001 \text{ g/mg})}{6.30 \times 10^{-7} \text{ mol}} = 1.42 \times 10^{4} \text{ g/mol}$$

COLLOIDS

!

Dip a glass into water from a muddy stream, and shortly you will see particles in the water settling out. This is a heterogeneous mixture where the particles are large (in excess of 1000 nm), and it is called a **suspension.** In contrast, dissolving sodium chloride in water results in a true homogeneous **solution,** with solute particles less than 1 nm in diameter. True solutions do not settle out, because of the very small particle size. But there is a homogeneous mixture whose solute diameters fall in between solutions and suspensions. These are called **colloids** and have solute particles in the range of 1 to 1000 nm diameter. Table 11.1 shows some representative colloids.

Many times it is difficult to distinguish a colloid from a true solution. The most common method is to shine a light through the mixture under investigation. A light shone through a true solution is invisible, but a light shown through a colloid is visible because the light reflects off the larger colloid particles. This is called the **Tyndall effect.**

Table 11.1 Common Colloid Types

Colloid Type	Substance Dispersed	Dispersing Medium	Examples
aerosol	solid	gas	smoke
aerosol	liquid	gas	fog
solid foam	gas	solid	marshmallow
foam	gas	liquid	whipped cream
emulsion	liquid	liquid	milk, mayonnaise
solid emulsion	liquid	solid	cheese, butter
sol	solid	liquid	paint, gelatin

EXPERIMENTAL

Experimental procedures for solutions fall into two broad categories. One group involves concentration units, and the other involves colligative properties. In both cases, keeping close track of the units may simplify the problem.

Concentration problems are concerned with the definitions of the various units. It is possible to calculate the mass and/or volume of the solvent and solute by taking the difference between the final and initial measurements. The density, if not given, is calculated, not measured. It is important to recognize the difference between the values that must be measured and those that can be calculated. Moles are also calculated, not measured.

Do not forget that nearly all the concentration units use the total for the solution in the denominator. For these units it is important to remember to combine the quantities for the solvent and all solutes present. Molal concentrations are exceptions. Molality uses only the kilograms of solvent in the denominator. Do not make the mistake of using the entire solution in the denominator for molal concentrations.

Colligative properties may involve changes in the melting or boiling points. Changes cannot be measured; only "before" and "after" values can be measured. In an experiment, ΔT is not measured. The freezing, or boiling, point of the solution is measured and compared to that of the pure solvent. The difference is then calculated.

The vapor pressure of a solution and the osmotic pressure are measurable quantities.

Many errors are associated with electrolytes. The van't Hoff factor is often forgotten. The van't Hoff factor is a calculated value, not a measured value. As a calculated value, it may or may not be a whole number.

COMMON MISTAKES TO AVOID

1. When dealing with percentage solutions, be sure you know what type of percentage (mass, mass/volume, volume/volume) is being used.
2. Percentage solutions use amount of solute per hundred parts of solution.
3. In molarity problems, be sure to use liters of solution.
4. Molality problems deal with moles of solute per kilogram of **solvent.**
5. In colligative property problems, be sure to incorporate the van't Hoff factor for electrolytes.
6. In freezing point depression and boiling point elevation problems, be sure to use the molality of the solution.
7. In freezing point depression and boiling point elevation problems, to find the actual freezing/boiling point, calculate the ΔT (change in temperature), then subtract that amount from the solvent's freezing point, or add it to the solvent's boiling point.
8. Make sure your units cancel, leaving you with the units desired in your final answer.

9. Round off your numerical answers to the correct number of significant figures.
10. Remember, most molecular compounds—compounds containing only nonmetals—do not ionize in solution.

 REVIEW QUESTIONS

 You have 25 minutes to answer the following questions. You will be expected to do your calculations without a calculator.

1. A solution is prepared by dissolving 1.25 g of an unknown substance in 100.0 mL of water. Which procedure from the following list could be used to determine if the solute is an electrolyte?

   A. Measure the specific heat of the solution.
   B. Measure the volume of the solution.
   C. Measure the freezing point of the solution.
   D. Determine the specific heat of the solution.
   E. Determine the volume of the solute.

2. What is the final K^+ concentration in a solution made by mixing 300.0 mL of 1.0 M KNO_3 and 700.0 mL of 2.0 M K_3PO_4?

   A. 1.5 M
   B. 5.0 M
   C. 3.0 M
   D. 2.0 M
   E. 4.5 M

3. Strontium sulfate ($SrSO_4$) will precipitate when a solution of sodium sulfate is added to a strontium nitrate solution. What will be the strontium ion, Sr^{2+}, concentration remaining after 30.0 mL of 0.10 M Na_2SO_4 solution are added to 70.0 mL of 0.20 M $Sr(NO_3)_2$ solution?

   A. 0.14 M
   B. 0.15 M

C. 0.11 M
D. 0.20 M
E. 0.030 M

4. Which of the following is a strong electrolyte when it is mixed with water?

   A. HNO_2
   B. KNO_3
   C. C_2H_5OH
   D. CH_3COOH
   E. NH_3

5. A solution with a total chloride ion, Cl^-, concentration of 1.0 M is needed. Initially, the solution is 0.30 M in $MgCl_2$. How many moles of solid $CaCl_2$ must be added to 400 mL of the $MgCl_2$ solution to achieve the desired concentration of chloride ion?

   A. 0.10
   B. 0.080
   C. 0.20
   D. 0.15
   E. 0.16

6. Assuming the volumes are additive, what is the final $H^+(aq)$ concentration produced by adding 30.0 mL of 0.50 M HNO_3 to 70.0 mL of 1.00 M HCl?

   A. 0.75 M
   B. 1.50 M
   C. 1.25 M
   D. 0.85 M
   E. 0.43 M

7. The molality of a 1.0-molar ethyl alcohol solution may be determined if which of the following is supplied?

   A. density of the solution
   B. van't Hoff factor for ethyl alcohol
   C. temperature of the solution
   D. volume of the solution
   E. solubility of ethyl alcohol

8. A solution of chloroform, $CHCl_3$, in carbon tetrachloride, CCl_4, is nearly ideal. The vapor pressure of chloroform is 170 mm Hg at 20° C, and the vapor pressure of carbon tetrachloride is 87 mm Hg at this temperature. What is the mole fraction of carbon tetrachloride in the vapor over an equimolar solution of these two liquids?

   A. 0.25
   B. 0.87
   C. 0.66
   D. 0.50
   E. 0.34

9. To prepare 3.0 L of a 0.20-molar K_3PO_4 solution (molecular weight 212), a student should follow which of the following procedures?

   A. The student should weigh 42 g of solute and add sufficient water to obtain a final volume of 3.0 L.
   B. The student should weigh 42 g of solute and add 3.0 Kg of water.
   C. The student should weigh 130 g of solute and add sufficient water to obtain a final volume of 3.0 L.
   D. The student should weigh 42 g of solute and add 3.0 L of water.
   E. The student should weigh 130 g of solute and add 3.0 L of water.

10. A 5.2 molal aqueous solution of methyl alcohol, CH_3OH, is supplied. What is the mole fraction of methyl alcohol in this solution?

   A. 0.10
   B. 0.19

   C. 0.086
   D. 0.050
   E. 0.094

11. Choose the aqueous solution with the highest boiling point.

   A. 0.10 M HI
   B. 0.10 M $(NH_4)_3PO_4$
   C. 0.20 M C_2H_5OH
   D. 0.10 M NH_4Cl
   E. 0.10 M NaI

12. How many grams of $MgSO_4$ (molecular weight 120.4) are in 100.0 mL of a 5.0-molar solution?

   A. 600 g
   B. 5.0 g
   C. 12 g
   D. 60 g
   E. 120 g

13. How many milliliters of concentrated nitric acid (16.0-molar HNO_3) are needed to prepare 0.500 L of 6.0-molar HNO_3?

   A. 0.19 mL
   B. 250 mL
   C. 375 mL
   D. 190 mL
   E. 100 mL

14. I. the molal freezing point constant, K_f, of the solvent

   II. the freezing point of the pure solvent and the freezing point of the solution

When using the freezing point depression method of determining the molar mass of a nonelectrolyte, what information is needed in addition to the above?

   A. the mass of the solute
   B. the volume of the solvent and the mass of the solute

C. the mass of the solvent and the boiling point of the solvent

D. the mass of the solvent and the mass of the solute

E. no additional information is needed

15. A student has a solution with a mole fraction of 0.20 of chloroform (molecular weight 119.4) in carbon tetrachloride (molecular weight 153.8). What is the molality of chloroform in the solution?

A. 1.7 m

B. 0.17 m

C. 0.20 m

D. 1.3 m

E. 1.20 m

16. A solution is 10 percent urea by mass. Which item(s) from the following list are needed to calculate the molarity of this solution?

I.   the density of the solution

II. the density of the solvent

III. the molecular weight of urea

    A. I and III

    B. I only

    C. II only

    D. III only

    E. I and II

17. Which of the following aqueous solutions would have the greatest freezing point depression?

A. 0.10 m $(NH_4)_2SO_4$

B. 0.10 m $MnSO_4$

C. 0.10 m NaF

D. 0.10 m KCl

E. 0.10 m CH_3OH

18. Which of the following aqueous solutions would have the greatest conductivity?

A. 0.2 M $NaOH$

B. 0.2 M $RbCl$

C. 0.2 M NH_4NO_3

D. 0.2 M HNO_2

E. 0.2 M K_3PO_4

19. An aqueous KNO_3 solution is cooled from 75° C to 15° C. Which statement from the following list is true?

A. The molarity of the solution does not change.

B. The molality of the solution decreases.

C. The density of the solution does not change.

D. The molality of the solution does not change.

E. The mole fraction of the solute increases.

20. How many milliliters of water must be added to 50.0 mL of 10.0 M HNO_3 to prepare 4.00 M HNO_3?

A. 50.0 mL

B. 125 mL

C. 500 mL

D. 250 mL

E. 75.0 mL

21. Pick the pair of substances that will most likely obey Raoult's law.

A. $CH_3CH_2CH_2CH_2COOH(l)$ and $C_5H_{12}(l)$

B. $C_5H_{12}(l)$ and $H_2O(l)$

C. $CH_3CH_2CH_2CH_2COOH(l)$ and $H_2O(l)$

D. $H_3PO_4(l)$ and $H_2O(l)$

E. $C_5H_{12}(l)$ and $C_6H_{14}(l)$

22. The best method to isolate pure $MgSO_4$ from an aqueous solution of $MgSO_4$ is?

A. Evaporate the solution to dryness.

B. Titrate the solution.

C. Electrolyze the solution.

D. Use paper chromatography.

E. Filter the solution.

23. Pick the conditions that would yield the highest concentration of $N_2(g)$ in water.

    A. partial pressure of gas = 1.0 atm; temperature of water = 25° C
    B. partial pressure of gas = 0.50 atm; temperature of water = 55° C

    C. partial pressure of gas = 2.0 atm; temperature of water = 25° C
    D. partial pressure of gas = 2.0 atm; temperature of water = 85° C
    E. partial pressure of gas = 1.0 atm; temperature of water = 85° C

ANSWERS AND EXPLANATIONS

✓

1. **C.** If the solute is an electrolyte, the solution will conduct electricity and the van't Hoff factor, i, will be greater than 1. The choices do not include any conductivity measurements; therefore, the van't Hoff factor would need to be determined. This determination is done by measuring the osmotic pressure, the boiling point elevation, or the freezing point depression. The freezing point depression may be found by measuring the freezing point of the solution.

2. **E.** The potassium ion contribution from the KNO_3 is:

$$(300.0 \text{ mL})(1.0 \text{ mol } KNO_3/1000 \text{ mL})(1 \text{ mol } K^+/1 \text{ mol } KNO_3)$$
$$= 0.300 \text{ mol } K^+$$

   The potassium ion contribution from K_3PO_4 is:

$$(700.0 \text{ mL})(2.0 \text{ mol } K_3PO_4/1000 \text{ mL})(3 \text{ mol } K^+/1 \text{ mol } K_3PO_4)$$
$$= 4.20 \text{ mol } K^+$$

   The total potassium is 4.50 mol in a total volume of 1.000 L. Thus, the potassium concentration is 4.50 M.

3. **C.** The reaction is:

$$Sr^{2+}(aq) + SO_4^{2-}(aq) \rightarrow SrSO_4(s)$$

   The strontium nitrate solution contains:

$$(70.0 \text{ mL})(0.20 \text{ mol } Sr(NO_3)_2/1000 \text{ mL})(1 \text{ mol } Sr^{2+}/1 \text{ mol } Sr(NO_3)_2)$$
$$= 0.014 \text{ mol } Sr^{2+}$$

The sodium sulfate solution contains:

$$(30.0 \text{ mL})(0.10 \text{ mol Na}_2\text{SO}_4/1000 \text{ mL})(1 \text{ mol SO}_4^{2-}/1 \text{ mol Na}_2\text{SO}_4)$$
$$= 0.0030 \text{ mol SO}_4^{2-}$$

The strontium and sulfate ions react in a 1:1 ratio, so 0.0030 mol of sulfate ion will combine with 0.0030 mol of strontium ion leaving 0.011 mol of strontium in a total volume of 100.0 mL. The final strontium ion concentration is:

$$\frac{(0.011 \text{ mol Sr}^{2+})(1000 \text{ mL})}{(100.0 \text{ mL})(1 \text{ L})} = 0.11 \text{ M Sr}^{2+}$$

4. **B.** A (nitrous acid) and D (acetic acid) are weak acids, and E (ammonia) is a weak base. Weak acids and bases are weak electrolytes. C (ethanol) is a nonelectrolyte. Potassium nitrate (B) is a water soluble ionic compound.

5. **B.** The number of moles of chloride ion needed is:

$$(400 \text{ mL})(1.0 \text{ mol Cl}^-/1000 \text{ mL}) = 0.40 \text{ mol Cl}^-$$

The initial number of moles of chloride ion in the solution is:

$$(400 \text{ mL})(0.30 \text{ mol MgCl}_2/1000 \text{ mL})(2 \text{ mol Cl}^-/\text{mol MgCl}_2)$$
$$= 0.24 \text{ mol Cl}^-$$

The number of moles needed = $[(0.40 - 0.24) \text{ mol Cl}^-]$
$(1 \text{ mol CaCl}_2/2 \text{ mol Cl}^-) = 0.080 \text{ mol}$

6. **D.** Both of the acids are strong acids and yield 1 mol of H^+ each. Calculate the number of moles of H^+ produced by each of the acids. Divide the total number of moles by the final volume.

$$(30.0 \text{ mL})(0.50 \text{ mol H}^+/1000 \text{ mL}) + (70.0 \text{ mL})(1.00 \text{ mol H}^+/1000 \text{ mL})$$
$$= 0.085 \text{ mol H}^+$$

$$\frac{(0.085 \text{ mol H}^+)(1000 \text{ mL})}{(100.0 \text{ mL})(1 \text{ L})} = 0.85 \text{ M H}^+$$

7. **A.** To calculate the molality of a solution both the moles of solute and the kilograms of solvent are needed. A liter of solution would contain a known number of moles of solute. To convert this liter to mass, a mass to volume relationship (density) is needed.

8. **E.** The mole fraction may be determined by dividing the vapor pressure of the desired substance by the sum of all the vapor pressures.

$$(87 \text{ mm Hg}/87 \text{ mm Hg} + 170 \text{ mm Hg}) = 0.34$$

9. **C.** To produce a molar solution of any type, the final volume must be the desired volume. This eliminates answers D and E. B involves mass of water instead of volume. A calculation of the required mass will allow a decision between A and B.

$$(3.0 \text{ L})(0.20 \text{ mol K}_3\text{PO}_4/\text{L})(212 \text{ g K}_3\text{PO}_4/1 \text{ mol K}_3\text{PO}_4) = 130 \text{ g K}_3\text{PO}_4$$

10. **C.** A 5.2 molal solution has 5.2 mol of methyl alcohol in one Kg (1000 g) of water. The moles of water are needed.

$$(1000 \text{ g H}_2\text{O})(1 \text{ mol H}_2\text{O}/18.0 \text{ g H}_2\text{O}) = 55.6 \text{ mol H}_2\text{O}$$

The mole fraction may now be determined.

$$(5.2 \text{ mol CH}_3\text{OH})/(5.2 + 55.6) \text{ mol} = 0.086$$

11. **B.** The boiling point depends on the boiling point elevation (a colligative property). All colligative properties depend on the concentration of particles present. C is a nonelectrolyte, thus, the concentration of the particles is 0.20 M. All of the other substances are strong electrolytes. The concentration of particles in each of these may be determined by multiplying the molarity given by the van't Hoff factor. Each of these is calculated as follows:

A: $2 \times 0.10 = 0.20$ B: $4 \times 0.10 = 0.40$

D: $2 \times 0.10 = 0.20$ E: $2 \times 0.10 = 0.20$

12. **D.**

$$(5.0 \text{ mole MgSO}_4/1000 \text{ mL})(100.0 \text{ mL})(120.4 \text{ g MgSO}_4/\text{mol MgSO}_4)$$
$$= 60 \text{ g MgSO}_4$$

13. **D.** This is a dilution problem. $V_{before} = (M_{after})\ (V_{after})/(M_{before})$

$$(6.0 \text{ M HNO}_3)(0.500 \text{ L})(1000 \text{ mL}/1 \text{ L})/(16.0 \text{ M HNO}_3) = 190 \text{ mL}$$

14. **D.** To calculate the molar mass, the mass of the solute and the moles of the solute are needed. The molality of the solution may be determined from the freezing point depression, and the freezing point depression constant (I and II). If the mass of the solvent is known, the moles of the solute may be calculated from the molality. These moles, along with the mass of the solute, can be used to determine the molar mass.

15. **A.** If the mole fraction of chloroform is 0.20 then the solution has a 0.80 mol fraction of carbon tetrachloride. The moles of chloroform and the kilograms of carbon tetrachloride are needed. If 0.20 mol of chloroform are present, the number of kilograms of carbon tetrachloride is:

$(0.80 \text{ mol } CCl_4)(153.8 \text{ g } CCl_4/1 \text{ mol } CCl_4)(1 \text{ kg}/1000 \text{ g}) = 0.12 \text{ kg}$

$m \text{ } CHCl_3 = (0.20 \text{ mol } CHCl_3)/(0.12 \text{ kg}) = 1.7 \text{ m}$

16. **A.** To calculate the molarity, the moles of urea and the volume of the solution are needed. Density is an intensive property, so any arbitrary volume of solution may be used. One liter is a convenient volume. Using this volume and the density of the solution, you can calculate the mass of the solution. Ten percent of this is the mass of urea. The mass of urea and the molecular weight of urea give the moles of urea.

17. **A.** Freezing point depression is a colligative property, which depends on the number of particles present. The solution with the greatest concentration of particles will have the greatest depression. The concentration of particles in E (a nonelectrolyte) is 0.10 m. All other answers are strong electrolytes, and the concentration of particles in these may be calculated by multiplying the concentration by the van't Hoff factor.

    A: $3 \times 0.10 = 0.30$ B, C, and D: $2 \times 0.10 = 0.20$

18. **E.** The strong electrolyte with the greatest concentration of ions is the best conductor. D is a weak electrolyte, not a strong electrolyte. The number of ions for the strong electrolytes may be found by simply counting the ions: A—2, B—2, C—2, E—4. The best conductor has the greatest value when the molarity is multiplied by the number of ions.

19. **D.** Cooling the solution will change the temperature and the volume of the solution. Volume is important in the calculation of molarity and density. A volume change eliminates answers A and C. The mass and the number of moles are not affected by the temperature change. Mole fraction and molality will not change. This eliminates B and E.

20. **E.** This is a dilution problem. $V_{after} = (M_{before} V_{before})/(M_{after})$

    $(10.0 \text{ M } HNO_3 \times 50.0 \text{ mL})/(4.0 \text{ M } HNO_3) = 125 \text{ mL}$

    The final volume is 125 mL. Since the original volume was 50.0 mL, an additional 75.0 mL must be added.

21. **E.** The two most similar substances will be most likely to be ideal.

22. **A.** Solutions cannot be separated by titrations or filtering. Electrolysis of the solution would produce hydrogen and oxygen gas. Chromatography might achieve a minimal separation.

23. **C.** The solubility of a gas is increased by increasing the partial pressure of the gas, and by lowering the temperature.

FREE-RESPONSE QUESTIONS

You have 20 minutes to answer the following questions. You may not use a calculator.

Five beakers each containing 100.0 mL of an aqueous solution are placed on a lab bench. The solutions are all at 25° C. Solution 1 contains 0.20 M KNO_3. Solution 2 contains 0.10 M $BaCl_2$. Solution 3 contains 0.15 M $C_2H_4(OH)_2$. Solution 4 contains 0.20 M $(NH_4)_2SO_4$. Solution 5 contains 0.25 M $KMnO_4$.

a. One of the solutions could oxidize two of the other solutions. Which solution is it? Which solutions could it oxidize?

b. Which solution has the lowest pH? Explain.

c. Which pair of solutions would give a precipitate if they are mixed? What is the formula for this precipitate?

d. Which solution would be the poorest conductor of electricity? Explain.

e. Rank the solutions in order of increasing boiling point. Explain.

ANSWERS AND EXPLANATIONS

a. 1 point for picking solution 5, and 1 point for picking solutions 2 and 3.

b. 1 point for picking solution 4, and 1 point for saying the ammonium ion (NH_4^+) is a weak acid, or that it undergoes hydrolysis.

c. 1 point for picking solutions 2 and 4, and 1 point for $BaSO_4$.

d. 1 point for picking solution 3, and 1 point for saying it is a non-electrolyte or that it does not ionize.

e. 1 point for the order: $3 < 2 < 1 < 5 < 4$, and 1 point for the explanation. The explanation must relate the order to the number (concentration) of solute particles in the solution.

There is a total of 10 points possible.

RAPID REVIEW

- A solution is a homogeneous mixture composed of a solvent and one or more solutes. A solute is a substance present in smaller amount.

- The general rule of solubility is "like dissolves like." This means that polar solvents dissolve polar solutes and nonpolar solvents dissolve nonpolar solutes.

- A saturated solution is one in which the maximum amount of solute is dissolved for a given amount of solvent at a given temperature. Any solution with less than the maximum solute is called unsaturated. A solution with greater than maximum solute is supersaturated (an unstable state).

- Solution concentration may be expressed as a percentage, which is the amount of solute dissolved per 100 units of solvent. It may be expressed as mass %, mass/volume %, or volume/volume %. Know how to calculate the appropriate percentage concentration for a solution.

- For the chemist the most useful unit of concentration is molarity (M), which is the moles of solute per liter of solution. Know how to work molarity problems.

- Another concentration unit is the molality (m), which is the moles of solute per kilogram of solvent. Know how to work molality problems.

- Electrolytes conduct an electrical current when melted or dissolved in pure water, whereas nonelectrolytes do not.

- Colligative properties are properties of solutions that depend simply on the number of solute particles and not the types. Colligative properties include:

  1. Vapor pressure lowering—The vapor pressure of the solvent is lower in a solution than in the pure solvent.
  2. Freezing point depression—The freezing point of a solution is lower than the pure solvent.
  3. Boiling point elevation—The boiling point of a solution is always higher than the boiling point of the pure solvent.
  4. Osmotic pressure—Solvent molecules pass through a semipermeable membrane from the less concentrated side to the more concentrated side. The osmotic pressure is the amount of pressure needed to stop this osmosis.

- Know how to use the appropriate colligative properties equation to calculate the amount of vapor pressure lowering, freezing point lowering, van't Hoff factor, etc.

- A colloid is a homogeneous mixture in which the solute particle size is intermediate between true solutions and suspensions. If a light is shown through a colloid, the light beam is visible. This is the Tyndall effect.

Kinetics

KEYWORDS AND EQUATIONS

$$\text{Rate} = k[A]^m [B]^n \dots$$

$$\ln \frac{[A]_0}{[A]_t} = kt \text{ or } \ln[A]_t - \ln[A]_0 = -kt \text{ (first order)}$$

$$\frac{1}{[A]_t} - \frac{1}{[A]_0} = kt \quad \text{(second order)}$$

$$t_{1/2} = \frac{\ln 2}{k} = \frac{0.693}{k}$$

$$k = Ae^{-E_a/RT} \text{ or } \ln k = \frac{-E_a}{R}\left(\frac{1}{T}\right) + \ln A$$

E_a = activation energy

k = rate constant

A = frequency factor

INTRODUCTION

Thermodynamics (Chapter 7) often can be used to predict whether a reaction will occur spontaneously, but it gives very little information about the speed at which a reaction occurs. **Kinetics** is the study of the speed of reactions and is largely an experimental science. Some general qualitative ideas about reaction speed may be developed, but accurate quantitative relationships require that experimental data to be collected.

For a chemical reaction to occur, there must be a collision between the reactants. That collision is necessary to transfer kinetic energy, to

214

break old chemical bonds and reform new ones. If the collision doesn't transfer enough energy, no reaction will occur. And the collision must take place at the correct place on the molecule, the **reactive site.**

Five factors affect the rates of chemical reaction:

1. *Nature of the reactants*—Large complex molecules tend to react slower than smaller ones because statistically there is a greater chance of collisions occurring somewhere else on the molecule rather than at the reactive site.
2. *The temperature*—Temperature is a measure of the average kinetic energy of the molecules. The higher the temperature, the higher the kinetic energy and the greater the chance that enough energy will be transferred to cause the reaction. Also, the higher the temperature, the greater the number of collisions and the greater the chance of a collision at the reactive site.
3. *The concentration of reactants*—The higher the concentration of reactants, the greater the chance of collision and (normally) the greater the reaction rate. For gaseous reactants, the pressure is directly related to the concentration; the greater the pressure, the greater the reaction rate.
4. *Physical state of reactants*—When reactants are in the same physical state, the reaction rates should be higher than if they are in different states because there is greater chance of collision. Also, gases and liquids tend to react faster than solids because of the increase in surface area. The more chance for collision, the faster the reaction rate.
5. *Catalysts*—A **catalyst** is a substance that speeds up the reaction rate and is (at least theoretically) recoverable at the end of the reaction in an unchanged form. Catalysts accomplish this by reducing the activation energy of the reaction. **Activation energy** is that minimum amount of energy that must be supplied to the reaction in order to initiate or start the reaction. Many times the activation energy is supplied by the kinetic energy of the reactants.

RATES OF REACTION

The rate (or speed) of reaction is related to the change in concentration of either a reactant or product with time. Consider the general reaction: $A + B \rightarrow C + D$. As the reaction proceeds, the concentrations of reactants A and B will decrease and the concentrations of products C and D will increase. Thus, the rate can be expressed in the following ways:

$$\text{Rate} = -\frac{\Delta[A]}{\Delta t} = -\frac{\Delta[B]}{\Delta t} = \frac{\Delta[C]}{\Delta t} = \frac{\Delta[D]}{\Delta t}$$

The first two expressions involving the reactants are negative because their concentrations will decrease with time. The square brackets represent moles per liter concentration (molarity).

The rate of reaction decreases during the course of the reaction. The rate, r, which is calculated above can be expressed as the average rate of reaction over a given time frame or, more commonly, as the initial reaction rate—the rate of reaction at the instant the reactants are mixed.

The Rate Equation

The rate of reaction may depend upon reactant concentration, product concentration, and temperature. Cases in which the product concentration affects the rate of reaction are rare and are not covered on the AP exam. Therefore, we will not address those reactions. We will discuss temperature effects on the reaction later in this chapter. For the time being, let's just consider those cases in which the reactant concentration may affect the speed of reaction. For the general reaction: $a A + b B + \cdots \rightarrow c C + d D + \ldots$ where the lower case letters are the coefficients in the balanced chemical equation; the upper case letters stand for the reactant; and product chemical species and initial rates are used, the rate equation (rate law) is written:

$$\text{Rate} = k[A]^m[B]^n \ldots .$$

In this expression, k is the **rate constant**—a constant for each chemical reaction at a given temperature. The exponents m and n, called the **orders of reaction,** indicate what effect a change in concentration of that reactant species will have on the reaction rate. Say, for example, m = 1 and n = 2. That means that if the concentration of reactant A is doubled, then the rate will also double ($[2]^1 = 2$), and if the concentration of reactant B is doubled, then the rate will increase fourfold ($[2]^2 = 4$). We say that it is first order with respect to A and second order with respect to B. If the concentration of a reactant is doubled and that has no effect on the rate of reaction, then the reaction is zero order with respect to that reactant ($[2]^0 = 1$). Many times the overall order of reaction is calculated; it is simply the sum of the individual coefficients, third order in this example. The rate equation would then be shown as:

$$\text{Rate} = k[A][B]^2 \quad \text{(If the exponent is 1, it is generally not shown.)}$$

It is important to realize the rate law (the rate, the rate constant, and the orders of reaction) is determined experimentally.

The rate of reaction may be measured in a variety of ways, including taking the slope of the concentration versus time plot for the reaction. Once the rate has been determined, the orders of reaction can be determined by conducting a series of reactions in which the reactant species concentrations are changed one at a time, and mathematically determining the effect on the reaction rate. Once the orders of reaction have been determined, it is easy to calculate the rate constant.

Consider the reaction:

$$2 \text{ NO(g)} + \text{O}_2\text{(g)} \rightarrow 2 \text{ NO}_2\text{(g)}$$

The following kinetics data were collected:

Experiment	Initial [NO]	Initial [O_2]	Rate of NO_2 formation (M/s)
1	0.01	0.01	0.05
2	0.02	0.01	0.20
3	0.01	0.02	0.10

There are a couple of ways to interpret the data to generate the rate equation. If the numbers involved are simple (as above and on most tests, including the AP exam) you can reason out the orders of reaction. You can see that in going from experiment 1 to experiment 2, the [NO] was doubled ([O_2] held constant) and the rate increased fourfold. This means that the reaction is second order with respect to NO. Comparing experiments 1 and 3, you see that the [O_2] was doubled ([NO] was held constant) and the rate doubled. Therefore, the reaction is first order with respect to O_2 and the rate equation can be written as:

$$Rate = k[NO]^2[O_2]$$

The rate constant can be determined by substituting the values of the concentrations of NO and O_2 from any of the experiments into the rate equation above and solving for k.

Using experiment 1:

$$0.05 \text{ M/s} = k(0.01 \text{ M})^2(0.01 \text{ M})$$

$$k = 0.05 \text{ M/s}/(0.01 \text{ M})^2(0.01 \text{ M})$$

$$k = 5 \times 10^4/M^2s$$

Sometimes, because of the numbers' complexity, you must set up the equations mathematically. The ratio of the rate expressions of two experiments will be used in determining the reaction orders. The equations will be chosen so that the concentration of only one reactant has changed while the others remain constant. In the example above, the ratio of experiments 1 and 2 will be used to determine the effect of a change of the concentration of NO on the rate, and then experiments 1 and 3 will be used to determine the effect of O_2. Experiments 2 and 3 cannot be used because both chemical species have changed concentration.

Remember: in choosing experiments to compare, choose two in which the concentration of only one reactant has changed while the others have remained constant.

Comparing experiments 1 and 2:

$$\frac{0.05 \text{ M/s} = k[0.01]^m[0.01]^n}{0.20 \text{ M/s} = k[0.02]^m[0.01]^n}$$

Canceling the rate constants and the $[0.01]^n$ and simplifying:

$$\frac{1}{4} = \left(\frac{1}{2}\right)^m$$

m = 2 (can use logarithms to solve for m)

Comparing experiments 1 and 3:

$$\frac{0.05 \text{ M/s} = k[0.01]^m[0.01]^n}{0.10 \text{ M/s} = k[0.01]^m[0.02]^n}$$

Canceling the rate constants and the $[0.01]^n$ and simplifying:

$$\frac{1}{2} = \left(\frac{1}{2}\right)^n$$

$$n = 1$$

Writing the rate equation:

$$\text{Rate} = k[NO]^2[O_2]$$

Again, the rate constant k could be determined by choosing any of the three experiments, substituting the concentrations, rate, and orders into the rate expression, and then solving for k.

INTEGRATED RATE LAWS

Thus far, only cases in which instantaneous data are used in the rate expression have been shown. These expressions allow us to answer questions concerning the speed of the reaction at a particular moment, but not questions about how long it might take to use up a certain reactant, etc. If changes in the concentration of reactants or products over time are taken into account, as in the **integrated rate laws,** these questions can be answered.

Consider the following reaction:

$$A \rightarrow B$$

Assuming that this reaction is first order, then the rate of reaction can be expressed as the change in concentration of reactant A with time:

$$\text{Rate} = -\frac{\Delta[A]}{\Delta t}$$

and also as the rate law:

$$\text{Rate} = k[A]$$

Setting these terms equal to each other gives:

$$-\frac{\Delta[A]}{\Delta t} = k[A]$$

and integrating over time gives:

$$\ln\frac{[A]_0}{[A]_t} = kt$$

where ln is the natural logarithm, $[A]_0$ is the concentration of reactant A at time = 0 and $[A]_t$ is the concentration of reactant A at some time t.

If the reaction is second order in A, then the following equation can be derived using the same procedure:

$$\frac{1}{[A]_t} - \frac{1}{[A]_0} = kt$$

Consider the following problem: Hydrogen iodide, HI, decomposes through a second-order process to the elements. The rate constant is 2.40×10^{-21}/M s at 25° C. How long will it take for the concentration of HI to drop from 0.200 M to 0.190 M at 25° C?

Answer: 1.10×10^{20} s. This is a simple plug-in problem, with $k = 2.40 \times 10^{-21}$/M s, $[A]_0 = 0.200$ M, and $[A]_t = 0.190$ M. You can simply plug in the values and solve for t, or you first can rearrange the equation to give $t = (1/[A]_t - 1/[A]_0)/k$. You will get the same answer in either case. If you get a negative answer, you interchanged $[A]_t$ and $[A]_0$. A common mistake is to use the first-order equation instead of the second-order equation. The problem will always give you the information needed to determine if the first-order or second-order equation is required.

The order of reaction can be determined graphically through the use of the integrated rate law. If a plot of the ln[A] versus time yields a straight line, then the reaction is first order with respect to reactant A. If a plot of $\frac{1}{[A]}$ versus time yields a straight line, then the reaction is second order with respect to reactant A.

The reaction **half-life, $t_{1/2}$,** is the amount of time that it takes for a reactant concentration to decrease to one-half its initial concentration. For a first-order reaction, the half-life is a constant, independent of reactant concentration, and can be shown to have the following mathematical relationship:

$$t_{1/2} = \frac{\ln 2}{k} = \frac{0.693}{k}$$

For second-order reactions, the half-life does depend on the reactant concentration and can be calculated using the following formula:

$$t_{1/2} = \frac{1}{k[A]_0}$$

This means that as a second-order reaction proceeds, the half-life increases.

Radioactive decay is a first-order process, and the half-lives of the radioisotopes are well documented (see Chapter 15 for a discussion of half-lives with respect to nuclear reactions).

Consider the following problem: The rate constant for the radioactive decay of thorium-232 is 5.0×10^{-11}/year. Determine the half-life of thorium-232.

Answer: 1.4×10^{10} yr. This is a radioactive decay process. Radioactive decay follows first-order kinetics. The solution to the problem simply requires the substitution of the k-value into the appropriate equation:

$$t_{1/2} = 0.693/k = 0.693/5.0 \times 10^{-11} \text{yr}^{-1} = 1.386 \times 10^{10} \text{yr}$$

which rounds to the answer reported.

Hydrogen iodide, HI, decomposes through a second-order process to the elements. The rate constant is 2.40×10^{-21}/M s at 25° C. What is the half-life for this decomposition for a 0.200 M of HI at 25° C?

Answer: 2.08×10^{21} s.

The problem specifies that this is a second-order process. Thus, you must simply plug in the appropriate values into the second-order half-life equation:

$$t_{1/2} = 1/k[A]_0 = 1/(2.40 \times 10^{-21}/\text{M s})(0.200 \text{ M}) = 2.08333 \times 10^{21} \text{ seconds}$$

which rounds to the answer reported.

If you are unsure about your work in either of these problems, just follow your units. You are asked for time, so your answer must have time units only and no other units.

ACTIVATION ENERGY

A change in the temperature at which a reaction is taking place affects the rate constant k. As the temperature increases, the value of the rate constant increases and the reaction is faster. The Swedish scientist Arrhenius derived a relationship in 1889 that related the rate constant and temperature. The Arrhenius equation has the form: $k = Ae^{-E_a/RT}$ where k is the rate constant, A is a term called the frequency factor that accounts for molecular orientation, e is the natural logarithm base, R is universal gas constant, T is the Kelvin temperature and E_a is the **activation energy,** the minimum amount of energy that is needed to initiate or start a chemical reaction.

The Arrhenius equation is most commonly used to calculate the activation energy of a reaction. One way this can be done is to plot the ln of k versus 1/T. This gives a straight line whose slope is $-E_a/R$. Knowing the value of R allows the calculation of the value of E_a.

Normally, high activation energies are associated with slow reactions. Anything that can be done to lower the activation energy of a reaction will tend to speed up the reaction.

REACTION MECHANISMS

In the introduction to this chapter we discussed how chemical reactions occurred. Recall that there must be a collision between reactants at the reactive site that transfers enough energy to provide the activation energy before a reaction can occur. However, many reactions do not take place in quite this simple a way. Many reactions proceed from reactants to products through a sequence of reactions. This sequence of reactions is called the **reaction mechanism.** For example, consider the reaction

$$A + 2 B \rightarrow E + F$$

Most likely, E and F are not formed from the simple collision of an A and two B molecules. This reaction might follow this reaction sequence:

$$A + B \rightarrow C$$

$$C + B \rightarrow D$$

$$D \rightarrow E + F$$

If you add together the three equations above, you will get the overall equation $A + 2 B \rightarrow E + F$. C and D are called **reaction intermediates,** chemical species that are produced and consumed during the reaction, but that do not appear in the overall reaction.

Each individual reaction in the mechanism is called an **elementary step** or reaction. Each reaction step has its own rate of reaction. Usually, one of the reaction steps is much slower than the rest and is called the **rate-determining step.** The rate-determining step limits how fast the overall reaction can occur. Therefore, the rate law of the rate-determining step is the rate law of the overall reaction.

The rate equation for an elementary step can be determined from the reaction stoichiometry, unlike the overall reaction. The reactant coefficients in the elementary step become the reaction orders in the rate equation for that elementary step.

Many times a study of the kinetics of a reaction gives clues to the reaction mechanism. For example, consider the following reaction:

$$NO_2(g) + CO(g) \rightarrow NO(g) + CO_2(g)$$

It has been determined experimentally that the rate law for this reaction is: Rate = $k[NO_2]^2$. This indicates that the reaction does not occur with a simple collision between NO_2 and CO. The following mechanism has been proposed for this reaction:

$$NO_2(g) + NO_2(g) \rightarrow NO_3(g) + NO(g)$$

$$NO_3(g) + CO(g) \rightarrow NO_2(g) + CO_2(g)$$

Notice that if you add these two steps together, you get the overall reaction. The first step has been shown to be the slow step in the mechanism, the rate-determining step. If we write the rate law for this elementary step it is: Rate = $k[NO_2]^2$, which is identical to the experimentally determined rate law for the overall reaction.

Also note that both of the steps in the mechanism are **bimolecular reactions**, reactions that involve the collision of two chemical species. In **unimolecular reactions** a single chemical species decomposes or rearranges. Both bimolecular and unimolecular reactions are common, but the collision of three or more chemical species is quite rare. Therefore, in developing or assessing a mechanism, it is best to consider only unimolecular or bimolecular elementary steps.

CATALYSTS

A **catalyst** is a substance that speeds up the rate of reaction without being consumed in the reaction. A catalyst may take part in the reaction and even be changed during the reaction, but at the end of the reaction it is at least theoretically recoverable in its original form. It will not produce more of the product, but it allows the reaction to proceed more quickly. In equilibrium reactions (see Chapter 13), the catalyst speeds up both the forward and reverse reactions. Catalysts speed up the rates of reaction by providing a different mechanism that has a lower activation energy. The higher the activation energy of a reaction, the slower the reaction will proceed. Catalysts provide an alternate pathway that has a lower activation energy and thus will be faster. In general, there are two distinct types of catalysts.

Homogeneous Catalysts

Homogeneous catalysts are catalysts that are in the same phase or state of matter as the reactants. They provide an alternate reaction pathway (mechanism) with a lower activation energy.

The decomposition of hydrogen peroxide is a slow, one-step reaction, especially if the solution is kept cool and in a dark bottle:

$$2\,H_2O_2 \rightarrow 2\,H_2O + O_2$$

However, if ferric ion is added, the reaction speeds up tremendously. The proposed reaction sequence for this new reaction is:

$$2\,Fe^{3+} + H_2O_2 \rightarrow 2\,Fe^{2+} + O_2 + 2\,H^+$$

$$2\,Fe^{2+} + H_2O_2 + 2\,H^+ \rightarrow 2\,Fe^{3+} + 2\,H_2O$$

Notice that in the reaction the catalyst, Fe^{3+}, was reduced to the ferrous ion, Fe^{2+}, in the first step of the mechanism, but in the second step it was oxidized back to the ferric ion. Overall, the catalyst remained unchanged. Notice also that although the catalyzed reaction is a two-step reaction, it is significantly faster than the original uncatalyzed one-step reaction.

Heterogeneous Catalysts

A **heterogeneous catalyst** is in a different phase or state of matter than the reactants. Most commonly, the catalyst is a solid and the reactants are liquids or gases. These catalysts lower the activation energy for the reaction by providing a surface for the reaction, and also providing a better orientation of one reactant so its reactive site is more easily hit by the other reactant. Many times these heterogeneous catalysts are finely divided metals. The Haber process, by which nitrogen and hydrogen gases are converted into ammonia, depends upon an iron catalyst, while the hydrogenation of vegetable oil to margarine uses a nickel catalyst.

EXPERIMENTAL

Unlike other experiments, a means of measuring time is essential to all kinetics experiments. This may be done with a clock or a timer. The initial concentration of each reactant must be determined. Often this is done through a simple dilution of a stock solution. The experimenter must then determine the concentration of one or more substances later, or record some measurable change in the solution. Unless there will be an attempt to measure the activation energy, the temperature should be kept constant. A thermometer is needed to confirm this.

"Clock" experiments are common kinetics experiments. They do not require a separate experiment to determine the concentration of a substance in the reaction mixture. In clock experiments, after a certain amount of time, the solution suddenly changes color. This occurs when one of the reactants has disappeared, and another reaction involving a color change can begin.

In other kinetics experiments, the volume or pressure of a gaseous product is monitored. Again, it is not necessary to analyze the reaction mixture. Color changes in a solution may be monitored with a spectrophotometer. Finally, as a last resort, a sample of the reaction mixture may be removed at intervals and analyzed.

The initial measurement and one or more later measurements are required. (Remember, you measure times; you calculate changes in time (Δt)). Glassware, for mixing and diluting solutions, and a thermometer are the equipment needed for a clock experiment. Other kinetics experiments will use additional equipment to measure volume, temperature, etc. Do not forget: In all cases you measure a property, then calculate a change. You never measure a change.

COMMON MISTAKES TO AVOID

1. When working mathematical problems, be sure your units cancel to give you the desired unit in your answer.
2. Be sure to round your answer off to the correct number of significant figures.
3. In working rate law problems, be sure to use molarity for your concentration unit.
4. In writing integrated rate laws, be sure to include the negative sign with the change in *reactant* concentration, since it will be decreasing with time.
5. Remember that the rate law for an overall reaction must be derived from experimental data.
6. In mathematically determining the rate law, be sure to set up the ratio of two experiments such that the concentration of only one reactant has changed.
7. Remember that in most of these calculations the base e logarithm (ln) is used and not the base 10 logarithm (log).

REVIEW QUESTIONS

You have 15 minutes. You may not use a calculator.

1. A reaction follows the rate law: Rate = $k[A]^2$. Which of the following plots will give a straight line?

   A. 1/[A] versus 1/time
   B. $[A]^2$ versus time
   C. 1/[A] versus time
   D. ln[A] versus time
   E. [A] versus time

2. For the following reaction: $NO_2(g) + CO(g) \rightarrow NO(g) + CO_2(g)$ the rate law is Rate = $k[NO_2]^2$. If a small amount of gaseous carbon monoxide (CO) is added to a reaction mixture that was 0.10 molar in NO_2 and 0.20 molar in CO, which of the following statements is true?

   A. Both k and the reaction rate remain the same.
   B. Both k and the reaction rate increase.
   C. Both k and the reaction rate decrease.
   D. Only k increases, the reaction rate remains the same.
   E. Only the reaction rate increases; k remains the same.

3. The specific rate constant, k, for radio-active beryllium-11 is 0.049 s^{-1}. What mass of a 0.500 mg sample of beryllium-11 remains after 28 seconds?

   A. 0.250 mg
   B. 0.125 mg
   C. 0.0625 mg
   D. 0.375 mg
   E. 0.500 mg

4. The slow rate of a particular chemical reaction might be attributed to which of the following?

   A. a low activation energy
   B. a high activation energy
   C. the presence of a catalyst
   D. the temperature is high
   E. the concentration of the reactants are high

5. The steps below represent a proposed mechanism for the catalyzed oxidation of CO by O_3.

   Step 1: $NO_2(g) + CO(g) \rightarrow NO(g) + CO_2(g)$

   Step 2: $NO(g) + O_3(g) \rightarrow NO_2(g) + O_2(g)$

   What are the overall products of the catalyzed reaction?

   A. CO_2 and O_2
   B. NO and CO_2
   C. NO_2 and O_2
   D. NO and O_2
   E. NO_2 and CO_2

6. The decomposition of ammonia to the elements is a first-order reaction with a half-life of 200 s at a certain temperature. How long will it take the partial pressure of ammonia to decrease from 0.100 atm to 0.00625 atm?

   A. 200 s
   B. 400 s
   C. 800 s
   D. 1000 s
   E. 1200 s

7. The energy difference between the reactants and the transition state is

   A. the free energy
   B. the heat of reaction
   C. the activation energy
   D. the kinetic energy
   E. the reaction energy

8. The purpose of striking a match against the side of a box to light the match is

   A. to supply the free energy for the reaction
   B. to supply the activation energy for the reaction
   C. to supply the heat of reaction
   D. to supply the kinetic energy for the reaction
   E. to catalyze the reaction

9. The table below gives the initial concentrations and rate for three experiments.

Experiment	Initial [CO] (mol L^{-1})	Initial [Cl$_2$] (mol L^{-1})	Initial rate of formation of COCl$_2$ (mol L^{-1} min^{-1})
1	0.200	0.100	3.9×10^{-25}
2	0.100	0.200	3.9×10^{-25}
3	0.200	0.200	7.8×10^{-25}

   The reaction is $CO(g) + Cl_2(g) \rightarrow COCl_2(g)$. What is the rate law for this reaction?

   A. Rate = k[CO]
   B. Rate = k[CO]^2[Cl$_2$]
   C. Rate = k[Cl$_2$]
   D. Rate = k[CO][Cl$_2$]^2
   E. Rate = k[CO][Cl$_2$]

10. The reaction $(CH_3)_3CBr(aq) + H_2O(l) \rightarrow (CH_3)_3COH(aq) + HBr(aq)$ follows the rate law Rate = k[(CH$_3$)$_3$CBr]. What will be the effect of decreasing the concentration of $(CH_3)_3CBr$?

    A. The rate of the reaction will increase.
    B. More HBr will form.
    C. The rate of the reaction will decrease.

D. The reaction will shift to the left.

E. The equilibrium constant will increase.

11. When the concentration of $H^+(aq)$ is doubled for the reaction $H_2O_2(aq) + 2 Fe^{2+}(aq) + 2 H^+(aq) \rightarrow 2 Fe^{3+}(aq) + 2 H_2O(g)$, there is no change in the reaction rate. This indicates

A. the H^+ is a spectator ion

B. the rate-determining step does not involve H^+

C. the reaction mechanism does not involve H^+

D. the H^+ is a catalyst

E. the rate law is first-order with respect to H^+

12. The mechanism below has been proposed for the reaction of $CHCl_3$ with Cl_2.

Step 1: $Cl_2(g) \rightleftharpoons 2 Cl(g)$ fast

Step 2: $Cl(g) + CHCl_3(g)$
         $\rightarrow CCl_3(g) + HCl(g)$ slow

Step 3: $CCl_3(g) + Cl(g) \rightarrow CCl_4(g)$ fast

Which of the following rate laws is consistent with this mechanism?

A. Rate = $k[Cl_2]$

B. Rate = $k[CHCl_3][Cl_2]$

C. Rate = $k[CHCl_3]$

D. Rate = $k[CHCl_3]/[Cl_2]$

E. Rate = $k[CHCl_3][Cl_2]^{1/2}$

ANSWERS AND EXPLANATIONS

✓

1. **C.** The "2" exponent means this is a second-order rate law. Second-order rate laws give a straight-line plot for 1/[A] versus t.

2. **A.** The value of k remains the same unless the temperature is changed or a catalyst is added. Only materials that appear in the rate law, in this case NO_2, will affect the rate. Adding NO_2 would increase the rate, and removing NO_2 would decrease the rate. CO has no effect on the rate.

3. **B.** The half-life is $0.693/k = 0.693/0.049 \text{ s}^{-1} = 14 \text{ s}$. The time given, 28 s, represents two half-lives. The first half-life uses one-half of the isotope, and the second half-life uses one-half of the remaining material, so only one-fourth of the original material remains.

4. **B.** Slow reactions have high activation energies. High activation energies are often attributed to strong bonds within the reactant molecules. All the other choices give faster rates.

5. **A.** Add the two equations together:

$$NO_2(g) + CO(g) + NO(g) + O_3(g) \rightarrow NO(g) + CO_2(g) + NO_2(g) + O_2(g)$$

Then cancel identical species that appear on opposite sides:

$$CO(g) + O_3(g) \rightarrow CO_2(g) + O_2(g)$$

6. **C.** The value will be decreased by one-half for each half-life. Using the following table:

Half-lives	Remaining
0	0.100
1	0.0500
2	0.0250
3	0.0125
4	0.00625

Four half-lives = 4(200 s) = 800 s

7. **C.** This is the definition of the activation energy.

8. **B.** The friction supplies the energy needed to start the reaction. The energy needed to start the reaction is the activation energy.

9. **E.** Beginning with the generic rate law: Rate = $k[CO]^m[Cl_2]^n$, it is necessary to determine the values of m and n (the orders). Comparing Experiments 2 and 3, the rate doubles when the concentration of CO is doubled. This direct change means the reaction is first order with respect to CO. Comparing Experiments 1 and 3, the rate doubles when the concentration of Cl_2 is doubled. Again, this direct change means the reaction is first order. This gives: Rate = $k[CO]^1[Cl_2]^1 = k[CO][Cl_2]$.

10. **C.** The compound appears in the rate law, and so a change in its concentration will change the rate. The reaction is first order in $(CH_3)_3CBr$, so the rate will change directly with the change in concentration of this reactant.

11. **B.** All substances involved, directly or indirectly, in the rate-determining step will change the rate when their concentrations are changed. The ion is required in the balanced chemical equation, so it cannot be a spectator ion, and it must appear in the mechanism. Catalysts will change the rate of a reaction. Since H^+ does not effect the rate, the reaction is zero order with respect to this ion.

12. **E.** The rate law depends on the slow step of the mechanism. The reactants in the slow step are Cl and $CHCl_3$ (one of each). The rate law is first order with respect to each of these. The Cl is half of the original reactant molecule Cl_2. This replaces the [Cl] in the rate law with $[Cl_2]^{1/2}$. Do not make the mistake of using the overall reaction to predict the rate law.

3 FREE-RESPONSE QUESTIONS

You have 15 minutes for this question. You may use a calculator.

$$2\ ClO_2(aq) + 2\ OH^-(aq) \rightarrow ClO_3^-(aq) + ClO_2^-(aq) + H_2O(l)$$

A series of experiments were conducted to study the above reaction. The initial concentrations and rates are reported in the table below.

	Initial Concentration (mol/L)		Initial Rate of Formation
Experiment	$[OH^-]$	$[ClO_2]$	of ClO_3^- (mol/L min)
1	0.030	0.020	0.166
2	0.060	0.020	0.331
3	0.030	0.040	0.661

a. i. Determine the order of the reaction with respect to each reactant. Make sure you explain your reasoning.

ii. Give the rate law for the reaction.

b. Determine the value of the rate constant, making sure the units are included.

c. Calculate the initial rate of disappearance of ClO_2 in experiment 1.

d. The following has been proposed as a mechanism for this reaction.

$$\text{Step 1: } ClO_2 + ClO_2 \rightarrow Cl_2O_4$$

$$\text{Step 2: } Cl_2O_4 + OH^- \rightarrow ClO_3^- + HClO_2$$

$$\text{Step 3: } HClO_2 + OH^- \rightarrow ClO_2^- + H_2O$$

Which step is the rate-determining step? Show that this mechanism is consistent with both the rate law for the reaction and with the overall stoichiometry.

ANSWERS AND EXPLANATIONS

✓

a. i. This part of the problem begins with a generic rate equation: Rate = k[ClO₂]ᵐ[OH⁻]ⁿ. The values of the exponents, the orders, must be determined. It does not matter which is done first. If you want to begin with ClO₂, you must pick two experiments from the table where its concentration changes but the OH⁻ concentration does not change. These are experiments 1 and 3. Experiment 3 has twice the concentration of ClO₂ as experiment 1. This doubling of the ClO₂ concentration has quadrupled the rate. The relationship between the concentration ($\times 2$) and the rate ($\times 4 = \times 2^2$) indicates that the order for ClO₂ is 2 ($= m$). Using experiments 1 and 2 (only the OH⁻ concentration changes), we see that doubling the concentration simply doubles the rate. Thus, the order for OH⁻ is 1 ($= n$). Give yourself 1 point for each order you got correct.

ii. Plugging the orders into the generic rate law gives: Rate = $k[ClO_2]^2[OH^-]^1$ which is usually simplified to: Rate = $k[ClO_2]^2[OH^-]$. Give yourself 1 point if you got this correct.

b. Any one of the three experiments may be used to calculate the rate constant. If the problem asked for an average rate constant, you would need to calculate a value for each of the experiments and then average the values.

The rate law should be rearranged to: $k = \text{Rate}/[ClO_2]^2[OH^-]$. Then the appropriate values are plugged into the equation. Using experiment 1 as an example:

$$k = (0.166 \text{ mol/L min})/[(0.020 \text{ M})^2(0.030 \text{ M})]$$

$$= 1.3833 \times 10^4 \text{ M/M}^3 \text{ min} = 1.4 \times 10^4/\text{M}^2 \text{ min}$$

The answer could also be reported as $1.4 \times 10^4 \text{ L}^2/\text{mol}^2\text{min}$. You should not forget that M = mol/L.

Give yourself 1 point for the correct numerical value. Give yourself 1 point for the correct units.

c. The coefficients from the equation say that for every mole of ClO₃⁻ that forms, 2 mol of ClO₂ reacted. Thus the rate of ClO₂ is twice the rate of ClO₃⁻. Do not forget that since ClO₃⁻ is forming, it has a positive rate, and since ClO₂ is reacting it has a negative rate. This gives:

$$-2 \Delta[ClO_2]/\Delta t = \Delta[ClO_3]/\Delta t$$

Rearranging and plugging in the rate from experiment 1 gives:

$$\Delta[ClO_2]/\Delta t = -0.5(0.166 \text{ mol/L min}) = -0.0830 \text{ mol/L min}$$

Give yourself 2 points if you got the entire answer correct. You only get 1 point if the sign or units are missing.

d. The rate-determining step must match the rate law. One approach is to determine the rate law for each step in the mechanism. This gives:

$$\text{Step 1: Rate} = k[ClO_2]^2$$

$$\text{Step 2: Rate} = k[Cl_2O_4][OH^-] = k[Cl_2O]^2[OH^-]$$

$$\text{Step 3: Rate} = k[HClO_2][OH^-] = k[ClO_2][OH^-]^2$$

For steps 2 and 3 the intermediates must be replaced with reactants. Step 2 gives a rate-law matching the one derived in part a. Give yourself 1 point if you picked step 2, or if you picked a step with a rate-law that matches a wrong answer for part a. Give yourself 1 more point if you explained the substitution of reactants for intermediates.

To see if the stoichiometry is correct, simply add the three steps together and cancel the intermediates (materials that appear on both sides of the reaction arrow).

$$\text{Step 1: } ClO_2 + ClO_2 \rightarrow Cl_2O_4$$

$$\text{Step 2: } Cl_2O_4 + OH^- \rightarrow ClO_3^- + HClO_2$$

$$\text{Step 3: } HClO_2 + OH^- \rightarrow ClO_2^- + H_2O$$

$$\text{Total: } 2\,ClO_2 + Cl_2O_4 + 2\,OH^- + HClO_2$$
$$\rightarrow Cl_2O_4 + ClO_3^- + HClO_2 + ClO_2^- + H_2O$$

After removing the intermediates (Cl_2O_4 and $HClO_2$):

$$2\,ClO_2 + 2\,OH^- \rightarrow ClO_3^- + ClO_2^- + H_2O$$

As this matches the original reaction equation, the mechanism fulfills the overall stoichiometry requirement. Give yourself 1 point if you have done this.

The total is 10 points for this question.

RAPID REVIEW

- Kinetics is a study of the speed of a chemical reaction.

- The five factors that can affect the rates of chemical reaction are the nature of the reactants, the temperature, the concentration of the reactants, the physical state of the reactants, and catalysts.

- The rate equation relates the speed of reaction to the concentration of reactants and has the form: Rate = $k[A]^m[B]^n$ . . . where k is the rate constant and m and n are the orders of reaction with respect to that specific reactant.

- The rate law must be determined from experimental data. Review how to determine the rate law from kinetics data.

- When mathematically comparing two experiments in the determination of the rate equation, be sure to choose two in which all reactant concentrations except one remain constant.

- Rate laws can be written in the integrated form.

- If a reaction is first order, it has the rate law of Rate = k[A]; a plot of ln[A] versus time gives a straight line.

- If a reaction is second order, it has the form of Rate $= \dfrac{1}{[A]_t} - \dfrac{1}{[A]_0} = kt$; a plot of $\dfrac{1}{[A]}$ versus time gives a straight line.

- The reaction half-life is the amount of time that it takes the reactant concentration to decrease to one-half its initial concentration.

- The half-life can be related to concentration and time by these two equations (first and second order, respectively): $t_{1/2} = \dfrac{\ln 2}{k} = \dfrac{0.693}{k}$ and $t_{1/2} = \dfrac{1}{k[A]_0}$. Know how to apply these equations.

- The activation energy is the minimum amount of energy needed to initiate or start a chemical reaction.

- Many reactions proceed from reactants to products by a series of steps called elementary steps. All these steps together describe the reaction mechanism, the pathway by which the reaction occurs.

- The slowest step in a reaction mechanism is the rate-determining step. It determines the rate law.

- A catalyst is a substance that speeds up a reaction without being consumed in the reaction.

- A homogeneous catalyst is in the same phase as the reactants, whereas a heterogeneous catalyst is in a different phase than the reactants.

Chapter 13

Equilibrium

KEYWORDS AND EQUATIONS

✓

Q = reaction quotient

$$Q = \frac{[C]^c[D]^d}{[A]^a[B]^b}, \quad \text{where } aA + bB \rightleftharpoons cC + dD$$

equilibrium constants:

K_a (weak acid) K_b (weak base) K_w (water)

K_p (gas pressure) K_c (molar concentrations)

$$K_a = \frac{[H^+][A^-]}{[HA]} \qquad K_b = \frac{[OH^-][HB^+]}{[B]}$$

$K_w = [OH^-][H^+] = 1.0 \times 10^{-14} = K_a \times K_b$ at 25°C

$pH = -\log[H^+]$, $pOH = -\log[OH^-]$

$14 = pH + pOH$

$$pH = pK_a + \log\frac{[A^-]}{[HA]}$$

$$pOH = pK_b + \log\frac{[HB^+]}{[B]}$$

$pK_a = -\log K_a$, $pK_b = -\log K_b$

$K_p = K_c(RT)^{\Delta n}$, where Δn = moles product gas – moles reactant gas

INTRODUCTION

We've been discussing chemical reactions for several chapters. In Chapter 12 you saw how chemical reactions take place and some of the factors that affect the reaction's speed. In this chapter we will discuss another aspect of chemical reactions, equilibrium.

A few chemical reactions proceed to completion, using up one or more of the reactants and then stopping. However, most reactions behave in a different way. Consider the general reaction:

$$a\,A + b\,B \rightarrow c\,C + d\,D$$

Reactants A and B are forming C and D. Then C and D start to react to form A and B:

$$c\,C + d\,D \rightarrow a\,A + b\,B$$

These two reactions proceed until the two rates of reaction become equal. That is, the speed of production of C and D in the first reaction is equal to the speed of production of A and B in the second reaction. Since these two reactions are occurring simultaneously in the same container, the amounts of A, B, C, and D become constant. A **chemical equilibrium** has been reached, in which two exactly opposite reactions are occurring at the same place, at the same time, and with the same rates of reaction. When a system reaches the equilibrium state, the reactions do not stop. A and B are still reacting to form C and D; C and D are still reacting to form A and B. But because the reactions proceed at the same rate, the amounts of each chemical species are constant. This state is sometimes called a *dynamic* equilibrium state to emphasize the fact that the reactions are still occurring—it is a dynamic, not a static state. An equilibrium state is indicated by a double arrow instead of a single arrow. For the reaction above it would be shown as:

$$a\,A + b\,B \rightleftharpoons c\,C + d\,D$$

It is important to remember that at equilibrium the concentrations of the chemical species are constant, not necessarily equal. There may be a lot of C and D and a little A and B, or vice versa. The concentrations are constant, unchanging, but not necessarily equal.

If the temperature is held constant, then the ratio of the two reactions, the forward and reverse, should be a constant. This constant is called the **reaction quotient,** Q, and has the following form:

$$Q_c = \frac{[C]^c[D]^d}{[A]^a[B]^b}$$

!

The reaction quotient is a fraction. In the numerator is the product of the chemical species on the right-hand side of the equilibrium arrow, each raised to the power of that species' coefficient in the balanced chemical equation. It is called the Q_c in this case, because molar concentrations are being used. If this was a gas phase reaction, gas pressures could be used and it would become a Q_p.

Remember: products over reactants.

EQUILIBRIUM EXPRESSIONS

The reactant quotient can be written at any point during the reaction, but the most useful point is when the reaction has reached equilibrium. At equilibrium, the reaction quotient becomes the **equilibrium constant, K_c** (or K_p if gas pressures are being used). Usually this equilibrium constant is expressed simply as a number without units, since it is a ratio of concentrations or pressures. In addition, the concentrations of solids or pure liquids (not in solution) that appear in the equilibrium expression are assumed to be 1 since their concentrations do not change.

Consider the Haber process for the production of ammonia:

$$N_2(g) + 3\ H_2(g) \rightleftharpoons 2\ NH_3(g)$$

The equilibrium constant expression would be written as:

$$K_c = \frac{[NH_3]^2}{[N_2][H_2]^3}$$

If the partial pressures of the gases were used, then the K_p would be written in the following form:

$$K_p = \frac{P_{NH_3}^2}{P_{N_2} \times P_{H_2}^3}$$

There is a relationship between the K_c and the K_p: $K_p = K_c(RT)^{\Delta n_{gas}}$ where R is the ideal gas constant (0.08206 L atm / mol K) and Δn_{gas} is the change in the number of moles of gas in the reaction.

!

Remember: Be sure that your value of R is consistent with the units chosen for the partial pressures of the gases.

For the following equilibrium $K_p = 1.90$: $C(s) + CO_2(g) \rightleftharpoons 2\ CO(g)$ Calculate K_c for the this equilibrium at 25° C.

$$C(s) + CO_2(g) \rightleftharpoons 2\ CO(g) \quad K_p = 1.90$$

$$K_p = K_c(RT)^{\Delta n_{gas}}$$

$$1.90 = K_c \frac{[(0.08206\ L\ atm)(298\ K)]^{(2-1)}}{[(mol\ K)]}$$

$$K_c = 0.0777$$

The numerical value of the equilibrium constant can give an indication of the extent of the reaction after equilibrium has been reached. If the value of the K_c is large, that means the numerator is much larger than the denominator and the reaction has produced a relatively large amount of products (reaction lies far to the right). If the K_c is small, then the numerator is much smaller than the denominator and not much product has been formed (reaction lies far to the left).

LE CHATELIER'S PRINCIPLE

At a given temperature, a reaction will reach equilibrium with the production of a certain amount of product. If the equilibrium constant is small, that means that not much product will be formed. But is there anything that can be done to produce more? Yes there is—through the application of **Le Chatelier's principle.** Le Chatelier, a French scientist, discovered that if a chemical system at equilibrium is stressed (disturbed) it will reestablish equilibrium by shifting the reactions involved. This means that the amounts of the reactants and products will change, but the final ratio will remain the same. The equilibrium may be stressed in a number of ways: changes in concentration, pressure, and temperature. Many times the use of a catalyst is mentioned. However a catalyst will have no effect on the equilibrium amounts because it affects both the forward and reverse reactions equally. It will, however, cause the reaction to reach equilibrium faster.

Changes in Concentration

If the equilibrium system is stressed by a change in concentration of one of the reactants or products, the equilibrium will react to remove that stress. If the concentration of a chemical species is decreased, the equilibrium will shift to produce more of it. In doing so, the concentration of chemical species on the other side of the reaction arrows will be decreased. If the concentration of a chemical species is increased, the equilibrium will shift to consume it, increasing the concentration of chemical species on the other side of the reaction arrows.

For example, again consider the Haber process:

$$N_2(g) + 3\ H_2(g) \rightleftharpoons 2\ NH_3(g)$$

If one increases the concentration of hydrogen gas, then the equilibrium shifts to the right to consume some of the added hydrogen. In doing so, the concentration of ammonia (NH_3) will increase and the concentration of nitrogen gas will decrease. On the other hand, if the concentration of nitrogen gas was decreased, the equilibrium would shift to the left to form more, the concentration of ammonia would decrease, and the concentration of hydrogen would increase.

Again, remember that the concentrations may change, but the value of K_c or K_p would remain the same.

Changes in Pressure

Changes in pressure are only significant if gases are involved. The pressure may be changed by changing the volume of the container or by changing the concentration of a gaseous species (although this is really a change in concentration and can be treated as a concentration effect, as above). If the container becomes smaller, the pressure increases because there is an increased number of collisions on the inside walls of the container. This stresses the equilibrium system, and it will shift to reduce the pressure. This can be accomplished by shifting the equilibrium toward the side of the equation that has the lesser number of moles of gas. If the container size is increased, the pressure decreases and the equilibrium will shift to the side containing more moles of gas to increase the pressure. If the number of moles of gas is the same on both sides, changing the pressure will not affect the equilibrium.

Once again, consider the Haber reaction:

$$N_2(g) + 3\ H_2(g) \rightleftharpoons 2\ NH_3(g)$$

Note that there are 4 mol of gas (1 of nitrogen and 3 of hydrogen) on the left side and 2 mol on the right. If the container is made smaller, the pressure will increase and the equilibrium will shift to the right because 4 mol would be converted to 2 mol. The concentrations of nitrogen and hydrogen gases would decrease, and the concentration of ammonia would increase.

Remember: Pressure effects are only important for gases.

Changes in Temperature

Changing the temperature changes the amount of heat in the system and can be treated as a concentration effect. To treat it this way, one must know which reaction, forward or reverse, is exothermic (releasing heat).

One last time, let's consider the Haber reaction:

$$N_2(g) + 3\ H_2(g) \rightleftharpoons 2\ NH_3(g)$$

The formation of ammonia is exothermic (liberating heat), so the reaction could be written as:

$$N_2(g) + 3\ H_2(g) \rightleftharpoons 2\ NH_3(g) + heat$$

If the temperature of the reaction mixture were increased, the amount of heat would be increased and the equilibrium would shift to the left to consume the added heat. In doing so, the concentration of nitrogen and hydrogen gases would increase and the concentration of ammonia gas would decrease. If you were in the business of selling ammonia, you would probably want to operate at a reduced temperature, in order to shift the reaction to the right.

Given the following equilibrium (endothermic as written), predict what changes, if any, would occur if the following stresses are applied after equilibrium was established.

$$CaCO_3(s) \rightleftharpoons CaO(s) + CO_2(g)$$

a. add CO_2
b. remove CO_2
c. add CaO
d. increase T
e. decrease V
f. add a catalyst

Answers:
a. Left—the equilibrium shifts to remove some of the excess CO_2.
b. Right—the equilibrium shifts to replace some of the CO_2.
c. No change—solids do not shift equilibria unless they are totally removed.
d. Right—endothermic reactions shift to the right when heated.
e. Left—a decrease in volume, or an increase in pressure, will shift the equilibrium toward the side with less gas.
f. No change—catalysts do not affect the position of an equilibrium.

ACID–BASE EQUILIBRIUM

In Chapter 4 we introduced the concept of acids and bases. Recall that acids are proton (H^+) donors and bases are proton acceptors. Also recall that acids and bases may be strong or weak. **Strong acids** completely dissociate in water; **weak acids** only partially dissociate. For example, consider two acids HCl (strong) and CH_3COOH (weak). If each is added to water to form aqueous solutions the following reactions take place:

$$HCl(aq) + H_2O(l) \rightarrow H_3O^+(aq) + Cl^-(aq)$$

$$CH_3COOH(aq) + H_2O(l) \rightleftharpoons H_3O^+(aq) + CH_3COO^-(aq)$$

The first reaction essentially goes to completion—there is no HCl left in solution. The second reaction is an equilibrium reaction—there are appreciable amounts of both reactants and products left in solution.

There are generally only two strong bases to consider: the hydroxide and the oxide ion (OH^- and O^{2-}, respectively). All other bases are weak. **Weak bases** also establish an equilibrium system, as in aqueous solutions of ammonia:

$$NH_3(aq) + H_2O(l) \rightleftharpoons OH^-(aq) + NH_4^+(aq)$$

In the Brønsted-Lowery acid–base theory, there is competition for an H^+. Consider the acid–base reaction between acetic acid, a weak acid, and ammonia, a weak base:

$$CH_3COOH(aq) + NH_3(aq) \rightleftharpoons CH_3COO^-(aq) + NH_4^+(aq)$$

Acetic acid donates a proton to ammonia in the forward (left-to-right reaction) of the equilibrium to form the acetate and ammonium ions. But in the reverse (right-to-left) reaction, the ammonium ion donates a proton to the acetate ion to form ammonia and acetic acid. The ammonium ion is acting as an acid, and the acetate ion a base. Under the Brønsted-Lowery system, acetic acid (CH_3COOH) and the acetate ion (CH_3COO^-) are called a conjugate acid–base pair. **Conjugate acid–base pairs** differ by only a single H^+. Ammonia (NH_3) and the ammonium ion (NH_4^+) are also a conjugate acid–base pair. In this reaction there is a competition for the H^+ between acetic acid and the ammonium ion. To predict on which side the equilibrium will lie, this general rule applies: *The equilibrium will favor the side in which the weakest acid and base are present.* Figure 13.1 shows the relative strengths of the conjugate acid–base pairs.

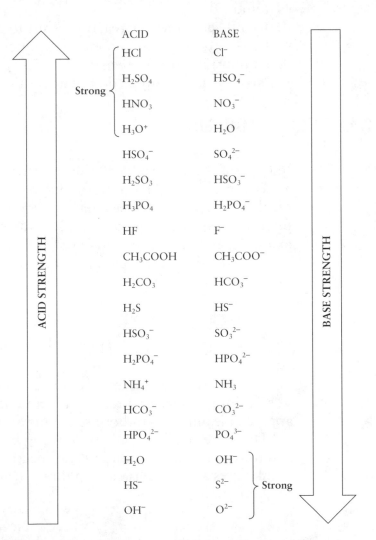

Figure 13.1 Conjugate acid–base pair strengths.

In Figure 13.1 you can see that acetic acid is a stronger acid than the ammonium ion and ammonia is a stronger base than the acetate ion. Therefore, the equilibrium will lie to the right.

The reasoning above allows us to find good qualitative answers, but in order to be able to do quantitative problems (how much is present, etc.), the extent of the dissociation of the weak acids and bases must be known. That is where a modification of the equilibrium constant is useful.

The K_a—The Acid Dissociation Constant

Strong acids completely dissociate (ionize) in water. Weak acids partially dissociate and establish an equilibrium system. But as you saw in Figure 13.1, there is a large range of weak acids based upon their ability to donate protons. Consider the general weak acid, HA, and its reaction when placed in water:

$$HA(aq) + H_2O(l) \rightleftharpoons H_3O^+(aq) + A^-(aq)$$

An equilibrium constant expression can be written for this system:

$$K_c = \frac{[H_3O^+][A^-]}{[HA]}$$

The $[H_2O]$ is assumed to be a constant and is incorporated into the K_a value. It is not shown in the equilibrium constant expression.

Since this is the equilibrium constant associated with a weak acid dissociation, this particular K_c is most commonly called the **acid dissociation constant,** the K_a. The K_a expression is then:

$$K_a = \frac{[H_3O^+][A^-]}{[HA]}$$

Many times the weak acid dissociation reaction will be shown in a shortened notation, omitting the water:

$$HA(aq) \rightleftharpoons H^+(aq) + A^-(aq) \qquad \text{with the } K_a = \frac{[H^+][A^-]}{[HA]}$$

The greater the amount of dissociation is, the larger the value of the K_a. Table 13.1 shows the K_a values of some common weak acids.

Here are a couple of tips: For every H^+ formed, an A^- is formed, so the numerator of the K_a expression can be expressed as $[H^+]^2$ (or $[A^-]^2$, although it is rarely done this way). Also, the $[HA]$ is the equilibrium molar concentration of the undissociated weak acid, not its initial concentration. The exact expression would then be $[HA] = M_{initially} - [H^+]$, where $M_{initially}$ is the initial concentration of the weak acid. This is true because for every H^+ that is formed, an HA must have dissociated. However, many times if the K_a is small, you can approximate the equilibrium concentration of the weak acid by its initial concentration, $[HA] \approx M_{initially}$.

Table 13.1 K_a Values for Selected Weak Acids

Name (Formula)	Lewis Structure	K_a
Iodic acid (HIO_3)		1.6×10^{-1}
Chlorous acid ($HClO_2$)		1.12×10^{-2}
Nitrous acid (HNO_2)		7.1×10^{-4}
Hydrofluoric acid (HF)		6.8×10^{-4}
Benzoic acid (C_6H_5COOH)		6.3×10^{-5}
Acetic acid (CH_3COOH)		1.8×10^{-5}
Propanoic acid (CH_3CH_2COOH)		1.3×10^{-5}
Hypochlorous acid (HClO)		2.9×10^{-8}
Hypobromous acid (HBrO)		2.3×10^{-9}
Phenol (C_6H_5OH)		1.0×10^{-10}
Hypoiodous acid (HIO)		2.3×10^{-11}

If the initial molarity and K_a of the weak acid are known, the $[H^+]$ (or $[A^-]$) can be calculated easily. And if the initial molarity and $[H^+]$ are known, the K_a can be calculated.

Calculate the $[H^+]$ of a 0.300 M acetic acid solution.

$$K_a = 1.8 \times 10^{-5}$$

$$HC_2H_3O_2(aq) \rightleftharpoons H^+(aq) + C_2H_3O_2^-(aq)$$
$$0.300 - x \qquad x \qquad x$$

$$K_a = \frac{[H^+][C_2H_3O_2^-]}{[HC_2H_3O_2]} = 1.8 \times 10^{-5}$$

$$= \frac{(x)(x)}{0.300 - x} = 1.8 \times 10^{-5}$$

$$x = [H^+] = 2.3 \times 10^{-3} \text{ M}$$

For **polyprotic acids,** acids that can donate more than one proton, the K_a for the first dissociation is much larger than the K_a for the second dissociation. If there is a third K_a, it is much smaller still. For most practical purposes you can simply use the first K_a.

The K_w—The Water Dissociation Constant

Before examining the equilibrium behavior of aqueous solutions of weak bases, let's look at the behavior of water itself. In the initial discussion of acid–base equilibrium above, we showed water acting both as an acid (proton donor when put with a base) and a base (proton acceptor when put with an acid). Water is **amphoteric,** it will act as either an acid or a base, depending on whether the other species is a base or acid. But in pure water the same amphoteric nature is noted. In pure water a very small amount of proton transfer is taking place:

$$H_2O(l) + H_2O(l) \rightleftharpoons H_3O^+(aq) + OH^-(aq)$$

This is commonly written as:

$$H_2O(l) \rightleftharpoons H^+(aq) + OH^-(aq)$$

There is an equilibrium constant, called the **water dissociation constant, K_w,** which has the form:

$$K_w = [H^+][OH] = 1.00 \times 10^{-14} \text{ at } 25°C$$

Again, the concentration of water is a constant and is incorporated into the K_w.

The numerical value of the K_w of 1.00×10^{-14} is true for the product of the $[H^+]$ and $[OH^-]$ in pure water and for aqueous solutions of acids and bases.

In the discussion of weak acid, we indicated that the $[H^+] = [A^-]$. Now that you know about the dissociation of water, you know that that is not exactly the case. There are two sources of H^+ in the system, the weak acid and water. However, the amount of H^+ that is due to the water dissociation is very small and can be easily ignored.

pH

Because the concentration of the hydronium ion, H_3O^+, can vary tremendously in solutions of acids and bases, a scale to easily represent the acidity of a solution was developed. It is called the pH scale and is related to the $[H_3O^+]$:

$$pH = -\log [H_3O^+] \text{ or } -\log [H^+] \text{ using the shorthand notation}$$

Remember that in pure water $K_w = [H_3O^+][OH^-] = 1.00 \times 10^{-14}$. Since both the hydronium ion and hydroxide ions are formed in equal amounts, the K_w expression can be expressed as:

$$[H_3O^+]^2 = 1.00 \times 10^{-14}$$

Solving for $[H_3O^+]$ gives us $[H_3O^+] = 1.00 \times 10^{-7}$. If you then calculate the pH of pure water:

$$pH = -\log [H_3O^+] = -\log [1.00 \times 10^{-7}] = -(-7.00) = 7.00$$

The pH of pure water is 7.00. On the pH scale this is called **neutral.** A solution whose $[H_3O^+]$ is greater than in pure water will have a pH less than 7.00 and is called **acidic.** A solution whose $[H_3O^+]$ is less than in pure water will have a pH greater than 7.00 and is called **basic.** Figure 13.2 shows the pH scale and the pH values of some common substances.

The pOH of a solution can also be calculated. It is defined as $pOH = -\log[OH^-]$. The pH and the pOH are related:

$$pH + pOH = pK_w = 14.00 \text{ at } 25° \text{ C}$$

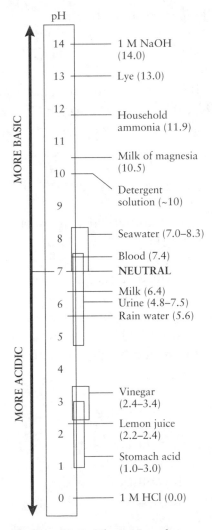

Figure 13.2 The pH scale.

In any of the problems above in which [H⁺] or [OH⁻] was calculated, you can now calculate the pH or pOH of the solution.

The K_b—The Base Dissociation Constant

Weak bases (B), when placed into water, also establish an equilibrium system much like weak acids:

$$B(aq) + H_2O(l) \rightleftharpoons HB^+(aq) + OH^-(aq)$$

The equilibrium constant expression is called the weak **base dissociation constant, K_b**, and has the form:

$$K_b = \frac{[HB^+][OH^-]}{[HB]}$$

The same reasoning that was used in dealing with weak acids is also true here: $[HB^+] = [OH^-]$; $[HB] \approx M_{initially}$; the numerator can be represented as $[OH^-]^2$; and knowing the initial molarity and K_b of the weak base, the $[OH^-]$ can easily be calculated. And if the initial molarity and $[OH^-]$ is known, the K_b can be calculated.

A 0.500 M solution of ammonia has a pH of 11.48. What is the K_b of ammonia?

pH = 11.48

$[H^+] = 10^{-11.48}$

$[H^+] = 3.3 \times 10^{-12}$

$K_w = [H^+][OH^-] = 1.00 \times 10^{-14}$

$[OH^-] = 3.0 \times 10^{-3}$

$$NH_3 + H_2O \rightleftharpoons NH_4^+ + OH^-$$
$$0.500 - x \qquad x \qquad x$$

$$K_b = \frac{[NH_4^+][OH^-]}{[NH_3]}$$

$$[OH^-] = [NH_4^+] = 3.0 \times 10^{-3} M$$

$$[NH_3] = 0.500 - 3.0 \times 10^{-3} = 0497\ M$$

$$K_b = \frac{(3.0 \times 10^{-3})^2}{(0.497)} = 1.8 \times 10^{-5}$$

The K_a and K_b of conjugate acid–base pairs are related through the K_w expression:

$$K_a \times K_b = K_w$$

Determine the pH of a solution made by adding 0.400 mol of strontium acetate to sufficient water to produce 2.000 L of solution.

Solution:
The initial molarity is 0.400 mol/2.000 L = 0.200 M.
When a salt is added to water dissolution will occur:

$$Sr(C_2H_3O_2)_2 \rightarrow Sr^{2+}(aq) + 2\ C_2H_3O_2^-(aq)$$

The resultant solution, since strontium acetate is soluble, has 0.200 M Sr^{2+} and 0.400 M $C_2H_3O_2^-$.

Ions such as Sr^{2+}, that come from strong acids or strong bases, may be ignored in this type of problem. Ions such as $C_2H_3O_2^-$, from weak acid or bases, will undergo hydrolysis. The acetate ion is the conjugate BASE of acetic acid ($K_a = 1.74 \times 10^{-5}$). Since acetate is not a strong base this will be a K_b problem, and OH^- will be produced. The equilibrium is:

$$C_2H_3O_2^- + H_2O \rightleftharpoons OH^- + HC_2H_3O_2$$
$$0.400 - x \qquad\qquad + x \qquad + x$$

Determining K_b from K_a (using $K_w = K_aK_b$) gives:

$$\frac{[x][x]}{0.400 - x} = K_b = 5.75 \times 10^{-10}$$

with $x = 1.52 \times 10^{-5} = [OH^-]$, and pH = 9.180

BUFFERS

Buffers are solutions that resist a change in pH when an acid or base is added to them. The most common type of buffer is a mixture of a weak acid and its conjugate base. The weak acid will neutralize any base added, and the weak base of the buffer will neutralize any acid added to the solution. The hydronium ion concentration of a buffer can be calculated using an equation derived from the K_a expression:

$$[H_3O^+] = K_a \times \frac{[HA]}{[A^-]}$$

Taking the negative log of both sides yields the **Henderson-Hasselbalch equation,** which can be used to calculate the pH of a buffer:

$$pH = pK_a + \log \frac{[A^-]}{[HA]}$$

The weak base K_b expression can also be used giving:

$$[OH^-] = K_b \times \frac{[B]}{[HB^+]} \quad \text{and} \quad pOH = pK_b + \log \frac{[HB^+]}{[B]}$$

These equations allow us to calculate the pH of the buffer solution knowing the K_a of the weak acid and the concentrations of the weak acid and its conjugate base. Also, if the desired pH is known, along with the K_a of the weak acid, the ratio of base to acid can be calculated. The more concentrated these species are, the more acid or base can be neutralized and the less the change in buffer pH. This is a measure of the **buffer capacity,** the ability to resist a change in pH.

What is the pH of a solution containing 2.00 mol of ammonia and 3.00 mol of ammonium chloride in a volume of 1.00 L?

$$K_b = 1.81 \times 10^{-5}$$

$$NH_3 + H_2O \rightleftharpoons NH_4^+ + OH^-$$

There are two ways to solve this problem.

$$K_b = \frac{[NH_4^+][OH^-]}{[NH_3]} = \frac{(3.00 + x)(x)}{(2.00 - x)} = 1.81 \times 10^{-5}$$

Assume x small

$$1.81 \times 10^{-5} = \frac{3.00\ x}{2.00}$$

$$x = 1.21 \times 10^{-5}$$

$$pOH = 4.918$$

$$pH = 14.000 - 4.918 = 9.082$$

Alternate solution:

$$pOH = pK_b + \log \frac{[NH_4^+]}{[NH_3]}$$

$$= 4.742 + \log \frac{3.00}{2.00}$$

$$= 4.918 \qquad pH = 9.082$$

TITRATION EQUILIBRIA

An acid–base **titration** is a laboratory procedure commonly used to determine the concentration of an unknown solution. A base solution of known concentration is added to an acid solution of unknown concentration (or vice versa) until an acid–base **indicator** visually signals that the **equivalence point** of the titration has been reached. The equivalence point is the point at which a stoichiometric amount of the base has been added to the acid. This may be commonly called the **endpoint** of the titration.

If the acid being titrated is a weak acid, then there are equilibria which will be established and accounted for in the calculations. Typically, a plot of pH of the weak acid solution being titrated versus the volume of the strong base added (the **titrant**) starts at a low pH and gradually rises until close to the equivalence point, where the curve rises dramatically. After the equivalence point region, the curve returns to a gradual increase. This is shown in Figure 13.3.

In many cases, one may know the initial concentration of the weak acid, but may be interested in the pH changes during the titration. To study the changes one can divide the titration curve into four distinctive areas in which the pH is calculated.

1. Calculating the initial pH of the weak acid solution is accomplished by treating it as a simple weak acid solution of known concentration and K_a.

2. As base is added, a mixture of weak acid and conjugate base is formed. This is a buffer solution and can be treated as one in the calculations. Figure the moles of acid consumed from the moles of titrant added— that will be the moles of conjugate base formed. Then figure the molar concentration of weak acid and conjugate base taking into consideration the volume of titrant added. Finally, apply your buffer equations.

3. At the equivalence point all the weak acid has been converted to a weak base. The weak base will react with water, so treat it as a weak base solution and calculate the [OH$^-$] using the K_b. Finally, calculate the pH of the solution.

4. After the equivalence point, you have primarily the excess strong base that will determine the pH.

A 100.0 mL sample of 0.150 M nitrous acid (pK_a = 3.35) was titrated with 0.300 M sodium hydroxide. Determine the pH of the solu-

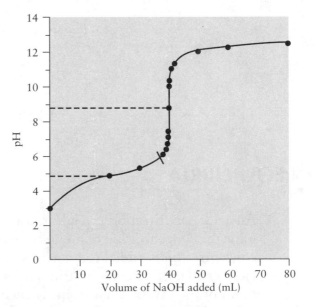

Figure 13.3 Titration of a weak acid with a strong base.

tion after the following quantities of base have been added to the acid solution:

a. 0.00 mL
b. 25.00 mL
c. 49.50 mL
d. 50.00 mL
e. 55.00 mL
f. 75.00 mL

a. 0.00 mL. Since no base has been added, only HNO_2 is present. HNO_2 is a weak acid so this can only be a K_a problem.

$$HNO_2 \rightleftharpoons H^+(aq) + NO_2^-$$
$$0.150 - x \qquad x \qquad x$$

$$K_a = 10^{-3.35} = 4.5 \times 10^{-4} = \frac{(x)\,(x)}{0.150 - x}$$

Quadratic needed: $x^2 + 4.47 \times 10^{-5}x - 6.70 \times 10^{-5} = 0$

(extra sig. figs.)

$$x = [H^+] = 8.0 \times 10^{-3}M \quad pH = 2.10$$

b. 25.00 mL. Since both an acid and a base are present (and they are not conjugates) this must be a stoichiometry problem. Stoichiometry requires a balanced chemical equation and moles.

$$HNO_2 + NaOH \rightarrow Na^+ + NO_2^- + H_2O$$

$Na^+ + NO_2^-$ this could be written as $NaNO_2$, but the separated ions are more useful.

Acid: $\dfrac{1.150 \text{ mol}}{1000 \text{ mL}}$ 100.00 mL = 0.0150 mol (This number will be used in all remaining steps.)

Base: $\dfrac{1.300 \text{ mol}}{1000 \text{ mL}}$ 25.00 mL = 0.00750 mol

Based on the stoichiometry of the problem, and on the moles of acid and base, NaOH is the limiting reagent.

	HNO_2 +	NaOH	$\longrightarrow$	Na^+ +	NO_2^- +	H_2O
init.	0.0150	0.00750 mol		0	0	
react.	−0.00750	−0.00750		+0.00750	+0.00750	
final	0.00750	0.000		-----	0.00750	

The stoichiometry part of the problem is finished.

The solution is no longer HNO_2 and $NaOH$, but HNO_2 and NO_2^- (a conjugate acid–base pair).

Since a CA/CB pair is present, this is now a buffer problem, and the Henderson-Hasselbalch equation may be used.

$$pH = pK_a + \log (CB/CA) = 3.35 + \log (0.00750/0.00750) = 3.35$$

Note the simplification in the CB/CA concentrations. Both moles are divided by exactly the same volume (since they are in the same solution), so the identical volumes cancel.

$$\frac{\dfrac{0.00750 \text{ mol base}}{0.12500 \text{ L solution}}}{\dfrac{0.00750 \text{ mol acid}}{0.12500 \text{ L solution}}}$$

c. 49.50 mL. Since both an acid and a base are present (and they are not conjugates), this must be a stoichiometry problem again. Stoichiometry requires a balanced chemical equation and moles.

$$HNO_2 + NaOH \rightarrow Na^+ + NO_2^- + H_2O$$

$$\text{Base:} \frac{0.300 \text{ mol}}{1000 \text{ mL}} \; 49.50 \text{ mL} = 0.0148 \text{ mole}$$

Based on the stoichiometry of the problem, and on the moles of acid and base, $NaOH$ is the limiting reagent.

	HNO_2 +	$NaOH$ ⟶	Na^+ +	NO_2^- + H_2O
init.	0.0150	0.0148 mol	0	0
react.	−0.0148	−0.0148	+0.0148	+ 0.0148
final	0.0002	0.000	––––	0.0148

The stoichiometry part of the problem is finished.

The solution is no longer HNO_2 and $NaOH$, but HNO_2 and NO_2^- (a conjugate acid base pair).

Since a CA/CB pair is present this is now a buffer problem, and the Henderson-Hasselbalch equation may be used.

$$pH = pK_a + \log (CB/CA) = 3.35 + \log (0.0148/0.0002) = 5.2$$

d. 50.00 mL. Since both an acid and a base are present (and they are not conjugates), this must be a stoichiometry problem. Stoichiometry requires a balanced chemical equation and moles.

$$HNO_2 + NaOH \rightarrow Na^+ + NO_2^- + H_2O$$

$$\text{Base: } \frac{0.300 \text{ mol}}{1000 \text{ mL}} \; 50.00 \text{ mL} = 0.0150 \text{ mol}$$

Based on the stoichiometry of the problem, and on the moles of acid and base, both are limiting reagent.

$$HNO_2 + NaOH \longrightarrow Na^+ + NO_2^- + H_2O$$

init.	0.0150	0.0150 mol	0	0
react.	−0.0150	−0.0150	+0.0150	+0.0150
final	0.0000	0.000	————	0.0150

$$[NO_2] = 0.0150 \text{ mol} / 0.0150 \text{ L} = 0.100 \text{ M}$$

The stoichiometry part of the problem is finished.

The solution is no longer HNO_2 and NaOH, but a NO_2^- solution (a conjugate base of a weak acid).

Since the CB of a weak acid is present this is a K_b problem.

$$pK_b = 14.000 - pK_a = 14.000 - 3.35 = 10.65$$

$$NO_2^- + H_2O \rightleftharpoons OH^- + HNO_2$$
$$0.100 - x \qquad\qquad x \qquad x$$

$$K_b = 10^{-10.65} = 2.24 \times 10^{-11} = \frac{(x)(x)}{0.100 - x} \quad \text{neglect } x$$

$$x = [OH] = 1.50 \times 10^{-6} \text{ M} \qquad pOH = 5.82$$

$$pH = 14.00 - pOH = 14.00 - 5.82 = 8.18$$

e. 55.00 mL. Since both an acid and a base are present (and they are not conjugates), this must be a stoichiometry problem. Stoichiometry requires a balanced chemical equation and moles.

$$HNO_2 + NaOH \rightarrow Na^+ + NO_2^- + H_2O$$

$$\text{Base: } \frac{0.300 \text{ mol}}{1000 \text{ mL}} \; 55.00 \text{ mL} = 0.0165 \text{ mol}$$

Based on the stoichiometry of the problem, and on the moles of acid and base, the acid is now the limiting reagent.

$$HNO_2 + NaOH \longrightarrow Na^+ + NO_2^- + H_2O$$

init.	0.0150	0.0165 mol	0	0
react.	−0.0150	−0.0150	+0.0150	+0.0150
final	0.0000	0.0015	————	0.0150

The strong base will control the pH.

$$[OH^-] = 0.0015 \text{ mol} / 0.155 \text{ L} = 9.7 \text{ x } 10^{-3} \text{ M}$$

The stoichiometry part of the problem is finished.
Since this is now a solution of a strong base, this is now a simple pOH/pH problem.

$$pOH = - 9.7 \text{ x } 10^{-3} = 2.01$$

$$pH = 14.00 - pOH = 14.00 - 2.01 = 11.99$$

f. 75.00 mL. Since both an acid and a base are present (and they are not conjugates), this must be a stoichiometry problem. Stoichiometry requires a balanced chemical equation and moles.

$$HNO_2 + NaOH \rightarrow Na^+ + NO_2^- + H_2O$$

$$\text{Base: } \frac{0.300 \text{ mol}}{1000 \text{ mL}} \, 75.00 \text{ mL} = 0.0225 \text{ mol}$$

Based on the stoichiometry of the problem, and on the moles of acid and base, the acid is now the limiting reagent.

	HNO_2	+ NaOH	$\longrightarrow$	Na^+	+ NO_2^-	+ H_2O
init.	0.0150	0.0225 mol		0	0	
react.	−0.0150	−0.0150		+0.0150	+ 0.0150	
final	0.0000	0.0075		−−−−	0.0150	

The strong base will control the pH.

$$[OH^-] = 0.0075 \text{ mol} / 0.175 \text{ L} = 4.3 \times 10^{-2} \text{ M}$$

The stoichiometry part of the problem is finished.
Since this is now a solution of a strong base, this is now a simple pOH/pH problem.

$$pOH = -\log 4.3 \times 10^{-2} = 1.37$$

$$pH = 14.00 - pOH = 14.00 - 1.37 = 12.63$$

SOLUBILITY EQUILIBRIA

Many salts are soluble in water, but some are only slightly soluble. These salts, when placed in water, quickly reach their solubility limit and the ions establish an equilibrium system with the undissolved solid. For example $PbSO_4$, when dissolved in water, establishes the following equilibrium:

$$PbSO_4(s) \rightleftharpoons Pb^{2+}(aq) + SO_4^{2-}(aq)$$

The equilibrium constant expression for systems of slightly soluble salts is called the **solubility product constant, K_{sp}**. It is the product of the ionic concentrations, each one raised to the power of the coefficient in the balanced chemical equation. It contains no denominator since the concentration of a solid is, by convention, 1 and does not appear in the equilibrium constant expressions. (Some textbooks will say that the concentrations of solids, liquids, and solvents are included in the equilibrium constant.) The K_{sp} expression for the $PbSO_4$ system would be:

$$K_{sp} = [Pb^{2+}][SO_4^{2-}]$$

For this particular salt the numerical value of the K_{sp} is 1.6×10^{-8} at $25°$ C. Note that the Pb^{2+} and SO_4^{2-} ions are formed in equal amounts, so the right-hand side of the equation could be represented as $[Pb^{2+}]^2 = [SO_4^{2-}]^2$. If the numerical value of the solubility product constant is known, then the concentration of the ions can be determined. And if one of the ion concentrations can be determined, then the K_{sp} can be calculated.

The K_{sp} of magnesium fluoride in water is 8×10^{-8}. How many grams of magnesium fluoride will dissolve in 0.250 L of water?

$$MgF_2(s) \rightleftharpoons Mg^{2+} + 2\ F^-$$

$$K_{sp} = [Mg^{2+}][F^-]^2 = 8 \times 10^{-8}$$

$$= (x)(2x)^2 = 4x^3 = 8 \times 10^{-8}$$

$$x = 3 \times 10^{-3} = [Mg^{2+}]$$

$$\frac{(3 \times 10^{-3}\ \text{mol Mg}^{2+})}{(L)} (0.250\ L) \frac{(1\ \text{mol MgF}_2)(62.3\ \text{g MgF}_2)}{(1\ \text{mol Mg}^{2+})(1\ \text{mol MgF}_2)}$$

$$= 0.05\ g$$

If a slightly soluble salt solution is at equilibrium and a solution containing one of the ions involved in the equilibrium is added, the solubility of the slightly soluble salt is decreased. For example, let's again consider the $PbSO_4$ equilibrium:

$$PbSO_4(s) \rightleftharpoons Pb^{2+}(aq) + SO_4^{2-}(aq)$$

Suppose a solution of Na_2SO_4 is added to this equilibrium system. The additional sulfate ion will disrupt the equilibrium by Le Chatelier's principle and shift it to the left, decreasing the solubility. The same would be true if you tried to dissolve $PbSO_4$ in a solution of Na_2SO_4 instead of pure water—the solubility would be less. This application of Le Chatelier's principle to equilibrium systems of slightly soluble salt is called the **common-ion effect.** Calculations like the ones above involving finding concentrations and K_{sp}'s can still be done, but the concentration of the additional common ion will have to be inserted into the solubility product constant expression. Sometimes, if the K_{sp} is very small and the common ion concentration is large, the concentration of the common ion can simply be approximated by the concentration of the ion added.

Calculate the silver ion concentration in each of the following solutions:

a. $Ag_2CrO_4(s)$ + water
b. $Ag_2CrO_4(s)$ + 1.00 M Na_2CrO_4

$K_{sp} = 1.9 \times 10^{-12}$

a. $Ag_2CrO_4(s) \rightleftharpoons 2\ Ag^+ + CrO_4^{2-}$
$2\ x \ x$

$K_{sp} = (2x)^2(x) = 1.9 \times 10^{-12} = 4x^3$

$x = 7.8 \times 10^{-5}$

$[Ag^+] = 2x = 1.6 \times 10^{-4}$ M

b. 1.00 M $Na_2CrO_4 \rightarrow$ 1.00 M CrO_4^{2-} (common ion)

$Ag_2CrO_4(s) \rightleftharpoons 2Ag^+ + CrO_4^{2-}$
$2\ x 1.00 + x$

$K_{sp} = (2x)^2(1.00 + x) = 1.9 \times 10^{-12} = 4x^2$
$\phantom{K_{sp} = (2x)^2(1.00 + x) = 1.9 \times 10^{-12} = }$ neglect x

$x = 6.9 \times 10^{-7}$

$[Ag^+] = 2\ x = 1.4 \times 10^{-6}$ M

Knowing the value of the solubility product constant can also allow us to predict whether a precipitate will form if two solutions, each containing an ion component of a slightly soluble salt, are mixed. The **ion-product,** sometimes represented as Q (same form as the solubility product constant), is calculated taking into consideration the mixing of the volumes of the two solutions, and this ion-product is compared to the K_{sp}. If it is greater than the K_{sp}, precipitation will occur until the ion concentrations have been reduced to the solubility level.

If 10.0 mL of a 0.100 M $BaCl_2$ solution is added to 40.0 mL of a 0.0250 M Na_2SO_4 solution, will $BaSO_4$ precipitate? K_{sp} for $BaSO_4 = 1.1 \times 10^{-10}$

To answer this question, the concentration of the barium ion and the sulfate ion *before* precipitation must be used. These may be determined simply from $M_{dil} = M_{con} V_{con} / V_{dil}$.

For Ba^{2+}: $M_{dil} = (0.100 \text{ M})(10.0 \text{ mL}) / (10.0 + 40.0 \text{ mL}) = 0.0200 \text{ M}$

For SO_4^{2-}: $M_{dil} = (0.0250 \text{ M})(40.0 \text{ mL}) / (50.0 \text{ mL}) = 0.0200 \text{ M}$

Plugging these values into the following relation produces:

$$Q = [Ba^{2+}][SO_4^{2-}] = (0.0200)(0.0200) = 0.000400$$

Since Q is greater than K_{sp}, precipitation will occur.

OTHER EQUILIBRIA

Other types of equilibria can be treated in much the same way as the ones discussed above. For example, there is an equilibrium constant associated with the formation of complex ions. This equilibrium constant is called the **formation constant, K_f**. $Zn(H_2O)_4^{2+}$ reacts with ammonia to form the $Zn(NH_3)_4^{2+}$ complex ion according to the following equation:

$$Zn(H_2O)_4^{2+}(aq) + 4 \, NH_3(aq) \rightleftharpoons Zn(NH_3)_4^{2+}(aq) + 4 \, H_2O(l)$$

The K_f of $Zn(NH_3)_4^{2+}(aq)$ is 7.8×10^8, indicating that the equilibrium lies to the right.

EXPERIMENTAL

Equilibrium experiments directly, or indirectly, involve filling a table like the following:

Reactants and Products

Initial amount
Change
Equilibrium amount

The initial amounts—concentrations or pressures—are normally zero for the products, and a measured or calculated value for the reactants. Once equilibrium has been established, the amount of at least one of the substances is determined. Based on the change in this one substance and the stoichiometry, the amounts of the other materials may be calculated.

Measurements may include the pressure, the mass (to be converted to moles), the volume (to be used in calculations), and the pH (to be converted into either the hydrogen ion or hydroxide ion concentration). Some experiments measure the color intensity (with a spectrophotometer), which may be converted to a concentration.

Do not make the mistake of "measuring" a change. Changes are never measured, they are always calculated.

COMMON MISTAKES TO AVOID

1. Be sure to check the units and significant figures of your final answer.
2. When writing equilibrium constant expressions use products over reactants. Each concentration is raised to the power of the coefficient in the balanced chemical equation
3. In converting from K_c to K_p be sure to use the ideal gas constant, R, whose units are consistent with the units of the partial pressures of the gases.
4. Remember, in working Le Chatelier problems, pressure effects are only important for gases that are involved in the equilibrium.
5. Be sure, when working weak-base problems, to use the K_b and not the K_a.
6. In titration problems, make sure you compensate for dilution when mixing two solutions together.
7. A K_a expression *must* have $[H^+]$ in the numerator, and a K_b expression *must* have $[OH^-]$ in the numerator.

3 REVIEW QUESTIONS

Answer the following questions in 35 minutes. You may not use a calculator.

1. A 0.1-molar solution of acetic acid (CH_3COOH) has a pH of about

   A. 1
   B. 3
   C. 7
   D. 10
   E. 14

2.

Acid	K_a, acid dissociation constant
H_3PO_4	7.2×10^{-3}
$H_2PO_4^-$	6.3×10^{-8}
HPO_4^{2-}	4.2×10^{-13}

   Using the above information, chose the best answer for preparing a pH = 8 buffer.

   A. $K_2HPO_4 + KH_2PO_4$
   B. H_3PO_4
   C. $K_2HPO_4 + K_3PO_4$
   D. K_3PO_4
   E. $K_2HPO_4 + H_3PO_4$

3. The K_a, acid dissociation constant, for an acid is 9×10^{-4} at room temperature. At this temperature, what is the approximate percent dissociation of the acid in a 1.0 M solution?

   A. 0.03%
   B. 0.09%
   C. 3%
   D. 5%
   E. 9%

Use the following information for questions 4–6.

   A. a solution with pH = 7.
   B. a solution with a pH < 7, which is not a buffer
   C. a solution with a pH < 7, which is a buffer
   D. a solution with a pH > 7, which is not a buffer

E. a solution with a pH > 7, which is a buffer

Ionization Constants:

HCOOH	$K_a = 1.8 \times 10^{-4}$
CH_3NH_2	$K_b = 4.4 \times 10^{-4}$
H_3PO_2	$K_{a1} = 3 \times 10^{-2}$
	$K_{a2} = 1.7 \times 10^{-7}$

4. A solution with an initial HCOOK concentration of 1 M, and an initial K_2HPO_2 concentration of 1 M.

5. A solution with an initial H_3PO_2 concentration of 1 M, and an initial KH_2PO_2 concentration of 1 M.

6. A solution with an initial CH_3NH_2 concentration of 1 M, and an initial CH_3NH_3Cl concentration of 1 M.

7. A solution of a weak base is titrated with a solution of a standard strong acid. The progress of the titration is followed with a pH meter. Which of the following observations would occur?

A. The pH of the solution gradually decreases throughout the experiment.
B. Initially the pH of the solution drops slowly, and then it drops much more rapidly.
C. At the equivalence point the pH is 7.
D. After the equivalence point, the pH becomes constant because this is the buffer region.
E. The pOH at the equivalence point equals the pK_b of the base.

8. What is the ionization constant, K_a, for a weak monoprotic acid if a 0.30-molar solution has a pH of 4.0?

A. 9.7×10^{-10}
B. 4.7×10^{-2}
C. 1.7×10^{-6}
D. 3.0×10^{-4}
E. 3.3×10^{-8}

9. Phenol, C_6H_5OH, has $K_a = 1.0 \times 10^{-10}$. What is the pH of a 0.010 M solution of phenol?

A. between 3 and 7
B. 10
C. 2
D. between 7 and 10
E. 7

10. You are given equimolar solutions of each of the following. Which has the lowest pH?

A. NH_4Cl
B. NaCl
C. K_3PO_4
D. Na_2CO_3
E. KNO_3

11. When sodium nitrite is dissolved in water

A. the solution is acidic because of hydrolysis of the sodium ion
B. the solution is neutral
C. the solution is basic because of hydrolysis of the sodium ion
D. the solution is acidic because of hydrolysis of the NO_2^- ion
E. the solution is basic because of hydrolysis of the NO_2^- ion

Questions 12–15 refer to the following aqueous solutions. All concentration are 1 M.

A. $H_2C_2O_4$ (oxalic acid) and KHC_2O_4 (potassium hydrogen oxalate)
B. KNO_3 (potassium nitrate) and HNO_3 (nitric acid)
C. NH_3 (ammonia) and NH_4NO_3 (ammonium nitrate)
D. $C_2H_5NH_2$ (ethylamine) and KOH (potassium hydroxide)
E. CH_3NH_2 (methylamine) and $HC_2H_3O_2$ (acetic acid)

12. The most acidic solution (lowest pH)

13. The solution with a pH nearest 7

14. A buffer with a pH > 7

15. A buffer with a pH < 7

16. Determine the OH^-(aq) concentration in 1.0 M aniline ($C_6H_5NH_2$) solution. (The K_b for aniline is 4.0×10^{-10}.)

    A. 2.0×10^{-5} M
    B. 4.0×10^{-10} M
    C. 3.0×10^{-6} M
    D. 5.0×10^{-7} M
    E. 1.0×10^0 M

17. A student wishes to reduce the zinc ion concentration in a saturated zinc iodate solution to 1×10^{-6} M. How many moles of solid KIO_3 must be added to 1.00 liter of solution? (K_{sp} $Zn(IO_3)_2$ = 4×10^{-6} at 25° C)

    A. 1 mol
    B. 0.5 mol
    C. 0.0001 mol
    D. 4 mol
    E. 2 mol

18. At constant temperature, a change in volume will NOT affect the moles of substances present in which of the following?

    A. $H_2(g) + I_2(g) \rightleftharpoons 2\,HI(g)$
    B. $CO(g) + Cl_2(g) \rightleftharpoons COCl_2(g)$
    C. $PCl_5(g) \rightleftharpoons PCl_3(g) + Cl_2(g)$
    D. $N_2(g) + 3\,H_2(g) \rightleftharpoons 2\,NH_3(g)$
    E. $CH_4(g) + CO_2(g) \rightleftharpoons 2\,CO(g)$ $+ 2\,H_2(g)$

19. The equilibrium constant for the hydrolysis of $C_2O_4^{2-}$ is best represented by which of the following?

    A. $K = [OH^-][C_2O_4^{2-}] / [HC_2O_4^-]$
    B. $K = [H_3O^+][C_2O_4^{2-}] / [HC_2O_4^-]$
    C. $K = [HC_2O_4^-][OH^-] / [C_2O_4^{2-}]$
    D. $K = [C_2O_4^{2-}] / [HC_2O_4^-][OH^-]$
    E. $K = [C_2O_4^{2-}] / [HC_2O_4^-][H_3O^+]$

20. $IO_3^- + HC_2H_3O_2 \rightleftharpoons HIO_3 + C_2H_3O_2^-$

    The above equation has an equilibrium constant that is less than 1. What are the relative strengths of the acids and bases?

	Acids	Bases
A.	$HIO_3 < HC_2H_3O_2$	$IO_3^- < C_2H_3O_2^-$
B.	$HIO_3 < HC_2H_3O_2$	$IO_3^- > C_2H_3O_2^-$
C.	$HIO_3 > HC_2H_3O_2$	$IO_3^- > C_2H_3O_2^-$
D.	$HIO_3 > HC_2H_3O_2$	$IO_3^- < C_2H_3O_2^-$
E.	$HIO_3 = HC_2H_3O_2$	$IO_3^- = C_2H_3O_2^-$

21. $ZnS(s) + 2\,H^+(aq) \rightleftharpoons Zn^{2+}(aq) + H_2S(aq)$

    What is the equilibrium constant for the above reaction? The successive acid dissociation constants for H_2S are 9.5×10^{-8} (K_{a1}) and 1×10^{-19} (K_{a2}). The K_{sp}, the solubility product constant, for ZnS equals 1.6×10^{-24}.

    A. $1.6 \times 10^{-24} / 9.5 \times 10^{-8}$
    B. $1 \times 10^{-19} / 1.6 \times 10^{-24}$
    C. $9.5 \times 10^{-27} / 1.6 \times 10^{-24}$
    D. $9.5 \times 10^{-8} / 1.6 \times 10^{-24}$
    E. $1.6 \times 10^{-24} / 9.5 \times 10^{-27}$

22. $H_2PO_4^- + H_2O \rightleftharpoons H_3O^+ + HPO_4^{2-}$

    Which species, in the above equilibrium, behave as bases?

    I. HPO_4^{2-}
    II. $H_2PO_4^-$
    III. H_2O

    A. I only
    B. I and II
    C. II and III
    D. I and III
    E. III only

23. $H_2C_3H_2O_4 + 2\,H_2O \rightleftharpoons 2\,H_3O^+ + C_3H_2O_4^{2-}$

    As shown above, malonic acid is a diprotic acid. The successive equilibrium constants are 1.5×10^{-3} (K_{a1}) and 2.0×10^{-6} (K_{a2}). What is the equilibrium constant for the above reaction?

A. 1.0×10^{-14}
B. 2.0×10^{-6}
C. 4.0×10^{-12}
D. 3.0×10^{-9}
E. 1.5×10^{-3}

24. $C(s) + H_2O(g) \rightleftharpoons CO(g) + H_2O(g)$
$$\text{endothermic}$$

An equilibrium mixture of the reactants is placed in a sealed container at 150° C. The amount of the products may be increased by which of the following changes?

I.   raising the temperature of the container
II. increasing the volume of the container
III. adding 1 mol of C(s) to the container

    A. II only
    B. I and II
    C. I only
    D. II and III
    E. III only

25. $C_2H_4(g) + 3 O_2(g) \rightleftharpoons 2 CO_2(g) + 2 H_2O(g)$

An equal number of moles of each of the reactants are sealed in a container and allowed to come to the equilibrium shown above. At equilibrium which of the following must be true?

I. $[CO_2]$ must equal $[H_2O]$
II. $[O_2]$ must be less than $[C_2H_4]$
III. $[CO_2]$ must be greater than $[C_2H_4]$

    A. II and III
    B. I only
    C. III only
    D. II only
    E. I and II

26. $CH_4(g) + CO_2(g) \rightleftharpoons 2 CO(g) + 2 H_2(g)$

A 1.00-L flask is filled with 0.30 mol of CH_4 and 0.40 mol of CO_2, and allowed to come to equilibrium. At equilibrium,

there are 0.20 mol of CO in the flask. What is the value of K_c, the equilibrium constant, for the reaction?

A. 1.2
B. 0.027
C. 0.30
D. 0.060
E. 3.0

27. $NO_2(g) \rightleftharpoons 2 NO(g) + O_2(g)$

The above materials were sealed in a flask and allowed to come to equilibrium at a certain temperature. A small quantity of $O_2(g)$ was added to the flask, and the mixture allowed to return to equilibrium at the same temperature. Which of the following has increased over its original equilibrium value?

A. the quantity of $NO_2(g)$ present
B. the quantity of NO(g) present
C. the equilibrium constant, K, increases
D. the rate of the reaction
E. the partial pressure of NO(g)

28. $2 CH_4(g) + O_2(g) \rightleftharpoons 2 CO(g) +$
$$4 H_2(g) \ \Delta H < 0$$

In order to increase the value of the equilibrium constant, K, which of the following changes must be done to the above equilibrium?

A. increase the temperature
B. increase the volume
C. decrease the temperature
D. add CO(g)
E. add a catalyst

29. $HC_3H_5O_2(aq) + HCOO^-(aq)$
$\rightleftharpoons HCOOH(aq) + C_3H_5O_2^-(aq)$

The equilibrium constant, K, for the above equilibrium is 7.2×10^{-2}. This value implies which of the following?

A. A solution with equimolar amounts of $HC_3H_5O_2(aq)$ and $HCOO^-(aq)$ is neutral.

B. $C_3H_5O_2^-$(aq) is a stronger base than HCOO⁻(aq).

C. $HC_3H_5O_2$(aq) is a stronger acid than HCOOH(aq).

D. HCOO⁻(aq) is a stronger base than $C_3H_5O_2^-$(aq).

E. The value of the equilibrium does not depend on the temperature.

30. The addition of nitric acid increases the solubility of which of the following compounds?

A. KCl(s)
B. $Pb(CN)_2$(s)

C. $Cu(NO_3)_2$(s)
D. NH_4NO_3(s)
E. $FeSO_4$(s)

31. The K_{sp} for $Mn(OH)_2$ is 1.6×10^{-13}. What is the molar solubility of this compound in water?

A. $\sqrt[3]{4.0 \times 10^{-14}}$
B. 1.6×10^{-13}
C. $\sqrt[3]{1.6 \times 10^{-13}}$
D. $\sqrt[2]{4.0 \times 10^{-14}}$
E. 4.0×10^{-14}

ANSWERS AND EXPLANATIONS

✓

1. **B.** An acid, any acid, will give a pH below 7; thus, answers C–E are eliminated. A 0.1-molar solution of a strong acid would have a pH of 1. Acetic acid is not a strong acid, so answer A is eliminated.

2. **A.** The K nearest 10^{-8} will give a pH near 8. The answer must involve the $H_2PO_4^-$ ion.

3. **C.** The generic K_a is: $K_a = [H^+][A^-]/[HA] = 9 \times 10^{-4} = x^2/1.0 - x$

    $x = 3 \times 10^{-2}$ M and the percent dissociation is $(3 \times 10^{-2}/1.0)$ $\times 100\% = 3\%$

    You will need to be able to do calculations at this level without a calculator.

4. **D.** The two substances are not a conjugate acid–base pair, so this is not a buffer. Both compounds are salts of a strong base and a weak acid; such salts are basic (pH > 7).

5. **C.** The two substances constitute a conjugate acid–base pair, so this is a buffer. The pH should be near $-\log K_{a1}$. This is about 2 (acid).

6. **E.** The two substances constitute a conjugate acid–base pair, so this is a buffer. The pOH should be near $-\log K_b$. This is about 4. The pH would be about $14 - 4 = 10$.

7. **B.** Any time an acid is added, the pH will drop. The reaction of the weak base with the acid produces the conjugate acid of the weak base. The combination of the weak base and its conjugate is a buffer, so the pH will not change very much until all the base is used. After all the base has reacted, the pH will drop much more rapidly. The equivalence point of a weak base–strong acid titration is always below 7 (only strong base–strong acid titrations will give a pH of 7

at the equivalence point). The value of pOH is equal to pK_b half-way to the equivalence point.

8. **E.** If pH = 4.0, then $[H^+] = 1 \times 10^{-4} = [A^-]$, and $[HA] = 0.30 - 1 \times 10^{-4}$. The generic K_a is $[H^+][A^-]/[HA]$, and when the values are plugged into this equation: $(1 \times 10^{-4})^2/0.30 = 3.3 \times 10^{-8}$.

9. **A.** This is an acid-dissociation constant, thus the solution must be acidic (pH < 7). The pH of a 0.010 M strong acid would be 2.0. This is not a strong acid, thus, the pH must be above 2.

10. **A.** A is the salt of a strong acid and a weak base; it is acidic. B and E are salts of a strong acid and a strong base; they are neutral. C and D are salts of a weak acid and a strong base; they are basic. The lowest pH would be the acidic choice.

11. **E.** Sodium nitrite is a salt of a weak acid and a strong base. Ions from strong bases, Na^+ in this case, do not undergo hydrolysis, and do not affect the pH. Ions from weak acids, NO_2^- in this case, undergo hydrolysis to produce basic solutions.

12. **B.** The presence of a strong acid, HNO_3, would make this the most acidic (lowest pH).

13. **E.** The weak acid and the weak base partially cancel each other to give a nearly neutral solution.

14. **C.** Both A and C are buffers because they have conjugate acid–base pairs of either a weak acid (A) or a weak base (C). The weak acid buffer would have a pH below 7, and the weak base buffer would have a pH above 7.

15. **A.** See the answer to question 14.

16. **A.** The equilibrium constant expression is: $K_b = 4.0 \times 10^{-10} = [OH^-][C_6H_5NH_3^+]/[C_6H_5NH_2]$. This expression becomes: $(x)(x)/(1.0-x) = 4.0 \times 10^{-10}$, which simplifies to: $x^2/1.0 = 4.0 \times 10^{-10}$. Taking the square root of each side gives: $x = 2.0 \times 10^{-5} = [OH^-]$.

17. **E.** The solubility-product constant expression is: $K_{sp} = [Zn^{2+}][IO_3^-]^2 = 4 \times 10^{-6}$. This may be rearranged to: $[IO_3^-]^2 = 4 \times 10^{-6}/[Zn^{2+}]$. Plugging in the desired zinc ion concentration gives: $[IO_3^-]^2 = 4 \times 10^{-6}/(1 \times 10^{-6}) = 4$. Taking the square root of each side leaves a desired IO_3^- concentration of 2 M. 2 mol of KIO_3 must be added to 1.00 L of solution to produce this concentration.

18. **A.** When dealing with gaseous equilibria, volume changes are important when there is a difference in the total number of moles of gas on opposite sides of the equilibrium arrow. All the answers, except A, have differing numbers of moles of gas on opposite sides of the equilibrium arrow.

19. **C.** Hydrolysis of any ion begins with the interaction of that ion with water. Thus, both the ion and water must be on the left side of the

equilibrium arrow, and hence in the denominator of the equilibrium constant expression (water, as all solvents, will be left out of the expression). The oxalate ion is the conjugate base of a weak acid. As a base it will produce OH^- in solution along with the conjugate acid ($HC_2O_4^-$) of the base. The equilibrium reaction is: $C_2O_4^{2-}(aq) + H_2O(l) \rightleftharpoons OH^-(aq) + HC_2O_4^-(aq)$.

20. **D.** The low value for the equilibrium constant means that the equilibrium lies to the left. For this to be true, the weaker acid and the weaker base must be on the left side.

21. **E.** The equilibrium given is actually the sum of the following three equilibria:

$ZnS(s) \rightleftharpoons Zn^{2+}(aq) + S^{2-}(aq)$ $K_{sp} = 1.6 \times 10^{-24}$

$S^{2-}(aq) + H^+(aq) \rightleftharpoons HS^-(aq)$ $K = 1/K_{a2} = 1/1 \times 10^{-19}$

$HS^-(aq) + H^+(aq) \rightleftharpoons H_2S(aq)$ $K' = 1/K_{a1} = 1/9.5 \times 10^{-8}$

Summing these equations means you need to multiply the equilibrium constants:

$K_{sum} = K_{sp}KK' = K_{sp}/K_{a2}K_{a1} = 1.6 \times 10^{-24} / [(1 \times 10^{-19})(9.5 \times 10^{-8})]$

22. **D.** As the reaction moves to the left, the H_2O behaves as a base (accepts H^+). When the reaction moves to the right, HPO_4^{2-} behaves as a base.

23. **D.** The equilibrium constant for the two successive ionizations will be the product of the two equilibrium constants given. Thus, $K = K_{a1}K_{a2} = (1.5 \times 10^{-3})(2.0 \times 10^{-6})$.

24. **B.** The addition or removal of some solid, as long as there is some present, will not change the equilibrium. An increase in volume will cause the equilibrium to shift towards the side with more moles of gas (right). Raising the temperature of an endothermic process will shift the equilibrium to the right. Any shift to the right will increase the amounts of the products.

25. **E.** Assuming 1 mol of each reactant is used, the equilibrium quantities would be: $[C_2H_4] = 1 - x$, $[O_2] = 1 - 3x$, $[CO_2] = 2x$, and $[H_2] = 2x$. Unless the value of x is known, it is not possible to relate the actual concentrations of any reactant to any product.

26. **B.** Using the following table:

	[CH₄]	[CO₂]	[CO]	[H₂]
Initial	0.30	0.40	0	0
Change	− x	− x	+ 2 x	+ 2 x
Equilibrium	0.30 − x	0.40 − x	2 x	2 x

The presence of 0.20 mol of CO (0.20 M) at equilibrium means that $2x = 0.20$ and that $x = 0.10$. Using this value for x the bottom line of the table becomes:

	$[CH_4]$	$[CO_2]$	$[CO]$	$[H_2]$
Equilibrium	0.20	0.30	0.20	0.20

The equilibrium expression is: $K = [CO]^2[H_2]^2/[CH_4][CO_2]$. Plugging the equilibrium values into the equilibrium expression gives: $K = (0.20)^2(0.20)^2 / (0.20)(0.30)$

27. **A.** The addition of a product will cause the equilibrium to shift to the left. The amounts of all the reactants will increase, and the amounts of all the products will decrease (the O_2 will not go below its earlier equilibrium value since excess was added). The value of K is constant, unless the temperature is changed. The rates of the forward and reverse reactions are equal at equilibrium.

28. **C.** The only way to change the value of K is to change the temperature. For an exothermic process ($\Delta H < 0$), K is increased by a decrease in temperature.

29. **B.** The low value of K means that the equilibrium lies to the left. The equilibrium always lies away from the stronger acid and the stronger base.

30. **B.** Nitric acid, being an acid, will react with a base. In addition to obvious bases containing OH^-, the salts of weak acids are also bases. All of the anions, except CN^-, are from strong acids.

31. **A.** The equilibrium constant expression for the dissolving of manganese(II) hydroxide is:

$$K_{sp} = [Mn^{2+}][OH^-]^2 = 1.6 \times 10^{-13}$$

If s is used to indicate the molar solubility, the equilibrium express becomes:

$$K_{sp} = (s)(2s)^2 = 4 s^3 = 1.6 \times 10^{-13}$$

This rearranges to:

$$s = \sqrt[3]{K/4}$$

FREE-RESPONSE QUESTIONS

You have 15 minutes. You may use a calculator.

$$CdI_4^{2-}(aq) \rightleftharpoons Cd^{2+}(aq) + 4 I^-(aq)$$

An aqueous solution is prepared that is initially 0.100 M in CdI_4^{2-}. After equilibrium is established, the solution is found to be 0.013 M in Cd^{2+}.

a. Derive the expression for the dissociation constant, K_d, and determine the value of the constant.

b. What will be the cadmium ion concentration arising when 0.400 mol of KI is added to 1.00 L of the solution in part a?

c. A solution is prepared by mixing 0.500 L of the solution from part b and 0.500 L of 2.0×10^{-5} M NaOH. Will cadmium hydroxide, $Cd(OH)_2$, precipitate? The K_{sp} for cadmium hydroxide is 2.2×10^{-14}.

d. When the initial solution is heated the cadmium ion concentration increases. Is the equilibrium an exothermic or an endothermic process? Explain how you arrived at your conclusion.

ANSWERS AND EXPLANATIONS

✓

a. $K_d = [Cd^{2+}][I^-]^4 / [CdI_4^{2-}]$ Give yourself 1 point for this expression.

Using the following table:

	CdI_4^{2-}(aq)	Cd^{2+}(aq)	I^-(aq)
Initial	0.100 M	0	0
Change	$-x$	$+x$	$+4x$
Equilibrium	$0.100 - x$	x	$4x$

The value of $[Cd^{2+}]$ is given ($= 0.013$), and this is x. This changes the last line of the table to:

	CdI_4^{2-}(aq)	Cd^{2+}(aq)	I^-(aq)
Equilibrium	$0.100 - x = 0.087\ x$	$= 0.013$	$4x = 0.052$

Plugging these values into the K_d expression gives: $(0.013)(0.052)^4 / (0.087) = 1.1 \times 10^{-6}$.

Give yourself 1 point for this answer. You can also get 1 point if you correctly plug your values into the wrong equation.

b. The table in part a changes to the following:

	CdI_4^{2-}(aq)	Cd^{2+}(aq)	I^-(aq)
Initial	0.100 M	0	0.400
Change	$-x$	$+x$	$+4x$
Equilibrium	$0.100 - x$	x	$0.400 + 4x$

$$K_d = [Cd^{2+}][I^-]^4/[CdI_4^{2-}] = 1.1 \times 10^{-6} = (x)(0.400 + 4x)^4/(0.100 - x)$$

$$= (x)(0.400)^4/(0.100)$$

$$x = 4.3 \times 10^{-6}\ M = [Cd^{2+}]$$

Give yourself 1 point for the correct setup and 1 point for the correct answer.

c. The equilibrium is $Cd(OH)_2 \rightleftharpoons Cd^{2+}(aq) + 2\ OH^-(aq)$

The dilution reduces both the Cd^{2+} and OH^- concentration by a factor of 2. This gives:

$[Cd^{2+}] = 4.3 \times 10^{-6} / 2 = 2.2 \times 10^{-6}$ and $[OH^-] = 2.0 \times 10^{-5} / 2 = 1.0 \times 10^{-5}$

The reaction quotient is: $Q = [Cd^{2+}][OH^-]^2 = (2.2 \times 10^{-6})(1.0 \times 10^{-5})^2$
$$= 2.2 \times 10^{-16}$$

This value is less than the K_{sp}, so no precipitate will form.

Give yourself 1 point for a correct calculation, and another point for the correct conclusion.

d. Since the cadmium ion concentration increases, the equilibrium must shift to the right. Endothermic processes shift to the right when they are heated. This is in accordance to Le Chatelier's principle.

Give yourself 1 point for endothermic. Give yourself 1 point for mentioning Le Chatelier's principle.

Your score is based on a total of 8 points.

RAPID REVIEW

- A chemical equilibrium is established when two exactly opposite reactions occur at the same place, the same time, and the same rates of reaction.

- At equilibrium the concentration of the chemical species become **constant,** but not necessarily equal.

- For the reaction $aA + bB \rightleftharpoons cC = dD$, the equilibrium constant expression would be: $K_c = \dfrac{[C]^c[D]^d}{[A]^a[B]^b}$. Know how to apply this equation.

- Le Chatelier's principle says that if an equilibrium system is stressed, it will reestablish equilibrium by shifting the reactions involved. A change in concentration of a species will cause the equilibrium to shift to reverse that change. A change in pressure or temperature will cause the equilibrium to shift to reverse that change.

- Strong acids completely dissociate in water, whereas weak acids only partially dissociate.

- Weak acids and bases establish an equilibrium system.

- Under the Brønsted-Lowery acid–base theory, acids are proton (H^+) donors and bases are proton acceptors.

- Conjugate acid–base pairs differ only in a single H^+; the one that has the extra H^+ is the acid.

- The equilibrium for a weak acid is described by the K_a, the acid dissociation constant. It has the form: $K_a = \dfrac{[H_3O^+][A^-]}{[HA]}$. Know how to apply this equation.

- Most times the equilibrium concentration of the weak acid, $[HA]$, can be approximated by the initial molarity of the weak acid.

- Knowing the K_a and the initial concentration of the weak acid allows the calculation of the $[H^+]$.

- Water is an amphoteric substance, acting either as an acid or a base.

- The product of the $[H^+]$ and $[OH^-]$ in a solution or in pure water is a constant, K_w, called the water dissociation constant, 1.00×10^{-14}. $K_w = [H^+][OH^-] = 1.00 \times 10^{-14}$ at $25°$ C. Know how to apply this equation.

- The pH is a measure of the acidity of a solution. $pH = -\log[H^+]$. Know how to apply this equation.

- On the pH scale 7 is neutral; pH > 7 is basic; and pH < 7 is acidic.

- $pH + pOH = pK_w = 14.00$. Know how to apply this equation.

- The K_b is the ionization constant for a weak base. $K_b = \dfrac{[HB^+][OH^-]}{[HB]}$. Know how to apply this equation.

- $K_a \times K_b = K_w$ for conjugate acid–base pairs. Know how to apply this equation.

- Buffers are solutions that resist a change in pH by neutralizing either an added acid or an added base.

- The Henderson-Hasselbalch equation allows the calculation of the pH of a buffer solution: $pH = pK_a + \log \dfrac{[A^-]}{[HA]}$. Know how to apply this equation.

- The buffer capacity is a quantitative measure of the ability of a buffer to resist a change in pH. The more concentrated the acid–base components of the buffer, the higher its buffer capacity.

- A titration is a laboratory technique to determine the concentration of an acid or base solution.

- An acid–base indicator is used in a titration and changes color in the presence of an acid or base.

- The equivalence point or endpoint of a titration is the point at which an equivalent amount of acid or base has been added to the base or acid being neutralized.

- Know how to determine the pH at any point of an acid–base titration.

- The solubility product constant, K_{sp}, is the equilibrium constant expression for sparingly soluble salts. It is the product of the ionic concentration of the ions, each raised to the power of the coefficient of the balanced chemical equation.

- Know how to apply ion-products and K_{sp} values to predict precipitation.

- Formation constants describe complex ion equilibria.

Chapter 14

Electrochemistry

KEYWORDS AND EQUATIONS

✓ A table of half-reactions is given in the exam booklet.

I = current (amperes) q = charge (coulombs)

E° = standard reduction potential K = equilibrium constant

1 faraday (F) = 96,500 coulombs (C)

Faraday's constant, F = 96,500 coulombs per mole of electrons

$$I = q/t \qquad \log K = \frac{nE°}{0.0592}$$

$$E_{cell} = E°_{cell} - \left(\frac{RT}{nF}\right) \ln Q = E°_{cell} - \left(\frac{0.0592}{n}\right) \log Q \text{ at } 25°C$$

INTRODUCTION

Electrochemistry is the study of chemical reactions that produce electricity and chemical reactions that take place because electricity is supplied. Electrochemical reactions may be of many types. Electroplating is an electrochemical process. So are the electrolysis of water, the production of aluminum metal, and the production and storage of electricity in batteries. All these processes involve the transfer of electrons and redox reactions.

REDOX REACTIONS

Electrochemical reactions involve redox reactions. In Chapter 4 we discussed redox reactions, but here is a brief review: Redox is a term that stands for reduction and oxidation. Reduction is the gain of electrons, and oxidation is the loss of electrons. For example, suppose a piece of zinc metal is placed in a solution containing the Cu^{2+} cation. Very quickly, a reddish solid forms on the surface of the zinc metal. That substance is copper metal. At the molecular level the zinc metal is losing electrons to form the Zn^{2+} cation and the Cu^{2+} ion is gaining electrons to form copper metal. These two processes can be shown as:

$$Zn \rightarrow Zn^{2+}(aq) + 2e^- \qquad \text{(oxidation)}$$
$$Cu^{2+}(aq) + 2e^- \rightarrow Cu \qquad \text{(reduction)}$$

The electrons that are being lost by the zinc metal are the same electrons that are being gained by the cupric cation. The zinc metal is being oxidized, and the cupric ion is being reduced.

Something must cause the oxidation (taking of the electrons), and that substance is called the oxidizing agent (the reactant being reduced). In the example above, the oxidizing agent is the Cu^{2+} ion. The reactant undergoing oxidation is called the reducing agent because it is furnishing the electrons used in the reduction half-reaction. Zinc metal is the reducing agent above. The two half-reactions, oxidation and reduction, can be added together to give you the overall redox reaction. The electrons must cancel—that is, there must be the same number of electrons lost as electrons gained:

$$Zn + Cu^{2+}(aq) + 2e^- \rightarrow Zn^{2+}(aq) + 2e^- + Cu \qquad \text{or}$$
$$Zn + Cu^{2+}(aq) \rightarrow Zn^{2+}(aq) + Cu$$

In these redox reactions, like the electrochemical reactions we will show you, there is a simultaneous loss and gain of electrons. In the oxidation reaction (commonly called a half-reaction) electrons are being lost, but in the reduction half-reaction those very same electrons are being gained. So, in redox reactions electrons are being exchanged as reactants are being converted into products. This electron exchange may be direct, as when copper metal plates out on a piece of zinc, or it may be indirect, as in an electrochemical cell (battery). In this chapter we will show you both processes and the calculations associated with each.

The complete balancing of redox reactions has never appeared on the AP exam, but we have included the half-reaction method of balancing redox reaction in the Appendix, just in case you are having trouble with the technique in your chemistry class.

The definitions for oxidation and reduction given above are the most common and the most useful ones. A couple of others might also be useful: Oxidation is the gain of oxygen or loss of hydrogen and involves an increase in oxidation number. Reduction is the gain of hydrogen or loss of oxygen and involves a decrease in oxidation number.

ELECTROCHEMICAL CELLS

In the example above, the electron transfer was direct, that is, the electrons were exchanged directly from the zinc metal to the cupric ions. But such a direct electron transfer doesn't allow for any useful work to be done by the electrons. Therefore, in order to use these electrons, indirect electron transfer must be done. The two half-reactions are physically separated and connected by a wire. The electrons that are lost in the oxidation half-reaction are allowed to flow through the wire to get to the reduction half-reaction. While those electrons are flowing through the wire they can do useful work, like powering a calculator or a pacemaker. **Electrochemical cells** use indirect electron transfer to produce electricity by a redox reaction, or they use electricity to produce a desired redox reaction.

Galvanic (Voltaic) Cells

Galvanic (voltaic) cells produce electricity by using a redox reaction. Let's take that zinc/copper redox reaction that we studied before (the direct electron transfer reaction) and make it a galvanic cell by separating the oxidation and reduction half-reactions. (See Figure 14.1)

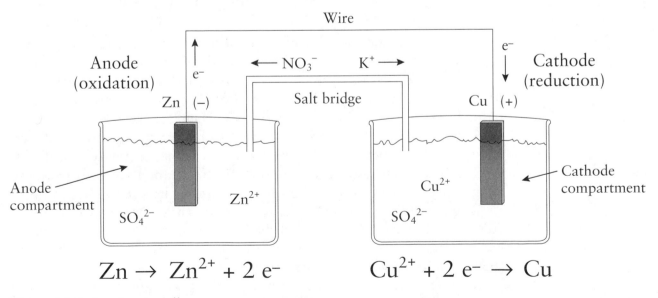

Figure 14.1 A galvanic cell.

Instead of one container, as before, two will be used. A piece of zinc metal will be placed in one, a piece of copper metal in another. A solution of aqueous zinc sulfate will be added to the beaker containing the zinc electrode and an aqueous solution of copper(II) sulfate will be added to the beaker containing the copper metal. The zinc and copper metals will form the **electrodes** of the cell, the solid portion of the cell that conducts the electrons involved in the redox reaction. The solutions in which the electrodes are immersed are called the **electrode compartments.** The electrodes are connected by a wire and . . . nothing happens. If the redox reactions were to proceed, the beaker containing the zinc metal would build up a positive charge due to the zinc cations being produced in the oxidation half-reaction. The beaker containing the copper would build up a negative charge due to the loss of the copper(II) ions. The solutions (compartments) must maintain electrical neutrality. To accomplish this, a salt bridge will be used. A **salt bridge** is often an inverted U tube that holds a gel containing a concentrated electrolyte solution, such as KNO_3 in this example. Any electrolyte could be used as long as it is not reactive in the redox reaction. The anions in the salt bridge will migrate through the gel into the beaker containing the zinc metal, and the salt-bridge cations will migrate in the opposite direction. In this way electrical neutrality is maintained. In electrical terms, the circuit has been completed and the redox reaction can occur. The zinc electrode is being oxidized in one beaker and the copper(II) ions in the other beaker are being reduced to copper metal. The same redox reaction is happening in this indirect electron transfer as happened in the direct one:

$$Zn + Cu^{2+}(aq) \rightarrow Zn^{2+}(aq) + Cu$$

The difference is that the electrons are now flowing through a wire from the oxidation half-reaction to the reduction half-reaction. And electrons flowing through a wire is electricity, which can do work. If a voltmeter was connected to the wire connecting the two electrodes, a current of 1.10 V would be measured. This galvanic cell shown in Figure 14.1 is commonly called a Daniell cell.

In the Daniell cell shown in Figure 14.1, note that the compartment with the oxidation half-reaction is on the left and the compartment undergoing reduction is on the right. This is a convention that you will have to follow. The AP graders look for this. The electrode at which oxidation is taking place is called the **anode,** and the electrolyte solution in which it is immersed is called the **anode compartment.** The electrode at which reduction takes place is called the **cathode,** and its solution is the **cathode compartment.** The anode is labeled with a negative sign (−), while the cathode has a positive sign (+). The electrons flow from the anode to the cathode.

Remember: Oxidation is an anode process.

Sometimes the half-reaction(s) involved in the cell lack a solid conductive part to act as the electrode, so an **inert (inactive) electrode,** a solid conducting electrode that does not take part in the redox reaction, is used. Graphite and platinum are commonly used as inert electrodes.

Cell Notation

Cell notation is a shorthand notation representing a galvanic cell. To write the cell notation in Figure 14.1:

1. Write the chemical formula of the anode: **Zn(s)**
2. Draw a single vertical line to represent the phase boundary between the anode and the anode compartment: **Zn(s)|**
3. Write the reactive part of the anode compartment with its initial concentration (if known) in parenthesis (assume 1 M in this case): **Zn(s) | Zn²⁺(1 M)**
4. Draw a double vertical line to represent the salt bridge connecting the two electrode compartments: **Zn(s) | Zn²⁺(1 M) ||**
5. Write the reactive part of the cathode compartment with its initial concentration (if known) shown in parentheses: **Zn(s)| Zn²⁺(1 M)|| Cu²⁺(1 M)**
6. Draw a single vertical line representing the phase boundary between the cathode compartment and the cathode: **Zn(s)| Zn²⁺ (1 M)|| Cu²⁺(1 M) |**
7. Finally, write the chemical formula of the cathode: **Zn(s)| Zn²⁺(1 M)|| Cu²⁺(1 M)| Cu(s)**

If an inert electrode is used because one or both redox half-reactions do not have solid associated with the reaction, the inert electrode is shown with its phase boundary. If the electrode components are in the same phase, they are separated by commas; if not, a vertical phase boundary line. For example, consider the following redox reaction:

$$Ag^{+}(aq) + Fe^{2+}(aq) \rightarrow Fe^{3+}(aq) + Ag(s)$$

The oxidation of the ferrous ion to ferric doesn't involve a solid, so an inert electrode, such as platinum, would be used. The cell notation would then be:

$$Pt(s)|Fe^{2+}(aq), Fe^{3+}(aq)\|Ag^{+}(aq)|Ag(s)$$

Cell Potential

In the discussion of the Daniell cell we indicated that this cell produces 1.10 volts. This voltage is really the difference in potential between the two half-cells. There are half-cell potentials associated with many half-cells. A list of all possible combinations of half-cells would be tremendously long. Therefore, a way of combining desired half-cells has been developed. The cell potential (really the half-cell potentials) depends on concentration and temperature, but initially we'll simply look at the half-cell potentials at standard state of 298 K (25° C) and all components in their standard states (1 M concentration of all solutions, 1 atmosphere pressure for any gases, and pure solid electrodes). All the half-cell potentials are tabulated as the reduction potentials, that is, the potentials associated with the reduction reaction. The hydrogen half-reaction has been defined as the standard and has been given a value of exactly 0.00 V. All the other half-reactions have been measured relative to it, some positive and some negative. The table of **standard reduction potentials** provided on the AP exam is shown in Table 14.1.

Here are some things to be aware of in looking at this table:

- All reactions are shown in terms of the reduction reaction relative to the standard hydrogen electrode.
- The more positive the value of the voltage associated with the half-reaction (E°), the more readily the reaction occurs.
- The strength of the oxidizing agent increases as the value becomes more positive, and the strength of the reducing agent increases as the value becomes more negative.

This table of standard reduction potentials can be used to write the overall cell reaction and to calculate the **standard cell potential,** the potential (voltage) associated with the cell at standard conditions. There are a few things to remember when using these standard reduction potentials to generate the cell reaction and cell potential:

1. Because the standard cell potential is for the galvanic cell, it must be a positive value, E° > 0.
2. Because one half-reaction must involve oxidation, one of the half-reactions shown in the table of reduction potentials must be reversed to indicate the oxidation. If the half-reaction is reversed, the sign of the standard reduction potential must be reversed. However, this is not necessary to calculate the standard cell potential.
3. Because oxidation occurs at the anode and reduction at the cathode, the standard cell potential can be calculated from the standard reduction potentials of the two half-reactions involved in the overall reaction by using the equation:

$$E^{\circ}_{cell} = E^{\circ}_{cathode} - E^{\circ}_{anode} > 0$$

But remember, both the $E^{\circ}_{cathode}$ and E°_{anode} are shown as reduction potentials, used directly from the table without reversing.

Once the standard cell potential has been calculated, the reaction can be written by reversing the half-reaction associated with the anode and adding the half-reactions together, using appropriate multipliers if needed to ensure that the number of electrons lost and gained are equal.

Table 14.1 Standard Reduction Potentials in Aqueous Solution at 25°C

Half-reaction			$E°(V)$
$Li^+ + e^-$	$\rightarrow$	$Li(s)$	-3.05
$Cs^+ + e^-$	$\rightarrow$	$Cs(s)$	-2.92
$K^+ + e^-$	$\rightarrow$	$K(s)$	-2.92
$Rb^+ + e^-$	$\rightarrow$	$Rb(s)$	-2.92
$Ba^{2+} + 2\,e^-$	$\rightarrow$	$Ba(s)$	-2.90
$Sr^{2+} + 2\,e^-$	$\rightarrow$	$Sr(s)$	-2.89
$Ca^{2+} + 2\,e^-$	$\rightarrow$	$Ca(s)$	-2.87
$Na^+ + e^-$	$\rightarrow$	$Na(s)$	-2.71
$Mg^{2+} + 2\,e^-$	$\rightarrow$	$Mg(s)$	-2.37
$Be^{2+} + 2\,e^-$	$\rightarrow$	$Be(s)$	-1.70
$Al^{3+} + 3\,e^-$	$\rightarrow$	$Al(s)$	-1.66
$Mn^{2+} + 2\,e^-$	$\rightarrow$	$Mn(s)$	-1.18
$Zn^{2+} + 2\,e^-$	$\rightarrow$	$Zn(s)$	-0.76
$Cr^{3+} + 3\,e^-$	$\rightarrow$	$Cr(s)$	-0.74
$Fe^{2+} + 2\,e^-$	$\rightarrow$	$Fe(s)$	-0.44
$Cr^{3+} + e^-$	$\rightarrow$	Cr^{2+}	-0.41
$Cd^{2+} + 2\,e^-$	$\rightarrow$	$Ce(s)$	-0.40
$Tl^+ + e^-$	$\rightarrow$	$Tl(s)$	-0.34
$Co^{2+} + 2\,e^-$	$\rightarrow$	$Co(s)$	-0.28
$Ni^{2+} + 2\,e^-$	$\rightarrow$	$Ni(s)$	-0.25
$Sn^{2+} + 2\,e^-$	$\rightarrow$	$Sn(s)$	-0.14
$Pb^{2+} + 2\,e^-$	$\rightarrow$	$Pb(s)$	-0.13
$2\,H^+ + 2\,e^-$	$\rightarrow$	$H_2(g)$	0.00
$S(s) + 2\,H^+ + 2\,e^-$	$\rightarrow$	$H_2S(g)$	0.14
$Sn^{4+} + 2\,e^-$	$\rightarrow$	Sn^{2+}	0.15
$Cu^{2+} + e^-$	$\rightarrow$	Cu^+	0.15
$Cu^{2+} + 2\,e^-$	$\rightarrow$	$Cu(s)$	0.34
$Cu^+ + e^-$	$\rightarrow$	$Cu(s)$	0.52
$I_2(s) + 2\,e^-$	$\rightarrow$	$2\,I^-$	0.53
$Fe^{3+} + e^-$	$\rightarrow$	Fe^{2+}	0.77
$Hg_2^{2+} + 2\,e^-$	$\rightarrow$	$2\,Hg(l)$	0.79
$Ag^+ + e^-$	$\rightarrow$	$Ag(s)$	0.80
$Hg^{2+} + 2\,e^-$	$\rightarrow$	$Hg(l)$	0.85
$2\,Hg^{2+} + 2\,e^-$	$\rightarrow$	Hg_2^{2+}	0.92
$Br_2(l) + 2\,e^-$	$\rightarrow$	$2\,Br^-$	1.07
$O_2(g) + 4\,H^+ + 4\,e^-$	$\rightarrow$	$2\,H_2O(l)$	1.23
$Cl_2(g) + 2\,e^-$	$\rightarrow$	$2\,Cl^-$	1.36
$Au^{3+} + 3\,e^-$	$\rightarrow$	$Au(s)$	1.50
$Co^{3+} + e^-$	$\rightarrow$	Co^{2+}	1.82
$F_2(g) + 2\,e^-$	$\rightarrow$	$2\,F^-$	2.87

Suppose a galvanic cell was to be constructed utilizing the following two half-reactions taken from Table 14.1:

$$Ni^{2+} + 2e^- \rightarrow Ni(s) \qquad E° = -0.25 \text{ V}$$

$$Ag^+ + e^- \rightarrow Ag(s) \qquad E° = 0.80 \text{ V}$$

First, the cell voltage can be calculated using:

$$E°_{cell} = E°_{cathode} - E°_{anode} > 0$$

Since the cell potential must be positive (a galvanic cell) there is only one arrangement of −0.25 and 0.80 volts than can result in a positive value:

$$E°_{cell} = 0.80 \text{ v} - (-0.25 \text{ v}) = 1.05 \text{ V}$$

This means that the Ni electrode is the anode and must be involved in oxidation, so the reduction half-reaction can be reversed, changing the sign of the standard half-cell potential and added to the silver half-reaction. **Note that the silver half-reaction must be multiplied by two to equalize electron loss and gain, but the half-cell potential is not:**

$$Ni(s) \rightarrow Ni^{2+} + 2e^- \qquad\qquad E° = 0.25 \text{ V}$$

$$2 \times (Ag^+ + e^- \rightarrow Ag(s)) \qquad\qquad E° = 0.80 \text{ V}$$

$$\overline{Ni(s) + 2Ag^+ \rightarrow Ni^{2+} + Ag(s) \qquad E°_{cell} = 1.05 \text{ V}}$$

Note that the same cell potential is obtained as using the: $E°_{cell} = E°_{cathode} - E°_{anode} > 0$

If, for example, you are given the cell notation, you could use this method to determine the cell potential.

Electrolytic Cells

Electrolytic cells use electricity from an external source to produce a desired redox reaction. Electroplating and the recharging of an automobile battery are examples of electrolytic cells.

Figure 14.2 shows a comparison of a galvanic and electrolytic cell for the Sn/Cu system.

On the left-hand side of Figure 14.2, the galvanic cell is shown for this system. Note that this reaction produces 0.48 V. But what if we wanted the reverse reaction to occur, the nonspontaneous reaction? This can be accomplished by applying a voltage in excess of 0.48 V from an external electrical source. This is shown on the right-hand side of Figure 14.2. In this electrolytic cell, electricity is being used to produce the nonspontaneous redox reaction.

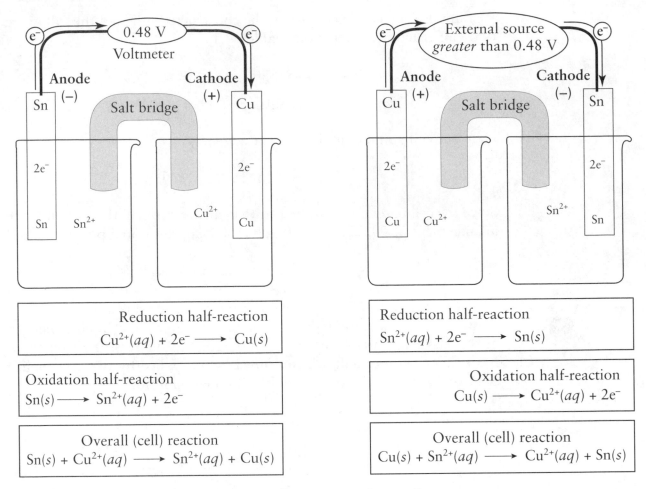

Figure 14.2 Comparison of a galvanic cell and an electrolytic cell.

QUANTITATIVE ASPECTS OF ELECTROCHEMISTRY

One of the most widely used applications of electrolytic cells is in **electrolysis,** the decomposition of a compound. Water may be decomposed into hydrogen and oxygen. Aluminum salts may be electrolyzed to produce aluminum metal. In these situations, several questions may be asked: *How long* will it take; *how much* can be produced; *what current* must be used? Given any two of these quantities, the third may be calculated. To answer these questions, the balanced half-reaction must be known. Then the following relationships can be applied:

$$1 \text{ Faraday} = 96,500 \text{ coulombs per mole of electron}$$
$$(F = 96,500 \text{ C/mol e}^-)$$

$$1 \text{ ampere} = 1 \text{ coulomb/second } (A = C/s)$$

Knowing the amperage and how long it is being applied (seconds), the coulombs can be calculated. Then the coulombs can be converted into moles of electrons, and the moles of electrons can be related to the moles (and then grams) of material being electrolyzed through the balanced half-reaction.

If liquid titanium(IV) chloride (acidified with HCl) is electrolyzed by a current of 1.000 amp for 2.000 h, how many grams of titanium will be produced?

Answer:

$$TiCl_4 \rightarrow Ti + 2\,Cl_2 \text{ (not necessary)}$$

$$Ti^{4+} + 4\,e^- \rightarrow Ti \text{ (necessary)}$$

$$(2.000 \text{ h}) \frac{(3600 \text{ s})(1.000 \text{ C})(1 \text{ mol } e^-)}{(h)\quad\quad (s)} \frac{(1 \text{ mol Ti})(47.90 \text{ g Ti})}{(96485 \text{ C})(4 \text{ mol } e^-)(\text{mol Ti})}$$

$$= 0.8936 \text{ g Ti}$$

Calculation of the $E°_{cell}$ also allows for the calculation of two other useful quantities—the Gibbs free energy ($\Delta G°$) and the equilibrium constant (K).

The Gibbs free energy is the best thermodynamic indicator of whether a reaction will be spontaneous (Review Chapter 7 on thermodynamics). The Gibbs free energy for a reaction can be calculated from the $E°$ of the reaction using the following equation:

$$\Delta G° = -nFE°_{cell}$$

where F is Faraday's constant of 96,500 C/mol e^- = 96,500 J/V.

If the redox reaction is at equilibrium, the equilibrium constant may be calculated by:

$$E°_{cell} = \frac{0.0592 \text{ V}}{n} \log K \quad \text{or} \quad \log K = \frac{nE°_{cell}}{0.0592 \text{ V}}$$

Determine $\Delta G°$ and K for the following reaction:

$$Ni(s) + 2Ag^+ \rightarrow Ni^{2+} + Ag(s) \quad E°_{cell} = 1.05 \text{ V}$$

Answer:

For this reaction, two electrons are transferred from the Ni to the Ag. Thus, n is 2 for this reaction. The value of F (96,500 J/V) is given on the exam, so you will not need to memorize it.

The first answer is:

$$\Delta G° = -nFE°_{cell} = -2(96,500 \text{ J/V})(1.05 \text{ V}) = -2.03 \times 10^5 \text{ J}$$

The second answer is:

$$\log K = \frac{nE°_{cell}}{0.0592 \text{ V}} = \frac{2(1.05 \text{ V})}{0.0592 \text{ V}} = 35.5$$

This gives a K of about 10^{35} (actually K = 3×10^{35}). In many cases, the approximate value will be all you need for the AP exam.

NERNST EQUATION

Thus far, all of our calculations have been based on the standard cell potential or standard half-cell potentials—that is, the standard state conditions that were defined previously. However, many times the cell is not at standard conditions—commonly the concentrations are not 1 M. The actual cell potential, E_{cell}, can be calculated by the use of the **Nernst equation**:

$$E_{cell} = E°_{cell} - \left(\frac{RT}{nF}\right) \ln Q = E°_{cell} - \left(\frac{0.0592}{n}\right) \log Q \text{ at } 25°C$$

where R is the ideal gas constant, T is the Kelvin temperature, n is the number of electrons transferred, F is Faraday's constant, and Q is the activity quotient discussed in Chapter 13. The second form, involving the log Q, is the more useful form. If one knows the cell reaction, the concentrations of ions, and the $E°_{cell}$, then the actual cell potential can be calculated. Another useful application of the Nernst equation is in calculating the concentration of one of the reactants from cell potential measurements. Knowing the actual cell potential and the $E°_{cell}$ allows calculation of Q, the activity quotient. Knowing Q and all but one of the concentrations allows the calculation of the unknown concentration. Another application of the Nernst equation is in concentration cells. A **concentration cell** is an electrochemical cell in which the same chemical species are used in both cell compartments, but differing in concentration. Because the half-reactions are the same, the $E°_{cell} = 0.00$ V. Simply substituting the appropriate concentrations into the activity quotient allows calculation of the actual cell potential.

When using the Nernst equation on a cell reaction in which the overall reaction is not supplied, only the half-reactions and concentrations, there are two equivalent methods to work the problem. The first way is to write the overall redox reaction based upon $E°$ values and then apply the Nernst equation. If the E_{cell} turns out to be negative, it indicates that the reaction is not a spontaneous one (an electrolytic cell), or that the reaction is written backwards if it supposed to be a galvanic cell. If it is supposed to be a galvanic cell, all you need to do is to reverse the overall reaction and change the sign on the E_{cell} to positive. The other method involves using the Nernst equation with the individual half-reactions, then combining them depending on whether or not it is a galvanic cell. The only disadvantage to the second method is that you must use the Nernst equation twice. Either method should lead you to the correct answer.

Calculate the potential of a half-cell containing 0.10 M $K_2Cr_2O_7$, 0.20 M $Cr^{3+}(aq)$, and 1.0×10^{-4} M $H^+(aq)$.

Answer:

$$Cr_2O_7^{2-} + 14\,H^+(aq) + 6\,e^- \rightarrow 2\,Cr^{3+}(aq) + 7\,H_2O \qquad E° = 1.33\,V$$

$$E = E° - \frac{0.0592}{n} \log \frac{[Cr^{3+}]^2}{[Cr_2O_7^{2-}][H^+]^{14}} \qquad \text{ignore } H_2O$$

$$= 1.33\,V - \frac{0.0592}{6} \log \frac{[.20]^2}{[.10]\,[1.0 \times 10^{-4}]^{14}}$$

$$= 0.78\,V$$

EXPERIMENTAL

Electrochemical experiments fall into two broad categories. Some experiments are concerned with standard cell voltages, while other experiments use the Nernst equation directly or indirectly.

Measurements of the cell potential are essential and require a voltmeter (potentiometer). These measurements may be taken from different combinations of half-cells, or from measurements before and after changes of some aspect of the cell were made.

Using measurements of different half-cell combinations, a set of "standard" reduction potential may be constructed. This set will be similar to a table of standard reduction potentials. The solutions used in the half-cells must be of known concentration. These solutions are produced by weighing reagents and diluting to volume. These measurements will require a balance and a volumetric flask. It is also possible to produce known concentrations by diluting solutions. This method requires a pipette and a volumetric flask. Review Chapter 11 for solution techniques.

Experiments involving the Nernst equation are primarily concerned with concentrations. One or more of the concentrations in the Q portion of the Nernst equation are calculated by measuring the nonstandard cell potential and comparing this to the standard cell potential. Remember, you calculate the concentration from a measured voltage. Once the concentration is determined, it may be combined with other concentrations and used to calculate an equilibrium constant.

COMMON MISTAKES TO AVOID

1. Be sure your units cancel to give the unit wanted in your final answer.
2. Be sure to round your answer off to the correct number of significant figures.
3. Remember that oxidation is the loss of electrons and reduction the gain, and that in redox reactions the same number of electrons is lost and gained.
4. Be sure that what you determine to be the oxidizing and reducing agents are *reactant* species.
5. When diagramming an electrochemical cell, be sure the electrons go from anode to cathode.
6. Be sure that for a galvanic cell, the cell potential is greater than 0.
7. Be sure to label the anode as (−) and the cathode (+) in a galvanic cell.
8. In cell notation, be sure to write anode, anode compartment, salt bridge, cathode compartment, cathode.
9. When using a multiplier to equalize electron loss and gain in reduction half-cell potentials, **do not** use the multiplier on the voltage of the half-cell.
10. When using the Nernst equation, be sure to use the correct form of the activity quotient, products over reactants, and each concentration raised to the power the same as the coefficient in the balanced reaction.

  ## REVIEW QUESTIONS

Answer the following questions in 25 minutes. You may not use a calculator.

Choose one of the following for questions 1–4.

   A. There is no change in the voltage.
   B. The voltage becomes zero.
   C. The voltage increases.
   D. The voltage decreases, but stays positive.
   E. The voltage becomes negative.

The following reaction takes place in a voltaic cell.

$$Zn(s) + Cu^{2+}(1\ M) \rightarrow Cu(s) + Zn^{2+}(1\ M)$$

The cell has a voltage is measured and found to be +1.10 v.

1. What happens to the voltage when a saturated $ZnSO_4$ solution is added to the zinc compartment of the cell?

2. What happens to the cell voltage when the copper electrode is made smaller?

3. What happens to the cell voltage when the salt bridge is filled with deionized water instead of 1 M KNO_3?

4. What happens to the cell voltage after the cell has operated for 10 minutes?

5. $MnO_4^-(aq) + H^+(aq) + C_2O_4^{2-}(aq)$

    $\rightarrow Mn^{2+}(aq) + H_2O(l) + CO_2(g)$

    What is the coefficient of H^+ when the above reaction is balanced?

    A. 16
    B. 2
    C. 8
    D. 5
    E. 32

6. $S_2O_3^{2-} + OH^- \rightarrow SO_4^{2-} + H_2O + e^-$

    After the above half-reaction is balanced, which of the following are the respective coefficients of OH^- and SO_4^{2-} in the balanced half-reaction?

    A. 8 and 3
    B. 6 and 2
    C. 10 and 2
    D. 5 and 2
    E. 5 and 1

7. How many moles of Pt may be deposited on the cathode when 0.80 F of electricity is passed through a 1.0 M solution of Pt^{4+}?

    A. 1.0 mol
    B. 0.60 mol
    C. 0.20 mol
    D. 0.80 mol
    E. 0.40 mol

8. All of the following may serve as reducing agents, EXCEPT:

    A. Mg
    B. Cs
    C. Fe^{2+}
    D. MnO_4^-
    E. Br^-

9. $Cr_2O_7^{2-} + 14 H^+ + 3 S^{2-}$

    $\rightarrow 2 Cr^{3+} + 3 S + 7 H_2O$

    For the above reaction, pick the true statement from the following.

A. The S^{2-} is reduced by $Cr_2O_7^{2-}$.
B. The oxidation number of chromium changes from +7 to +3.
C. The oxidation number of sulfur remains −2.
D. The S^{2-} is oxidized by $Cr_2O_7^{2-}$.
E. The H^+ oxidized the S.

10. $H^+ + NO_3^- + e^- \rightarrow NO + H_2O$

    What is the coefficient for water arising when the above half-reaction is balanced?

    A. 3
    B. 4
    C. 2
    D. 1
    E. 6

11. $Co^{2+} + 2 e^- \rightarrow Co \quad E° = -0.28 \text{ v}$

    $Cd^{2+} + 2 e^- \rightarrow Cd \quad E° = -0.40 \text{ v}$

    Given the above standard reduction potentials, estimate the approximate value of the equilibrium constant for the following reaction:

    $$Cd + Co^{2+} \rightarrow Cd^{2+} + Co$$

    A. 10^{-4}
    B. 10^{-2}
    C. 10^4
    D. 10^{16}
    E. 10^2

12. When a basic solution of $KMnO_4$ is added to a $SnCl_2$ solution, a brown precipitate of MnO_2 forms and Sn^{4+} remains in solution. When the same basic solution of $KMnO_4$ is added to a NaF solution, no reaction occurs. Which of the substances involved in these reactions serves as the best reducing agent?

    A. $SnCl_2$
    B. $KMnO_4$
    C. NaF

D. MnO_2
E. Sn^{4+}

13. A sample of silver is to be purified by electrorefining. This will separates silver from an impurity of gold. The impure silver is made into an electrode. Which of the following is the best way to set up the electrolytic cell?

A. an impure silver cathode and an inert anode
B. an impure silver cathode and a pure gold anode
C. a pure silver cathode with an impure silver anode
D. a pure gold cathode with an impure silver anode
E. an impure silver cathode with a pure silver anode

14. $2\,MnO_4^- + 16\,H^+ + 5\,S^{2-}$

$\rightarrow 2\,Mn^{2+} + 5\,S + 8\,H_2O$

The reducing agent in the above reaction is which of the following?

A. MnO_4^-
B. H^+
C. S
D. S^{2-}
E. Mn^{2+}

15. $2\,Fe^{3+} + Zn \rightarrow Zn^{2+} + 2\,Fe^{2+}$

The reaction shown above was used in an electrolytic cell. The voltage measured for the cell was not equal to the calculated $E°$ for the cell. This discrepancy could be caused by which of the following?

A. The anion in the anode compartment was chloride, instead of nitrate as in the cathode compartment.
B. One or more of the ion concentrations was not 1 M.
C. Both of the solutions were at 25° C instead of 0° C.
D. The solution in the salt bridge was Na_2SO_4 instead of KNO_3.

E. The anode and cathode were different sizes.

16. How many grams of mercury could be produced by electrolyzing a 1.0 M $Hg(NO_3)_2$ solution with a current of 2.00 A for 3.00 h?

A. 22.4 g
B. 201 g
C. 11.2 g
D. 44.8 g
E. 6.00 g

17. An electrolysis cell was constructed with two platinum electrodes in a 1.00 M aqueous solution of KCl. An odorless gas evolves from one electrode, and a gas with a distinctive odor evolves from the other electrode. Choose the correct statement from the following list.

A. The gas with the distinctive odor was evolved at the anode.
B. The odorless gas was oxygen.
C. The gas with the distinctive odor was evolved at the negative electrode.
D. The odorless gas was evolved at the positive electrode.
E. The odorless gas was evolved at the anode.

18. $H_2O_2(aq) + KIO_4(aq) \rightarrow KIO_3(aq)$

$+ O_2(g) + H_2O(l)$

Choose the true statement from the following list.

A. The iodine is reduced from +8 to +6.
B. This is not an oxidation-reduction reaction.
C. H_2O_2 behaves as a reducing agent.
D. Hydrogen is reduced from +2 to +1.
E. H_2O_2 behaves as an oxidizing agent.

Questions 19 and 20 are concerned with the following half-reaction in an electrolytic cell:

$$2 \text{ BrO}_3^- + 12 \text{ H}^+ + 10 \text{ e}^-$$
$$\rightarrow \text{ Br}_2 + 6 \text{ H}_2\text{O}$$

19. Choose the correct statement from the following list.

    A. The BrO_3^- undergoes oxidation at the anode.
    B. Br goes from a -1 oxidation to a 0 oxidation state.
    C. Br_2 is oxidized at the anode.
    D. H^+ is a catalyst.
    E. The BrO_3^- undergoes reduction at the cathode.

20. If a current of 5.0 A is passed through the electrolytic cell for 0.50 h, how should you calculate the grams of Br_2 to form?

    A. $(5.0)(0.50)(3600)(159.8) / (10)$
    B. $(5.0)(0.50)(3600)(159.8) / (96500)(10)$

C. $(5.0)(0.50)(60)(159.8) / (96500)(10)$
D. $(5.0)(0.50)(3600)(79.9) / (96500)(10)$
E. $(5.0)(0.50)(159.8) / (96500)(10)$

21. $2 \text{ M(s)} + 3 \text{ Zn}^{2+}(aq) \rightarrow 2 \text{ M}^{3+}(aq)$
    $+3 \text{ Zn}^{2+}(aq)$ $E° = 0.90 \text{ V}$

    $Zn^{2+}(aq) + 2 \text{ e}^-$
    $\rightarrow \text{ Zn(s)}$ $E° = -0.76 \text{ V}$

    Using the above information, determine the standard reduction potential for the following reaction:

    $$M^{3+}(aq) + 3 \text{ e}^- \rightarrow M(s)$$

    A. 0.90 V
    B. +1.66 V
    C. 0.00 V
    D. −0.62 V
    E. −1.66 V

ANSWERS AND EXPLANATIONS

1. **D.** The addition of zinc ion, from the $ZnSO_4$, increases the zinc concentration. This increases the numerator in the logarithm part of the Nernst equation. This is a negative term, thus, the cell voltage will decrease.

2. **A.** The size of the electrode is not important.

3. **B.** The salt bridge serves as an ion source to maintain charge neutrality. Deionized water would not be an ion source, so the cell could not operate.

4. **D.** As the cell operates, the copper ion concentration would decrease and the zinc ion concentration would increase. Both of these changes would make the logarithm term in the Nernst equation more negative. This would decrease the voltage.

5. **A.** The balanced equation is:

$$2 \text{ MnO}_4^-(aq) + 16 \text{ H}^+(aq) + 5 \text{ C}_2\text{O}_4^{2-}(aq)$$
$$\rightarrow 2 \text{ Mn}^{2+}(aq) + 8 \text{ H}_2\text{O(l)} + 10 \text{ CO}_2(g)$$

6. **C.** The balanced equation is:

$$S_2O_3^{2-} + 10\ OH^- \rightarrow 2\ SO_4^{2-} + 5\ H_2O + 8\ e^-$$

7. **C.** It takes 4 mol of electrons (4 F) to change the platinum ions to platinum metal. The calculation would be: (0.80 F)(1 mol Pt/4 F) = 0.20 mol Pt

8. **D.** For a substance to serve as a reducing agent, it must be capable of being oxidized. The manganese, in the MnO_4^-, is already in its highest oxidation state, so it could not be oxidized. All other answers contain a substance that may be oxidized.

9. **D.** The dichromate ion oxidizes the sulfide ion to elemental sulfur, as the sulfide ion reduces the dichromate ion to the chromium(III) ion. Chromium goes from +6 to +3 while sulfur goes from −2 to 0. The hydrogen remains +1, so it is neither oxidized nor reduced.

10. **C.** The balanced chemical equation is:

$$4\ H^+ + NO_3^- + 3\ e^- \rightarrow NO + 2\ H_2O$$

11. **C.** Using the equation:

$$\log K = \frac{nE^\circ}{0.0592} = \frac{2(0.12)}{0.0592} = 4.05$$

This will give a K of about 10^4 (actually, $K = 1.1 \times 10^4$).

12. **A.** The Sn^{2+}, from $SnCl_2$, reduces the manganese from +7 to +4. This makes $SnCl_2$ a reducing agent. The tin is oxidized to Sn^{4+}, so $KMnO_4$ is an oxidizing agent. NaF did nothing, so it behaves as neither an oxidizing nor as a reducing agent.

13. **C.** The impure silver must be oxidized so it will go into solution. Oxidation occurs at the anode. Reduction is required to covert the silver ions to pure silver. Reduction occurs at the cathode. The cathode must be pure silver, otherwise it could be contaminated with the cathode material.

14. **D.** The MnO_4^- oxidizes the sulfide ion to elemental sulfur while, the sulfide ion reduces the permanganate ion to the manganese(II) ion.

15. **B.** If the voltage was not equal to E°, then the cell was not standard. Standard cells have 1 M concentrations, and operate at 25° with a partial pressure of each gas equal to 1 atm. No gases are involved in this reaction, so the cell must be operating at a different temperature or a different concentration (or both).

16. **A.** $\left(\dfrac{2.00\ C}{s}\right)\left(\dfrac{3600\ s}{1\ h}\right)(3.00\ h)\left(\dfrac{1\ F}{96500\ C}\right)\left(\dfrac{1\ mol\ Hg}{2\ F}\right)\left(\dfrac{200.6\ g\ Hg}{1\ mol\ Hg}\right)$

17. **A.** The gases produced are hydrogen (at the cathode) and chlorine (at the anode). Hydrogen is odorless, while chlorine has a distinctive odor.

18. **C.** The KIO_4 oxidizes the H_2O_2. Thus, H_2O_2 is the reducing agent. The iodine is reduced from +7 to +5, while the oxygen in the H_2O_2, is oxidized from −1 to 0 (O_2).

19. **E.** The bromate ion, BrO_3^-, is gaining electrons so it is being reduced. Reduction always occurs at the cathode.

20. **B.** Recall that 5.0 amp is 5.0 C/s. The calculation would be:

$$\frac{5.0\ C\ (0.50\ h)\ 3600\ s\ (159.8\ g)\ 1\ F\quad (1\ mol\ Br_2)}{s\qquad\qquad h\quad (mol\ Br_2)\ 96500\ C\quad (10\ F)}$$

21. **E.** The half-reactions giving the overall reaction must be:

$$3[Zn^{2+}(aq) + 2\ e^- \to Zn(s)]\quad E° = -0.76\ V$$
$$\underline{2[M(s) \to M^{3+}(+3\ e^-)]\qquad E° = ?}$$
$$2\,M(s) + 3Zn^{2+}(aq)\qquad E° = 0.90\ V$$
$$\to 2\,M^{3+}(aq) + 3Zn^{2+}(aq)$$

Thus, −0.76 + ? = 0.90, giving ? = 1.66 V. The half-reaction under consideration is the reverse of the one used in this combination, thus the sign of the calculated voltage must be reversed. Do not make the mistake of multiplying the voltages when the half-reactions were multiplied to equalize the electrons.

FREE-RESPONSE QUESTIONS

Answer the following question in 15 minutes. You may not use a calculator.

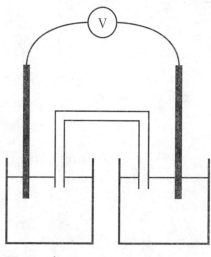

V = voltmeter

The above galvanic cell is constructed with a cobalt electrode in a 1.0 M $Co(NO_3)_2$ solution in the left compartment and a silver electrode in a 1.0 M $AgNO_3$ in the right compartment. The salt bridge contains a KNO_3 solution. The cell voltage is positive.

a. What is the balanced net ionic equation for the reaction, and what is the cell potential?

$$Co^{2+} + 2\ e^- \rightarrow Co \qquad E° = -0.28\ V$$

$$Ag^+ + 1\ e^- \rightarrow Ag \qquad E° = +0.80\ V$$

b. Which electrode is the anode? Justify your answer.

c. Could KCl be substituted for the KNO_3 in the salt bridge? Justify your answer.

d. If some solid $Co(NO_3)_2$ is added to the cobalt compartment, what will happen to the voltage? Justify your answer.

e. If the cell is allowed to operate until equilibrium is established, what will the potential be? Justify your answer.

ANSWERS AND EXPLANATIONS

✓   a. The cell reaction is:

$$Co(s) + 2\ Ag^+(aq) \rightarrow Co^{2+}(aq) + 2\ Ag(s)$$

Give yourself 1 point if you got this correct. The physical states are not necessary.

The calculation of the cell potential may be done in different ways. Here is one method:

$$Co \rightarrow Co^{2+} + 2\ e^- \qquad E° = +0.28\ V$$

$$(Ag^+ + 1\ e^- \rightarrow Ag) \qquad E° = +0.80\ V$$

$$Co(s) + 2\ Ag^+(aq) \qquad E° = +1.08\ V$$
$$\rightarrow Co^{2+}(aq) + 2\ Ag(s)$$

Give yourself 1 point for the correct answer regardless of the method used. The most common mistake is to multiply the silver voltage by two. You do not get the point for an answer of 1 V.

The half-reactions and their standard reductions potentials are supplied on the exam, not in the problem as given here. You will be expected to find the appropriate half-reactions in a table.

b. The cobalt is the anode. You get 1 point for this statement.

The reason Co is the anode is because the Co is oxidized. You get 1 point for this statement, or if you say the Co loses electrons.

c. KCl cannot be substituted for KNO_3 in this case. This is worth 1 point.

The Cl^- ion from the KCl would react with the silver ion to give insoluble AgCl. Give yourself 1 point for this explanation.

d. The voltage would decrease. Give yourself 1 point for this answer.

The excess Co^{2+}, from the $Co(NO_3)_2$, would make the cell nonstandard. The Nernst equation should be used to calculate the new voltage. The concentration of the cobalt ions appears in the numerator of the logarithm term of the Nernst equation. This makes the logarithm term more negative, yielding a lower voltage. Give yourself 1 point for any answer relating to this. It might be helpful if you wrote out the Nernst equation for this cell.

e. At equilibrium the cell voltage would be 0 V. This is worth 1 point.

At equilibrium no work is done, so the potential must be zero. Give yourself 1 point for this answer.

There are a total of 10 points possible on these questions.

RAPID REVIEW

- Electrochemistry is the study of redox reactions that produce electricity or the use of electricity to produce a desired redox reaction.

- In redox reactions electrons are lost and gained. Oxidation is the loss of electrons, and reduction is the gain of electrons.

- The reactant that is being reduced is the oxidizing agent, and the reactant being oxidized is the reducing agent.

- The same number of electrons is lost and gained in redox reactions.

- Galvanic (voltaic) cells produce electricity through the use of a redox reaction.

- The anode is the electrode at which the oxidation half-reaction takes place. The anode compartment is the solution that the anode electrode is immersed.

- The cathode is the electrode at which reduction takes place, and the cathode compartment is the solution in which the cathode is immersed.

- In a galvanic cell the anode is labeled as (−) and the cathode (+).

- A salt bridge is used in an electrochemical cell to maintain electrical neutrality in the cell compartments.

- Be able to diagram an electrochemical cell.

- The cell notation is a shorthand way of representing a cell. It has the form:

$$\text{anode}|\text{anode compartment}\|\text{cathode compartment}|\text{cathode}$$

- Standard reduction potentials are used to calculate the cell potential under standard conditions. All half-reactions are shown in the reduction form.

- For a galvanic cell $E^\circ_{cell} > 0$.

- The $E^\circ_{cell} = E^\circ_{cathode} - E^\circ_{anode} > 0$. Know how to use this equation to calculate the E°_{cell}.

- Electrolytic cells use an external source of electricity to produce a desired redox reaction.

- Review how to diagram an electrolytic cell.

- The following relationships can be used to calculate quantitative changes that occur in an electrochemical cell, especially an electrolytic one: 1 F = 96,500 C per mole of electron ($F = 96,500$ C/mol $e^- = 96,500$ J/V) and 1 amp = 1 C/s (A = C/s)

- The standard cell potential can be used to calculate the Gibbs free energy for the reaction: $\Delta G^\circ = -nFE^\circ_{cell}$. Know how to use this equation.

- The standard cell potential can also be used to calculate the equilibrium constant for a reaction: $\log K = \dfrac{nE^\circ_{cell}}{0.0592 \text{ V}}$. Know how to use this equation.

- The Nernst equation, $E_{cell} = E^\circ_{cell} - \left(\dfrac{0.0592}{n}\right) \log Q$ at 25° C, can be used to calculate the potential of a cell that is not at standard conditions, or to calculate the concentration of one cell compartment if the standard cell potential, the actual cell potential, and the other concentrations are known. Know how to use the Nernst equation for these purposes.

Chapter 15

Nuclear Chemistry

KEYWORDS AND EQUATIONS

No specific nuclear equations provided.

INTRODUCTION

Radioactivity, the spontaneous decay of an unstable isotope to a more stable one, was first discovered by Henri Becquerel in 1896. Marie Curie and her husband expanded on his work and developed most of the concepts that are used today.

Throughout this book you have been studying traditional chemistry and chemical reactions. This has involved the transfer or sharing of electrons from the electron clouds, especially the valence electrons. Little has been said to this point regarding the nucleus. Now we are going to shift our attention to nuclear reactions and, for the most part, ignore the electron clouds.

NUCLEAR REACTIONS

Balancing Nuclear Reactions

Most nuclear reactions involve breaking apart the nucleus into two or more different elements or subatomic particles. If all but one of the particles is known, the unknown particle can be determined by balancing the nuclear equation. When chemical equations are balanced, coefficients are added to ensure that there are the same number of each type of atom on both sides of the reaction arrow. To balance nuclear equations, we ensure that there is the same sum of both mass numbers and atomic numbers on both the left and right of the reaction arrow. Recall that a specific isotope of an element can be represented by the following symbolization:

$$^A_Z X$$

In this symbolization A is the mass number (sum of protons and neutrons), Z is the atomic number (number of protons) and X is the element symbol (from the periodic table). In balancing nuclear reactions, make sure the sum of all A values on the left of the arrow equals the sum of all A values to the right of the arrow. The same will be true of the sums of the atomic numbers. Knowing that these sums must equal allows one to predict the mass and atomic number of an unknown particle if all the others are known.

Consider the **transmutation**—creation of one element from another— of Cl-35. This isotope of chlorine is bombarded by a neutron and H-1 is created, along with an isotope of a different element. First, a partial nuclear equation is written:

$$^{35}_{17}Cl + {}^1_0n \rightarrow {}^1_1H + ?$$

The sum of the mass numbers on the left of the equation is 36 (35+1) and on the right is 1+x. The mass number of the unknown isotope must be 35. The sum of the atomic numbers on the left is 17 (17+0) and 1+x on the right. The atomic number of the unknown must then be 16. This atomic number identifies the element as sulfur, so a complete nuclear equation can be written:

$$^{35}_{17}Cl + {}^1_0n \rightarrow {}^1_1H + {}^{35}_{16}S$$

Sulfur-35 does not occur in nature; it is an artificially produced isotope.

Natural Radioactive Decay Modes

!

Three common types of radioactive decay are observed in nature, and two others are occasionally observed.

Alpha Emission

An alpha particle is essentially a helium nucleus with two protons and two neutrons. It is represented as: ^4_2He or α. As this particle is expelled from the nucleus of the radioisotope that is undergoing decay, it has no electrons and thus has a 2+ charge. However, it quickly acquires two electrons from its surroundings to form the neutral atom. Most commonly the alpha particle is shown as the neutral atom and not the cation.

Radon-222 undergoes alpha decay according to the following equation:

$$^{222}_{86}\text{Rn} \rightarrow {}^{218}_{84}\text{Po} + {}^{4}_{2}\text{He}.$$

Notice that in going from Rn-222 to Po-218, the atomic number has decreased by 2 and the mass number by 4.

Beta Emission

A beta particle is essentially an electron and can be represented as either $^{0}_{-1}\beta$ or $^{0}_{-1}\text{e}$. This electron comes from the nucleus, not the electron cloud, and results from the conversion of a neutron into a proton and an electron: $^{1}_{0}\text{n} \rightarrow {}^{1}_{1}\text{p} + {}^{0}_{-1}\text{e}$.

Nickel-63 will undergo beta decay according to the following equation:

$$^{63}_{28}\text{Ni} \rightarrow {}^{63}_{29}\text{Cu} + {}^{0}_{-1}\text{e}.$$

Notice that the atomic number has increased by 1 in going from Ni-63 to Cu-63, but the mass number has remained unchanged.

Gamma Emission

Gamma emission is the giving off of high-energy, short-wavelength photons similar to x-rays. This radiation is commonly represented as γ. Gamma emission commonly accompanies most other types of radioactive decay but is not shown in the balanced nuclear equation because it has neither appreciable mass nor charge.

Alpha, beta, and gamma emissions are the most common types of natural decay modes, but positron emission and electron capture are also observed occasionally.

Positron Emission

A positron is essentially an electron that has a positive charge instead of a negative one. It is represented as $^{0}_{1}\beta$ or $^{0}_{1}\text{e}$. Positron emission results from the conversion of a proton to a neutron and a positron: $^{1}_{1}\text{p} \rightarrow {}^{1}_{0}\text{n} + {}^{0}_{1}\text{e}$. It is observed in the decay of some natural radioactive isotopes, such as K-40: $^{40}_{19}\text{K} \rightarrow {}^{40}_{18}\text{Ar} + {}^{0}_{1}\text{e}$.

Electron Capture

The four decay modes described above all involve the emission or giving off of a particle; electron capture is the capturing of an electron from the energy level closest to the nucleus (1s) by a proton in the nucleus. This creates a neutron: $^{0}_{-1}\text{e} + {}^{1}_{1}\text{p} \rightarrow {}^{1}_{0}\text{n}$. This leaves a vacancy in the 1s energy level, and an electron from a higher energy level drops down to fill this vacancy. A cascading effect occurs as the electrons shift downward and, as they do so, energy is released. This energy falls in the x-ray part of the electromagnetic spectrum. These x-rays give scientists a clue that electron capture has taken place.

Polonium-204 undergoes electron capture: $^{204}_{84}Po + ^{0}_{-1}e \rightarrow ^{204}_{83}Bi +$ x-rays. Notice that the atomic number has decreased by 1, but the mass number has remained the same.

NUCLEAR STABILITY

!

Predicting whether a particular isotope is stable and what type of decay mode it might undergo can be tricky. All isotopes containing 83 or more protons are unstable and will undergo nuclear decay. For these large, massive isotopes alpha decay is observed most commonly. Alpha decay gets rid of four units of mass and two units of charge, thus helping to relieve the repulsive stress found in these nuclei. For other isotopes, with atomic numbers less than 83, stability is best predicted by the use of the neutron to proton (n/p) ratio.

If one plots the number of neutrons versus the number of protons for the known stable isotopes, the **nuclear belt of stability** is formed. At the low end of this belt of stability (Z < 20) the n/p ratio is 1. At the high end (Z ≈ 80), the n/p ratio is about 1.5. One can then use the n/p ratio of the isotope under question to predict whether or not it will be stable. If it is unstable, the isotope will utilize a decay mode that will bring it back onto the belt of stability.

For example, consider Ne-18. It has 10 p and 8 n, giving a n/p ratio of 0.8. That is less than 1, so the isotope is unstable. This isotope is neutron-poor, meaning it doesn't have enough neutrons (or has too many protons) to be stable. Decay modes that increased the number of neutrons, decreased the number of protons, or both would be favored. Both positron emission and electron capture accomplish this by converting a proton into a neutron. As a general rule, positron emission occurs with lighter isotopes and electron capture with heavier isotopes.

Isotopes that are neutron-rich, that have too many neutrons or not enough protons, lie above the belt of stability and tend to undergo beta emission because that decay mode converts a neutron into a proton.

A particular isotope may undergo a series of nuclear decays until finally a stable isotope is formed. For example, radioactive U-238 decays to stable Pb-206 in 14 steps, a majority of which are alpha emissions, as one might predict.

NUCLEAR DECAY CALCULATIONS

A radioactive isotope may be unstable, but it is impossible to predict when a certain atom will decay. However, if a statistically large enough sample is examined, some trends become obvious. The radioactive decay follows first-order kinetics (see Chapter 12 for a more in-depth discussion of first-order reactions). If the number of radioactive atoms in a sample is monitored, it can be determined that it takes a certain amount of time for half the sample to decay; it takes the same amount of time for half the remaining sample to decay; and so on. The amount of time it takes for half the sample to decay is called the half-life of the isotope and is given the symbol $t_{1/2}$. The table below shows the percentage of radioactive isotope remaining versus half-life.

Half-life, $t_{1/2}$	Percent radioactive isotope remaining
0	100
1	50
2	25
3	12.5
4	6.25
5	3.12
6	1.56
7	0.78
8	0.39
9	0.19
10	0.09

As a general rule, the amount of radioactivity at the end of 10 half-lives drops below the level of detection and the sample is said to be "safe."

Half-lives may be very short, 4.2×10^{-6} seconds for Po-213, or very long, 4.5×10^9 years for U-238. The very long half-lives of waste products is a major problem with nuclear fission reactors. Remember, it takes 10 half-lives for the sample to be safe.

If only multiples of half-lives are considered, the calculations are very straightforward. For example, I-131 is used in the treatment of thyroid cancer and has a $t_{1/2}$ of eight days. How long would it take to decay to 25% of its original amount? Looking at the chart, you see that 25% decay would occur at two half-lives or 16 days. However, since radioactive decay is not a linear process, you cannot use the chart to predict how much would still be radioactive at the end of 12 days or at some time (or amount) that is not associated with a multiple of a half-life. To solve these types of problems, one must use the mathematical relationships associated with first-order kinetics that were presented in Chapter 12. In general, two equations are used:

$$(1)\ \ln N_t/N_o = -kt$$

$$(2)\ t_{1/2} = \ln 2/k$$

In these equations, the ln is the natural logarithm; N_t is the amount of isotope radioactive at some time t; N_0 is the amount initially radioactive; and k is the rate constant for the decay. If you know initial and final amounts and are looking for the half-life, you would use equation (1) to solve for the rate constant and then use equation (2) to solve for $t_{1/2}$.

For example: What is the half-life of a radioisotope that takes 15 min to decay to 90% of its original activity?

Using equation (1): $\ln 90/100 = -k(15 \text{ min})$
$-0.1054 = -k(15 \text{ min})$
$7.02 \times 10^{-3} \text{ min}^{-1} = k$

Now equation (2): $t_{1/2} = \ln 2/7.02 \times 10^{-3} \text{ min}^{-1}$
$t_{12} = 0.693/7.02 \times 10^{-3} \text{ min}^{-1}$
$t_{12} = 98.7 \text{ min}$

If one knows the half-life and amount remaining radioactive, equation (2) can be used to calculate the rate constant k and equation (1) can then be used to solve for the time. This is the basis of C-14 dating, which is used to determine the age of objects that were once alive.

For example, suppose a wooden tool is discovered and its C-14 activity is determined to have decreased to 65% of the original. How old is the object?

The half-life of C-14 is 5730 yr. Substituting this into equation (2):

$5730 \text{ yr} = \ln 2/k$
$5730 \text{ yr} = 0.6931/k$
$k = 1.21 \times 10^{-4} \text{ yr}^{-1}$

Substituting this rate constant into equation (1):

$\ln 65/100 = -(1.21 \times 10^{-4} \text{ yr}^{-1})t$
$-0.4308 = -(1.21 \times 10^{-4} \text{ yr}^{-1})t$
$t = 3600 \text{ yr}$

MASS–ENERGY RELATIONSHIPS

Whenever a nuclear decay or reaction takes place, energy is released. This energy may be in the form of heat and light, gamma radiation, or kinetic energy of the expelled particle and recoil of the remaining particle. This energy results from the conversion of a very small amount of matter into energy. (Remember that in nuclear reaction there is no conservation of matter, as in ordinary chemical reactions.) The amount of energy that is produced can be calculated by using Einstein's equation $E = mc^2$, where E is the energy produced, m is the mass converted into energy (the mass defect), and c is the speed of light. The amount of matter that is converted into energy is normally very small, but when it is multiplied by the speed of light (a very large number) squared, the amount of energy produced is very large.

For example: When 1 mol of U-238 decays to Th-234, 5×10^{-6} Kg of matter is converted to energy (the mass defect). To calculate the amount of energy released:

$$E = mc^2$$
$$E = (5 \times 10^{-6} \text{ kg})(3.00 \times 10^8 \text{ m/s})^2$$
$$E = 5 \times 10^{11} \text{ kg-m}^2/\text{s}^2 = 5 \times 10^{11} \text{ J}$$

COMMON MISTAKES TO AVOID

1. Make sure your answer is reasonable. Don't just write down the answer from your calculator.
2. Make sure your units cancel in your calculations, leaving the unit you want.
3. When balancing nuclear equations, be sure the sum of all mass numbers on the left side of the arrow equals the sum of all mass numbers on the right side. The same will be true of the sums of the atomic numbers.
4. When balancing nuclear reactions, be sure you use the atomic number of the unknown and **not** the mass number to determine the element symbol.
5. Make sure that in alpha, beta, gamma, and positron emission the particle being emitted is on the right side of the reaction arrow. In electron capture, the electron should be on the left side of the arrow.
6. In half-life problems, don't omit the minus sign. Watch your units.
7. In half-life problems, be sure to use the amount of isotope still radioactive as N_t and not the amount decayed.

REVIEW QUESTIONS

You have 10 minutes. You may not use a calculator.

1. When $^{226}_{88}\text{Ra}$ decays, it emits 2 α particles, then a β particle, followed by an α particle. The resulting nucleus is:

   A. $^{212}_{83}\text{Bi}$

   B. $^{222}_{86}\text{Rn}$

   C. $^{214}_{82}\text{Pb}$

   D. $^{214}_{83}\text{Bi}$

   E. $^{212}_{85}\text{At}$

2. The formation of $^{230}_{90}\text{Th}$ from $^{234}_{92}\text{U}$ occurs by:

   A. electron capture
   B. α decay
   C. β decay
   D. position decay
   E. γ decay

3. Which of the following lists the types of radiation in the correct order of increasing penetrating power?

    A. α, γ, β
    B. β, α, γ
    C. α, β, γ
    D. β, γ, α
    E. γ, β, α

4. What is the missing product in the following nuclear reaction?

    $$_{92}^{236}U \rightarrow 4_0^1n + _{53}^{136}I + \underline{\quad}$$

    A. $_{39}^{90}Y$

    B. $_{38}^{96}Sr$

    C. $_{39}^{96}Y$

    D. $_{40}^{98}Zr$

    E. $_{41}^{98}Nb$

5. Which of the following statements are correct concerning β particles.

    I.   They have a mass number of zero and a charge of -1.
    II. They are electrons.

III. They are less penetrating than α particles.

    A. I and II
    B. I and III
    C. II and III
    D. I only
    E. II only

6. An atom of $_{92}^{234}U$ undergoes radioactive decay by α emission. What is the product nuclide?

    A. $_{90}^{230}Th$

    B. $_{90}^{234}Th$

    C. $_{92}^{230}U$

    D. $_{91}^{230}Pa$

    E. $_{94}^{238}Pu$

7. If 75% of a sample of pure $_1^3H$ decays in 24.6 years, what is the half-life of $_1^3H$?

    A. 24.6 yr
    B. 18.4 yr
    C. 12.3 yr
    D. 6.15 yr
    E. 3.07 yr

ANSWERS AND EXPLANATIONS

1. **D.** The mass should be $226 - (4 + 4 + 0 + 4) = 214$. The atomic number should be $88 - (2 + 2 - 1 + 2) = 83$.

2. **B.** Mass difference $= 234 - 230 = 4$, and atomic number difference $= 92 - 90 = 2$. These correspond to an α particle.

3. **C.** Alpha particles are the least penetrating, and gamma rays are the most penetrating.

4. **C.** Mass difference $= 236 - 4(1) - 136 = 96$. Atomic number difference $= 92 - 4(0) - 53 = 39$.

5. **A.** In nuclear reactions the mass of a β particle is treated as 0 and a charge of -1. Electrons and β particles are the same.

6. **A.** Mass number $= 234 - 4 = 230$, and atomic number $= 92 - 2 = 90$.

7. **C.** After one half-life, 50% would remain. After another half-life this would be reduced by one-half to 25%. The total amount decayed is 75%. Thus, 24.6 yr must be two half-lives of 12.3 yr each.

RAPID REVIEW

- Know how nuclear equations are balanced: The same sum of both mass and atomic numbers appear on both sides of the equation.

- Know the five naturally occurring decay modes:

   1. Alpha emission, in which a helium nucleus, $_2^4\text{He}$, is emitted from the nucleus.
   2. Beta emission, in which an electron, $_{-1}^0\text{e}$, is emitted from the nucleus. This is due to the conversion of a neutron into a proton plus the beta particle.
   3. Gamma emission, in which high-energy electromagnetic radiation is emitted from the nucleus. This commonly accompanies the other types of radioactive decay. It is due to the conversion of a small amount of matter into energy.
   4. Positron emission, in which a positron, $_{+1}^0\text{e}$, a particle having the same mass as an electron but a positive charge, is emitted from the nucleus. This is due to a proton converting into a neutron and the positron.
   5. Electron capture, in which an inner shell electron is captured by a proton in the nucleus with the formation of a neutron. X-rays are emitted as the electrons cascade down to fill the vacancy in the lower energy level.

- Know that nuclear stability is best related to the neutron-to-proton ratio (n/p), which starts at about 1/1 for light isotopes and ends at about 1.5/1 for heavier isotopes with atomic numbers up to 82. All isotopes of mass number greater than 83 are unstable and will commonly undergo alpha decay. Below atomic number 83, neutron-poor isotopes will probably undergo positron emission or electron capture, while neutron-rich isotopes will probably undergo beta emission.

- Know that the half-life, $t_{1/2}$, of a radioactive isotope is the amount of time it takes for one-half of the sample to decay. Know how to use the appropriate equations to calculate amounts of an isotope remaining at any given time or use similar data to calculate the half-life of an isotope.

- Know how to use Einstein's equation $E = mc^2$ to calculate the amount of energy produced from a mass defect (the amount of matter that was converted into energy).

Chapter 16

Organic Chemistry

 2 KEYWORDS AND EQUATIONS

No keywords or equations specific to this chapter are listed on the AP exam.

INTRODUCTION

Organic chemistry is the study of the chemistry of carbon. Almost all the compounds containing carbon are classified as organic compounds. Only a few—for example, carbonates and cyanides—are classified as inorganic. It used to be thought that all organic compounds had to be produced by living organisms, but this idea was proven wrong in 1828 when German chemist Friedrich Wöhler produced the first organic compound from inorganic starting materials. From that time, chemists have synthesized many organic compounds found in nature and have also made many never found naturally. It is carbon's characteristic of bonding strongly to itself and to other elements in long, complex chains and rings, that gives carbon the ability to form the many diverse and complex compounds needed to support life.

ALKANES

Alkanes are a member of a family of organic compounds called **hydro-carbons,** compounds of carbon and hydrogen. These hydrocarbons are the simplest of organic compounds, but are extremely important to our society as fuels and raw materials for chemical industries. We heat our homes and run our automobiles through the combustion (burning) of these hydrocarbons. Paints, plastics, and pharmaceuticals are all made from hydrocarbons. **Alkanes** are hydrocarbons that contain only single covalent bonds within the molecule. They are called **saturated hydrocarbons** because they are bonded to the maximum number of other atoms. These alkanes may be straight-chained hydrocarbons, in which the carbons are sequentially bonded; branched hydrocarbons, in which another hydrocarbon group is bonded to the hydrocarbon "backbone"; or they may be cyclic, in which the hydrocarbon is composed entirely or partially of a ring system. The straight-chained and branched alkenes have the general formula of C_nH_{2n+2}, whereas the cyclic alkenes have the general formula of C_nH_{2n}. The n stands for the number of carbon atoms in the compound. The first 10 straight-chained hydrocarbons are shown in Table 16.1.

There can be many more carbon units in a chain than are shown in Table 16.1. These are enough to allow us to study alkane nomenclature, the naming of alkanes.

Alkane Nomenclature

The naming of alkanes is based on choosing the longest carbon chain in the structural formula, then naming the hydrocarbon branches while indicating onto which carbon that branch is attached. Here are the specific rules for naming simple alkanes:

1. Find the continuous carbon chain in the compound that contains the most carbon atoms. This will be the base name of the alkane.
2. This base name will be modified by adding the names of the branches (substituent group) in front of the base name. Alkane branches are named by taking the name of the alkane that contains the same number of carbon atoms, dropping the *–ane* ending and adding *–yl*. Methane becomes methyl, propane becomes propyl, etc. If there is more than one branch, list them alphabetically.

Table 16.1 The First Ten Straight-Chained Hydrocarbons

Name	Molecular Formula	Structural Formula
methane	CH_4	CH_4
ethane	C_2H_6	CH_3-CH_3
propane	C_3H_8	$CH_3-CH_2-CH_3$
butane	C_4H_{10}	$CH_3-CH_2-CH_2-CH_3$
pentane	C_5H_{12}	$CH_3-CH_2-CH_2-CH_2-CH_3$
hexane	C_6H_{14}	$CH_3-CH_2-CH_2-CH_2-CH_2-CH_3$
heptane	C_7H_{16}	$CH_3-CH_2-CH_2-CH_2-CH_2-CH_2-CH_3$
octane	C_8H_{18}	$CH_3-CH_2-CH_2-CH_2-CH_2-CH_2-CH_2-CH_3$
nonane	C_9H_{20}	$CH_3-CH_2-CH_2-CH_2-CH_2-CH_2-CH_2-CH_2-CH_3$
decane	$C_{10}H_{22}$	$CH_3-CH_2-CH_2-CH_2-CH_2-CH_2-CH_2-CH_2-CH_2-CH_3$

3. The position where a particular substituent is attached to the chain is indicated by a location number. These numbers are assigned by consecutively numbering the carbons of the base hydrocarbon, starting at one end of the hydrocarbon chain. Choose the end that will result in the lowest sum of location numbers for the substituent groups. Place this location number in front of the substituent name and separate it from the name by a hyphen (2-methyl).

4. Place the substituent names with their location numbers in front of the base name of the alkane in alphabetical order. If there are identical substituents (two methyl groups, for example), give the location numbers of each, separated by commas using the common Greek prefixes (di-, tri-, tetra-, etc.) to indicate the number of identical substituent groups (i.e. 2,3-dimethyl). These Greek prefixes are not considered in the alphabetical arrangement.

5. The last substituent group becomes a part of the base name as a prefix.

Studying Figures 16.1 and 16.2 may help you learn the naming of substituted alkanes.

Structural Isomerism

Compounds that have the same molecular formulas but different structural formulas are called **isomers.** With hydrocarbons, this applies to a different arrangement of the carbon atoms. Isomers such as these are called **structural isomers.** Figure 16.3 shows the structural isomers of C_5H_{12}. Note that there are the same number of carbons and hydrogens in each structure. Only the way the carbons are bonded is different.

In writing structural isomers as well as any organic compound, remember that **carbon forms four bonds.** One of the most common mistakes that a chemistry student makes is writing an organic structure with a carbon

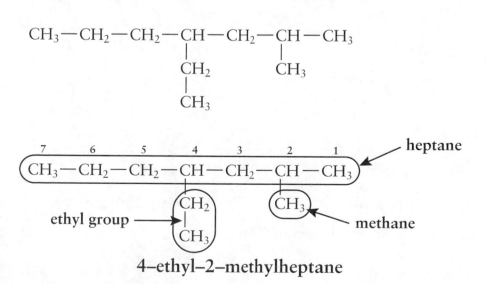

Figure 16.1 Naming an alkane.

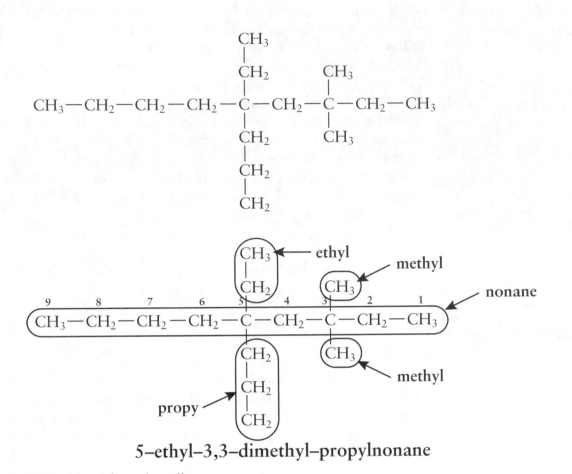

Figure 16.2 Naming of another alkane.

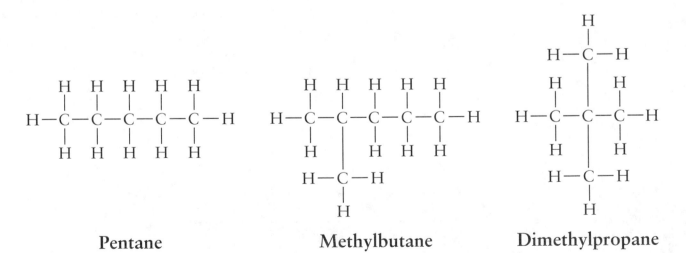

Figure 16.3 Structural isomers of C_5H_{12}.

atom having less or more than four bonds. Here is a problem in nomenclature just for practice:

Name the following compound:

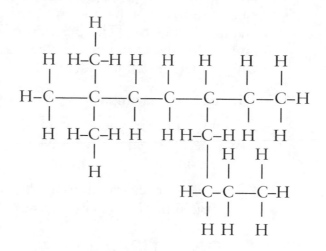

Answer: 5-ethyl-2,2-dimethylnonane

Solution:

First, pick the longest chain. This is bold-faced in this example. The carbons are attached by single bonds, thus this is an alkane. Because the longest chain has nine carbons, this is a nonane.

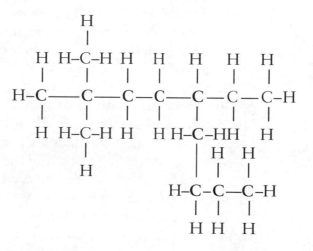

Next, the longest chain should be numbered from one end to the other with the lowest number(s) going to the branches. For the above example the numbering of the chain (boldface carbon atoms) would be:

1 2 3 4 5

6

7 8 9

Once these numbers have been assigned, do not alter them later.

All carbon atoms that are not part of the nine-atom main chain are branches. Branches have -yl endings. It may help you to circle the carbon atoms belonging in the branches. In the above example, there are three branches. Two consist of only one carbon and are called methyl groups. The remaining branch has two carbons, so it is an ethyl group. The branches are arranged alphabetically. If there is more than one of a particular type, use a prefix (di-, tri-, tetra-, etc.). The two methyl groups are designated dimethyl. The position of each branch is indicated with a number already determined for the main chain. Each branch must get its own number, even if it is identical to one already used.

In the above example this gives: 5-ethyl-2,2-dimethylnonane

a. ethyl before methyl (alphabetical—prefixes are ignored)
b. two methyl groups = dimethyl
c. three branches = three numbers

Numbers are separated from other numbers by commas, and numbers are separated from letters by a dash.

COMMON FUNCTIONAL GROUPS

If chemistry students had to learn the properties of each of the millions of organic compounds, they would face an impossible task. Luckily, chemists find that having certain arrangements of atoms in an organic molecule causes those molecules to react in a similar fashion. For example, methyl alcohol, CH_3–OH, and ethyl alcohol, CH_3–CH_2–OH, undergo the same types of reaction. The –OH group is the reactive part of these types of molecules. These reactive groups are called **functional groups.** Instead of learning the properties of individual molecules, one can simply learn the properties of functional groups.

In our study of the simple hydrocarbons, there are only two functional groups. One is a carbon-to-carbon double bond. Hydrocarbons that contain a carbon-to-carbon double bond are called **alkenes.** Naming alkenes is very similar to naming alkanes. The major difference is that the carbon base has an *-ene* ending instead of the *-ane* ending. The carbon backbone of the base hydrocarbon is numbered so the position of the double bond has the lowest location number.

The other hydrocarbon functional group is a carbon-to-carbon triple bond. Hydrocarbons that contain a triple bond are called **alkynes.** Alkynes use the *-yne* ending on the base hydrocarbon. The presence of a double or triple bond make these hydrocarbons **unsaturated,** that is they do not have the maximum number of bonds to other atoms.

The introduction of other atoms (N, O, Cl, etc.) to the organic compounds gives rise to many other functional groups. The major functional groups are shown in Table 16.2.

MACROMOLECULES

As we mentioned in the introduction to this chapter, carbon has the ability to bond to itself in long and complex chains. These large molecules,

Table 16.2 Common Functional Groups

Functional Group	Compound Type	Suffix or Prefix of Name	Example	Systematic Name (Common Name)
C=C	alkene	-ene	H₂C=CH₂ (structure)	ethene (ethylene)
—C≡C—	alkyne	-yne	H—C≡C—H	ethyne (acetylene)
—C—Ö—H	alcohol	-ol	H—C—Ö—H (structure)	methanol (methyl alcohol)
—C—Ẍ: (X=halogen)	haloalkane	halo-	H—C—Cl: (structure)	chloromethane (methyl chloride)
—C—N̈—	amine	-amine	H—C—C—N̈—H (structure)	ethylamine
—C(=O)—H	aldehyde	-al	H—C—C(=O)—H (structure)	ethanal (acetaldehyde)
—C—C(=O)—C—	ketone	-one	H—C—C(=O)—C—H (structure)	2-propanone (acetone)
—C(=O)—Ö—H	carboxylic acid	-oic acid	H—C—C(=O)—Ö—H (structure)	ethanoic acid (acetic acid)
—C(=O)—Ö—C—	ester	-oate	H—C—C(=O)—Ö—C—H (structure)	methyl ethanoate (methyl acetate)
—C(=O)—N̈—	amide	-amide	H—C—C(=O)—N̈—H (structure)	ethanamide (acetamide)
—C≡N:	nitrile	-nitrile	H—C—C≡N: (structure)	ethanenitrile (acetonitrile, methyl cyanide)

called **macromolecules,** may have molecular weights in the millions. They are large, complex molecules, but most are composed of repeating units called **monomers.** Figure 16.4 shows two macromolecules, cellulose and nylon, and indicates their repeating units.

Macromolecules are found in nature. Cellulose, wool, starch, and DNA are but a few of the macromolecules that occur naturally. Carbon's ability to form these large, complex molecules is necessary to provide the diversity of compounds needed to make up a tree or a human being. But many of the useful macromolecules that we use everyday are created in the lab and industrial complex by chemists. Nylon, rayon, polyethylene, and polyvinyl chloride are all synthetic macromolecules. They differ by what repeating units (monomers) are joined together in the polymerization process. Our society has grown to depend on these plastics, these synthetic fabrics. The complexity of carbon compounds is reflected by the complexity of our modern society.

EXPERIMENTAL

There have been no experimental applications of organic chemistry on recent AP exams.

COMMON MISTAKES TO AVOID

1. **When writing organic formulas, make sure that every carbon has four bonds.**

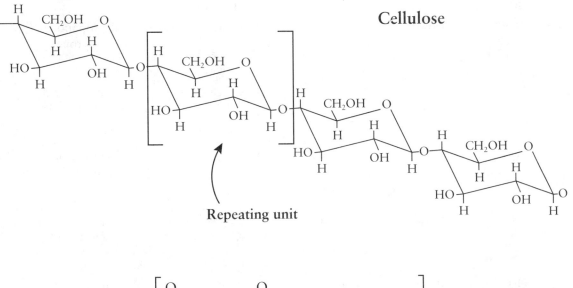

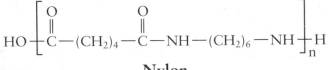

Figure 16.4 Two nylon macromolecules.

2. When naming the alkanes, make sure to number the carbon chain so the sum of all location numbers is as small as possible.
3. When naming branched alkanes, be sure to consider the branches when finding the longest carbon chain. The longest chain isn't the one in which the carbon atoms all lie in a horizontal line.
4. In naming identical substituents on the longest carbon chain, be sure to use repeating location numbers, separated by commas (2,2-dimethyl)
5. **Be sure that every carbon has four bonds!**

3 REVIEW QUESTIONS

You have 5 minutes. You may not use a calculator.

1. Cycloalkanes are hydrocarbons with the general formula C_nH_{2n}. If a 0.500 g sample of any alkene is combusted in excess oxygen, how many moles of water will form?

   A. 0.50
   B. 0.072
   C. 0.036
   D. 1.0
   E. 0.018

2.
$$\begin{array}{c} O\text{--}H \\ | \\ CH_3\text{--}CH\text{--}CH_2\text{--}CH_3 \end{array}$$

   The organic compound shown above would be classified as

   A. an organic base
   B. an ether
   C. an alcohol
   D. an aldehyde
   E. a ketone

3. Which of the following compounds is optically active?

   A. $CH_3CHClCH_2CH_2CH_3$
   B. $CH_3CH{=}CHCH_2CH_3$
   C. $CH_3CH_2CHClCH_2CH_3$
   D. $CH_3CH_2CH_2CH_2OH$
   E. $CH_3CH_2CH_2CH_2CH_3$

4. A carboxylic acid may be represented as:

   A. ROH
   B. RCHO
   C. R-O-R′
   D. RCOOH
   E. RCOOR′

ANSWERS AND EXPLANATIONS

✓

1. **C.** The general formula, C_nH_{2n}, means that 1 mol of H_2O will form per mole of empirical formula unit, regardless of the value of n. The moles of water formed is the mass of the alkene divided by the empirical formula mass.

(0.500 g alkene)(1 mol alkene/14 g alkene)(1 mol H_2O/mol alkene)

$$= 0.036 \text{ mol}$$

2. **C.** Organic bases are, in general, amines (contain N). An ether would have an oxygen single bonded to two carbons (R groups). An aldehyde has oxygen double bonded to a carbon at the end of a chain. Aldehydes (RCHO) and alcohols (ROH) are often confused because of the similarity in their general formulas. Ketones have oxygen double bonded to a carbon not at the end of a chain.

3. **A.** Redrawing the structures may help you recognize the correct answer. An optical isomer must be a carbon atom with four *different* groups attached to it. For A the groups on the second carbon are: CH_{3-}, H, Cl, and $-CH_2CH_2CH_3$. Answer C is misleading. It is similar to A, but two of the groups, the $-CH_2CH_3$ groups, are the same.

4. **D.** A = alcohol   B = aldehyde   C = ether   D = ester

FREE-RESPONSE QUESTIONS

You have 20 minutes to do the following questions. You may use a calculator.

The alkane hexane, C_6H_{14}, has a molecular weight of 86.17 g/mol.

a. Like all hydrocarbons, hexane will burn. Write a balanced chemical equation for the complete combustion of hexane. This reaction produces gaseous carbon dioxide and liquid water.

b. The complete combustion of 10.0 g of hexane produces 487 kJ. What is the molar heat of combustion (ΔH) of hexane?

c. Determine the pressure exerted by the carbon dioxide formed when 5.00 g of hexane is combusted. Assume the carbon dioxide is dry and stored in a 20.0-L container at 27° C.

d. Under identical conditions, hexane vapor diffuses at one-half the rate of the vapor of another compound. What is the molar mass of the other compound?

e. Hexane, like most alkanes, may exist in different isomeric forms. The structural formula of one of these isomers is pictured below. Draw the structural formula of any two other isomers of hexane. Make sure all carbons atoms and hydrogen atoms are shown.

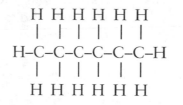

ANSWERS AND EXPLANATIONS

a. $2\ C_6H_{14} + 19\ O_2 \rightarrow 12\ CO_2 + 14\ H_2O$

Give yourself 2 points for the answer shown above, or for the coefficients: 1, 9/2, 6, and 7. Give yourself 1 point if you have one or more, not all, of the elements balanced.

b. $(-487\ kJ/10.0\ g\ \text{hexane})\ (86.17\ g\ \text{hexane/mol hexane}) = -4.20 \times 10^3\ kJ/mol$

Give yourself 2 points for the above setup and correct answer (this requires a negative sign in the answer). If the setup is partially correct, give yourself 1 point.

c. The ideal gas equation should be rearranged to the form $P = nRT/V$.

$n = (5.00\ g\ \text{hexane})\ (1\ mol\ \text{hexane}/86.17\ g\ \text{hexane})$

$(12\ mol\ CO_2/2\ mol\ \text{hexane}) = 0.3481\ mol\ CO_2$

This answer has an extra significant figure. The mole ratio should match the one given in your balanced equation. You will not be penalized again for an incorrectly balanced equation. You will lose a point if you do not include a hexane-to-CO_2 conversion.

$R = 0.0821\ L\ atm/mol\ K$

This value is given in your test booklet.

$$T = 27° + 273 = 300 \text{ K}$$

You will be penalized if your forget to use the Kelvin temperature.

$$V = 20.0 \text{ L}$$

$$P = (0.3481 \text{ mol CO}_2) (0.0821 \text{ L atm/mol K}) (300 \text{ K})/(20.0 \text{ L})$$
$$= 0.429 \text{ atm}.$$

Give yourself 2 points for the correct setup and answer. Give yourself 1 point if you did everything correctly, except the mole ratio or the Kelvin conversion.

d. This part requires Graham's law: $r_1/r_2 = (M_2/M_1)^{1/2}$

If we let "1" refer to hexane, and "2" refer to the unknown vapor, then: $r_1 = (1/2)r_2$, and $M_1 = 86.17 \text{ g/mol}$. When these values are plugged into the equation:

$$\frac{(1/2)r_2}{r_2} = \left(M_2/86.17 \text{ g/mol}\right)^{1/2}$$

Canceling and then squaring both sides gives:

$$(1/2)^2 = (1/4) = M_2/86.17 \text{ g/mol}$$

$$M_2 = (1/4)(86.17 \text{ g/mol}) = 21.54 \text{ g/mol}$$

Give yourself 2 points for the correct setup and the correct answer. It is not necessary to show all the intermediate steps. Give yourself 1 point if you make a mistake.

e. You may need to redraw one or more of your answers to match the answers shown below. Give yourself 1 point for each correct answer, with a 2-point maximum. There are no bonus points for additional answers.

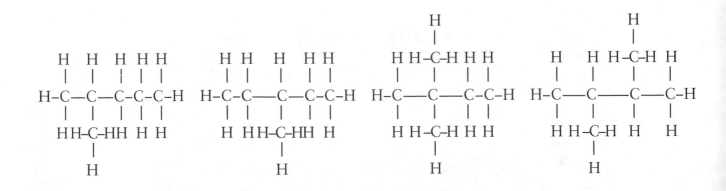

These compounds are 2-methylpentane, 3-methylpentane, 2,2-dimethylbutane and 2,3-dimethylbutane, respectively. These four, along with the original n-hexane are the only isomers. If you think you have another isomer, you have simply redrawn one of these. Try naming your answer and see if it matches one of these names.

Total your points. The maximum is 10 points.

RAPID REVIEW

- Organic chemistry is the chemistry of carbon.

- Hydrocarbons are organic compounds of just carbon and hydrogens.

- Alkanes are hydrocarbons in which there are only single bonds.

- Alkanes are named in a very systematic way. Review the rules for naming alkanes.

- Isomers are compounds that have the same molecular formulas but different structural formulas. Review the writing of the various structural isomers of alkanes. **Make sure that each carbon atom has four bonds.**

- A functional group is a group of atoms that is the reactive part of the molecule. Review the general functional groups.

- Macromolecules are large molecules that may have molecular weights in the millions. Macromolecules are generally composed of repeating units called monomers.

Chapter 17

Experimental

 KEYWORDS AND EQUATIONS

Beer's Law: A = abc (A = absorbance; a = molar absorbtivity; b = path length; c = concentration)

analytical balance	barometer	beaker(s)
buret	burner	calorimeter
capillary tubes	centrifuge	clamp
crucible and cover	cuvettes	desiccator
drying oven	electrodes	Erlenmeyer flask
evaporating dish	filter crucibles	filter flasks
forceps	and adapters	graduated cylinder
hot plate	funnel	ion exchange resin
Meker burner	ice	or silica gel
pipette	mortar and pestle	pH meter
rubber tubing	power supply (battery)	Pt or Ni test wire
stopwatch	spectrophotometer	stirrer
test tube rack	support stand	test tube(s)
triangle crucible	thermometer	tongs
support	voltmeter	volumetric flask
wash bottle	watch glass	water bath
wire gauze		

INTRODUCTION

The free-response portion of the AP exam routinely contains a question concerning an experiment, and there may also be a few multiple-choice questions on one or more of these experiments. This chapter reviews the basic experiments the AP Exam Committee believes to be important. You should look over all of the experiments in this chapter and pay particular attention to any experiments you did not perform. In some cases you may find, after reading the description, that you did a similar experiment. Not every AP class does every experiment, but any of these experiments may appear on the AP exam.

The free-response questions on recent exams have been concerned with the equipment, measurements, and calculations required. In some cases, sources of error are considered. To answer the question completely, you will need an understanding of the chemical concepts involved.

To discuss an experiment, you must be familiar with the equipment needed. In the keywords section at the beginning of this chapter is a complete list of equipment for the experiments. Make sure you are familiar with each item. You may know an item by a different name, or you may need to talk to your teacher to get additional information concerning an item.

In some cases, the exam question will request a list of the equipment needed, while in other cases you will get a list from which to choose the items you need. Certain items appear in many experiments. These include the analytical balance, beakers, support stands, pipettes, test tubes, and Erlenmeyer flasks. Burets, graduated cylinders, clamps, desiccators, drying ovens, pH meters, volumetric flasks, and thermometers are also commonly used. If you are not sure what equipment to choose, these serve as good guesses. Most of the remaining equipment appears in three or fewer experiments.

You will need to know the basic measurements required for the experiment. For example, you may need to measure the initial and final temperatures. Do not make the mistake of saying you measure the change in temperature. You *calculate* the change in temperature from your measured initial and final temperatures. You do not need to give a lot of detail when listing the required measurements, but you need to be very specific in what you *measure*.

The basic calculations fall into two categories. Simple calculations, such as the change in temperature or the change in volume, are the easiest to forget. Simple calculations may also include mass-to-mole conversions. The other calculations normally involve plugging into one of the equations given at the beginning of an earlier chapter in this book.

EXPERIMENT 1: FINDING THE FORMULA OF A COMPOUND

Synopsis

The formula of a compound is determined by using the mass of the original substance, usually a metal, and the mass of a compound of that substance, usually an oxide. (See Chapter 5.)

Equipment

analytical balance	burner	crucible and cover
support stand	tongs	triangle crucible support

Measurements

1. the mass of the crucible and cover
2. the mass of the original sample and the crucible and cover
3. the mass of the reacted sample and the crucible and cover

The last measurement must be done after the sample has cooled to room temperature.

Calculations

The mass of the sample is calculated by taking the difference between masses 1 and 2. The mass of the substance that combined with the original substance is calculated from the difference between masses 2 and 3. The moles of the substances must be calculated by dividing each mass by the atomic weight of the element. The empirical formula is calculated from the simplest ratio of the moles of the elements present.

Comments

This procedure will allow you to calculate the empirical formula of the substance. The experiment is often performed by reacting magnesium metal with atmospheric oxygen to form magnesium oxide.

EXPERIMENT 2: THE PERCENTAGE OF WATER IN A HYDRATE

Synopsis

The amount of water present in a sample is determined by weighing a compound before and after heating. The difference in mass is due to the loss of water. (See Chapter 5.)

Equipment

analytical balance	burner	crucible and cover
support stand	test tube(s)	tongs
triangle crucible support	wire gauze	

Measurements

1. the mass of the crucible and cover
2. the mass of the original sample and the crucible and cover
3. the mass of the heated (dried) sample and the crucible and cover

The last measurement must be done after the sample has cooled to room temperature.

Calculations

The mass of the hydrate is calculated from the difference between masses 1 and 2. The mass of the water lost is calculated from the difference between masses 2 and 3. The percentage of water is calculated by dividing the mass of the water lost by the mass of the hydrate and multiplying the result by 100%.

A variation of this experiment uses the mass of the anhydrous material (calculated from the difference between masses 1 and 3). The moles of the anhydrous material and water are then calculated from their respective masses and molar masses. The simplest ratio of the moles gives the empirical formula.

Comments

The experiment often uses copper(II) sulfate hydrate, magnesium sulfate hydrate, calcium sulfate hydrate, or barium chloride hydrate.

EXPERIMENT 3: MOLAR MASS BY VAPOR DENSITY

Synopsis

The molar mass (molecular weight) of a volatile substance is determined in this experiment. The mass of a sample of vapor is initially determined. This mass, along with the volume of the container, the pressure, and the temperature is used with the ideal gas equation to calculate the molar mass. (See Chapter 6.)

Equipment

analytical balance	barometer	beaker(s)
clamp	Erlenmeyer flask	graduated cylinder
support stand		

Measurements

1. the mass of the flask
2. the mass of the flask plus condensed vapor
3. the temperature of the water bath used to heat the flask
4. the barometric pressure
5. the number of milliliters of water required to fill the flask

Calculations

There are a variety of ways to do the calculations. Most of these, however, involve the calculation of the number of moles (n) from the ideal gas equation: $n = PV/RT$. The mass of the vapor sample is calculated from the difference between measurements 1 and 2. The temperature (measurement 3) is converted to Kelvin. The pressure (measurement 4) is converted to atmospheres. Measurement 5 is converted to liters. Plugging the various numbers into the ideal gas equation allows you to calculate the number of moles. The molar mass is calculated by dividing the mass of the sample by the moles.

Comments

Variations in this experiment usually combine the ideal gas equation with the mass of the sample.

EXPERIMENT 4: MOLAR MASS BY FREEZING POINT DEPRESSION

Synopsis

The molar mass (molecular weight) of a solute is determined by measuring its effect on the freezing point of a solvent. A cooling curve is constructed by plotting the temperature of a solution that is slowly cooling versus time. After the solution completely freezes, the difference between the solution's freezing point and the pure solvent's freezing point is calculated. The change in the freezing point is then related to the molality of the solution. (See Chapter 11.)

Equipment

beaker(s)	ice	pipette
stirrer	stopwatch	test tube(s)
thermometer		

Measurements

1. the mass of the empty test tube
2. the mass of the test tube plus the solvent
3. the mass of the test tube plus solute plus solvent

The solid solvent or solution is heated above its melting point and then allowed to cool.

4. repeated measurements of the temperature
5. the times at which the preceding measurements were made

The above series of measurements may be done one time for the solvent and one time for the solution, or the melting point of the solvent may be obtained (not measured) from a table.

Calculations

The mass of the solvent is calculated from the difference between measurements 1 and 2. The mass of the solute is calculated from the differences between masses 2 and 3. The mass of the solvent is converted to kilograms.

The temperature and time measurements (4 and 5) are plotted, and a smooth curve is drawn.

The temperature difference between the "level" regions of the solvent plot and the solution plot (or the difference between the solution plot and the tabulated freezing point of the solvent) is used to calculate the change in temperature (ΔT) between the freezing point of the solvent and the solution. The change in temperature divided by the freezing point depression constant (from a table) will give the molality of the solution. The molality of the solution times the kilograms of solvent yields the moles of solute. Finally, the mass of the solute divided by the moles of solute gives its molar mass.

Comments

One variation in this experiment is to add the solute to the test tube before the solvent.

EXPERIMENT 5: MOLAR VOLUME OF A GAS

Synopsis

The volume occupied by a mole of a gas is calculated in this experiment. A sample of a solid substance is heated, decomposing it into several products, including a gas. The mass of the gas is determined by the weight difference before and after heating and is then converted to moles. The volume of the gas, the pressure, and temperature are measured. (See Chapter 6.)

Equipment

analytical balance	barometer	beaker(s)
clamp	Erlenmeyer flask	graduated cylinder
rubber tubing	test tube(s)	thermometer

Measurements

1. the barometric pressure
2. the mass of the test tube plus solid sample (before the reaction)
3. the mass of the test tube plus sample after the reaction
4. the temperature of the water
5. volume of water displaced into the beaker, if the variation is used

The mass of the test tube after the reaction must be determined after the test tube has completely cooled to room temperature.

Calculations

The temperature must be converted to Kelvin (T_1), and the volume of water is normally expressed in liters.

The mass of gas generated is calculated by taking the difference between measurements 2 and 3. Using the molar mass of the gas, the mass of gas is converted to moles of gas (n).

For the variation, the vapor pressure of water at the recorded temperature is found in a table. The pressure of the gas (P_1) is the difference between the value in the table and measurement 1.

The volume of water in the beaker is the volume of the gas (V_1).

Calculate the volume (V_2) of the gas at STP (T_2 and P_2) using the combined gas law.

The molar volume of the gas is the volume at STP (V_2) divided by the moles of gas (n).

Comments

The most common procedure is to produce oxygen gas by decomposing $KClO_3$. A common variation is to measure the volume of gas produced by displacing water from a flask. The volume of water displaced is the volume of gas generated at that temperature and pressure. From a measurement of the atmospheric pressure and the temperature of the gas, the volume of gas at STP can be calculated.

EXPERIMENT 6: STANDARDIZATION OF A SOLUTION

Synopsis

The concentration of a solution (the titrant) is determined by using it to titrate a sample of known composition. (See Chapter 5.)

Equipment

analytical balance	buret	desiccator
drying oven	Erlenmeyer flask	pH meter
pipette	support stand	volumetric flask
wash bottle		

Measurements

1. the mass of an empty flask
2. the mass of the flask plus the sample
3. the initial reading of the buret
4. intermediate readings from the buret
5. the final reading of the buret
6. the pH of the solution at various times during the reaction

Calculations

The mass of the sample is calculated from the differences between masses 1 and 2. The volume added is calculated by taking the difference between measurement 3 and either measurement 4 or 5.

A plot of pH versus the volume added is made. This graph or the difference between measurements 3 and 5 gives the volume of titrant.

The volume of titrant is converted to liters.

The mass of the sample is converted to moles by using the molar mass. The moles of titrant may be calculated from a consideration of the moles of sample and the balanced chemical equation. The moles of titrant divided by the liters of solution gives the molarity of the solution.

Comments

A solution could be prepared by dissolving a known amount of solute in a volumetric flask and diluting to volume.

The course of the titration could be followed with an acid–base indicator instead of a pH meter.

EXPERIMENT 7: ACID–BASE TITRATION

Synopsis

The concentration of an acid or a base (titrant) may be determined by titrating a solution of an unknown concentration with a solution of a known concentration.

Equipment

analytical balance	buret	clamp
desiccator	drying oven	Erlenmeyer flask
pH meter	pipette	support stand
wash bottle		

Measurements

1. the volume of the solution of acid or base using a pipette
2. the initial reading of the buret
3. intermediate readings from the buret
4. the final reading of the buret
5. the pH of the solution at various times during the reaction

Calculations

The volume added is calculated by taking the difference between measurement 2 and either measurement 3 or 4.

A plot of pH versus the volume added is made. This graph or the difference between measurements 2 and 3 gives the volume of titrant.

The volume of titrant is converted to liters.

The pipetted volume is converted to moles by multiplying the liters of solution by its molarity. The moles of titrant are determined using the mole ratio in the balanced chemical equation for the acid–base reaction. The molarity of the solution is calculated by dividing the moles of titrant by the liters of titrant used.

Comments

It does not matter whether an acid is titrated by a base or vice versa.

EXPERIMENT 8: OXIDATION-REDUCTION TITRATION

Synopsis

The concentration of either an oxidizing or a reducing agent may be determined by titrating a solution of an unknown concentration versus a solution of a known concentration or containing a known mass of solute.

Equipment

analytical balance	buret	clamp
desiccator	drying oven	Erlenmeyer flask
pH meter	pipette	support stand
wash bottle		

Measurements

1. the volume of a solution of an oxidant or reductant using a pipette
2. the initial reading of the buret
3. the final reading of the buret

Calculations

The volume of titrant added is calculated by the difference between measurements 2 and 3.

The volume of titrant is then converted to liters.

The pipetted volume is converted to moles by multiplying the liters of solution by its molarity. The moles of titrant are determined from the mole ratio in the balanced chemical equation for the reaction. The molarity of the solution is calculated by dividing the moles of titrant by the liters of titrant used.

Comments

Common oxidants are potassium permanganate and potassium dichromate.

Iron(II) and oxalates are commonly chosen as reductants.

EXPERIMENT 9: MASS/MOLE RELATIONSHIPS IN A CHEMICAL REACTION

Synopsis

The initial masses of various reactants may be determined and then converted to moles. A similar calculation may be done for the products.

Equipment

analytical balance	beaker(s)	desiccator
Erlenmeyer flask	graduated cylinder	hot plate

Measurements

mass of samples of different reactants
mass of samples of different products

Calculations

Convert the masses of the reactants and products to moles using their molar masses. Using the mole ratios from the balanced chemical equation, it is possible to determine how much material should react or be produced. These calculated values can be compared to the observed values.

Comments

Nearly any reaction may be used.

EXPERIMENT 10: FINDING THE EQUILIBRIUM CONSTANT

Synopsis

The value of an equilibrium constant is calculated by measuring (or calculating) the equilibrium concentrations of the reactants and products. A calibration curve is constructed by measuring the absorbance of a colored solution versus its concentration. Known quantities of the reactants are mixed, and the calibration curve is used to determine the concentration of the colored substance in the resultant solution. (See Chapter 13.)

Equipment

analytical balance	pipette	spectrophotometer
test tube(s) or cuvettes	volumetric flask	

Spectrophotometers

Some of the AP recommended experiments require the use of a spectrophotometer. A spectrophotometer is an instrument that is used to measure the amount of light absorbed (or percentage transmitted) by a particular solute in a solution. In order to determine the absorbance (A) of a sample, the instrument is set to a particular wavelength; a solution, contained in a holder called a cuvette, is placed in a sample chamber and an absorbance reading is taken. This procedure may be repeated for other solutions or wavelengths. The cuvette is a standard size to ensure a given path length (b).

A plot of absorbance versus wavelength may be used to identify a component of a solution or to determine the wavelength of maximum absorbance (maximum molar absorptivity = a). A more common plot is one of absorbance versus concentration. For this type of plot the instrument is set at the wavelength of maximum molar absorptivity and the absorbances of solutions of various known concentrations (c) are measured. This plot should be a straight line. This linear relationship is called Beer's Law and has the form of A = abc. The concentration of an unknown solution may be determined by measuring its absorbance and using the plot to find its concentration.

Measurements

Calibration Curve

Quantities of one or more reactants are pipetted into a volumetric flask.
The solutions are diluted to a known volume in the volumetric flask.
Measurements of the absorbance are made with a spectrophotometer.

Equilibrium Concentrations

Different quantities of various reactants are pipetted into a volumetric flask and diluted to a known volume.
Measurements of the absorbance of these solutions are made with a spectrophotometer.

Calculations

Calibration Curve

The concentration of the absorbing species is calculated using the initial pipetted volumes and the final volumetric flask volume. These concentrations are plotted versus the absorbance of the solution.

Equilibrium Concentrations

The final concentration of each reactant is calculated from the final volume and the volume and concentration of the solution pipetted into the volumetric flask. The calibration curve is used to find the equilibrium concentration. Using the balanced chemical equation, the equilibrium concentrations of the other substances may be calculated.

The equilibrium concentrations are plugged into the reaction quotient expression, and the equilibrium constant is calculated.

Comments

Any equilibrium may be used, as long as one substance is colored.

EXPERIMENT 11: PH MEASUREMENTS AND INDICATORS FOR ACID–BASE TITRATIONS

Synopsis

The acidity of various substances is determined with a pH meter or acid–base indicators. This may also be done by mixing or diluting solutions. (See Chapter 13.)

Equipment

analytical balance	Erlenmeyer flask	graduated cylinder
pH meter	pipette	volumetric flask

Measurements

1. Weigh each acid or base into a volumetric flask, and dilute to volume.
2. Pipette a sample of an acid or base of known concentration into a volumetric flask, and dilute to volume.
3. Pipette different solutions into a flask.
4. Measure the pH of the solutions using a pH meter.

Calculations

All weighed samples are converted to moles by using the molar mass, and the moles are divided by the volume of the volumetric flask in liters to yield molarity.

The concentrations of the diluted solutions (measurement 2) are calculated by using the dilution equation.

The concentrations of the other solutions (measurement 3) are calculated from the balanced chemical equation and the dilution equation.

The pH may be estimated by adding an acid–base indicator to any of the prepared solutions.

The hydrogen ion concentration, hydroxide ion concentration, or pOH may be calculated from the pH. One or more of these may be used to determine the concentration of all other species in the solution.

Comments

The original acids and bases may all be solids or solutions, or a mixture of both.

EXPERIMENT 12: THE RATE AND ORDER OF A REACTION

Synopsis

The rate equation for a reaction is determined in this experiment. Known quantities of solutions are mixed, and the time required for a change is recorded. (See Chapter 12.)

Equipment

analytical balance   buret   clamp
Erlenmeyer flask   graduated cylinder   pipette
stopwatch   support stand   thermometer

Measurements

1. Weigh solid samples.
2. Use a pipette or a buret to measure the volume of any solutions.
3. Use the buret to measure the volume of any gas formed (multiple measurements at different times may be required).
4. Measure the temperature of the solutions.
5. Measure time intervals or record the time after mixing when an observable change occurs.

NOTE: When using a buret, an initial and a final measurement are always needed.

Calculations

Using the molar mass, calculate the moles of all weighed samples. The moles of substances are converted to molarities by dividing by the volume of the solution. Molarities may also be determined from pipette or buret readings using the dilution equation. (If a buret is used, one of the volumes is calculated from the difference between the initial and final readings.) The dilution equation may be needed to calculate the concentration of each reactant immediately after all the solutions are mixed.

If a gas is being generated, plot the volume of gas formed versus time. The volume of the gas formed is the difference between the initial buret reading and the buret reading at a particular time. The slope of this graph is the rate.

The rate may also be determined by taking the amount of any reactant divided by the time required.

Tabulate the concentrations of the reactant solutions and the rates for various trials. The rate law may be determined by comparing values in this table. (See Chapter 12.)

Comments

Many types of reactions may be used. The simple recording of the time required for a noticeable change is particularly applicable to "clock" reactions.

EXPERIMENT 13: ENTHALPY CHANGES

Synopsis

In this experiment the heat change associated with a process is calculated. Various substances are added to a calorimeter (usually a polystyrene cup), and the initial and the final temperatures are measured. (See Chapter 7.)

Equipment

analytical balance   calorimeter   graduated cylinder
thermometer

Measurements

1. The masses of various substances are determined.
2. The volume of a solution or solvent is determined with a graduated cylinder.
3. Measure the initial temperature.
4. Measure the final temperature.

Calculations

The masses are converted to moles using the molar mass. The volumes of solutions may be converted to moles using the molarity.

The mass of a solvent or solution may be calculated from the volume and density.

A total mass may need to be calculated by adding the individual masses together.

The change in temperature (ΔT) is calculated from the difference between the final and initial temperatures.

The energy (Joules or calories) is calculated by multiplying the mass times the change in temperature times the specific heat (from a table).

The enthalpy change is calculated by dividing the calculated energy by the moles, mass, or some other designated quantity.

Comments

Any reaction or phase change may be used.

EXPERIMENT 14: QUALITATIVE ANALYSIS OF CATIONS AND ANIONS

Synopsis

Solutions containing various ions are tested for the presence of certain specified ions. The formation of colors, gases, or precipitates indicates the presence or absence of certain ions. (See Chapter 4.)

Equipment

beaker(s)	centrifuge	evaporating dish
funnel	mortar and pestle	Pt or Ni test wire
test tube(s)	watch glass	

Measurements

This is primarily an observation experiment. No precise measurements are needed.

Calculations

No calculations are required.

Comments

A wide variety of cations or anions may be used. Many of the results are a simple application of the solubility rules.

EXPERIMENT 15: SYNTHESIS AND ANALYSIS OF A COORDINATION COMPOUND

Synopsis

A coordination compound is usually synthesized from a transition metal ion that is in solution. The compound is filtered from the solution and tested in various ways to determine the composition of the substance. (See Chapter 4.)

Equipment

analytical balance   beaker(s)   Erlenmeyer flask
evaporating dish   pipette   spectrophotometer
test tube(s) or cuvettes   volumetric flask

Measurements

Synthesis

Quantities of the reactants are weighed and added to a beaker. A solvent may or may not be present initially.

The mass of the product is determined by weighing.

Analysis

Weigh a sample of the compound into a volumetric flask, and dilute to volume.

Use a pipette to measure samples to be diluted.

Measure the absorbency of the diluted solutions with a spectrophotometer. This may or may not require the separate construction of a calibration curve.

Calculations

Calculate the moles of each reactant from the masses and molar masses. Then calculate the yield based on the limiting reagent. The mass of the product, determined at the end of the synthesis, divided by the mass calculated from the limiting reagent times 100%, gives the percent yield.

There are numerous possible analysis calculations.

Comments

Commonly synthesized coordination compounds include $K_3[Fe(C_2O_4)_3]$ and $[Co(NH_3)_6]Cl_3$.

EXPERIMENT 16: GRAVIMETRIC ANALYSIS

Synopsis

The amount of a substance present in a sample is determined by taking a solution containing that substance and precipitating a compound containing that substance. The precipitate is then dried and weighed. (See Chapter 5.)

Equipment

analytical balance	beaker(s)	crucible and cover
desiccator	drying oven	funnel
Meker burner	support stand	triangle crucible support

Measurements

1. A sample is weighed and then dissolved.
2. Excess (unmeasured) reactant is added to the solution to form a precipitate.
3. The empty crucible and cover are weighed.
4. The crucible and cover containing the dried precipitate are weighed.

Calculations

The mass of the precipitate is found as the difference between measurements 3 and 4.

The mass of the dried precipitate is converted into moles by using the molar mass. Through use of a stoichiometric ratio, the moles of precipitate are converted to the moles of the substance of interest. The moles of this substance are converted to its mass using the molar mass.

The mass of the substance of interest divided by the mass of the sample and then multiplied by 100% gives the percent of a substance in the sample.

Comments

Common precipitates include AgCl and $BaSO_4$.

EXPERIMENT 17: COLORIMETRIC ANALYSIS

Synopsis

This experiment involves determining the amount of a substance in a solution. A calibration curve is constructed plotting the measured absorbance versus the concentration of a colored substance. The concentration of an unknown solution may be determined by reversing this process.

Equipment

buret	pipette	spectrophotometer
support stand		test tube(s) or cuvettes

Measurements

Using either a pipette or a buret, quantities of standard solutions are measured. (If a buret is used, separate measurements of the initial and final volumes are needed.) Solvent may be added to dilute the samples if needed. These are the known solutions from which a calibration curve will be constructed.

The absorbance of each solution is determined with a spectrophotometer.

The absorbance of one or more unknown solutions is determined with a spectrophotometer.

Calculations

Concentrations of the known solutions are calculated using the dilution equation.

A plot of absorbance versus concentration for the known solutions is made.

The plot allows the absorbance of the unknown solution(s) to be converted to concentration.

Comments

Any colored substance may be used.

EXPERIMENT 18: CHROMATOGRAPHIC SEPARATION

Synopsis

Two or more substances are separated by the differences in their affinity to paper or some other material.

Equipment

beaker(s)   capillary tubes
pipette   test tube(s)
ion exchange resin or silica gel

Measurements

In some cases, the distance a spot travels on the chromatographic media is measured. This requires the use of a ruler.

Calculations

There are usually no calculations.

Comments

Instead of an ion exchange resin or silica gel, it is possible to use filter paper as a chromatographic media.

EXPERIMENT 19: PROPERTIES OF BUFFER SOLUTIONS

Synopsis

Buffer and non-buffer solutions are prepared. The pHs of these solutions are determined before and after other substances—usually acids or bases—are added.

Equipment

beaker(s)   pH meter   pipette
volumetric flask

Measurements

volumes of the pipetted solutions
pH of various solutions

Calculations

The concentrations of the solutions may be calculated by using the dilution equation. Concentrations may then be converted to moles by multiplying the concentration by the liters of solution. This procedure applies to buffer components or any reactant species.

The moles of substances may be determined from the initial moles and stoichiometry. Combined with the liters of solution, these may be used to determine the final concentrations.

Comments

The pH values of the solutions may be used in several ways, depending upon the goal of the experiment.

EXPERIMENT 20: AN ELECTROCHEMICAL SERIES

Synopsis

The reactivity of several metals with solutions containing ions of other metals is observed. (See Chapter 4.)

Equipment

beaker(s)	forceps	graduated cylinder
test tube(s)	test tube rack	

Measurements

This experiment is based on observations, not measurements.

Calculations

Observations, not calculations, are needed.

Comments

The more active metal will displace a less active metal from a solution. Hydrogen is usually included in the series by using acids.

EXPERIMENT 21: ELECTROCHEMICAL CELLS AND ELECTROPLATING

Synopsis

Electrochemical cells are constructed, and their cell potentials are deter-mined with a voltmeter. Electroplating is accomplished by using an external power supply, usually a battery, to plate a metal onto an electrode. (See Chapter 14.)

Equipment

beaker(s)	electrodes	filter crucibles and adapters
filter flasks	power supply (battery)	test tube(s)
voltmeter		

Measurements

The cell potentials are measured with a voltmeter.

Calculations

Normally, no calculations are required.

Comments

Cells may vary in composition or concentrations.

EXPERIMENT 22: SYNTHESIS AND PROPERTIES OF AN ORGANIC COMPOUND

Synopsis

Any of a number of chemical reactions can be used to synthesize an organic compound. After synthesis, the compound is purified and tested. (See Chapter 16.)

Equipment

analytical balance	buret	burner
capillary tubes	drying oven	Erlenmeyer flask
evaporating dish	filter flasks	support stand
thermometer	water bath	

Measurements

Quantities of reactants are measured by using either mass or volume measurements. In some cases, the mass of the product is measured.

Calculations

When the mass of the product (actual yield) is measured, normally a percent yield is required. The mass of the limiting reagent is converted, through moles, to the theoretical yield of product. The percent yield is calculated by dividing the actual yield by the theoretical yield, then multiplying the resulting value by 100%.

Comments

Many different compounds could be synthesized.

COMMON MISTAKES TO AVOID

1. You *measure* initial and final values, but *calculate* the change.
2. You use an analytical balance to weigh the mass (grams), but not the moles.

 REVIEW QUESTIONS

Multiple-choice questions concerning experiments have been embedded in the review questions in the appropriate chapters.

ANSWERS AND EXPLANATIONS

None

 FREE-RESPONSE QUESTIONS

First Free-Response Question

 Answer the following question. You have 15 minutes, and you may not use a calculator.

A water-soluble sample of a solid containing some barium nitrate is to be analyzed for barium. The barium is to be precipitated as barium sulfate. Answer the following questions about this experiment.

a. List the apparatus needed for this experiment.

b. Outline the steps in this experiment.

c. Set up the calculations needed to determine the percent barium in the sample.

d. What changes would be required in the procedure if the original sample also contained lead?

Second Free-Response Question

Answer the following question. You have 15 minutes, and you may not use a calculator.

A sample of a solid, weak monoprotic acid, HA, is supplied, along with solid sodium hydroxide, a phenolphthalein solution, and primary standard potassium hydrogen phthalate (KHP).

a. Describe how a standardized sodium hydroxide solution may be prepared for the titration.

b. Sketch a pH versus volume of base added for the titration.

c. Sketch the titration curve if the unknown acid was really a diprotic acid.

d. Describe the steps to determine K_a for HA.

e. What factor determines which indicator should be chosen for this titration?

ANSWERS AND EXPLANATIONS

First Free-Response Question

a.
analytical balance	beaker(s)	crucible and cover
desiccator	drying oven	funnel
Meker burner	support stand	triangle crucible support

You get 1 point for the following set: analytical balance, crucible and cover, and funnel.

You get 1 point for any others you list. There is a maximum of 2 points.

You can only get the second point if you have the entire first set.

b. *Weigh a sample of the solid (into a beaker).

Heat the crucible and lid with the Meker burner repeatedly until constant weight is achieved.

*Weigh the crucible and lid.

Add sufficient deionized water to dissolve the sample.
(Warm the solution).
*Slowly add a solution containing the sulfate ion (usually sodium sulfate) to the solution.
Allow the precipitate to settle, and check for complete precipitation.
*Filter the precipitate and place it in the crucible.
Heat the crucible and lid with the sample to constant weight.
*Weigh the cooled crucible, lid, and sample.

You get 2 points for everything in order. Information in parentheses is optional. The first two items may be in any order. You get 1 point if the order is wrong or if any of the starred items is missing.

c. mass of precipitate = (crucible + lid + sample) − (crucible + lid)

$$\text{mass of barium in sample} = \frac{(\text{mass of precipitate})(1 \text{ mol BaSO}_4)(137.33 \text{ g Ba})}{(233.34 \text{ g BaSO}_4)(1 \text{ mol Ba})}$$

$$\text{percentage of barium} = \frac{(\text{mass of barium in sample}) \ 100\%}{(\text{mass of original sample})}$$

Give yourself 1 point for each correct equation. The values 137.33 and 233.34 are optional.

d. Lead would also precipitate as the sulfate. It would be necessary to remove the lead before the sulfate was added.

Give yourself 1 point for this answer.

There are a total of 8 points possible.

Second Free-Response Question

a. A sample of sodium hydroxide is weighed and dissolved in deionized water to give a solution of the approximate concentration desired. (Alternatively, a concentrated NaOH solution could be diluted.)

Samples of dried KHP are weighed into flasks and dissolved in deionized water.

A few drops of the appropriate acid–base indicator (phenolphthalein) are added to each sample.

A buret is rinsed with a little of the NaOH solution; then the buret is filled with NaOH solution.

An initial buret reading is taken.

NaOH solution is titrated into the KHP samples until the first permanent pink color.

A final buret reading is taken.

Using the molar mass of KHP, determine the moles of KHP present. This is equal to the moles of NaOH.

The difference in the buret readings is the volume of NaOH solution added (convert this to liters).

The molarity of the NaOH solution is the moles NaOH divided by the liters of NaOH solution added.

(Repeat the procedure for each sample.)

Give yourself 2 points for this entire list, if the items are in order. If three or more items are in the wrong order or missing, you only get 1 point. You get 0 points for three or fewer items.

b.

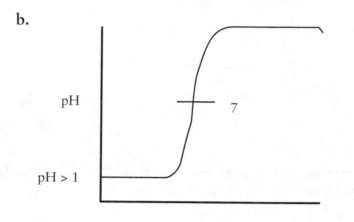

Volume Added

Equivalence point at pH < 7

You get 1 point for this graph. You get an additional point for noting that the equivalence point is greater than 7.

c.

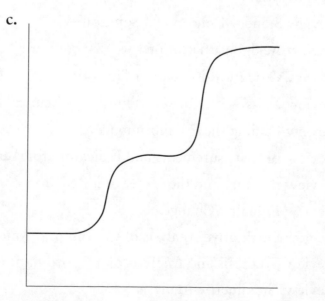

You get 1 point for this graph. You must show two regions.

d. There are several related ways to do this problem. One method is to split the sample into two portions. Titrate one portion to the equivalence point. Add the titrated sample to the un-titrated sample, and add a volume of deionized water equal to the volume of NaOH solution added. The pH of this mixture is equal to the pK_a of the acid (this corresponds to a half-titrated sample).

You get 1 point for anything concerning a half-titrated sample and an additional point for pH = pK_a.

e. The pH at the equivalence point must be close to the pK_a of the indicator.

You get 1 point for this answer.

There are 8 points possible.

RAPID REVIEW

Reviewing the experiments should include looking at the synopsis, apparatus, calculations and comments.

- Review Finding the Formula of a Compound
- Review the Percentage of Water in a Hydrate
- Review Molar Mass by Vapor Density
- Review Molar Mass by Freezing Point Depression
- Review Molar Volume of a Gas
- Review Standardization of a Solution
- Review Acid–Base Titration
- Review Oxidation-Reduction Titration
- Review Mass/Mole Relationships in a Chemical Reaction
- Review Finding the Equilibrium Constant
- Review pH Measurements and Indicators for Acid–Base Titrations
- Review the Rate and the Order of a Reaction
- Review Enthalpy Changes
- Review Qualitative Analysis of Cations and Anions
- Review Synthesis and Analysis of a Coordination Compound
- Review Gravimetric Analysis

- Review Colorimetric Analysis
- Review Chromatographic Separation
- Review Properties of Buffer Solutions
- Review an Electrochemical Series
- Review Electrochemical Cells and Electroplating
- Review Synthesis and Properties of an Organic Compound

PART IV

PRACTICE MAKES PERFECT

AP CHEMISTRY PRACTICE EXAM 1: THE FIRST OPPORTUNITY TO EXCEL

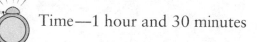

Time—1 hour and 30 minutes

Answer the following questions in the time allowed. You may use a periodic table while taking this exam. Write the answers on a separate sheet of paper.

1. Choose the strongest Lewis base from the following.

   A. Na^+
   B. Fe^{3+}
   C. NH_3
   D. Zn^{2+}
   E. BF_3

2. Which of the following CANNOT behave as both a Brønsted base and a Brønsted acid?

   A. HPO_4^{2-}
   B. $C_2O_4^{2-}$
   C. HSO_4^-
   D. $HC_2O_4^-$
   E. HCO_3^-

3. A species, molecule, or ion, is called a Lewis base if it does which of the following?

   A. It is an electron-pair donor.
   B. It donates an H^+.
   C. It accepts an H^+.
   D. It is an electron-pair accepter.
   E. It increase the H^+(aq) in water.

4. Which of the following are proper laboratory procedures for a titration?

   I.   Make sure the color change of the indicator persists for at least 30 s.
   II. Allow all materials to cool to room temperature before they are weighed.
   III. Rinse the buret with deionized water before it is filled with titrant for the first titration.
   A. I and III only
   B. I, II, and III
   C. II only
   D. II and III only
   E. I and II only

5. In most of its compounds, this element exists as a monatomic cation.

   A. F
   B. S
   C. N
   D. Ca
   E. Cl

6. In which of the following groups are the species listed correctly in order of increasing radius?

   A. Sr, Ca, Mg
   B. Se^{2-}, S^{2-}, O^{2-}
   C. Mn^{3+}, Mn^{2+}, Mn
   D. I^-, Br^-, Cl^-
   E. K, Ca, Sc

7. Which of the following elements has the lowest electronegativity?

   A. F
   B. I
   C. C
   D. K
   E. Al

8. Which of the following represents the correct formula for hex-amminechromium(III) chloride?

   A. $[Cr(NH_3)_6](ClO_3)_3$
   B. $(NH_3)_6Cr_3Cl$
   C. Am_6CrCl_3
   D. $[Cr(NH_3)_6]Cl_3$
   E. $[Cr_3(NH_3)_6]Cl_3$

9. ____ $Fe(OH)_3(s) +$ ____ $H_2SeO_4(aq)$
   $\rightarrow$ ____ $Fe_2(SeO_4)_3(s) +$ ____ $H_2O(l)$

   After the above chemical equation is balanced, the lowest whole-number coefficient for water is

   A. 1
   B. 6
   C. 9
   D. 12
   E. 3

10. Which of the following best represents the net ionic equation for the reaction of barium hydroxide with an aqueous potassium sulfate solution?

    A. $Ba(OH)_2 + KSO_4 \rightarrow BaSO_4 + KOH$
    B. $Ba^{2+} + K_2SO_4 \rightarrow BaSO_4 + 2\ K^+$
    C. $Ba^{2+} + SO_4^{2-} \rightarrow BaSO_4$
    D. $Ba(OH)_2 + SO_4^{2-} \rightarrow BaSO_4 + 2\ OH^-$
    E. $Ba(OH)_2 + K_2SO_4 \rightarrow BaSO_4 + 2\ KOH$

11. A sample of magnesium metal is heated in the presence of nitrogen gas. After the sample was heated, some water was added to it. Which of the following statements is false?

    A. The magnesium reacted with the nitrogen to produce magnesium nitride.
    B. No reaction occurred because nitrogen gas is so unreactive.
    C. The solid did not dissolve in the water.
    D. After the addition of the water, the distinctive odor of ammonia gas was present.
    E. The water converted some of the magnesium nitride to magnesium hydroxide.

12. A student mixes 50.0 mL of 0.10 M $Ni(NO_3)_2$ solution with 50.0 mL of 0.10 M NaOH. A green precipitate forms, and the concentration of the hydroxide ion becomes very small. Which of the following correctly places the concentrations of the remaining ions in order of decreasing concentration?

    A. $[Na^+] > [Ni^{2+}] > [NO_3^-]$
    B. $[Ni^{2+}] > [NO_3^-] > [Na^+]$
    C. $[Na^+] > [NO_3^-] > [Ni^{2+}]$
    D. $[NO_3^-] > [Na^+] > [Ni^{2+}]$
    E. $[Ni^{2+}] > [Na^+] > [NO_3^-]$

13. The addition of concentrated $Ba(OH)_2(aq)$ to a 1.0 M $(NH_4)_2SO_4$ solution will result in which of the following observations?

A. The odor of ammonia is detected, and a white precipitate forms.
B. The formation of a white precipitate takes place.
C. The solution becomes acidic.
D. The odor of ammonia is detected.
E. An odorless gas forms and bubbles out of the mixture.

14. Manganese, Mn, forms a number of oxides. A particular oxide is 69.6% Mn. What is the simplest formula for this oxide?

   A. MnO
   B. Mn_2O_3
   C. Mn_3O_4
   D. MnO_2
   E. Mn_2O_7

15. Sodium sulfate forms a number of hydrates. A sample of a hydrate is heated until all the water is removed. What is the formula of the original hydrate if it loses 56% of its mass when heated?

   A. $Na_2SO_4 \cdot H_2O$
   B. $Na_2SO_4 \cdot 2H_2O$
   C. $Na_2SO_4 \cdot 6H_2O$
   D. $Na_2SO_4 \cdot 8H_2O$
   E. $Na_2SO_4 \cdot 10H_2O$

16. $3\ Cu(s) + 8\ HNO_3(aq) \rightarrow$
    $3\ Cu(NO_3)_2(aq) + 2\ NO(g) + 4\ H_2O(l)$

   Copper metal reacts with nitric acid according to the above equation. A 0.30-mol sample of copper metal and 100.0 mL of 3.0 M nitric acid are mixed in a flask. How many moles of NO gas will form?

   A. 0.20 mol
   B. 0.038 mol
   C. 0.10 mol
   D. 0.075 mol
   E. 0.30 mol

17. Gold(III) oxide, Au_2O_3, can be decomposed to gold metal, Au, plus oxygen gas, O_2. How many moles of oxygen gas will form when 2.21 g of solid gold(III) oxide is decomposed? The formula weight of gold(III) oxide is 442.

   A. 0.00750 mol
   B. 0.0150 mol
   C. 0.00500 mol
   D. 0.00250 mol
   E. 0.0100 mol

18. ____ $C_4H_{11}N(l) +$ ____ $O_2(g) \rightarrow$
    ____ $CO_2(g) +$ ____ $H_2O(l) +$ ____ $N_2(g)$

   When the above equation is balanced, the lowest whole number coefficient for CO_2 is:

   A. 4
   B. 16
   C. 27
   D. 22
   E. 2

19. $2\ KMnO_4 + 5\ H_2C_2O_4 + 3\ H_2SO_4 \rightarrow$
    $K_2SO_4 + 2\ MnSO_4 + 10\ CO_2 + 8\ H_2O$

   How many moles of $MnSO_4$ are produced when 2.0 mol of $KMnO_4$, 5.0 mol of $H_2C_2O_4$, and 1.5 mol of H_2SO_4 are mixed?

   A. 2.0 mol
   B. 1.5 mol
   C. 1.0 mol
   D. 3.0 mol
   E. 2.5 mol

20. ____ $KClO_3 \rightarrow$ ____ $KCl +$ ____ O_2

   After the above equation is balanced, how many moles of O_2 can be produced from 1.0 mol of $KClO_3$?

   A. 1.5 mol
   B. 3.0 mol

C. 1.0 mol
D. 3.0 mol
E. 6.0 mol

21. $Sr + 2 H_2O \rightarrow Sr(OH)_2 + H_2$

Strontium reacts with water according to the above reaction. What volume of hydrogen gas, at standard temperature and pressure, is produced from 0.100 mol of strontium?

A. 3.36 L
B. 5.60 L
C. 2.24 L
D. 4.48 L
E. 1.12 L

22. A sample of nitrogen gas is placed in a container with constant volume. The temperature is changed until the pressure doubles. Which of the following also changes?

A. density
B. moles
C. average velocity
D. number of molecules
E. potential energy

23. An experiment to determine the molecular weight of a gas begins by heating a solid to produce a gaseous product. The gas passes through a tube and displaces water in an inverted, water-filled bottle. The mass of the solid is measured, as is the volume and the temperature of the displaced water. Once the barometric pressure has been recorded, what other information is needed to finish the experiment?

A. the heat of formation of the gas
B. the density of the water

C. the mass of the displaced water
D. the vapor pressure of the water
E. the temperature to which the solid was heated

24. Determine the final temperature of a sample of hydrogen gas. The sample initially occupied a volume of 6.00 L at 127° C and 875 mm Hg. The sample was heated, at constant pressure, until it occupied a volume of 15.00 L.

A. 318° C
B. 727° C
C. 45° C
D. 160° C
E. 1000° C

25. From the following, choose the gas that probably shows the least deviation from ideal gas behavior?

A. Kr
D. CH_4
C. O_2
D. H_2
E. NH_3

Choose from the following types of energy for questions 26–28.

A. free energy
B. lattice energy
C. kinetic energy
D. activation energy
E. ionization energy

26. The maximum energy available for useful work from a spontaneous reaction

27. The energy needed to separate the ions in an ionic solid

28. The energy difference between the transition state and the reactants

1. $2 ClF(g) + O_2(g)$ $\quad \Delta H° = 167.5$ kJ
    $\rightarrow Cl_2O(g) + OF_2(g)$

2. $2 F_2(g) + O_2(g)$ $\quad \Delta H° = -43.5$ kJ
    $\rightarrow 2 OF_2(g)$

3. $2 ClF_3(l) + 2 O_2(g)$ $\quad \Delta H° = 394.1$ kJ
    $\rightarrow Cl_2O(g) + 3 OF_2(g)$

29. Using the information given above, calculate the enthalpy change for the following reaction:

    $$ClF(g) + F_2(g) \rightarrow ClF_3(l)$$

    A. -135.1 kJ
    B. $+135.1$ kJ
    C. 270.2 kJ
    D. -270.2 kJ
    E. 0.0 kJ

30. When lithium sulfate, Li_2SO_4, is dissolved in water, the temperature increases. Which of the following conclusions may be related to this?

    A. Lithium sulfate is less soluble in hot water.
    B. The hydration energies of lithium ions and sulfate ions are very low.
    C. The heat of solution for lithium sulfate is endothermic.
    D. The solution is not an ideal solution.
    E. The lattice energy of lithium sulfate is very low.

31. What is the energy required to completely separate the ions in an ionic solid?

    A. ionization energy
    B. kinetic energy
    C. activation energy
    D. lattice energy
    E. free energy

32. $C_2H_4(g) + H_2O(g)$
    $\rightarrow C_2H_5OH(g)$ $\quad \Delta H = -46$ kJ

    Determine ΔH for the above reaction if $C_2H_5OH(l)$ was formed in the above

    reaction instead of $C_2H_5OH(g)$. The ΔH of vaporization for C_2H_5OH is 43 kJ/mol.

    A. $+3$ kJ
    B. $+89$ kJ
    C. -3 kJ
    D. $+43$ kJ
    E. -89 kJ

33. The ground-state configuration of Ni^{2+} is which of the following?

    A. $1s^2 2s^2 2p^6 3s^2 3p^6 3d^8 4s^2$
    B. $1s^2 2s^2 2p^6 3s^2 3p^6 3d^{10} 4s^2$
    C. $1s^2 2s^2 2p^6 3s^2 3p^6 3d^{10}$
    D. $1s^2 2s^2 2p^6 3s^2 3p^6 3d^8$
    E. $1s^2 2s^2 2p^6 3s^2 3p^6 3d^5 4s^2$

34. A ground-state electron in a calcium atom might have which of the following sets of quantum numbers?

    A. $n = 3; l = 2; m_l = 0; m_s = -1/2$
    B. $n = 5; l = 0; m_l = 0; m_s = -1/2$
    C. $n = 4; l = 1; m_l = 0; m_s = -1/2$
    D. $n = 4; l = 0; m_l = 0; m_s = -1/2$
    E. $n = 4; l = 0; m_l = +1; m_s = -1/2$

The following answers are to be used for questions 35–38.

    A. Pauli exclusion principle
    B. electron shielding
    C. the wave properties of matter
    D. Heisenberg uncertainty principle
    E. Hund's rule

35. The diffraction of electrons

36. The maximum number of electrons in an atomic orbital is two.

37. An oxygen atom is paramagnetic in the ground state.

38. The position and momentum of an electron cannot be determined exactly.

39. Magnesium reacts with element X to form an ionic compound. If the ground-state electron configuration of X is $1s^2 2s^2 2p^5$, what is the simplest formula for this compound?

    A. Mg_2X_3
    B. MgX_2
    C. MgX_4
    D. Mg_2X_5
    E. MgX

40. VSEPR predicts that a BF_3 molecule will be which of the following shapes?

    A. tetrahedral
    B. trigonal bipyramidal
    C. square pyramid
    D. trigonal planar
    E. square planar

41. Which of the following is polar?

    A. BF_3
    B. IF_5
    C. CF_4
    D. XeF_4
    E. AsF_5

42. The only substance listed below that contains ionic, σ, and π bonds is:

    A. C_2H_4
    B. NaH
    C. NH_4Cl
    D. $NaC_2H_3O_2$
    E. H_2O

43. Which molecule or ion in the following list has the greatest number of unshared electron pairs around the central atom?

    A. IF_7
    B. NO_3^-
    C. BF_3
    D. NH_3
    E. CBr_4

44. Which of the following processes does not involve breaking an ionic or a covalent bond?

    A. $2\,NO(g) + O_2 \rightarrow 2\,NO_2(g)$
    B. $NaNO_3(s) \rightarrow Na^+(aq) + NO_3^-(aq)$
    C. $Zn(s) \rightarrow Zn(g)$
    D. $2\,H_2(g) + O_2(g) \rightarrow 2\,H_2O(g)$
    E. $2\,KClO_3(s) \rightarrow 2\,KCl(s) + 3\,O_2(g)$

Choose from the following solids for questions 45–48.

    A. composed of atoms held together by delocalized electrons
    B. composed of molecules held together by intermolecular dipole–dipole interactions
    C. composed of positive and negative ions held together by electrostatic attractions
    D. composed of macromolecules held together by strong bonds
    E. composed of molecules held together by intermolecular London forces

45. Graphite

46. $Ca(s)$

47. $CaCO_3(s)$

48. $SO_2(s)$

49. The critical point represents

    A. the highest temperature and pressure where the substance may exist as discrete solid and gas phases.
    B. the highest temperature and pressure where the substance may exist as discrete liquid and gas phases.
    C. the temperature and pressure where the substance exists in equilibrium as solid, liquid, and gas phases.
    D. the highest temperature and pressure where the substance may exist as discrete liquid and solid phases.
    E. the highest temperature and pressure where a substance can sublime.

50. A sample of a pure liquid is placed in an open container and heated to the boiling point. Which of the following may increase the boiling point of the liquid?

    I.   The container is sealed.
    II. The size of the container is increased.
    III. More liquid is added.

    A. II and III
    B. I and III
    C. III only
    D. II only
    E. I only

51. Which point on the diagram below might represent the normal boiling point?

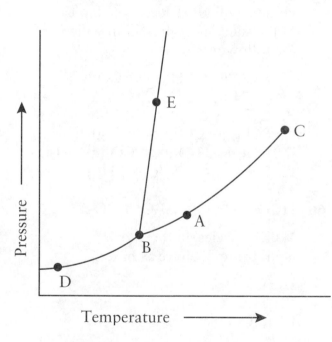

52. What is the total concentration of cations in a solution made by combining 700.0 mL of 3.0 M $(NH_4)_3PO_4$ with 300.0 mL of 2.0 M Na_2SO_4?

    A. 2.7 M
    B. 13 M
    C. 7.5 M
    D. 5.0 M
    E. 2.5 M

53. A stock solution that is 0.30 M in Na_2SO_4 is available. How many moles of solid Na_3PO_4 must be added to 800 mL of this solution to increase the sodium ion concentration to 0.90 M?

    A. 0.060
    B. 0.12
    C. 0.080
    D. 0.16
    E. 0.24

54. If a solution of ethyl ether, $(C_2H_5)_2O$, in ethanol, C_2H_5OH, is treated as an ideal solution. What is the mole fraction of ethyl ether in the vapor over an equimolar solution of these two liquids? The vapor pressure of ethyl ether is 480 mm Hg at 20° C, and the vapor pressure of ethanol is 50 mm Hg at this temperature.

    A. 0.50
    B. 0.76
    C. 0.91
    D. 0.27
    E. 0.09

55. How many milliliters of concentrated ammonia (7.0-molar NH_3) are needed to prepare 0.250 L of 3.0-molar NH_3?

    A. 110 mL
    B. 0.11 mL
    C. 200 mL
    D. 150 mL
    E. 75 mL

56. The plot of ln[A] versus time gives a straight line. This implies the rate law is

    A. rate = $k[A]^2$
    B. rate = $k[A]^{-2}$
    C. rate = $k[A]^0$
    D. rate = $k[A]^{-1}$
    E. rate = $k[A]$

57. The specific rate constant, k, for radioactive lawrencium-256 is 86 h^{-1}. What mass of a 0.0500 ng sample of lawrencium-256 remains after 58 s?

A. 0.0500 ng
B. 0.0250 ng
C. 0.0125 ng
D. 0.00625 ng
E. 0.0375 ng

58. The purpose of using a lit match to start the fire in a gas grill is

A. to supply the free energy for the reaction
B. to catalyze the reaction
C. to supply the heat of reaction
D. to supply the kinetic energy for the reaction
E. to supply the activation energy for the reaction

59.

Acid	K_a, acid dissociation constant
H_3PO_4	7.2×10^{-3}
$H_2PO_4^-$	6.3×10^{-8}
HPO_4^{2-}	4.2×10^{-13}

Using the above information, choose the best answer for preparing a pH = 7.9 buffer.

A. K_2HPO_4
B. K_3PO_4
C. $K_2HPO_4 + KH_2PO_4$
D. $K_2HPO_4 + K_3PO_4$
E. $H_3PO_4 + KH_2PO_4$

60. What is the ionization constant, K_a, for a weak monoprotic acid if a 0.6-molar solution has a pH of 2.0?

A. 1.7×10^{-4}
B. 1.7×10^{-2}
C. $6. \times 10^{-6}$
D. 2.7×10^{-3}
E. 3.7×10^{-4}

Questions 61–64 refer to the following aqueous solutions. All concentrations are 1 M.

A. CH_3NH_2 (methylamine) and LiOH (lithium hydroxide)

B. $C_2H_5NH_2$ (ethylamine) and $C_2H_5NH_3NO_3$ (ethylammonium nitrate)
C. CH_3NH_2 (methylamine) and $HC_3H_5O_2$ (propionic acid)
D. $KClO_4$ (potassium perchlorate) and $HClO_4$ (perchloric acid)
E. $H_2C_2O_4$ (oxalic acid) and KHC_2O_4 (potassium hydrogen oxalate)

61. The most basic solution (highest pH)

62. The solution with a pH nearest 7

63. A buffer with a pH > 7

64. A buffer with a pH < 7

65. At constant temperature, a change in volume will NOT affect the moles of the substances present in which of the following?

A. $2\ CO(g) + 2\ H_2(g) \rightleftharpoons CO_2(g) + CH_4(g)$
B. $CO(g) + Cl_2(g) \rightleftharpoons COCl_2(g)$
C. $PCl_3(g) + Cl_2(g) \rightleftharpoons PCl_5(g)$
D. $CO(g) + H_2O(g) \rightleftharpoons CO_2(g) + H_2(g)$
E. $2\ NH_3(g) \rightleftharpoons N_2(g) + 3\ H_2(g)$

66. $HCO_3^- + H_2O \rightleftharpoons H_3O^+ + CO_3^{2-}$

Which species, in the above equilibrium, behave as bases?

I. CO_3^{2-}
II. H_2O
III. HCO_3^-

A. I and III
B. II only
C. I and II
D. I only
E. II and III

67. $CO(g) + 2\ H_2(g) \rightleftharpoons CH_3OH(g)$

A 1.00-L flask is filled with 0.70 mol of H_2 and 0.60 mol of CO, and allowed to come to equilibrium. At equilibrium, there are 0.40 mol of CO in the flask. What is the value of K_c, the equilibrium constant, for the reaction?

A. 0.74
B. 3.2
C. 0.0050
D. 5.6
E. 1.2

68. $H_2O(l) + CrO_4^{2-}(aq) + HSnO_2^-(aq) \rightarrow CrO_2^-(aq) + OH^-(aq) + HSnO_3^-(aq)$

What is the coefficient of OH^- when the above reaction is balanced?

A. 10
B. 2
C. 5
D. 4
E. 1

69. $2\ Bi^{3+} + 3\ SnO_2^{2-} + 6\ OH^- \rightarrow 3\ SnO_3^{2-} + 3\ H_2O + 2\ Bi$

For the above reaction, pick the true statement from the following:

A. The oxidation number of tin changes from +2 to +4.
B. The oxidation number of tin changes from +4 to +2.
C. The Bi^{3+} is oxidized by the tin.
D. The OH^- reduces the Bi^{3+}.
E. The SnO_3^{2-} is formed by the reduction of SnO_2^{2-}.

70. An electrolysis cell was constructed with two platinum electrodes in a 1.00 M aqueous solution of KCl. An odorless gas evolved from one electrode and a gas with a distinctive odor evolved from the other electrode. Choose the correct statement from the following list.

A. The odorless gas was oxygen.
B. The odorless gas was evolved at the anode.
C. The gas with the distinctive odor was evolved at the anode.

D. The odorless gas was evolved at the positive electrode.
E. The gas with the distinctive odor was evolved at the negative electrode.

71. When $^{226}_{88}Ra$ decays, it emits 2 α particles, then a β particle, followed by an α particle. The resulting nucleus is:

A. $^{212}_{83}Bi$
B. $^{222}_{86}Rn$
C. $^{214}_{82}Pb$
D. $^{214}_{83}Bi$
E. $^{212}_{85}At$

72. Which of the following lists the types of radiation in the correct order of increasing penetrating power?

A. α, γ, β
B. β, α, γ
C. α, β, γ
D. β, γ, α
E. γ, β, α

73. Which of the following statements are correct concerning β particles?

I. They have a mass number of zero and a charge of −1.
II. They are electrons.
III. They are less penetrating than α particles.

A. I and II
B. I and III
C. II and III
D. I only
E. II only

74. If 75% of a sample of pure ^3_1H decays in 24.6 yr, what is the half-life of ^3_1H?

A. 24.6 yr
B. 18.4 yr
C. 12.3 yr
D. 6.15 yr
E. 3.07 yr

75. Alkenes are hydrocarbons with the general formula C_nH_{2n}. If a 0.453 g sample of any alkene is combusted in excess oxygen, how many moles of water will form?

A. 0.0648
B. 0.452
C. 0.0133
D. 0.324
E. 0.0324

Answers and Explanations for AP Chemistry Practice Exam 1

✓

1. **C.** This is the only one that has a pair of electrons to donate.

2. **B.** All can behave as Brønsted bases. Only B cannot behave as an acid.

3. **A.** This is the definition of a Lewis base.

4. **E.** The buret should be rinsed with titrant, not water.

5. **D.** The others are normally monatomic anions.

6. **C.** Increasing sizes indicate decreasing charge, lower position in a column on the periodic table, or position to the left in a period on the periodic table.

7. **D.** The element furthest away from F.

8. **D.** Hexammine = $(NH_3)_6$; chromium(III) = Cr^{3+}; chloride = Cl^-

9. **B.** $2\,Fe(OH)_3(s) + 3\,H_2SeO_4(aq) \rightarrow Fe_2(SeO_4)_3(s) + 6\,H_2O(l)$

10. **C.** The soluble compounds should be separated and the spectator ions eliminated.

11. **B.** Magnesium nitride does form.

12. **D.** Some of the nickel remains, the sodium does not change, and two nitrates are formed per nickel(II) nitrate.

13. **A.** The reactions are: $NH_4^+ + OH^- \rightarrow NH_3 + H_2O$ and $Ba^+ + SO_4^{2-} \rightarrow BaSO_4$

14. **B.** Percentages: (A) 77.8; (B) 69.6; (C) 72.0; (D) 63.2; (E) 49.5

15. **E.** Percentage of water: (A) 11; (B) 20; (C) 43; (D) 50; (E) 56

16. **D.** Nitric acid is the limiting reagent.

17. **A.** $(2.21\ g)(1\ mol/442\ g)(3\ mol\ O_2/2\ mol) = 7.50 \times 10^{-3}\ mol$

18. **B.** $4\,C_4H_{11}N(l) + 27\,O_2(g) \rightarrow 16\,CO_2(g) + 22\,H_2O(l) + 2\,N_2(g)$

19. **C.** Sulfuric acid is the limiting reagent.

20. **A.** $(1.0\ mol\ KClO_3)(3\ mol\ O_2/2\ mol\ KClO_3) = 1.5\ mol$

21. **C.** $(0.100\ mol\ Sr)(1\ mol\ H_2/1\ mol\ Sr)(22.4\ L/mol) = 2.24\ L$

22. **C.** The average velocity is related to temperature.

23. **D.** Water, whenever present, will contribute its vapor pressure.

24. **B.** $T_2 = (V_2 T_1)/V_1 = (15.00\ L \times 400\ K)/(6.00\ L) - 273 = 727\ ^\circ C$

25. **D.** Small and nonpolar

26. **A.** Definition

27. **B.** Definition

28. **D.** Definition

29. **A.**

$\frac{1}{2}[2\ ClF(g) + O_2(g) \rightarrow Cl_2O(g) + OF_2(g)]$	$\frac{1}{2}(167.5\ kJ)$
$\frac{1}{2}[2\ F_2(g) + O_2(g) \rightarrow 2\ OF_2(g)]$	$\frac{1}{2}(-43.5\ kJ)$
$\frac{1}{2}[Cl_2O(g) + 3\ OF_2(g) \rightarrow 2\ ClF_3(l) + 2\ O_2(g)]$	$-\frac{1}{2}(394.1\ kJ)$

$ClF(g) + F_2(g) \rightarrow ClF_3(l)$ $-135.1\ kJ$

30. **A.** Exothermic processes shift toward the starting materials when heated.

31. **D.** Definition

32. **E.** Subtract the heat of vaporization from the original value.

33. **D.** Ni^{2+} has 26 electrons. The first electrons to leave are the 4s electrons.

34. **D.** This describes one of the 4s electrons.

35. **C.** Diffraction is a wave phenomenon.

36. **A.** Definition

37. **E.** Electrons fill the orbitals individually before pairing. Unpaired electrons = paramagnetic.

38. **D.** Definition

39. **B.** X is F and forms a –1 ion. Magnesium forms a +2 ion.

40. **D.** BF_3 has three electron pairs around the B.

41. **B.** Using VSEPR, all the others are nonpolar.

42. **D.** Ionic bonding needs a metal and a nonmetal (usually). Only the acetate ion has resonating bonds (σ and π).

43. **D.** All the others have no unshared electron pairs.

44. **C.** Sublimation usually does not involve bond breaking. In any case, Zn is a metal, and it has no ionic or covalent bonds to break.

45. **D.** Both diamond and graphite are covalent network solids.

46. **A.** This is a description of metallic bonding.

47. **C.** This is a description of ionic bonding.

48. **B.** SO_2 consists of polar molecules.

49. B. Definition

50. E. This will increase the pressure and, therefore, the boiling point.

51. A. This is the only point on the liquid–gas transition line.

52. C. (0.7000 L)(3.0 mol/L)(3 cations/mol) + (0.3000 L)(2.0 mol) (2 cations/mol)

53. C. (0.800 L)(0.90 mol Na^+/L)–(0.800 L)(0.30 mol/L)(2 Na^+/mol)
$$= 0.24 \text{ mol } Na^+ \text{ needed}$$

(0.24 mol Na^+)(1 mol Na_3PO_4/3 mol Na^+) = 0.080 mol Na_3PO_4

54. C. Equimolar gives a mole fraction of 0.5.

0.5×480 mm Hg $+ 0.5 \times 50$ mm Hg $= 265$ mm Hg (total vapor pressure)

mole fraction ethyl ether = $(0.5 \times 480$ mm Hg)/265 mm Hg

55. A. $V_{con} = M_{dll}V_{dll}/M_{con} = (3.0 \text{ M} \times 250 \text{ mL})/7.0 \text{ M}$

56. E. This plot only gives a straight-line for a first-order reaction.

57. C. $t_{1/2} = (0.693/86 \text{ h}^-)(3600 \text{ s/h}) = 29$ s. The time is equivalent to two half-lives, so one-fourth of the sample should remain.

58. E. Energy is required to initiate the reaction.

59. C. The pK_a for $H_2PO_4^-$ is nearest to the pH value needed. Thus, the simplest buffer would involve this ion. The phosphoric acid in E would lower the pH too much.

60. A. $K_a = [H^+][A^-]/[HA]$ $[H^+] = [A^-] = 1.0 \times 10^{-2}$ $[HA] = 0.6$

61. A. LiOH is a strong base.

62. C. A solution of a weak acid and a weak base would be nearly neutral.

63. B. Only B and E are buffers. B is basic, and E is acidic.

64. E. Only B and E are buffers. B is basic, and E is acidic.

65. D. If there are equal numbers of moles of gas on each side of the equilibrium arrow, then volume or pressure changes will not affect the equilibrium.

66. C. HCO_3^- behaves as an acid.

67. D. The loss of 0.20 mol of CO means that 0.40 mol of H_2 reacted (leaving 0.30 mol) and 0.20 mol of CH_3OH formed. Dividing all the moles by the volume gives the molarity, and:

$$K_c = (0.20)/(0.40)(0.30)^2 = 5.6$$

68. B.
$$H_2O(l) + 2\ CrO_4{}^{2-}(aq) + 3\ HSnO_2{}^-(aq)$$
$$\rightarrow 2\ CrO_2{}^-(aq) + 2\ OH^-(aq) + 3\ HSnO_3{}^-(aq)$$

69. A. Assigning oxidation numbers and definitions are required.

70. C. Hydrogen (odorless) evolves at the cathode, and chlorine (distinctive odor) evolves at the anode.

71. D. The mass should be $226 - (4 + 4 + 0 + 4) = 214$. The atomic number should be $88 - (2 + 2 - 1 + 2) = 83$.

72. C. Alpha particles are the least penetrating, and gamma rays are the most penetrating.

73. A. In nuclear reactions, the mass of a β particle is treated as 0 and a charge of −1. Electrons and β particles are the same.

74. C. After one half-life, 50% would remain. After another half-life, this would be reduced by one-half to 25%. The total amount decayed is 75%. Thus, 24.6 years must be two half-lives of 12.3 years each.

75. E.

Count the answers you got correct. Then count the answers you got wrong (skip those you did not answer). Multiply the number of wrong answers by 0.25 and subtract this value for the number of correct answers. This gives you your score on this set of questions.

AP CHEMISTRY PRACTICE EXAM 1: FREE-RESPONSE QUESTIONS

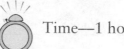

Time—1 hour and 30 minutes

Answer the following questions in the time allowed. You may use the equation/symbol pages, the list of reduction potentials, and a periodic table while taking this exam. Write the answers on a separate sheet of paper.

Part A. Time — 40 minutes

You may use a calculator for part A.

Question 1.

Compound	K_{sp}
$Cr(OH)_2$	1.0×10^{-17}
$Cr(OH)_3$	6.3×10^{-31}
$Fe(OH)_2$	7.9×10^{-16}
$Pb(OH)_2$	1.1×10^{-20}
$Mg(OH)_2$	6.0×10^{-10}
$Mn(OH)_2$	1.9×10^{-13}
$Sn(OH)_2$	6.3×10^{-27}

Use the K_{sp} data given above to answer the following questions.

a. Excess manganese(II) hydroxide, $Mn(OH)_2$, is added to 100.0 mL of deionized water. What is the pH of the solution?

b. A solution that is 0.10 M in Mg^{2+} and 0.10 M in Fe^{2+} is slowly made basic. What is the concentration of Fe^{2+} when Mg^{2+} begins to precipitate?

c. Two beakers are filled with water. Excess chromium(III) hydroxide is added to one and excess tin(II) hydroxide is added to the other. Which beaker has the higher concentration of metal ions? Calculate the concentration of metal ion in each beaker to support your prediction.

d. Chromium(III) hydroxide, $Cr(OH)_3$, is less soluble than chromium(II) hydroxide, $Cr(OH)_2$. Explain.

e. Calculate the grams of lead(II) hydroxide, $Pb(OH)_2$, that will dissolve in 1.00 L of water.

Answer either question 2 or question 3.

Question 2.

$$2\ PCl_3(g) + O_2(g) \rightarrow 2\ POCl_3(g)$$

Thermodynamic values related to the above reaction are given in the table below.

Substance	ΔH_f° (kJ/mol)	S° (J/mol K)	Bonds	Bond energies (kJ/mol)
PCl₃(g)	−287	312	P–Cl	331
O₂(g)	0	205.0	O=O	498
POCl₃(g)	−542.2	325	O–O	204

a. Determine the enthalpy change for the above reaction.
b. Estimate the PO bond energy.
c. Is the PO bond a single or a double bond? Justify your answer.
d. Calculate the entropy change for the reaction.
e. Is this reaction spontaneous or nonspontaneous at 25° C? Justify your prediction.

Question 3.

The following materials are made available for the determination of the molar mass of an unknown nonvolatile solid.

analytical balance   thermometer   beaker   support stand and clamp
test tube   stopwatch   hot plate

Phenol (melting point = 43° C and K_f = 7.40° C/m) is available as the solvent. The unknown behaves as a nonelectrolyte in phenol.

a. Plot a cooling curve for phenol on the axes below, and plot the cooling curve for a solution of the unknown in phenol.

Pure Phenol: Solution:

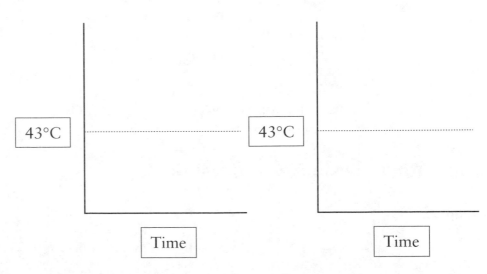

    b. What information must be obtained from the two graphs in order to calculate the molar mass?

    c. What additional information is needed to determine the molar mass of the unknown solid?

    d. Show how the above information may be used to calculate the molar mass of the unknown solid.

STOP

Part B. Time — 50 minutes

You may not use a calculator for part B.

Question 4.

Choose FIVE of the following eight questions. Place your answers in the appropriate boxes. There is no extra credit for answering more than five. Formulas for reactants and products are needed. Do not include formulas for substances that remain unchanged during the reaction. It is not necessary to balance the equations. Unless otherwise noted, assume all the reactions occur in aqueous solution. If a substance is present as ions in solution, write its formula as an ion.

Example: Hydrochloric acid is added to a lead(II) nitrate solution.

$$Pb^{2+} + Cl^- \rightarrow PbCl_2$$

    a. An acidified potassium permanganate solution is added to an iron(II) sulfate solution.

    b. Excess potassium cyanide is added to an iron(III) nitrate solution.

    c. Concentrated hydrobromic acid is added to a potassium nitrite solution.

    d. A clean magnesium strip is immersed in a copper(II) sulfate solution.

    e. Dinitrogen pentoxide is mixed with water.

    f. Concentrated hydrochloric acid is added to manganese(IV) oxide.

    g. Chlorine gas is bubbled through a solution of calcium iodide.

    h. An iron(III) nitrate solution is made basic with potassium hydroxide.

Question 5.

Five beakers are placed in a row on a countertop. Each beaker is half filled with a 0.20 M aqueous solution. The solutes, in order, are: (1) potassium sulfate, (2) methyl alcohol, (3) sodium carbonate, (4) ammonium chromate, and (5) barium chloride. The solutions are all at 25° C.

Answer the following questions with respect to the five solutions listed above.

a. Which solution will form a precipitate when ammonium chromate is added to it? Give the formula of the precipitate.
b. Which solution is the most basic? Explain.
c. Which solution will exhibit the lowest boiling point elevation? Explain.
d. Which solution is colored?
e. Which solution will not react with solution (5) barium chloride?

Question 6.

A sample of a solid, weak monoprotic acid, HA, is supplied along with standard sodium hydroxide solution.

The sodium hydroxide solution was standardized with potassium hydrogen phthalate (KHP).

a. List the apparatus required to titrate an HA solution.
b. Sketch a pH versus volume of base added curve for the titration.
c. Sketch the titration curve if the unknown acid was really a diprotic acid.
d. Describe the steps required to determine the molar mass of HA.
e. How would the molar mass of HA be changed if the KHP contained an inert impurity?

Answer either question 7 or question 8.

Question 7.

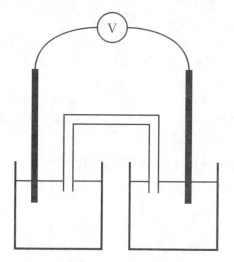

V = voltmeter

The above galvanic cell is constructed with a cadmium electrode in a 1.0 M $Cd(NO_3)_2$ solution in the left compartment and a silver electrode in a 1.0 M $AgNO_3$ in the right compartment. The salt bridge contains a KNO_3 solution. The cell voltage is positive.

a. What is the balanced net-ionic equation for the reaction, and what is the cell potential?
b. Show how to calculate the equilibrium constant for the cell.
c. Write the expression for Q that would be needed in the Nernst equation. Explain why any substances from the net-ionic equation do not appear in Q.
d. Show how to calculate the free energy for the reaction.
e. Identify the anode, the cathode, the oxidizing agent, and the reducing agent.

Question 8.

Relate each of the following to atomic properties and the principles of bonding.

a. The ionization energy of nitrogen atoms is higher than expected.
b. Draw the Lewis electron-dot structures for CO_2 and CO. Explain the polarity of these compounds.
c. The compound C_2H_3F is polar, but compounds with the general formula $C_2H_2F_2$ are sometimes polar and sometimes nonpolar. Show the structures and explain.
d. There are two isomers with the formula C_2H_6O. One of the isomers is more soluble in water than the other. Use the structures of these two compounds to explain the difference in solubility.
e. Why does SiF_4 react with fluoride ion, and CF_4 not react?

Answers and Explanations for AP Chemistry Free-Response Exam 1

Question 1.

✓   a. The volume of the solution is irrelevant. The equilibrium $Mn(OH)_2(s)$ $\rightleftharpoons Mn^{2+}(aq) + 2\,OH^-(aq)$ is important. The mass action expression for this equilibrium is: $K_{sp} = [Mn^{2+}][OH^-]^2 = 1.9 \times 10^{-13}$. Setting $[Mn^{2+}]$ $= x$ and $[OH^-] = 2x$, and plugging into the mass action expression gives: $(x)(2x)^2 = 4x^3 = 1.9 \times 10^{-13}$. Solving for x gives $x = 3.6 \times 10^{-5}$, and $[OH^-] = 2x = 7.2 \times 10^{-5}$.

   You get 1 point for the correct $[OH^-]$.
   There are two common ways to finish the problem. You do not need to show both.

   (i) $pOH = -\log[OH^-] = -\log 7.5 \times 10^{-5} = 4.14$
   $pH = 14.00 - pOH = 14.00 - 4.14 = 9.86$
   (ii) $[H^+] = K_w / [OH^-] = 1.0 \times 10^{-14} / 7.5 \times 10^{-5} = 1.4 \times 10^{-10}$
   $pH = -\log[H^+] = -\log 1.4 \times 10^{-10} = 9.86$

   You get 1 point for the correct pH. If you got the wrong $[OH^-]$ value, but used it correctly, you still get 1 point.

   b. The important equilibria are: $M(OH)_2(s) \rightleftharpoons M^{2+}(aq) + 2\,OH^-(aq)$, where M = Mg or Fe. It is necessary to determine the hydroxide ion concentration when the iron begins to precipitate.

$$K_{sp} = [Mg^{2+}][OH^-]^2 = 6.0 \times 10^{-10}$$

$$[OH^-]^2 = K_{sp}/[Mg^{2+}] = 6.0 \times 10^{-10}/0.10 = 6.0 \times 10^{-9}$$

$$[OH^-] = 7.7 \times 10^{-5}$$

   Using this value with the magnesium equilibrium gives:

$$K_{sp} = [Fe^{2+}][OH^-]^2 = 7.9 \times 10^{-16}$$

$$[Fe^{2+}] = K_{sp}/[OH^-]^2 = (7.9 \times 10^{-16})/(7.7 \times 10^{-5})^2 = 1.3 \times 10^{-7}\ M$$

   You get 1 point for the correct $[OH^-]$ and 1 point for the correct $[Fe^{2+}]$. Alternately, you get 1 point if you did only part of the procedure correctly. There is a maximum of 2 points for this part.

   c. Using the appropriate mass action expressions:

$$K_{sp} = [Sn^{2+}][OH^-]^2 = 6.3 \times 10^{-27}$$

$$[Sn^{2+}] = x \text{ and } [OH^-]^2 = 2x$$

$$(x)(2x)^2 = 4x^3 = 6.3 \times 10^{-27}$$

$$x = 1.2 \times 10^{-9} \text{ M} = [Sn^{2+}]$$

$$K_{sp} = [Cr^{3+}][OH^-]^3 = 6.3 \times 10^{-31}$$

$$[Cr^{3+}] = x \text{ and } [OH^-] = 3x$$

$$(x)(3x)^3 = 27x^4 = 6.3 \times 10^{-31}$$

$$x = 1.2 \times 10^{-8} \text{ M} = [Cr^{3+}]$$

The tin(II) hydroxide beaker has the lower metal ion concentration. You get 1 point for the correct beaker. You also get 1 point for each metal ion concentration you got correct. Your answers do not need to match exactly, but they should round to the same value.

d. The higher the charge on the cation, the less soluble a substance is.

You get 1 point for this answer.

e. The mass action expression is:

$$K_{sp} = [Pb^{2+}][OH^-]^2 = 1.1 \times 10^{-20}$$

$$[Pb^{2+}] = x \text{ and } [OH^-] = 2x$$

$$(x)(2x)^2 = 4x^3 = 1.1 \times 10^{-20}$$

$$x = 1.4 \times 10^{-7} \text{ M}$$

$$(1.4 \times 10^{-7} \text{ mol/L})(1.00 \text{ L})(241.2 \text{ g/mol}) = 3.4 \times 10^{-5} \text{ g}$$

You get 1 point for the correct answer (or an answer that rounds to this answer). You get 1 point for the setup.

Total your points for the different parts. There is a maximum of 10 points possible.

Question 2.

a. $\Delta H_{rxn}° = [2(-542.2)] - [2(-287) + 1(0)] = -510. \text{ kJ}$

The setup (products – reactants) is worth 1 point, and the answer is worth 1 point. You do not need to get the exact answer, but your answer should round to this one.

b. The answer from part a equals the bonds broken minus the bonds formed. Both phosphorus molecules have three P–Cl bonds, and O_2 has an O=O bond.

$$[(2 \times 3 \times 331) + (498)] - [(2\ PO) + (2 \times 3 \times 331)] = -510.\ kJ$$

$$PO = 504\ kJ$$

The setup (broken − formed) is worth 1 point, and the answer is worth 1 point. You do not need to get the exact answer, but your answer should round to this one.

c. It is a double bond. The value from part b is much higher than the single bond values from the table.

You get 1 point for the correct prediction, and 1 point for the explanation. If you got the wrong answer for part b, you can still get 1 or 2 points if you used the answer correctly on this part.

d. $\Delta S_{rxn}° = [2(325)] - [2(312) + 1(205.0)] = -179\ J/K$

The setup (products − reactants) is worth 1 point, and the answer is worth 1 point. You do not need to get the exact answer, but your answer should round to this one.

e. The free energy change must be calculated.

$$\Delta G_{rxn}° = \Delta H_{rxn}° - T\Delta S_{rxn}° = -510.\ kJ - (298\ K)(1\ kJ/1000\ J)(-179\ J/K)$$

$$= -457\ kJ$$

The negative value means the reaction is spontaneous.

You get 1 point for the prediction that the reaction is spontaneous. The setup (plugging into the equation) is worth 1 point if you remember to change the temperature to Kelvin and the joule to kilojoule conversion. An additional 1 point comes from the answer. If you got the wrong value in either part a or b, but used it correctly, you will still get the point for the answer. The free energy equation is part of the material supplied in the exam booklet.

Question 3.

a.

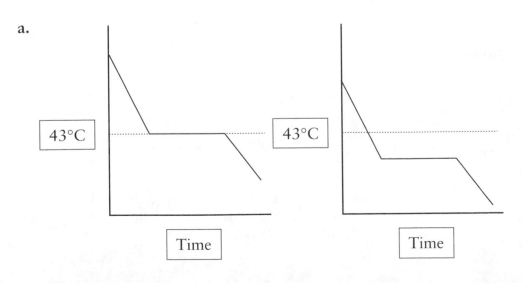

You get 1 point for the first plot. You get 1 point for the second plot only if the level region is definitely below 43° C.

b. The difference in the temperatures of the two level regions (ΔT) is needed.

You get 1 point for this answer.

c. The mass (in grams) of the unknown solid and the mass (in kilograms) of the phenol are required.

You get 1 point for each of these answers.

d. The required equation is: $\Delta T = K_f m$

Calculate the molality of the solution by dividing the change in temperature (ΔT) by the freezing point depression constant (K_f).
Calculate the moles of the unknown by multiplying the molality of the solution by the kilograms of phenol.
Calculate the molar mass by dividing the grams of the unknown by the moles of the unknown.
You get 1 point for each correct calculation you listed.

Total your points. There are 8 possible points.

Question 4.

Only the five answers will be graded. If you do more than five, only the first five will be graded. No extra points will be given for doing more than five. There are no extra points for balancing.

a. $H^+ + MnO_4^- + Fe^{2+} \rightarrow Fe^{3+} + Mn^{2+} + H_2O$

You get 1 point for the correct formulas for the reactants and 2 points for the correct formulas for the products. No variations are allowed.

b. $CN^- + Fe^{3+} \rightarrow [Fe(CN)_6]^{3-}$

You get 1 point for the correct formulas for the reactants and 2 points for the correct formula for the product. No variations are allowed.

c. $H^+ + NO_2^- \rightarrow HNO_2$

You get 1 point for the correct formulas for the reactants and 2 points for the correct formula for the product. No variations are allowed.

d. $Mg + Cu^{2+} \rightarrow Mg^{2+} + Cu$

You get 1 point for the correct formulas for the reactants and 2 points for the correct formulas for the products. No variations are allowed.

e. $N_2O_5 + H_2O \rightarrow HNO_3$

You get 1 point for the correct formulas for the reactants and 2 points for the correct formulas for the products. No variations are allowed.

f. $H^+ + Cl^- + MnO_2 \rightarrow Cl_2 + Mn^{2+} + H_2O$

You get 1 point for the correct formulas for the reactants and 2 points for the correct formulas for the products. No variations are allowed.

g. $Cl_2 + I^- \rightarrow Cl^- + I_2$

You get 1 point for the correct formulas for the reactants and 2 points for the correct formulas for the products. No variations are allowed.

h. $Fe^{3+} + OH^- \rightarrow Fe(OH)_3$

You get 1 point for the correct formulas for the reactants and 2 points for the correct formula for the product. No variations are allowed.

Question 5.

a. Solution (5) barium chloride will give a precipitate. The formula of the precipitate is $BaCrO_4$.

You get 1 point for picking the correct solution, and 1 point for the correct formula for the precipitate.

b. Solution (3) sodium carbonate is the most basic. Since the carbonate ion is the conjugate base of a weak acid, it will undergo significant hydrolysis to produce a basic solution.

You get 1 point for picking the correct solution, and 1 point for the correct formula for the explanation.

c. Solution (2) methyl alcohol will show the least boiling point elevation. Methyl alcohol is the only nonelectrolyte.

You get 1 point for picking the correct solution, and 1 point for the correct formula for the explanation.

d. Solution (4) ammonium chromate is yellow.

You get 1 point for picking the correct solution.

e. Solution (2) methyl alcohol is the only solution that will not form a precipitate with barium chloride.

You get 1 point for picking the correct solution.

Question 6.

a. *analytical balance   *buret   clamp
desiccator   drying oven   *Erlenmeyer flask
pH meter   pipette   support stand
wash bottle

You get 1 point if you have ALL the starred items. You get 1 point for the other items. There is a maximum of 2 points. If you only have some of the starred items, your maximum is 1 point.

b.

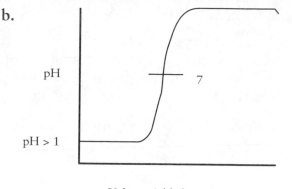

Equivalence point at pH < 7

You get 1 point for this graph. You get 1 point for noting that the equivalence point is greater than 7.

c.

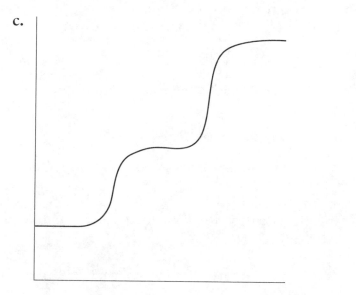

You get 1 point for this graph. You must show two regions.

d. 1. Weigh a sample of HA.
   2. Titrate HA versus standard NaOH to find the volume of NaOH solution required to neutralize the acid.
   3. Multiply the concentration of the NaOH solution times the volume used to get the moles of NaOH.
   4. The moles of HA is the same as the moles of NaOH.
   5. Divide the mass of HA by the moles of HA.

You get 2 points if you list all five steps. If you miss one or more steps you only get 1 point. You get 0 points if you get none of the steps correct. There are no bonus points for more steps or more details.

e. If the KHP contained an inert impurity, the concentration of the NaOH solution would be too low. If the concentration of the NaOH solution is low, then more solution would be needed for the titration of HA. This would yield a lower number of moles of HA, giving a higher molar mass.

You get 1 point for the NaOH concentration being low. You get 1 point for predicting a higher molar mass. If you incorrectly predicted the NaOH concentration to be too high, you can get 1 point if you predicted a lower molar mass.

Total your points. There is a maximum of 9 possible points.

Question 7.

a. The following reduction half-reactions are provided on the AP exam:

$$Cd^{2+} + 2\ e^- \rightarrow Cd \qquad E° = -0.40\ V$$

$$Ag^+ + 1\ e^- \rightarrow Ag \qquad E° = +0.80\ V$$

The first reaction needs to be reversed, the silver half-reaction needs to be doubled, and the reactions and voltages added.

$$
\begin{array}{ll}
Cd \rightarrow Cd^{2+} + 2\ e^- & E° = +0.40\ V \\
2(Ag^+ + 1\ e^- \rightarrow Ag) & E° = +0.80\ V \\
\hline
2\ Ag^+ + Cd \rightarrow Cd^{2+} + 2\ Ag & E° = +1.20\ V
\end{array}
$$

You get 1 point for the correct equation. You also get 1 point for the correct cell voltage.

b. Use the equation $\log K = nE°/0.0592$ (This equation is given on the AP exam.)

$$\log K = (2 \times 1.20)/0.0592$$

You get 1 point for plugging the values into the correct equation. You get the point even if you plugged in a wrong answer for E° from part a. The question does not ask you to do any calculations, thus, there are no points for showing any work beyond what is shown.

c. $Q = [Cd^{2+}]/[Ag^+]^2$ This answer is worth 1 point.

The remaining substances (Cd and Ag) are solids. Solids do not appear in Q expressions.
You get 1 point for the explanation.

d. Use the equation $\Delta G° = -nFE°$ (This equation is given on the AP exam.)

$$\Delta G° = -nFE° = -(2)(96500)(1.20)$$

You get 1 point for plugging the values into the correct equation. The question does not ask you to do any calculations, thus, there are no points for showing any work beyond what is shown.

e. Anode   Cd
   Cathode   Ag
   Oxidizing Agent   Ag$^+$
   Reducing Agent   Cd^{2+}

You get 1 point for each correctly identified item.

Total your points. There are 10 possible points.

Question 8.

a. Nitrogen atoms have a half-filled set of p-orbitals. Half-filled sets of orbitals have an increased stability.

You get 1 point for this answer.

b. :Ö::C::Ö: :C:::O:

CO$_2$ is linear and nonpolar. The different electronegativities of C and O make CO polar.
   You get 1 point for each correct Lewis structure and 1 point if you explain both polarities correctly. There is a maximum of 3 points.
   You may use a double line between the C and each of the O's in CO$_2$, and a triple line between the C and O in CO.

c. There is one compound with the formula C$_2$H$_3$F, and there are three compounds with the formula C$_2$H$_2$F$_2$. The structures are:

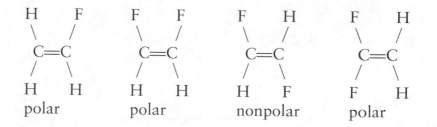

The fluorines are the most electronegative atoms present, and the bonds to them are polar covalent. The only nonpolar compound is the result of the polar C–F bonds pulling equally in opposite directions.
   You get 1 point for ALL the structures, and 1 point for a correct explanation. There is a maximum of 2 points.

d. The structures are: CH$_3$–O–CH$_3$ and   CH$_3$CH$_2$OH.

The first compound (dimethyl ether) is polar, but not as soluble in water as the second compound (ethanol) which is capable of hydrogen bonding to water.

You get 1 point if you show both structures, and you get 1 point for a correct explanation. The names shown in parentheses are not required.

e. Silicon tetrafluoride is capable of reacting with the fluoride ion (to produce SiF_6^{2-}) because silicon can expand its octet. Carbon tetrafluoride does not react because carbon cannot expand its octet.

An alternate explanation would be that silicon has d orbitals available for reacting and carbon does not.

You get 1 point for either explanation.

Total your points for the problem. There is a maximum of 9 possible points.

TOTAL SCORE:

Question 1   _____

Question 2 or 3   _____

Question 4   _____

Question 5   _____

Question 6   _____

Question 7 or 8   _____

AP CHEMISTRY PRACTICE EXAM 2: THE SECOND OPPORTUNITY TO EXCEL

5

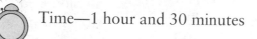

Time—1 hour and 30 minutes

Answer the following questions in the time allowed. You may use a periodic table while taking this exam. Write the answers on a separate sheet of paper.

1. Choose the strongest Lewis acid from the following.

   A. SO_4^{2-}
   B. Fe^{3+}
   C. Cl^-
   D. Na^+
   E. NO_3^-

2. Chlorine forms a number of oxyacids. Which of the following is the correct order of increasing acid strength?

   A. $HClO_3 < HClO_4 < HClO < HClO_2$
   B. $HClO_4 < HClO_3 < HClO_2 < HClO$
   C. $HClO < HClO_2 < HClO_3 < HClO_4$
   D. $HClO_4 < HClO_3 = HClO_2 < HClO$
   E. $HClO_4 = HClO_3 < HClO_2 < HClO$

3. Oxidation of which of the following substances will yield a stronger acid?

   A. H_2CO_3
   B. HNO_3
   C. HIO
   D. HIO_4
   E. H_2SO_4

4. A student prepared five vinegar samples by pipetting 10.00-mL samples of vinegar into five separate beakers. Each of the samples was diluted with deionized water, and phenolphthalein was added as an indicator. The samples were then titrated with standard sodium hydroxide until the appearance of a permanent pink color indicated the end point of the titration. The following volumes were obtained.

   Volumes of standard NaOH

   Sample 1: 43.28 mL
   Sample 2: 43.27 mL
   Sample 3: 50.00 mL no color change
   Sample 4: 43.26 mL
   Sample 5: 43.24 mL

Which of the following is the most likely cause for the variation in the results?

A. To much deionized water was added to the third sample.
B. The student forgot to add phenolphthalein to the third sample.
C. More acetic acid was present in the third vinegar sample.
D. The student did not properly rinse the buret with sodium hydroxide solution.
E. Too much indicator was in the third sample.

5. Choose the group that does not contain isotopes of the same element.

	Number of protons	Number of neutrons
A. Atom I	17	18
Atom II	18	19
B. Atom I	25	30
Atom II	25	31
C. Atom I	37	42
Atom II	37	41
D. Atom I	82	126
Atom II	82	128
E. Atom I	20	18
Atom II	20	20

6. Choose the ion with the largest ionic radius.

A. S^{2-}
B. H^+
C. Li^+
D. O^{2-}
E. Mg^{2+}

7. You are given an aqueous solution of $BaCl_2$. The simplest method for the separation of $BaCl_2$ from the solution is

A. filtration of the solution
B. osmosis of the solution
C. evaporation of the solution to dryness
D. electrolysis of the solution
E. centrifuging the solution

Choose one of the following for questions 8–10.

A. Cu^{2+}
B. CO_3^{2-}
C. Fe^{3+}
D. Al^{3+}
E. Pb^{2+}

8. This ion is amphoteric.

9. This ion does give a white precipitate when added to a calcium nitrate solution.

10. Solutions containing this ion give a reddish brown precipitate upon standing.

11. Which of the following is the correct net ionic equation for the addition of aqueous potassium sulfate to a solution of barium chloride?

A. $Ba^{2+} + SO_4^{2-} \rightarrow BaSO_4$
B. $Ba^{2+} + K_2SO_4 \rightarrow BaSO_4 + 2\ K^+$
C. $BaCl_2 + K_2SO_4 \rightarrow BaSO_4 + 2\ KCl$
D. $BaCl_2 + SO_4^{2-} \rightarrow BaSO_4 + 2\ Cl^-$
E. $BaCl_2 + P_2SO_4 \rightarrow BaSO_4 + 2\ PCl$

12. A solution is prepared for qualitative analysis. The solution contains the following ions: Pb^{2+}, Ni^{2+}, and Al^{3+}. Which of the following will cause no observable reaction?

A. Dilute $HCl(aq)$ is added.
B. Dilute $K_2CrO_4(aq)$ is added.
C. Dilute $KCl(aq)$ is added.
D. Dilute $NH_3(aq)$ is added.
E. Dilute $HNO_3(aq)$ is added.

13. The addition of concentrated $BaCl_2(aq)$ to a 1.0 M $(NH_4)_2SO_4$ solution will result in which of the following observations?

A. Nothing happens because the two solutions are immiscible.
B. The formation of a white precipitate takes place.

C. An odorless gas forms and bubbles out of the mixture.

D. The solution becomes basic.

E. The odor of ammonia will be detected.

14. How many milliliters of 0.300 M H_2SO_4 are required to neutralize 50.0 mL of 0.600 M KOH?

A. 20.0 mL

B. 25.0 mL

C. 30.0 mL

D. 60.0 mL

E. 50.0 mL

15. How many grams of hydrogen are in 25 g of $(NH_4)_2SO_4$?

A. 2.0 g

B. 8.0 g

C. 1.5 g

D. 3.0 g

E. 0.75 g

16. Gold(III) oxide, Au_2O_3, can be decomposed to gold metal, Au, plus oxygen gas, O_2. How many moles of oxygen gas will form when 22.1 g of solid gold(III) oxide is decomposed? The formula weight of gold(III) oxide is 442.

A. 0.100 mol

B. 0.0750 mol

C. 0.0500 mol

D. 0.150 mol

E. 0.0250 mol

17. ____ $C_4H_{11}N(l)$ + ____ $O_2(g) \rightarrow$ ____ $CO_2(g)$ + ____ $H_2O(l)$ + ____ $N_2(g)$

When the above equation is balanced, the lowest whole number coefficient for N_2 is:

A. 2

B. 22

C. 16

D. 27

E. 4

18. $2 KMnO_4 + 5 H_2C_2O_4 + 3 H_2SO_4 \rightarrow K_2SO_4 + 2 MnSO_4 + 10 CO_2 + 8 H_2O$

How many moles of $MnSO_4$ are produced when 2.0 mol of $KMnO_4$, 10 mol of $H_2C_2O_4$, and 6.0 mol of H_2SO_4 are mixed?

A. 1.0 mol

B. 2.0 mol

C. 3.5 mol

D. 2.5 mol

E. 3.0 mol

19. When the following equation is balanced, it is found that 2.00 mol of C_8H_{18} reacts with how many moles of O_2?

____ C_8H_{18} + ____ $O_2 \rightarrow$ ____ CO_2 + ____ H_2O

A. 37.5 mol

B. 2.00 mol

C. 25.0 mol

D. 1.00 mol

E. 12.5 mol

20. $Ra + 2 H_2O \rightarrow Ra(OH)_2 + H_2$

Radium reacts with water according to the above reaction. What volume of hydrogen gas, at standard temperature and pressure, is produced from 0.0100 mol of radium?

A. 0.560 L

B. 0.224 L

C. 0.448 L

D. 0.112 L

E. 0.336 L

21. Three flexible containers are used for gases. The containers are at the same temperature and pressure. One container has 2.0 g of hydrogen, another has 32.0 g of oxygen and the third has 44.0 g of carbon dioxide. Pick the **false** statement from the following list:

A. The densities increase in the order
   hydrogen < oxygen < carbon dioxide.
B. The number of molecules in the
   containers is the same.
C. The average kinetic energy of all the
   molecules is the same.
D. The volume of the three containers
   is the same.
E. The average speed of all the molecules is the same.

22. If a sample of SO_2 effuses at a rate of
    0.0035 mol per hour at 20° C, which of
    the gases below will effuse at approxi-
    mately double the rate under the same
    conditions?

    A. H_2
    B. O_2
    C. CO
    D. He
    E. CH_4

**Choose from the following types of energy
for questions 23–26.**

    A. free energy
    B. lattice energy
    C. kinetic energy
    D. activation energy
    E. ionization energy

23. The energy required to produce
    a gaseous cation from a gaseous atom
    in the ground state

24. The average _____ is the same
    for any ideal gas at a given temperature.

25. The maximum energy available for use-
    ful work from a spontaneous reaction

26. The energy required to separate cations
    from anions in an ionic solid

27. When cerium(III) acetate, $Ce(C_2H_3O_2)_3$,
    is dissolved in water, the temperature
    increases. Which of the following
    conclusions may be related to this?

A. The hydration energies of cerium(III)
   ions and acetate ions are very low.
B. Cerium(III) acetate is less soluble in
   hot water.
C. The solution is not an ideal solution.
D. The heat of solution for cerium(III)
   acetate is endothermic.
E. The lattice energy of cerium(III)
   acetate is very low.

28. Choose the reaction expected to have
    the greatest increase in entropy.

    A. $2 H_2(g) + O_2(g) \rightarrow 2 H_2O(g)$
    B. $2 Mn_2O_7(l) \rightarrow 4 MnO_2(s) + 3 O_2(g)$
    C. $C(s) + O_2(g) \rightarrow CO_2(g)$
    D. $2 Ca(s) + O_2(g) \rightarrow 2 CaO(s)$
    E. $NH_3(g) \rightarrow NH_3(l)$

29. A certain reaction is nonspontaneous
    under standard conditions, but
    becomes spontaneous at lower temper-
    atures. What conclusions may be
    drawn under standard conditions?

    A. $\Delta H < 0$, $\Delta S < 0$ and $\Delta G = 0$
    B. $\Delta H > 0$, $\Delta S < 0$ and $\Delta G > 0$
    C. $\Delta H < 0$, $\Delta S > 0$ and $\Delta G > 0$
    D. $\Delta H > 0$, $\Delta S > 0$ and $\Delta G > 0$
    E. $\Delta H < 0$, $\Delta S < 0$ and $\Delta G > 0$

30. $4 NO_2(g) + O_2(g) \rightarrow 2 N_2O_5(g) \Delta H$
    $= -111$ kJ

    Determine ΔH for the above reaction
    if $N_2O_5(s)$ were formed in the above
    reaction instead of $N_2O_5(g)$. The ΔH of
    sublimation for N_2O_5 is 54 kJ/mol.

    A. +54 kJ
    B. +219 kJ
    C. +165 kJ
    D. –219 kJ
    E. –165 kJ

31. Which of the following groups only
    contains atoms that are diamagnetic in
    their ground state?

    A. He, Co, and Sr
    B. Zn, Mg, and Xe

C. O, Be, and Ne
D. Ca, Mn, and Ar
E. As, Ba, and Rn

The following ground-state electron configurations are to be used for questions 32–35:

A. $1s^2 1p^6 2s^2 2p^3$
B. $1s^2 2s^2 2p^6 3s^2 3p^6 4s^2 3d^{10} 4p^6 5s^2 4d^1$
C. $1s^2 2s^2 2p^6 3s^2 3p^6 3d^3$
D. $1s^2 2s^2 2p^5$
E. $1s^2 2s^2 2p^6 3s^2 3p^6 4s^2 3d^{10} 4p^6$

32. It is not possible for this electron configuration to exist.

33. A halogen has this electron configuration.

34. A transition metal atom might have this configuration.

35. A transition metal ion could have this configuration.

The following answers are to be used for questions 36–39:

A. Pauli exclusion principle
B. electron shielding
C. the wave properties of matter
D. Heisenberg uncertainty principle
E. Hund's rule

36. The exact position of an electron is not known.

37. Nitrogen atoms, in their ground state, are paramagnetic.

38. An atomic orbital can hold no more than two electrons.

39. The 4s orbital fills before the 3d.

40. Which of the following does not have one or more π bonds?

A. HNO_2
B. N_2
C. N_2H_4

D. HNO_3
E. N_2H_2

For questions 41 and 42, pick the best choice from the following:

A. ionic bonds
B. hybrid orbitals
C. resonance structures
D. hydrogen bonding
E. van der Waals attractions

41. The unusually high melting point of hydrogen fluoride is due to

42. The presence of which explains why the bonds in BF_3 are all the same.

43. Which of the following has more than one unshared pair of valence electrons on the central atom?

A. NH_2^-
B. N_2O_5
C. NH_3
D. NO_2^-
E. NO_3^-

44. What types of hybridization of carbon are in the compound propane, $CH_3CH_2CH_3$?

I. sp^3
II. sp^2
III. sp

A. I only
B. II and III
C. I, II, and III
D. II only
E. I and II

45. The approximate boiling points for hydrogen compounds of some of the elements in the nitrogen family are: (SbH_3 15° C), (AsH_3 −62° C), (PH_3 −87° C), and (NH_3 −33° C). The best explanation for the fact that NH_3 does not follow the trend of the other hydrogen compounds is

A. NH_3 is the only one that is nearly ideal in the gas phase.
B. NH_3 is the only one that is a base.
C. NH_3 is the only one that is water-soluble.
D. NH_3 is the only one to exhibit hydrogen bonding.
E. NH_3 is the only one that is nonpolar.

Choose the appropriate answer from the following list for questions 46 and 47.

A. London dispersion forces
B. covalent bonding
C. hydrogen bonding
D. metallic bonding
E. ionic bonding

46. This is why copper is ductile.

47. This is why acetic acid molecules exist as dimers in the gaseous phase.

48. Which of the following best explains why 1-butanol, $CH_3CH_2CH_2CH_2OH$, has a higher boiling point (117° C) than its isomer, methyl propyl ether, $CH_3OCH_2CH_2CH_3$ (39° C)?

A. the lack of hydrogen bonding in 1-butanol
B. the presence of hydrogen bonding in 1-butanol
C. the higher molecular mass of 1-butanol
D. the lower specific heat of 1-butanol
E. the higher density of 1-butanol

49. What additional information is needed to convert the molality of a 1.00 m Na_2SO_4 solution to the molarity?

A. the volume of the solution
B. the density of the solution
C. the boiling point of the solution
D. the osmotic pressure of the solution
E. the mass of the solution

50. All the following substances will dissolve in water. Pick the nonelectrolyte.

A. $Ca(NO_3)_2$
B. KOH
C. C_2H_5OH
D. HCl
E. CH_3COOH

51. To prepare 4.0 L of a 0.50-molar $KClO_3$ solution (molecular weight 122.6), a student should follow which of the following procedures?

A. The student should weigh 245.2 g of solute and add 4.0 L of water.
B. The student should weigh 61.3 g of solute and add sufficient water to obtain a final volume of 4.0 L.
C. The student should weigh 61.3 g of solute and add 4.0 Kg of water.
D. The student should weigh 245.2 g of solute and add sufficient water to obtain a final volume of 4.0 L.
E. The student should weigh 61.3 g of solute and add 4.0 L of water.

52. Choose the aqueous solution with the highest boiling point.

A. 0.20 M HNO_3
B. 0.20 M HClO
C. 0.40 M C_3H_7OH
D. 0.20 M KI
E. 0.20 M Na_2SO_4

53. Which of the following aqueous solutions freezes at the lowest temperature?

A. 0.25 m $NaNO_3$
B. 0.25 m $FeSO_4$
C. 0.25 m $C_{12}H_{22}O_{11}$
D. 0.25 m $(NH_4)_2CrO_4$
E. 0.25 m KCl

54. For the following reaction, $H_2(g) + I_2(g) \rightarrow 2\ HI(g)$, the rate law is Rate = $k[H_2][I_2]$. If a small amount of iodine vapor (I_2) is added to a reaction mixture that was 0.10 molar in H_2 and

0.20 molar in I_2, which of the following statements is true?

A. Both k and the reaction rate decrease.
B. Both k and the reaction rate increase.
C. Both k and the reaction rate remain the same.
D. Only k increases, the reaction rate remains the same.
E. Only the rate increases, k remains the same.

55. Step 1: $(CH_3)_3CBr(aq) \rightarrow (CH_3)_3C^+(aq) + Br^-(aq)$

   Step 2: $(CH_3)_3C^+(aq) + H_2O(l)$
   $\rightarrow (CH_3)_3COH_2^+(aq)$

   Step 3: $(CH_3)_3COH_2^+(aq) \rightarrow H^+(aq) + (CH_3)_3COH(aq)$

   The above represents a proposed mechanism for the hydrolysis of $(CH_3)_3CBr$. What are the overall products of the reaction?

   A. $(CH_3)_3C^+$ and Br^-
   B. $(CH_3)_3COH_2^+$ and H^+
   C. $(CH_3)_3COH$ and H^+
   D. $(CH_3)_3COH$, H^+, and Br^-
   E. H^+ and Br^-

56. The table below gives the initial concentrations and rate for three experiments.

Experiment	Initial $[H_2]$ (mol L^{-1})	Initial $[NO]$ (mol L^{-1})	Initial rate of formation of N_2O (mol L^{-1} s^{-1})
1	0.100	0.100	2.80×10^5
2	0.200	0.100	5.60×10^5
3	0.200	0.200	2.24×10^6

The reaction is $H_2(g) + 2\,NO(g) \rightarrow N_2O(g) + H_2O(g)$. What is the rate law for this reaction?

A. Rate = $k[NO]$
B. Rate = $k[NO]^2[H_2]^2$
C. Rate = $k[H_2]$

D. Rate = $k[NO]^2[H_2]$
E. Rate = $k[NO][H_2]$

57. A solution of a weak base is titrated with a solution of a standard strong acid. The progress of the titration is followed with a pH meter. Which of the following observations would occur?

A. At the equivalence point, the pH is below 7.
B. The pH of the solution gradually decreases throughout the experiment.
C. At the equivalence point, the pH is 7.
D. The pOH at the equivalence point equals the pK_b of the base.
E. After the equivalence point, the pH becomes constant because this is the buffer region.

58. When potassium carbonate is dissolved in water

A. the solution is neutral.
B. the solution is basic because of hydrolysis of the CO_3^{2-} ion.
C. the solution is basic because of hydrolysis of the K^+ ion.
D. the solution is acidic because of hydrolysis of the K^+ ion.
E. the solution is acidic because of hydrolysis of the CO_3^{2-} ion.

59. Determine the $OH^-(aq)$ concentration in 0.10 M pyridine (C_5H_5N) solution. (The K_b for pyridine is 9×10^{-9}.)

A. 9×10^{-9} M
B. 5×10^{-6} M
C. 7×10^{-3} M
D. 1×10^{-1} M
E. 3×10^{-5} M

60. $FeS(s) + 2\,H^+(aq) \rightleftharpoons Fe^{2+}(aq) + H_2S(aq)$

What is the equilibrium constant for the above reaction? The successive acid dissociation constants for H_2S are 9.5×10^{-8} (K_{a1}) and 1×10^{-19} (K_{a2}). The K_{sp}, the solubility product constant, for FeS equals 5.0×10^{-18}.

A. $9.5 \times 10^{-27} / 5.0 \times 10^{-18}$
B. $5.0 \times 10^{-18} / 9.5 \times 10^{-27}$
C. $5.0 \times 10^{-18} / 9.5 \times 10^{-8}$
D. $9.5 \times 10^{-8} / 5.0 \times 10^{-18}$
E. $1 \times 10^{-19} / 5.0 \times 10^{-18}$

61. $C_2H_2(g) + H_2O(g) \rightleftharpoons CH_3CHO(g)$
    exothermic

An equilibrium mixture of the reactants is placed in a sealed container at 150° C. The amount of the product may be increased by which of the following changes?

I.   adding 1 mol of Ar(g) to the container
II. decreasing the volume of the container
III. raising the temperature of the container

   A. I only
   B. II and III
   C. III only
   D. I and II
   E. II only

62. The K_{sp} for $Cr(OH)_3$ is 1.6×10^{-30}. What is the molar solubility of this compound in water?

   A. $\sqrt[4]{1.6 \times 10^{-30}}$

   B. $\sqrt[4]{1.6 \times 10^{-30} / 27}$

   C. 1.6×10^{-30}

   D. $1.6 \times 10^{-30} / 27$

   E. $\sqrt[2]{1.6 \times 10^{-30}}$

Choose one of the following for questions 63–66.

   A. There is no change in the voltage.
   B. The voltage becomes zero.
   C. The voltage increases.
   D. The voltage decreases, but stays positive.
   E. The voltage becomes negative.

The following reaction takes place in a voltaic cell:

$$Zn(s) + Cu^{2+}(1\ M) \rightarrow Cu(s) + Zn^{2+}(1\ M)$$

The cell has its voltage measured and found to be +1.10 volts.

63. What happens to the voltage when deionized water is added to the zinc compartment?

64. What happens to the cell voltage when the copper electrode is made larger?

65. What happens to the cell voltage when the salt bridge is replaced with a zinc wire?

66. What happens to the cell voltage after the cell has operated for 15 min?

67. How many moles of Cr may be deposited on the cathode when 0.60 F of electricity is passed through a 1.0 M solution of Cr^{3+}?

   A. 0.60 mol
   B. 0.80 mol
   C. 1.0 mol
   D. 0.30 mol
   E. 0.20 mol

68. $Co^{2+} + 2\ e^- \rightarrow Co \qquad E° = -0.28\ v$

    $Zn^{2+} + 2\ e^- \rightarrow Zn \qquad E° = -0.76\ v$

Given the above standard reduction potentials, estimate the approximate value of the equilibrium constant for the following reaction:

$$Zn + Co^{2+} \rightarrow Zn^{2+} + Co$$

   A. 10^4
   B. 10^{16}
   C. 10^{-16}
   D. 10^{-8}
   E. 10^8

69. $2 \, Bi^{3+} + 3 \, SnO_2^{2-} + 6 \, OH^- \rightarrow 3 \, SnO_3^{2-} + 3 \, H_2O + 2 \, Bi$

The reducing agent in the above reaction is which of the following?

A. Bi^{3+}
B. SnO_2^{2-}
C. Bi
D. H_2O
E. OH^-

Questions 70 and 71 are concerned with the following half-reaction in an electrolytic cell:

$2 \, IO_3^+ + 6 \, H_2O + 10 \, e^- \rightarrow I_2 + 12 \, OH^-$

70. Choose the correct statement from the following list.

A. This reaction occurs at the anode.
B. The iodine is reduced from +5 to –1.
C. The iodine is oxidized from –1 to 0.
D. This reaction occurs at the cathode.
E. Water is a catalyst.

71. If a current of 7.50 amp is passed through the electrolytic cell for 0.45 h, how should you calculate the grams of I_2 to form?

A. (7.50)(0.45)(3600)(253.8)/(10)
B. (7.50)(0.45)(3600)(126.9)/ (96500)(10)
C. (7.50)(0.45)(60)(253.8)/(96500)(10)
D. (7.50)(0.45)(3600)(253.8)/ (96500)(10)
E. (7.50)(0.45)(126.9)/(96500)(10)

72. The formation of $^{230}_{90}Th$ from $^{234}_{92}U$ occurs by

A. electron capture
B. α decay
C. β decay
D. position decay
E. γ decay

73. What is the missing product in the following nuclear reaction?

$$^{236}_{92}U \rightarrow 4 \, ^{1}_{0}n + ^{136}_{53}I + \underline{\hspace{1cm}}$$

A. $^{99}_{39}Y$
B. $^{96}_{38}Sr$
C. $^{96}_{39}Y$
D. $^{98}_{40}Zr$
E. $^{98}_{41}Nb$

74.

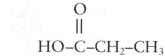

The above compound would be classified as

A. an aldehyde
B. a ketone
C. an ester
D. a carboxylic acid
E. an alcohol

75. The transition state is higher in energy than the reactants by an amount called

A. the heat of reaction
B. the reaction energy
C. the free energy
D. the kinetic energy
E. the activation energy

Answers and Explanations for AP Chemistry Practice Exam 2

1. **B.** All but D are Lewis bases. The higher charge on iron makes the difference.

2. **C.** More O = stronger acid.

3. **C.** Only C can be oxidized.

4. **B.** The phenolphthalein is the source of the color change.

5. **A.** If the numbers of protons are equal, the atoms are isotopes.

6. **A.** Anions are usually larger than cations. S is lower on the periodic table than O.

7. **C.** Solutions do not readily separate.

8. **D.** This is a property of aluminum.

9. **B.** The precipitate is $CaCO_3$.

10. **C.** Iron slowly hydrolyzes to form solid $Fe(OH)_3$.

11. **A.** Soluble compounds and spectator ions should not be present.

12. **E.** A and C precipitate $PbCl_2$. B precipitates $PbCrO_4$. D precipitates $Al(OH)_3$.

13. **B.** $BaSO_4$ forms.

14. **E.** (50.0 mL)(0.600 mol KOH/1000 mL)(1 mol H_2SO_4/2 mol KOH) (1000 mL/0.300 mol H_2SO_4)

15. **C.** (25 g $(NH_4)_2SO_4$)(1 mol$(NH_4)_2SO_4$/132 g $(NH_4)_2SO_4$)(8 mol H/ 1 mol $(NH_4)_2SO_4$)(1 g H/mol H)

16. **B.** (22.1 oxide)(1 mol oxide/442 g)(3 mol O_2/2 mol oxide) = 0.0750 mol

17. **A.** 4 $C_4H_{11}N$(l) + 27 O_2(g) → 16 CO_2(g) + 22 H_2O(l) + 2 N_2(g)

18. **B.** $KMnO_4$ is the limiting reactant.

19. **C.** 2 C_8H_{18} + 25 O_2 → 16 CO_2 + 18 H_2O

20. **B.** (0.0100 mol Ra)(1 mol H_2/1 mol Ra)(22.4 L/mol H_2) = 0.224 L

21. **E.** The average kinetic energy, not the average speed, is the same.

22. **E.** Use Graham's Law.

23. **E.** Definition

24. **C.** kinetic molecular theory

25. **A.** definition—a property of free energy

26. **B.** Definition

27. **B.** This is an exothermic process, and exothermic processes do not proceed as well at higher temperatures.

28. **B.** The reaction that has the greatest increase in the number of moles of gas.

29. **E.** To become spontaneous at a lower temperature means entropy impeded the reaction (entropy was negative). The enthalpy must be negative. Nonspontaneous under standard conditions means: $\Delta G > 0$

30. **D.** Subtract 54×2 mol N_2O_5 from the observed value (use Hess's law).

31. **B.** These have completely filled shells or subshells – all the electrons are paired = diamagnetic.

32. **A.** No such thing as a 1p.

33. **D.** All halogens are ns^2np^5.

34. **B.** A partially filled d orbital is required with an s^1 or s^2.

35. **C.** This is V^{2+}.

36. **D.** Definition

37. **E.** The electrons enter the orbitals separately (unpaired) until forced to pair. Unpaired = paramagnetic

38. **A.** Application of the definition.

39. **B.** This is a consequence of the better shielding of d electrons over s electrons.

40. **C.** There are only single bonds (σ) present.

41. **D.** Hydrogen bonding may occur when hydrogen is attached directly to N, O, or F.

42. **B.** B has three equivalent sp^2 orbitals.

43. **A.** C and D have one unshared pair, whereas E has none.

44. **A.** All three carbons have four single bonds.

45. **D.** Hydrogen bonding is possible when hydrogen is attached to N, O, and F.

46. **D.** A consequence of metallic bonding.

47. **C.** The two molecules are hydrogen bonded together.

48. **B.** The presence of the -OH group makes hydrogen bonding possible.

49. **B.** This is a dimensional analysis problem.

50. **C.** A is a soluble ionic compound; all the others are acids or bases. C is a neutral molecular compound.

51. **D.** (0.50 mol/L)(4.0 L)(122.6 g/mol) = 245.2 g and dilute to volume.

52. **E.** The substance producing the largest concentration of ions will have the highest boiling point.

53. **D.** The substance producing the largest concentration of ions will have the lowest freezing point.

54. **E.** Placing a larger number into the rate law will give a larger rate. The rate constant, k, is constant (unless the temperature changes or a catalyst is added).

55. **D.** Add the equations together and cancel any species that appear on both sides.

56. **D.** The reaction is first order in H_2 and second order in NO.

57. **A.** Strong acids and weak bases have pH = 7 at the equivalence point. The presence of a weak base lowers this value.

58. **B.** The carbonate ion is the conjugate base of a weak acid, and will produce a basic solution. The potassium ion comes from a strong base and will not undergo hydrolysis or change the pH.

59. **E.** $[OH^-] = (0.10 \times 9 \times 10^{-9})^{1/2} = 3 \times 10^{-5}$ M

60. **B.** $K = K_{sp}/K_{a1}K_{a2} = 5.0 \times 10^{-18}/(9.5 \times 10^{-8})(1 \times 10^{-19})$

61. **E.** I will yield no change, and III will decrease the amount of product.

62. **B.** $K_{sp} = [Cr^{3+}][OH^-]^3 = [x][3x]^3 = 27\ x^4 = 1.6 \times 10^{-30}$. Solve for x.

63. **C.** This will lower the concentration of Zn^{2+}, causing a shift to the right.

64. **A.** The size of the electrode is irrelevant.

65. **B.** A source of cations and anions is needed.

66. **D.** As the cell begins to run, the voltage decreases.

67. **E.** (0.60 F)(1 mol Cr/3 F)

68. **B.** $\log K = nE°/0.0592 = [2 \times (0.76 - 0.28)]/0.0592 = 16$

69. **B.** Bi^{3+} is the oxidizing agent.

70. **D.** Reduction reactions like this one always occur at the cathode.

71. **D.** Dimensional analysis:

$$(7.50\ coul/s)(0.45\ h)(3600\ s/h)(253.8\ g\ I_2/mol\ I_2)/(96500\ coul/F)(10\ F)$$

72. **B.** Mass difference = 234 − 230 = 4, and atomic number difference = 92 − 90 = 2. These correspond to an α particle.

73. **C.** Mass difference = 236 − 4(1) − 136 = 96. Atomic number difference = 92 − 4(0) − 53 = 39.

74. **D.** Based on classification of organic compounds.

75. **E.** Definition

Count the answers you got correct. Then count the answers you got wrong (skip those you did not answer). Multiply the number of wrong answers by 0.25 and subtract this value for the number of correct answers. This gives you your score on this set of questions.

AP CHEMISTRY PRACTICE EXAM 2: FREE-RESPONSE QUESTIONS

Time—1 hour and 30 minutes

Answer the following questions in the time allowed. You may use the equation/symbol pages, the list of reduction potentials, and a periodic table while taking this exam. Write the answers on a separate sheet of paper.

Part A. Time — 40 minutes

You may use a calculator for part A.

Question 1.

$$C(s) + 2\ H_2(g) \rightleftharpoons CH_4(g)$$

The value of K_p for the above equilibrium is 0.262 at 1270 K.

a. Write the equilibrium constant expression for the above equation.
b. Determine the value of K_c for the above equation at this temperature.
c. What is the value of K_p for the following equilibrium at 1270 K? Justify your answer.

$$CH_4(g) \rightleftharpoons C(s) + 2\ H_2(g)$$

d. Methane gas is introduced to a rigid container. The container is heated to 1270 K, and the initial partial pressure of the methane is 0.200 atm. What is the partial pressure of H_2 once equilibrium has been established?
e. In a separate experiment, a container with the initial equilibrium established is heated to 1350 K. At the higher temperature, the amount of CH_4 present has decreased, and the amount of H_2 present has increased. Is the initial equilibrium endothermic or exothermic? Justify your answer.
f. A small amount of carbon is introduced to a rigid container that is already at equilibrium. What changes, if any, would there be in the partial pressure of H_2? Justify your answer.

Answer either question 2 or question 3.

Question 2.

$$I^-(aq) + ClO^-(aq) \rightarrow IO^-(aq) + Cl^-(aq)$$

The above reaction occurs in basic solution. The following data were obtained from a series of experiments.

	Initial concentrations (molarities)			Initial rate (mol/L s)
	[I⁻]	[ClO⁻]	[OH⁻]	
Experiment 1	0.200	0.200	0.200	1.22
Experiment 2	0.400	0.200	0.200	2.44
Experiment 3	0.200	0.400	0.200	2.44
Experiment 4	0.200	0.200	0.400	0.610

Answer the following questions.

a. Determine the order of the reaction for I⁻, ClO⁻, and OH⁻. Justify your answers.
b. Write the rate law for the reaction.
c. Calculate the value of the rate constant. Include the units on the rate constant.
d. Assuming the reaction is exothermic, draw and label the potential energy level diagram for the reaction.

Question 3.

$$4 \ HCN(g) + 5 \ O_2(g) \rightarrow 4 \ CO_2(g) + 2 \ H_2O(g) + 2 \ N_2(g)$$

Thermodynamic values related to the above reaction are given in the table below.

Substance	$\Delta H_f°$ (kJ/mol)	S° (J/mol K)
$CO_2(g)$	−393.5	213.7
$HCN(g)$	135	201.7
$H_2O(g)$	−241.83	188.72
$H_2O(l)$	−285.84	69.94
$O_2(g)$	0	205.0
$N_2(g)$	0	191.5

a. Calculate the enthalpy change for this reaction.
b. Calculate the entropy change for this reaction.
c. Calculate the standard free energy for this reaction at 25° C.
d. Calculate the standard free energy change, at 25° C, if liquid water formed instead of water vapor.

STOP

Part B. Time — 50 minutes

You may not use a calculator for part B.

Question 4.

Choose FIVE of the following eight questions. Place your answers in the appropriate boxes. There is no extra credit for answering more than five. Formulas for reactants and products are needed. Do not include formulas for substances that remain unchanged during the reaction. It is not necessary to balance the equations. Unless otherwise noted, assume all the reactions occur in aqueous solution. If a substance is present as ions in solution, write its formula as an ion. Example: Hydrochloric acid is added to a lead(II) nitrate solution.

$$Pb^{2+} + Cl^- \rightarrow PbCl_2$$

a. Lithium metal is added to water.
b. Sulfur dioxide is bubbled through a lithium hydroxide solution.
c. Potassium oxide is mixed with water.
d. Nitric acid is added to a solution of methylamine.
e. Excess ammonia is added to a silver acetate solution.
f. Pentanol is combusted in oxygen.
g. Solid ammonium nitrate is heated.
h. An ammonium sulfate solution is mixed with a barium hydroxide solution.

Question 5.

$$5\ C_2O_4^{2-} + 2\ MnO_4^- + 16\ H^+ \rightarrow Mn^{2+} + 10\ CO_2 + 8\ H_2O$$

The above reaction is to be used in the analysis of an oxalate sample.

a. Outline the general procedure for the standardization of a potassium permanganate solution beginning with primary standard sodium oxalate.
b. Outline the calculation of the concentration of the potassium permanganate solution.
c. Show how to calculate the percent sodium oxalate in an unknown.
d. List the problems arising if the primary sodium oxalate solution was not dried before being weighed.
e. Normally, sulfuric acid is used to supply the hydrogen ions for the reaction. What would be the problem of substituting hydrochloric acid for sulfuric acid?

Question 6.

A sample containing $2/3$ mol of potassium chlorate, $KClO_3$, is heated until it decomposes to potassium chloride and oxygen gas. The oxygen is collected in an inverted bottle through the displacement of water. Answer the following questions using this information.

a. Write a balanced chemical equation for the reaction.
b. How many moles of oxygen gas are produced?
c. The temperature and pressure of the sample is adjusted to STP. The volume of the sample is found to be slightly greater than 22.4 L. Explain.
d. An excess of sulfur is burned in the oxygen. Write a balanced chemical equation and calculate the moles of gas formed.
e. After the sulfur had completely reacted, a sample of the residual water was removed from the bottle and found to be acidic. Explain.

Answer either question 7 or question 8.

Question 7.

Five beakers (A–E) are placed on a counter top. Each contains 200 mL of a 0.10 M solution. Beaker A contains $Ba(OH)_2$; beaker B contains $(NH_4)_2SO_4$; beaker C contains $(CH_3)_2CHOH$; beaker D contains K_3PO_4; and beaker E contains $FeSO_4$.

a. Which beaker has the lowest pH? Explain.
b. Which two beakers may be mixed to produce a gas with a characteristic odor? Write a chemical equation for the reaction.
c. Which of the solutions has its freezing point depressed the least? Explain.
d. Which two solutions are basic?
e. Which beaker will not give a precipitate when added to beaker A? Explain.

Question 8.

Answer the following questions about structure and bonding.

a. Which of the following tetrafluorides is polar? Use Lewis electron-dot structures to explain your conclusions.

$$SiF_4 \quad SF_4 \quad XeF_4$$

b. Rank the following compounds in order of increasing melting point. Explain. Lewis electron-dot structures may aid you.

$$SnF_2 \quad SeF_2 \quad KrF_2$$

c. Use Lewis electron-dot structures to show why the carbon oxygen bonds in the oxalate ion $(C_2O_4^{2-})$ are all equal.

d. When PCl_5 is dissolved in a polar solvent, the solution conducts electricity. Explain. Use an appropriate chemical equation to illustrate.

Answers and Explanations for AP Chemistry Free-Response Exam 2

Question 1.

✓ a. $K_p = P_{CH_4}/P_{H_2}^2 = 0.262$

You get 1 point for the correct equation. The "= 0.262" is optional.

b. $K_c = K_p/(RT)^{\Delta n}$ (This is from one of the equations given in the AP Exam booklet.)

$$\Delta n = 1 - 2 = -1$$

$$K_c = 0.262/[(0.0821)(1270)]^{-1} = 27.3$$

You get 1 point for the correct answer, and 1 point for choosing the correct equation.

c. $K_{new} = 1/K_p = 1/0.262 = 3.82$

When the equilibrium is reversed, you take the reciprocal of the equilibrium constant.

You get 1 point for the answer and 1 point for the explanation.

d. $K_p = P_{CH_4}/P_{H_2}^2 = 0.262$

	P_{H_2}	P_{CH_4}
initial	0.000	0.200
change	+2x	−x
equilibrium	2x	0.200 − x

Substituting: $K_p = (0.200 - x)/(2 x)^2 = 0.262$
$x = 0.170$
$P_{H_2} = 2 x = 0.340$ atm

You get 1 point for the correct answer, you get 1 point for the table, and you get 1 point for the setup. You could correctly use the equation and answer from part c.

e. The reaction is exothermic. The change in the amounts of CH_4 and H_2 indicate the reaction has shifted to the left. Exothermic reactions shift to the left as the temperature increases.

You get 1 point for answering exothermic, and 1 point for the explanation. You may get the explanation point even if you answered endothermic.

f. There would be no change. Solids do not shift equilibria.

You get 1 point for "no change," and 1 point for the explanation.

Total your points for each part. There are 12 possible points.

Question 2.

a. The orders for I^- and ClO^- are 1. The order for OH^- is -1. If you get all three of these correct, you get 1 point.

Comparing Experiments 1 and 2: The concentration of I^- is doubled, and the rate is doubled. This leads to I^- having an order of 1. You get 1 point for this reasoning.
    Comparing Experiments 1 and 3: The concentration of ClO^- is doubled, and the rate is doubled. This leads to ClO^- having an order of 1. You get 1 point for this reasoning.
    Comparing Experiments 1 and 4: The concentration of OH^- is doubled, and the rate is halved. This leads to OH^- having an order of -1. You get 1 point for this reasoning.

b. Rate $= k[I^-][ClO^-][OH^-]^{-1}$ This answer is worth 1 point. You will still get 1 point if you use incorrect orders from part a.

c. Rearrange the rate law to: $k = $ Rate$/[I^-][ClO^-][OH^-]^{-1}$ The values from any of the experiments may be plugged into this formula. Using Experiment 1:

$$k = 1.22/[0.200][0.200][0.200]^{-1} = 6.10 \text{ s}^{-1}$$

You get 1 point for plugging the values into the rearranged equation from part b. You get 1 point for the units.

d.

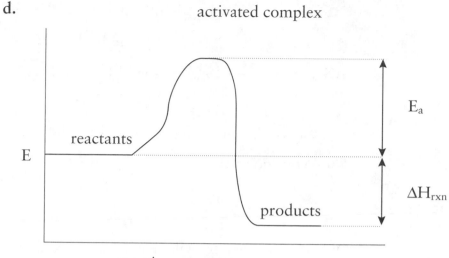

activated complex

reaction progress

You get 1 point for showing the products being lower than the reactants. You get 1 point for labeling the activation energy. You get 1 point for correctly labeling ΔH.

Total your points for the different parts. There are 10 possible points.

Question 3.

a. $\Delta H_{rxn}° = [4(-393.5) + 2(-241.83) + 2(0)] - [4(135) + 5(0)] = -2598 \text{ kJ}$

The setup (products – reactants) is worth 1 point, and the answer is worth 1 point. You do not need to get the exact answer, but you should be able to round to this one.

b. $\Delta S_{rxn}° = [4(213.7) + 2(188.72) + 2(191.5)] - [4(201.7) + 5(205.0)]$
$= -216.6 \text{ J/K}$

The setup (products – reactants) is worth 1 point, and the answer is worth 1 point. You do not need to get the exact answer, but you should round to this one.

c. $\Delta G_{rxn}° = \Delta H_{rxn}° - T\Delta S_{rxn}° = -2598 \text{ kJ} - (298 \text{ K})(1 \text{ kJ}/1000 \text{ J})(-216.6 \text{ J/K})$
$= -2533 \text{ kJ}$

The setup (plugging into the equation) is worth 1 point if you remember to change the temperature to Kelvin and the joule to kilojoule conversion. An additional 1 point comes from the answer. If you got the wrong value in either part a or b, but used it correctly, you will still get the point for the answer. The free energy equation is part of the material supplied in the exam booklet.

d. This requires a repeat of parts a–c using the values for $H_2O(l)$.

$\Delta H_{rxn}° = [4(-393.5) + 2(-285.84) + 2(0)] - [4(135) + 5(0)] = -2686 \text{ kJ}$

$$\Delta S_{rxn}° = [4(213.7) + 2(69.94) + 2(191.5)] - [4(201.7) + 5(205.0)]$$
$$= -454.1 \text{ J/K}$$

$$\Delta G_{rxn}° = \Delta H_{rxn}° - T\Delta S_{rxn}° = -2686 \text{ kJ} - (298 \text{ K})(1 \text{ kJ}/1000 \text{ J})(-454.1 \text{ J/K})$$
$$= -2551 \text{ kJ}$$

You get 1 point for the work and 1 point for the answer.

Total your points.

Question 4.

Only the five answers will be graded. If you do more than five, only the first five will be graded. No extra points will be given for doing more than five. There are no extra points for balancing.

a. $Li + H_2O \rightarrow Li^+ + OH^- + H_2$

You get 1 point for the correct formulas for the reactants and 2 points for the correct formulas for the products. No variations are allowed.

b. $SO_2 + OH^- \rightarrow SO_3^{2-} + H_2O$

You get 1 point for the correct formulas for the reactants and 2 points for the correct formulas for the products. No variations are allowed.

c. $K_2O + H_2O \rightarrow K^+ + OH^-$

You get 1 point for the correct formulas for the reactants and 2 points for the correct formulas for the products. No variations are allowed.

d. $H^+ + CH_3NH_2 \rightarrow CH_3NH_3^+$

You get 1 point for the correct formulas for the reactants and 2 points for the correct formulas for the products. No variations are allowed.

e. $NH_3 + Ag^+ \rightarrow [Ag(NH_3)_2]^+$

You get 1 point for the correct formulas for the reactants and 2 points for the correct formulas for the products. No variations are allowed.

f. $C_5H_{11}OH + O_2 \rightarrow CO_2 + H_2O$

You get 1 point for the correct formulas for the reactants and 2 points for the correct formulas for the products. No variations are allowed.

g. $NH_4NO_3 \rightarrow N_2O + H_2O$

or $NH_4NO_3 \rightarrow N_2 + O_2 + H_2O$

You get 1 point for the correct formulas for the reactants and 2 points for the correct formulas for the products. No variations are allowed;

you cannot use part of one line with the other line. This example was chosen to show that there may be more than one correct answer.

h. $NH_4^+ + SO_4^{2-} + Ba^{2+} + OH^- \rightarrow BaSO_4 + NH_3 + H_2O$

You get 1 point for the correct formulas for the reactants and 2 points for the correct formulas for the products. No variations are allowed.

Question 5.

a. 1. Samples of primary standard sodium oxalate are weighed into beakers, and deionized water is added to dissolve each of the samples. 2. A buret is rinsed with the potassium permanganate solution and then filled. 3. The potassium permanganate solution is titrated into the oxalate sample until a permanent pink color from the permanganate solution appears. All three of these will get you 2 points. One or two of these will get you 1 point. Other items, such as heating the oxalate solution before the titration, are not needed.

b. (gram sample)(1 mol $Na_2C_2O_4$/134 g)(2 mol MnO_4^-/5 mol $C_2O_4^{2-}$) (1/L MnO_4^- added)

This entire setup will get 2 points (the 134 is optional). You get 1 point if you miss a step.

c. Percent sodium oxalate = (grams sodium oxalate/grams sample) × 100%

You get 1 point for this answer.

d. If the primary standard was not dried, the sample would contain less sodium oxalate than indicated by the mass. The calculated concentration of the potassium permanganate solution would be too low. This item is worth 1 point.

A low concentration for the potassium permanganate solution would yield a low percentage of sodium oxalate in the sample. This item is worth 1 point.

e. Hydrochloric acid reacts with permanganate ion. This answer is worth 1 point.

Total your points for the various parts. There are 8 possible points.

Question 6.

a. $2 KClO_3(s) \rightarrow 2 KCl(s) + 3 O_2(g)$

You get 1 point if you have the above equation.

b. (⅔ mol $KClO_3$)(3 mol O_2/2 mol $KClO_3$) = 1 mol O_2

You get 1 point for the correct answer and 1 point for the work. You can get these points if you correctly use information from an incorrect equation in part a.

c. At STP the volume of 1 mol of O_2 should be 22.4 L. The volume is greater because oxygen was not the only gas in the sample. Water vapor was present. The presence of the additional gas leads to a larger volume.

You get 1 point for discussing STP and 22.4 L, and 1 point for discussing the presence of water vapor.

d. There are two acceptable equations; either will get you 1 point. You do not need both equations.

$$S(s) + O_2(g) \rightarrow SO_2(g)$$

$$2 S(s) + 3 O_2(g) \rightarrow 2 SO_3(g)$$

If you chose the first equation, the moles of gas produced would be:

$$(1 \text{ mol } O_2)(1 \text{ mol } SO_2/1 \text{ mol } O_2) = 1 \text{ mol } SO_2$$

If you chose the second equation, the moles of gas produced would be:

$$(1 \text{ mol } O_2)(2 \text{ mol } SO_3/3 \text{ mol } O_2) = 2/3 \text{ mol } SO_2$$

You get 1 point for either of these solutions. You will also get 1 point if you used an incorrect number of moles of O_2 from a wrong answer for part b.

e. Either of the possible sulfur oxides will dissolve in water to produce an acid. This will get you 1 point, as will a similar comment for either of the following equations:

$$SO_2 + H_2O \rightarrow H_2SO_3$$

$$SO_3 + H_2O \rightarrow H_2SO_4$$

Total your points for the different parts. There are 8 possible points.

Question 7.

a. Beaker B has the lowest pH. The NH_4^+ ion is the conjugate acid of a weak base, and as an acid (weak) it will lower the pH.

You get 1 point for the correct beaker. You get 1 point for the explanation.

b. Solutions A and B produce a gas with a characteristic odor when mixed. The reaction is:

$$NH_4^+(aq) + OH^-(aq) \rightarrow NH_3(g) + H_2O(l)$$

or

$$(NH_4)_2SO_4(aq) + Ba(OH)_2(aq) \rightarrow 2\ NH_3(g) + 2\ H_2O(l) + BaSO_4(s)$$

You get 1 point for the correct two solutions, and you get 1 point for either of the balanced equations.

c. Solution C has the lowest freezing point depression. This solution is the only nonelectrolyte present. The electrolytes depress the freezing point to a greater extent.

You get 1 point for the correct solution, and 1 point for the explanation.

d. Solutions A and D. You get 1 point for each of these you get correct.

e. Solution C will give no precipitate. Beaker B gives $BaSO_4$. Beaker D gives $Ba_3(PO_4)_2$. Beaker E gives $Fe(OH)_2$.

You get 1 point for choosing solution C. You get 1 point for listing the other precipitates or explaining that beaker C contains a nonelectrolyte that will not react with either barium ions or hydroxide ions.

Total your points for the different parts. There are 10 possible points.

Question 8.

a. Sulfur tetrafluoride is the only one of the three compounds that is polar.

    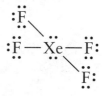

SiF₄ four bonding pairs and no lone pairs.	SF₄ four bonding pairs and one lone pair.	XeF₄ four bonding pairs and two lone pairs.
Tetrahedral	Seesaw	Square Planar

SiF_4 four bonding pairs and no lone pairs.

Tetrahedral

SF_4 four bonding pairs and one lone pair.

Seesaw

XeF_4 four bonding pairs and two lone pairs.

Square Planar

You get 1 point if you correctly predict SF_4 only to be nonpolar. You get 1 additional point for each correct Lewis structure.

b. The order is: $KrF_2 < SeF_2 < SnF_2$

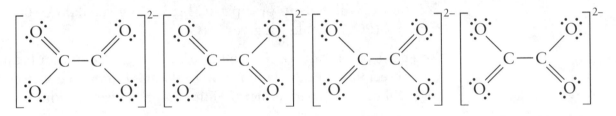

KrF₂ two bonding pairs and three nonbonding pairs

SeF₂ two bonding pairs and two nonbonding pairs

SnF₂ ionic

The Lewis structure indicates that KrF_2 is nonpolar. Thus, it only has very weak London dispersion forces between the molecules. SeF_2 is polar and the molecules are attracted by dipole-dipole attractions, which are stronger than London. SnF_2 has the highest melting point because of the presence of strong ionic bonds.

You get 1 point for the order, and 1 point for the discussion.

c. The following resonance structures may be drawn for the oxalate ion. The presence of resonance equalizes the bonds.

You get 1 point for any correct Lewis structure for $C_2O_4^{2-}$, and 1 point for showing or discussing resonance.

d. PCl_5 must ionize. There are two acceptable equations:

$$2\,PCl_5 \rightleftharpoons PCl_4^+ + PCl_6^- \quad \text{or} \quad PCl_5 \rightleftharpoons PCl_4^+ + Cl^-$$

You get 1 point for the explanation, and you get 1 point for either of the equations.

Total your points for the different parts. There are 10 possible points.

TOTAL SCORE:

Question 1 _____

Question 2 or 3 _____

Question 4 _____

Question 5 _____

Question 6 _____

Question 7 or 8 _____

PART V

APPENDIXES

SI Units

SI PREFIXES

Prefix	Abbreviation	Meaning
pico-	p	0.000000000001 or 10^{-12}
nano-	n	0.000000001 or 10^{-9}
micro-	μ	0.000001 or 10^{-6}
milli-	m	0.001 or 10^{-3}
centi-	c	0.01 or 10^{-2}
deci-	d	0.1 or 10^{-1}
deka-	da	10 or 10^{1}
hector-	h	100 or 10^{2}
kilo	k	1,000 or 10^{3}
Mega-	M	1,000,000 or 10^{6}
Giga-	G	1,000,000,000 or 10^{9}
Tera-	T	1,000,000,000,000 or 10^{12}

SI BASE UNITS AND SI/ENGLISH CONVERSIONS

Length

The base unit for length in the SI system is the *meter*.

1 kilometer (km) = 0.62 mile (mi)
1 mile (mi) = 1.61 kilometers (km)
1 yard (yd) = 0.914 meters (m)
1 inch (in) = 2.54 centimeters (cm)

Mass

The base unit for mass in the SI system is the *kilogram*.

1 pound (lb) = 454 grams (g)
1 metric ton (t) = 10^3 kg

Volume

The base unit for volume in the SI system is the *cubic meter*.

1 dm^3 = 1 liter (L) = 1.057 quarts (qt)
1 milliliter (mL) = 1 cubic centimeter (cm^3)
1 milliliter (mL) = 1,000 microliters (μL)
1 quart (qt) = 0.946 liters (L)
1 pint (pt) = 0.473 liter (L)
1 fluid ounce (fl oz) = 29.6 milliliters (mL)
1 gallon (gal) = 3.78 liters (L)

Temperature

The base unit for temperature in the SI system is *Kelvin*.

Celsius to Fahrenheit: °F = (9/5)°C + 32
Fahrenheit to Celsius: °C = (5/9)(°F − 32)
Celsius to Kelvin: °K = °C + 273.15

Pressure

The base unit for pressure in the SI system is the *pascal*.

1 millimeter of mercury (mm Hg) = 1 torr
1 Pa = 1 N/m^2 = 1 kg/m s^2
1 atm = 1.01325×10^5 Pa = 760 torr
1 bar = 1×10^5 Pa

Energy

The base unit for energy in the SI system is the *joule*.

1 J = 1 kg m^2/s^2 = 1 coulomb volt
1 calorie (cal) = 4.184 joules (J)
1 food Calorie (Cal) = 1 kilocalorie (kcal) = 4184 joules (J)
1 British thermal unit (BTU) = 252 calories (cal) = 1053 joules (J)

Balancing Redox Equations Using the Ion-Electron Method

The following steps may be used to balance oxidation-reduction (redox) equations by the ion-electron (half-reaction) method. While other methods may be successful, none is as consistently successful as is this particular method. The half-reactions used in this process will also be necessary when considering other electrochemical phenomena, thus the usefulness of half-reactions goes beyond balancing redox equations.

The basic idea of this method is to split a "complicated" equation into two parts called half-reactions. These simpler parts are then balanced separately, and recombined to produce a balanced overall equation. The splitting is done so that one of the half-reactions only deals with the oxidation portion of the redox process, whereas the other only deals with the reduction portion. What ties the two halves together is the fact that the total electrons lost by the oxidation process MUST equal the total gained by the reduction process (step 6).

It is very important that you follow each of the steps listed below completely, in order; do not try to take any short cuts. There are many modifications of this method. For example, a modification allows you to balance all the reactions as if they were in acidic solution followed by a step, when necessary, to convert to a basic solution. Switching to a modification before you completely understand this method very often leads to confusion, and an incorrect result.

1. ASSIGN OXIDATION NUMBERS AND BEGIN THE HALF-REACTIONS, ONE FOR OXIDATION AND ONE FOR REDUCTION

Beginning with the following example:

$$CH_3OH + Cr_2O_7^{2-} + H^+ \rightarrow HCOOH + Cr^{3+} + H_2O$$

(For many reactions, the substance oxidized, and the substance reduced will be obvious, so this step may be simplified. However, to be safe, at least do a partial check to confirm your predictions. Note: One substance may be both oxidized and reduced; do not let this situation surprise you–it is called disproportionation.)

Review the rules for assigning oxidation numbers if necessary, in Chapter 3. These numbers are only used in this step. Do not force them into step 5.

Start the half-reactions with the entire molecules or ions from the net ionic form of the reaction. Do not go back to the molecular form of the reaction or just pull out atoms from their respective molecules or ions. Thus from the example above, the initial half-reactions should be:

$$CH_3OH \rightarrow HCOOH$$

$$Cr_2O_7^{2-} \rightarrow Cr^{3+}$$

The carbon is oxidized (C^{2-} to C^{2+}) and the chromium is reduced (Cr^{6+} to Cr^{3+}). Check to make sure you get the same oxidation numbers for the carbon and the chromium (hydrogen and oxygen are +1 and −2 respectively).

2. BALANCE ALL ATOMS EXCEPT OXYGEN AND HYDROGEN

(In many reactions this will have been done in step 1; because of this many people forget to check this step. This is a very common reason why people get the wrong result.)

In the above example carbon (C) and chromium (Cr) are the elements to be considered. The carbon is balanced, so no change is required in the first half-reaction. The chromium needs to be balanced, and so the second half-reaction becomes:

$$Cr_2O_7^{2-} \rightarrow 2\ Cr^{3+}$$

 Note: To carry out the next two steps correctly, it is necessary to know if the solution is acidic or basic. A basic solution is one in which you are specifically told is basic, or one that contains a base of OH^- anywhere within the reaction. Assume that all other solutions are acidic (even if no acid is present).

3. BALANCE OXYGEN ATOMS

a. In Acidic Solutions Add 1 H_2O/O to the Side Needing Oxygen

b. In Basic Solutions Add 2 OH^- for Every Oxygen Needed on the Oxygen Deficient Side Plus 1 H_2O/O on the Opposite Side

Do not forget that two things (OH^- and H_2O) must be added in a basic solution. Also these must be added to opposite sides.

Examples:

acid:
$$Cr_2O_7^{2-} \rightarrow 2\ Cr^{3+}$$

becomes:

$$Cr_2O_7^{2-} \rightarrow 2\ Cr^{3+} + 7\ H_2O$$

Now an example in base:

base:
$$Cr_2O_7^{2-} \rightarrow 2\ CrO_2^{-}$$

becomes:

$$3\ H_2O + Cr_2O_7^{2-} \rightarrow 2\ CrO_2^{-} + 6\ OH^{-}$$

4. BALANCE HYDROGEN ATOMS

a. In Acidic Solutions Add H^+(aq)

b. In Basic Solutions Add 1 H_2O/H Needed Plus 1 OH^-/H on the Opposite Side

Again, do not forget that two things must be added in basic solutions (OH^- and H_2O). In this case they are still added to opposite sides, but with a different ratio.

Examples:

acid:
$$Cr_2O_7^{2-} \rightarrow 2\ Cr^{3+} + 7\ H_2O$$

becomes:

$$14\ H^+(aq) + Cr_2O_7^{2-} \rightarrow 2\ Cr^{3+} + 7\ H_2O$$

Now an example in base:

base:
$$6\ OH^- + C_2H_5OH \rightarrow 2\ CO_2 + 3\ H_2O$$

becomes:

$$6\ OH^- + 6\ OH^- + C_2H_5OH \rightarrow 2\ CO_2 + 3\ H_2O + 6\ H_2O$$

If the basic step is done correctly, the oxygens should remain balanced. This may be used as a check at this point.

5. BALANCE CHARGES BY ADDING ELECTRONS

The electrons must appear on opposite sides of the two half-reactions. They will appear on the left for the reduction, and on the right for the oxidation. Once added make sure you check and make sure that the total charge on each side is the same. Not being careful on this step is a major cause of incorrect answers. Do not forget to use both the coefficients and the overall charges on the ions (not the oxidation numbers from step 1).

Examples:

$$6 \, e^- + 14 \, H^+(aq) + Cr_2O_7^{2-} \rightarrow 2 \, Cr^{3+} + 7 \, H_2O$$

base:

$$6 \, OH^- + 6 \, OH^- + C_2H_5OH \rightarrow 2 \, CO_2 + 3 \, H_2O + 6 \, H_2O + 12 \, e^-$$

6. ADJUST THE HALF-REACTIONS SO THAT THEY BOTH HAVE THE SAME NUMBER OF ELECTRONS

(Find the lowest common multiple, and multiply each of the half-reactions by the appropriate factor to achieve this value. This is the key step, as the number of electrons lost MUST equal the number gained.)

Example:

Lowest common multiple = 12

$$3 \times (H_2O + CH_3OH \rightarrow HCOOH + 4 \, H^+(aq) + 4 \, e^-)$$

$$2 \times (6 \, e^- + 14 \, H^+(aq) + Cr_2O_7^{2-} \rightarrow 2 \, Cr^{3+} + 7 \, H_2O)$$

Giving:

$$3 \, H_2O + 3 \, CH_3OH \rightarrow 3 \, HCOOH + 12 \, H^+(aq) + 12 \, e^-$$

$$12 \, e^- + 28 \, H^+(aq) + 2 \, Cr_2O_7^{2-} \rightarrow 4 \, Cr^{3+} + 14 \, H_2O$$

7. ADD THE HALF-REACTIONS AND CANCEL

(The electrons must cancel)

Example (from step 6):

$$12 \, e^- + 3 \, H_2O + 3 \, CH_3OH + 28 \, H^+(aq) + 2 \, Cr_2O_7^{2-}$$
$$\rightarrow 4 \, Cr^{3+} + 14 \, H_2O + 3 \, HCOOH + 12 \, H^+(aq) + 12 \, e^-$$

Becomes:

$$3 \, CH_3OH + 16 \, H^+(aq) + 2 \, Cr_2O_7^{2-} \rightarrow 4 \, Cr^{3+} + 11 \, H_2O$$
$$+ 3 \, HCOOH$$

8. CHECK TO SEE IF ALL ATOMS BALANCE AND THAT THE TOTAL CHARGE ON EACH SIDE IS THE SAME

This step will let you know if you have done everything correctly.

If all the atoms and charges do not balance you have made a mistake. Look over your work. If you have made an obvious mistake, then you should correct it. If the mistake is not obvious, it may take less time to start over from the beginning. The most common mistakes are made in steps 2 and 5, or step 3 in a basic solution.

Make sure you learn to apply each of the above steps. Look over the individual examples and make sure you understand them separately. Then make sure you learn the order of these steps. Finally, balance redox reactions, this will take a lot of practice. Make sure that you reach the point of being able to consistently balance equations without looking at the rules.

Common Ions

IONS USUALLY WITH ONE OXIDATION STATE

Li^+	lithium ion	N^{3-}	nitride ion
Na^+	sodium ion	O^{2-}	oxide ion
K^+	potassium ion	S^{2-}	sulfide ion
Mg^{2+}	magnesium ion	F^-	fluoride ion
Ca^{2+}	calcium ion	Cl^-	chloride ion
Sr^{2+}	strontium ion	Br^-	bromide ion
Ba^{2+}	barium ion	I^-	iodide ion
Ag^+	silver ion		
Zn^{2+}	zinc ion		
Cd^{2+}	cadmium ion		
Al^{3+}	aluminum ion		

CATIONS WITH MORE THAN ONE OXIDATION STATE

	+1		+2
Cu^{1+}	copper(I) ion or cuprous ion	Cu^{2+}	copper(II) ion or cupric ion
Hg_2^{2+}	mercury(I) ion or mercurous ion	Hg^{2+}	mercury(II) ion or mercuric ion

	+2		+3
Fe^{2+}	iron(II) ion or ferrous ion	Fe^{3+}	iron(III) ion or ferric ion

Cr^{2+}	chromium(II) ion or chromous ion	Cr^{3+}	chromium(III) ion or chromic ion
Mn^{2+}	manganese(II) ion or manganous ion	Mn^{3+}	manganese(III) ion or manganic ion
Co^{2+}	cobalt(II) ion or cobaltous ion	Co^{3+}	cobalt(III) ion or cobaltic ion
	+2		+4
Sn^{2+}	tin(II) ion or stannous ion	Sn^{4+}	tin(IV) ion or stannic ion
Pb^{2+}	lead(II) ion or plumbous ion	Pb^{4+}	lead(IV) ion or plumbic ion

POLYATOMIC IONS AND ACIDS

Formula	Name	Ion	Ion name
H_2SO_4	sulfuric acid	SO_4^{2-}	sulfate ion
H_2SO_3	sulfurous acid	SO_3^{2-}	sulfite ion
HNO_3	nitric acid	NO_3^-	nitrate ion
HNO_2	nitrous acid	NO_2^-	nitrite ion
H_3PO_4	phosphoric acid	PO_4^{3-}	phosphate ion
H_2CO_3	carbonic acid	CO_3^{2-}	carbonate ion
$HMnO_4$	permanganic acid	MnO_4^-	permanganate ion
HCN	hydrocyanic acid	CN^-	cyanide ion
$HOCN$	cyanic acid	OCN^-	cyanate ion
$HSCN$	thiocyanic acid	SCN^-	thiocyanate ion
$HC_2H_3O_2$	acetic acid	$C_2H_3O_2^-$	acetate ion
$H_2C_2O_4$	oxalic acid	$C_2O_4^{2-}$	oxalate ion
H_2CrO_4	chromic acid	CrO_4^{2-}	chromate ion
$H_2Cr_2O_7$	dichromic acid	$Cr_2O_7^{2-}$	dichromate ion
$H_2S_2O_3$	thiosulfuric acid	$S_2O_3^{2-}$	thiosulfate ion
H_3AsO_4	arsenic acid	AsO_4^{3-}	arsenate ion
H_3AsO_3	arsenious acid	AsO_3^{3-}	arsenite ion

OXYHALOGEN ACIDS

Formula	Oxy name	Ion	Ion name
$HClO$	hypochlorous acid	ClO^-	hypochlorite ion
$HClO_2$	chlorous acid	ClO_2^-	chlorite ion
$HClO_3$	chloric acid	ClO_3^-	chlorate ion
$HClO_4$	perchloric acid	ClO_4^-	perchlorate ion

Br, I, can be substituted for chlorine Cl. F may form hypofluorous acid and the hypofluorite ion.

OTHER IONS

Ion	Ion name
O_2^{2-}	peroxide ion
OH^-	hydroxide ion
HSO_4^-	bisulfate ion; hydrogen sulfate ion
NH_4^+	ammonium ion
Hg_2^{2+}	mercury(I) ion
O_2^-	superoxide ion
HCO_3^-	bicarbonate ion; hydrogen carbonate ion
HPO_4^{2-}	hydrogen phosphate ion
$H_2PO_4^-$	dihydrogen phosphate ion

LIGANDS

Ligand	Formula(abbreviation)	Ligand name
Bromide ion	Br^-	bromo
Carbonate ion	CO_3^{2-}	carbonato
Chloride ion	Cl^-	chloro
Cyanide ion	CN^-	cyano
Fluoride ion	F^-	fluoro
Hydride ion	H^-	hydrido
Hydroxide ion	OH^-	hydroxo
Iodide ion	I^-	iodo
Nitrite ion	NO_2^-	nitrito
Oxalate ion	$C_2O_4^{2-}$	oxalato
Sulfide ion	S^{2-}	thio
Thiocyanate ion	SCN^-	thiocyanato
Ammonia	NH_3	ammine
Ethylenediamine	en	ethylenediamine
Water	H_2O	aqua

COLORS OF COMMON IONS IN AQUEOUS SOLUTION

Most common ions are colorless in solution, however, some have distinctive colors.

Fe^{2+} and Fe^{3+}	various colors
Cu^{2+}	blue to green

Cr^{2+}	blue
Cr^{3+}	green or violet
Mn^{2+}	faint pink
Ni^{2+}	green
Co^{2+}	pink
MnO_4^-	dark purple
CrO_4^{2-}	yellow
$Cr_2O_7^{2-}$	orange

Appendix D

Bibliography

Brown, Theodore L., H. Eugene LeMay, Jr. and Bruce E. Bursten, *Chemistry: The Central Science*, 7th ed., Prentice Hall, Upper Saddle Creek, NJ, 1997.

Cates, Charles R., Langley, Richard H. and Moore, John T. *Introductory Chemical Practice: A Quantitative Approach*, 6th ed., San Francisco, CA, 2003.

Goldberg, David E., *Fundamentals of Chemistry*, 3rd ed., McGraw-Hill, New York, NY, 2001.

Moore, John T., *Chemistry for Dummies*, Wiley Publishing, Inc., New York, NY, 2003.

Russo, Steve and Mile Silver, *Introductory Chemistry*, 2nd ed., Benjamin Cummings, San Francisco, CA, 2002.

Silberberg, Martin S., *Chemistry: The Molecular Nature of Matter and Change*, 3rd ed., McGraw-Hill, New York, NY, 2003.

Zumdahl, Steven S., *Chemistry*, Houghton Mifflin Company, Boston, MA, 1997.

Appendix E

Websites

Here is a list of Websites that contain information and links that you might find useful in your preparation for the AP Chemistry Exam:

www.acs.org/portal/chemistry
www.chemistry.about/com
www.webelements.com
www.chemclub.com
www.ice.chem.wisc.edu
www.collegeboard.com/ap/students/chemistry
www.shs.nebo.edu/Faculty/Haderlie/apchem/apchem.html
www.chemistrygeek.com/ap.htm
www.chem.purdue.edu/apchem/MainPage/AP_References/KEYS_TO_PASS.html

Appendix F

Glossary

absolute zero Absolute zero is 0 K and is the point at which all molecular motion ceases.

acidic A solution whose pH is *less* than 7.00 is said to be acidic.

acids Acids are proton (H^+) donors.

acid dissociation constant The acid dissociation constant is the equilibrium constant associated with the dissociation of a weak acid in water.

acid dissociation constant (K_a) The acid dissociation constant is the equilibrium constant associated with a weak acid dissociation in water.

activation energy Activation energy is the minimum amount of energy that must be supplied to initiate a chemical reaction.

activity series for metals The activity series lists metals in order of decreasing ease of oxidation.

actual yield The actual yield is the amount of product that is actually formed in a chemical reaction.

alkali metals Alkali metals are in the IA group on the periodic table.

alkaline earth metals Alkaline earth metals are in the IIA group on the periodic table.

alkanes Alkanes are hydrocarbons that contain only single covalent bonds within the molecule.

alkenes Alkenes are hydrocarbons that contain a carbon-to-carbon double bond.

alkynes Alkynes are hydrocarbons that contain a triple bond.

alpha particle An alpha particle is essentially a helium nucleus with two protons and two neutrons.

amorphous solids Amorphous solids are solids that lack extensive ordering of the particles.

amphoteric Amphoteric substances will act as either an acid or a base, depending on whether the other species is a base or acid.

amplitude Amplitude is the height of a wave and is related to the intensity (or brightness for visible light) of the wave.

amu An amu is $\frac{1}{12}$ the mass of a carbon atom that contains 6 protons and 6 neutrons (C-12).

angular momentum quantum number (l) The angular momentum quantum number is the quantum number that describes the shape of the orbital.

anions Anions are negatively charged ions.

anode The electrode at which oxidation is taking place is called the anode.

anode compartment The anode compartment is the electrolyte solution in which the anode is immersed.

aqueous solution An aqueous solution is a solution in which water is the solvent.

atomic number (Z) The atomic number of an element is the number of proton in the nucleus.

atomic orbital The atomic orbital is the region of space in which it is most likely to find a specific electron in an atom.

atomic solids In atomic solids, individual atoms are held in place by London forces.

Aufbau principle The Aufbau principle states that the electrons in an atom fill the lowest energy levels first.

Avogadro's law Avogadro's law states that there is a direct relationship between the volume and the number of moles of gas.

Avogadro's number Avogadro's number is the number of particles (atoms or molecules or ions) in a mole and is numerically equal to 6.022×10^{23} particles.

barometer A barometer is an instrument for measuring atmospheric pressure.

base dissociation constant, K_b The base dissociation constant is the equilibrium constant associated with the dissociation of a weak base in water.

bases Bases are defined as proton (H^+) acceptors.

basic A solution whose pH is *greater* than 7.00 is called basic.

beta particle A beta particle is essentially an electron.

bimolecular reactions Bimolecular reactions are chemical reactions that involve the collision of two chemical species.

binary compounds Binary compounds are compounds that consist of only two elements.

body-centered unit cell A body-centered unit cell has particles located at the corners of a cube and in the middle of the cube.

boiling The process of going from the liquid state to the gaseous state is called boiling.

boiling point the boiling point (b.p.) is the temperature at which a liquid boils.

bond order The bond order relates the bonding and antibonding electrons in the molecular orbital theory (# electrons in bonding MOs – # electrons in antibonding MOs)/2.

Boyle's law Boyle's law states that there is an inverse relationship between the volume and pressure of a gas, if the temperature and amount are kept constant.

buffer capacity The buffer capacity is the ability of the buffer to resist a change in pH.

buffers Buffers are solutions that resist a change in pH when an acid or base is added to them.

calorie The calorie is the amount of energy needed to raise the temperature of 1 gram of water 1° C.

calorimetry Calorimetry is the laboratory technique used to measure the heat released or absorbed during a chemical or physical change.

capillary action Capillary action is the spontaneous rising of a liquid through a narrow tube against the force of gravity.

catalyst A catalyst is a substance that speeds up the reaction rate and is (at least theoretically) recoverable at the end of the reaction in an unchanged form.

cathode The cathode is the electrode in an electrochemical cell at which reduction takes place.

cathode compartment The cathode compartment is the electrolyte solution in which the cathode is immersed.

cations Cations are positively charged ions.

cell notation Cell notation is a shorthand notation of representing a galvanic cell.

Charles's law Charles's law states that there is a direct relationship between the volume and temperature of a gas, if the pressure and amount are kept constant.

chemical equilibrium A chemical equilibrium has been reached in which two exactly opposite reactions are occurring at the same place, at the same time and with the same rates of reaction.

colligative properties Colligative properties are solution properties that are simply dependent upon the *number* of solute particles, and not the type of solute.

colloids Colloids are homogeneous mixtures in which solute diameters fall in between solutions and suspensions.

combined gas equation The combined gas equation relates the pressure, temperature, and volume of a gas, assuming the amount is held constant.

combination reactions Combination reactions are reactions in which two or more reactants (elements or compounds) combine to form one product.

combustion reactions Combustion reactions are redox reactions in which the chemical species rapidly combines with oxygen and usually emits heat and light.

common-ion effect The common-ion effect is an application of Le Chatelier's principle to equilibrium systems of slightly soluble salts.

complex A complex is composed of a central atom, normally a metal, surrounded by atoms or groups of atoms called ligands.

compounds Compounds are pure substances that have a fixed proportion of elements.

concentrated Concentrated is a qualitative way of describing a solution that has a relatively large amount of solute in comparison to the solvent.

concentration Concentration is a measure of the amount of solute dissolved in the solvent.

concentration cell A concentration cell is an electrochemical cell in which the same chemical species are used in both cell compartments, but differ in concentration.

conjugate acid–base pairs This is an acid–base pair that differs by only a single H^+.

continuous spectrum A continuous spectrum is a spectrum of light much like the rainbow.

coordinate covalent bonds Coordinate covalent bonds are covalent bonds in which one of the atoms furnishes both of the electrons for the bond.

coordination compounds Coordination compounds are a type of complex in which a metal atom is surrounded by ligands.

coordination number Coordination number is the number of ligands that can covalently bond to the metal ion in the complex ion.

covalent bonding In covalent bonding, one or more electron pairs are shared between two atoms.

crisscross rule The crisscross rule can be used to help determine the formula of an ionic compound.

critical point The critical point of a substance is the point on the phase diagram beyond which the gas and liquid phases are indistinguishable from each other.

crystal lattice The crystal lattice is a three-dimensional structure that crystalline solids occupy.

crystalline solids Crystalline solids display a very regular ordering of the particles (atoms, molecules, or ions) in a three-dimensional structure called the crystal lattice.

Dalton's law Dalton's law states that in a mixture of gases (A + B + C . . . . .) the total pressure is simply the sum of the partial pressures (the pressures associated with each individual gas).

decomposition reactions Decomposition reactions are reactions in which a compound breaks down into two or more simpler substances.

diamagnetism Diamagnetism is the repulsion of a molecule from a magnetic field due to the presence of all electrons in pairs.

dilute Dilute is a qualitative terms that refers to a solution that has a relatively small amount of solute in comparison to the amount of solvent.

dimensional analysis Dimensional analysis, sometimes called the factor label method, is a method for generating a correct setup for a mathematical problem.

dipole–dipole intermolecular force Dipole–dipole intermolecular forces occur between polar molecules.

double displacement (replacement) or metathesis reaction A double displacement (replacement) or metathesis reaction is a chemical reaction where at least one insoluble product is formed from the mixing of two solutions.

effective nuclear charge The overall attraction that an electron experiences is called the effective nuclear charge. This is less than the actual nuclear charge because other electrons interfere with attraction of the protons with the electron being considered.

electrochemistry Electrochemistry is the study of chemical reactions that produce electricity and chemical reaction that take place because electricity is supplied.

electrochemical cells Electrochemical cells use indirect electron transfer to produce electricity by a redox reaction or they use electricity to produce a desired redox reaction.

electrode The electrode is that solid part of the electrochemical cell that conducts the electrons that are involved in the redox reaction.

electrode compartment The solutions in which the electrodes are immersed are called the electrode compartments.

electrolysis Electrolysis is a reaction in which electricity is used to decompose a compound.

electrolyte An electrolyte is a substance which, when dissolved in water or melted, conducts an electrical current.

electrolytic cells Electrolytic cells use electricity from an external source to produce a desired redox reaction.

electromagnetic spectrum The electromagnetic spectrum is radiant energy, composed of gamma rays, x-rays, ultraviolet, visible, etc.

electron affinity The electron affinity is the energy change that results from adding an electron to an atom or ion.

electron capture Electron capture is a radioactive decay mode that involves the capturing of an electron from the energy level closest to the nucleus (1s) by a proton in the nucleus.

electronegativity The electronegativity (EN) is a measure of the attractive force that an atom exerts on a bonding pair of electrons.

electron cloud (density) The electron cloud or density is a volume of space in which the probability of finding the electron is high.

electronic configuration The electronic configuration is a condensed way of representing the pattern of electrons in an atom.

elementary step Elementary steps are the individual reactions in the reaction mechanism or pathway.

empirical formula The empirical formula is a chemical formula tells us what elements are present in the compound and the simplest whole-number ratio of elements.

endothermic Endothermic reactions absorb energy from their surroundings.

endpoint The endpoint of a titration is the point signaled by the indication that an equivalent amount of bases has been added to the acid sample or vice versa.

enthalpy The enthalpy change, ΔH, the heat gained or lost by the system during constant pressure conditions.

excited state An excited state of an atom is an energy state of higher energy.

entropy Entropy (S) is a measure of the disorder of a system.

equilibrium constant The quantity calculated when the equilibrium concentrations of the chemical species are substituted into the reaction quotient.

equivalence point The equivalence point is that point in the titration where the moles of H^+ in the acid solution has been exactly neutralized with the same number of moles of OH^-:

exothermic An exothermic reaction releases energy (heat) to its surroundings.

face-centered unit cell The face-centered unit cell has particles at the corners and one in the middle of each face of the cube, but not in the center.

First Law of Thermodynamics The First Law of Thermodynamics states that the total energy of the universe is constant.

formation constant The formation constant is the equilibrium constant for the formation of a complex ion from a metal ion and ligands.

frequency The frequency, ν, is defined as the number of waves that pass a point per second.

functional group Functional groups are reactive groups on a compound that react in a characteristic way no matter what the rest of the molecule.

galvanic (voltaic) cells Galvanic (voltaic) cells are electrochemical cells that produce electricity by a redox reaction.

gamma emission Gamma emission is a radioactive decay process in which high-energy, short-wavelength photons which are similar to x-rays are given off.

gas A gas is a state of matter that has neither no definite shape nor volume.

Gay-Lussac's law Gay-Lussac's law describes the direct relationship between the pressure of a gas and its Kelvin temperature, if the volume and amount are held constant.

Gibbs free energy The Gibbs free energy (G) is a thermodynamic function that combines the enthalpy, entropy, and temperature and is the best indicator about whether or not a reaction will be spontaneous.

Graham's law Graham's law says that the speed of gas diffusion (mixing of gases due to their kinetic energy) or effusion (movement of a gas through a tiny opening) is inversely proportional to the square root of the gases' molecular weight.

ground state The ground state of an atom is the lowest energy state that the electron can occupy.

groups Groups (families) are the vertical columns on the periodic table.

half-life The half-life, $t_{1/2}$, is the amount of time that it takes for a reactant concentration to decrease to one-half its initial concentration.

halogens Halogens are in the VIIA group on the periodic table.

heat capacity Heat capacity is the quantity of heat needed to change the temperature 1 K.

heat of vaporization The heat of vaporization is the heat need to transform the liquid into a gas.

Henderson-Hasselbalch equation The Henderson-Hasselbalch equation can be used to calculate the pH of a buffer.

Henry's law The solubility of a gas will increase with increasing partial pressure of the gas.

Hess's law Hess's law states that if a reaction occurs in a series of steps, then the enthalpy change for the overall reaction is simply the sum of the enthalpy changes of the individual steps.

heterogeneous catalyst A heterogeneous catalyst is a catalyst that is in a different phase or state of matter than the reactants.

homogeneous catalyst A homogeneous catalyst is a catalyst that is in the same phase or state of matter as the reactants.

Hund's rule Hund's rule states that electrons are added to the orbitals half filling them all before pairing.

hybrid orbitals Hybrid orbitals are atomic orbitals formed as a result of the mixing of the atomic orbitals of the atoms involved in the covalent bond.

hydrocarbons Hydrocarbons are organic compounds containing only carbon and hydrogen.

hydrogen bonding Hydrogen bonding is a specific type of dipole–dipole attraction in which a hydrogen atom is polar-covalently bonded to one of the following extremely electronegative elements: O, N, or F.

ideal gas An ideal gas is a gas that obeys the five postulates of the Kinetic Molecular Theory of Gases.

ideal gas equation The ideal gas equation relates the temperature, volume, pressure, and amount of a gas and has the mathematical form of $PV = nRT$.

indicators Indicators are substances that change their color during a titration to indicate the endpoint.

inert (inactive) electrode An inert (inactive) electrode is a solid conducting electrode in an electrochemical cell that does not take part in the redox reaction.

inner transition elements The inner transition elements are the two horizontal groups that have been pulled out of the main body of the periodic table.

integrated rate law The integrated rate law relates the change in the concentration of reactants or products over time.

intermediates Intermediates are chemical species that are produced and consumed during the reaction, but that do not appear in the overall reaction.

intermolecular forces Intermolecular forces are attractive or repulsive forces between molecules caused by partial charges.

ion–dipole intermolecular force Ion–dipole intermolecular forces are attractive forces that occur between ions and polar molecules.

ion-induced dipole intermolecular forces Ion-induced dipole intermolecular forces are attractive forces that occur between an ion and a nonpolar molecule.

ion-product The ion-product has the same form as the solubility product constant but represents a system that is not at equilibrium.

ionic bond Ionic bonds result from some metal losing electrons to form cations and some non-metal gaining those electrons to form an anion.

ionic equation The ionic equation shows the soluble reactants and products in the form of ions.

ionic solids Ionic solids have their lattices composed of ions held together by the attraction of opposite charges of the ions.

ionization energy The ionization energy (IE) is the energy needed to completely remove an electron from an atom.

isoelectronic Isoelectronic means having the same electronic configuration.

isomers Isomers are compounds that have the same molecular formulas but different structural formulas.

isotopes Isotopes are atoms of the same element (same number of protons) that have differing numbers of neutrons.

joule (J) The joule is the SI unit of energy.

kinetic energy Kinetic energy is energy of motion.

Kinetic Molecular Theory The Kinetic Molecular Theory attempts to represent the properties of gases by modeling the gas particles themselves at the microscopic level.

kinetics Kinetics is the study of the speed of reactions.

Law of Conservation of Matter The Law of Conservation of Matter says that in ordinary chemical reactions matter is neither created nor destroyed.

Lewis electron-dot structure The Lewis electron-dot structure is a structural formula that represents the element and its valence electrons.

Le Chatelier's principle Le Chatelier's principle states that if a chemical system at equilibrium is stressed (disturbed) it will reestablish equilibrium by shifting of the reactions involved.

limiting reactant The limiting reactant is the reactant that is used up first in a chemical reaction.

line spectrum A line spectrum is a series of fine lines of colors representing wavelengths of photons which are characteristic of a particular element.

liquid A liquid is a state of matter that has a definite volume but no definite shape.

macromolecules Macromolecules are extremely large molecules.

magnetic quantum number (m_l) The magnetic quantum number describes the orientation of the orbital around the nucleus.

main-group elements Main-group elements are the groups on the periodic table that are labeled with an A.

manometer A manometer is an instrument used to measure the gas pressure inside a container.

mass number The mass number is the sum of the proton and neutrons in an atom.

mass percent The mass percentage of a solution is the mass of the solute divided by the mass of the solution and then multiplied by 100% to get percentage.

mass-volume percent The mass/volume percent of a solution is the mass of the solute divided by the volume of the solution and then multiplied by 100% to yield percentage.

mechanism The mechanism is the sequence of steps that a reaction undergoes in going from reactants to products.

melting point The temperature at which the solid converts into the liquid state is called the melting point (m.p.) of the solid.

metallic bonding In metallic bonding the electrons of the atoms are delocalized and are free to move throughout the entire solid.

metallic solids Metallic solids have metal atoms occupying the crystal lattice held together by metallic bonding.

metalloids Metalloids are a group of elements that have properties of both metals and non-metals.

metals Metals are normally solids (mercury being an exception), shinny, and good conductors of heat and electricity. They can be hammered into thin sheets (malleable) and extruded into wires (ductile). Chemically, metals tend to lose electrons in reactions.

metathesis reaction In a metathesis reaction at least one insoluble product is formed from the mixing of two solutions.

molality (m) Molality is defined as the moles of solute per kilogram of solvent.

molar heat capacity The molar heat capacity (C) is the amount of heat needed to change the temperature of 1 mole of a substance 1 K.

molarity (M) Molarity is a concentration term that represents the moles of solute per liters of solution.

mole The mole (mol) is defined as the amount of a substance that contains the same number of particles as atoms in exactly 12 g of carbon-12.

molecular equation The molecular equation is an equation in which both the reactants and products are shown in the undissociated form.

molecular formula The molecular (actual) formula shows what elements are in the compound and the actual number of each element.

molecular orbital theory The molecular orbital (MO) theory of covalent bonding, atomic orbitals combine to form molecular orbitals that encompass the entire molecule.

molecular solids Molecular solids have their lattices composed of molecules held in place by London forces, dipole–dipole forces and hydrogen bonding.

molecule A molecule is a covalently bonded compound.

monomers Macromolecules are composed of repeating units, called monomers.

Nernst equation An equation that allows the calculation of the cell potential of a galvanic cell that is not at standard conditions.

net ionic equation The net ionic equation is written by dropping out the spectator ions and showing only those chemical species that are involved in the chemical reaction.

network covalent solids Network covalent solids have covalent bonds joining the atoms together in the extremely large crystal lattice.

neutral Neutral is 7.00 on the pH scale.

neutralization reactions Neutralization reactions are acid-base reactions in which an acid reacts with a base to give a salt and water.

noble gases Noble gases are in the VIIIA group on the periodic table. They are very unreactive due to their filled valence shell.

nonelectrolytes Nonelectrolytes are substances that do not conduct electricity when dissolved in water or melted.

nonmetals Nonmetals have properties that are generally the opposite of metals. Some are gases, are poor conductors of heat and electricity, are neither malleable nor ductile and tend to gain electrons in their chemical reactions.

nonpolar covalent bond In a nonpolar covalent bond the electrons are shared equally by the two atoms involved in the bond.

nuclear belt of stability The nuclear belt of stability is a plot of the # neutrons versus the # protons for the known stable isotopes.

nucleus The nucleus is a dense core of positive charge at the center of the atom that contained most of the mass of the atom.

orbital An orbital or wave function is a quantum mechanical mathematical description of the location of electrons. The electrons in a particular subshell are distributed among these volumes of space of equal energies.

octet rule The octet rule states that during chemical reactions, atoms lose, gain or share electrons in order to achieve a filled valence shell, to complete their octet.

order of reaction The order of reaction is the exponent in the rate equation that indicate what effect a change in concentration of that particular reactant species will have on the reaction rate.

organic chemistry Organic chemistry is the chemistry of carbon.

osmosis Osmosis is the passing of solvent molecules through a semipermeable membrane.

osmotic pressure The osmotic pressure is the amount of pressure that must be exerted on a solution in order to stop osmosis of solvent molecules through a semipermeable membrane.

oxidation Oxidation is the loss of electrons.

oxidation numbers Oxidation numbers are bookkeeping numbers that allows chemists to do things like balance redox equations.

oxidizing agent The oxidizing agent is the reactant being reduced.

paramagnetism Paramagnetism is the attraction of a molecule to a magnetic field due to unpaired electrons.

pascal The pascal is the SI unit of pressure.

percent yield The percent yield (% yield) is the actual yield divided by the theoretical yield and the resultant multiplied by 100.

periods Periods are the horizontal rows on the periodic table which have consecutive atomic numbers.

phase changes Phase changes are changes of state.

phase diagram A phase diagram is a graph representing the relationship of the states of matter of a substance to temperature and pressure.

pi (π) bonds Pi bonds result from the overlap of atomic orbitals above and below a line connecting the two atomic nuclei.

polar covalent bond Polar covalent bonds are covalent bonds in which there is an unequal sharing of the bonding pair of electrons.

polyprotic acids Polyprotic acids are acids that can donate more than one proton.

potential energy Potential energy is stored energy.

positron A positron is essentially an electron that has a positive charge instead of a negative one.

precipitate A precipitate is an insoluble product which forms in a solution; the formation of a solid from ions in solution.

precipitation reactions Precipitation reactions are reactions that involve the formation of an insoluble compound, a precipitate, from the mixing of two soluble compounds.

pressure Pressure is the force exerted per unit of surface area.

principal quantum number (n) The principal quantum number describes the size of the orbital and relative distance from the nucleus.

proof The proof of an aqueous ethyl alcohol solution is twice the volume percent.

quantized Quantized means that there could only be certain distinct energies associated with a state of the atom.

quantum numbers Quantum numbers are used to describe each electron within an atom corresponding to the orbital size, shape, and orientation in space.

radioactivity Radioactivity is the spontaneous decay of an unstable isotope to a more stable one.

rate constant (k) The rate constant is a proportionality constant that appears in the rate law and relates the concentration of reactants to the speed of reaction.

rate-determining step The rate-determining step is the slowest one of the reaction steps and controls the rate of the overall reaction.

rate equation The rate equation relates the speed of reaction to the concentration of reactants and has the form: Rate $= k[A]^m[B]^n$. . . . where k is the rate constant and m and n are the orders of reaction with respect to that specific reactant.

reactants The starting material in the chemical reaction that get converted into different substances called products.

reaction intermediate A reaction intermediate is a substance that is formed but then consumed during the reaction mechanism.

reaction mechanism The reaction mechanism is the sequence of individual reactions that occur in an overall reaction in going from reactants to products.

reaction quotient The reaction quotient, Q, is the numerical value that results when non-equilibrium concentrations are inserted into the equilibrium expression. When the system reaches equilibrium, the reaction quotient becomes the equilibrium constant.

reactive site The reactive site of a molecule is the place at which the reaction takes place.

redox reactions Redox reaction are chemical reactions in which electrons are lost and gained.

reducing agent The reactant undergoing oxidation in a redox reaction is called the reducing agent.

reduction Reduction is the gain of electrons in a redox reaction.

resonance Resonance is a way of describing a molecular structure which cannot be represented by a single Lewis structure. Several different Lewis structures are used, each differing only by the position of electron pairs.

reverse osmosis Reverse osmosis takes place when the pressure on the solution side exceeds the osmotic pressure and solvent molecules are forced back through the semipermeable membrane into the solvent side.

root mean square speed The average velocity of the gas particles is called the root mean square speed.

salt bridge A salt bridge is often an inverted U tube that contains a gel containing a concentrated electrolyte solution used in an electrochemical cell to maintain electrical neutrality in the cell compartments.

saturated hydrocarbons Saturated hydrocarbons are hydrocarbons that are single bonded to the maximum number of other atoms.

saturated solution A solution in which one has dissolved the maximum amount of solute per given amount of solvent at a given temperature is called a saturated solution.

Second Law of Thermodynamics The Second Law of Thermodynamics states that all processes that occur spontaneously move in the direction of an increase in entropy of the universe (system + surroundings).

semipermeable membrane A semipermeable membrane is a thin porous film which allows the passage of solvent molecules but not solute particles.

shells The electrons in an atom are located in various energy levels or **shells** that are located at different distances from the nucleus.

SI system The system of units used in science is the SI system (Système International) that is related to the metric system.

sigma bonds Sigma bonds have the orbital overlap on a line drawn between the two nuclei.

simple cubic unit cell The simple cubic unit cell has particles located at the corners of a simple cube.

single displacement (replacement) reactions Single displacement reactions are reactions in which atoms of an element replace the atoms of another element in a compound.

solid A solid is a state of matter that has both a definite shape and a definite volume.

solubility product constant, K_{sp} The solubility product constant is the equilibrium constant associated with sparingly soluble salts and is the product of the ionic concentrations, each one raised to the power of the coefficient in the balanced chemical equation.

solute The solute is the component of the solution that is there in smallest amount.

solution A solution is defined as a homogeneous mixture composed of solvent and one or more solutes.

solvation Solvation is the forming of a layer of bound solvent molecules around a solute.

solvent The solvent is that component of a solution that is present in largest amount.

specific heat capacity (or specific heat) (c) The specific heat capacity is the quantity of heat needed to raise the temperature of 1 g of the substance 1 K.

spectator ions Spectator ions are ions that are not actually involved in the chemical reaction taking place, but simply maintain electrical neutrality.

speed of light The speed of light is the speed that all electromagnetic radiation travels in a vacuum, 3.00×10^8 m/s.

spin quantum number The spin quantum number indicates the direction the electron is spinning.

standard cell potential The standard cell potential is the potential (voltage) associated with an electrochemical cell at standard conditions.

standard enthalpy of formation The standard enthalpy of formation of a compound (ΔH_f^0) is the change in enthalpy when 1 mol of the compound is formed from its elements when all substances are in their standard states.

standard molar entropies (S°) Standard molar enthalpies of elements and compounds are the entropies associated with 1 mole of a substance in its standard state.

standard reduction potentials The standard reduction potential is the voltage associated with a half-reaction shown in the form of reduction.

state function A state function is a function that doesn't depend on the pathway, only the initial and final states.

stoichiometry Stoichiometry is the calculation of the amount (mass, moles, particles) of one substance in the chemical reaction through the use of another.

strong acid A strong acid is an acid that ionizes completely in water.

strong base A strong base is a base that ionizes completely in water.

strong electrolytes Strong electrolytes completely ionize or dissociate in water.

structural isomers Structural isomers are compounds that have the same molecular formula but differ in how the groups are attached to each other.

sublimation Sublimation is going directly from the solid state to the gaseous state without ever having become a liquid.

subshells Within the shells, the electrons are grouped in subshells of slightly different energies.

supersaturated solution A supersaturated solution has more than the maximum amount of solute dissolved in the solvent.

surface tension Surface tension is the amount of force that it requires to break through the molecular layer at the surface of a liquid.

suspension A heterogeneous mixture in which the particles are large (in excess of 1000 nm).

surroundings The surroundings is a thermodynamics term that is the rest of the universe that is being affected by the change.

system The system is a thermodynamics term that is the part of the universe that we are studying.

ternary compounds Ternary compounds are those containing three (or more) elements.

thermochemistry Thermochemistry is the part of thermodynamics that deals with changes in heat that take place during chemical reactions.

thermodynamics Thermodynamics is the study of heat and its transformations.

theoretical yield The theoretical yield is the maximum amount of product that can be formed.

titrant The titrant is that solution in a titration that has a known concentration.

titration A titration is a laboratory procedure in which a solution of known concentration is used to determine the concentration of an unknown solution.

transition elements The B groups on the periodic table are called the transition elements.

transmutation Transmutation is a nuclear reaction which results in the creation of one element from another one.

triple point The triple point of a substance is the combination of temperature and pressure on a phase diagram at which all three states of matter can exist.

Tyndall effect The Tyndall effect is exhibited when a light is shone through a colloid and is visible due to the reflection of the light off the larger colloid particles.

unimolecular reactions Unimolecular reactions are reactions in which a single chemical species decomposes or rearranges.

unit cells Unit cells are the repeating units in a crystal lattice.

unsaturated Unsaturated organic compounds have carbons that do not have the maximum number of bonds to other atoms; there is at least one carbon-to-carbon double bond present.

unsaturated solution An unsaturated solution has less than that maximum amount of solute dissolved in a given amount of solvent.

valence bond theory The valence bond theory describes covalent bonding as the overlap of atomic orbitals to form a new kind of orbital, a hybrid orbital.

valence electrons Valence electrons are the electrons in the outermost energy level (outermost shell). Valence electrons are normally considered to be only the s and p electrons in the outermost energy level.

van der Waals equation van der Waals equation is an equation that is a modification of the ideal gas equation to compensate for the behavior of real gases.

van't Hoff factor The van't Hoff factor is the ratio of moles of solute particles formed to moles of solute dissolved in solution.

vapor pressure The pressure exerted by the gaseous molecules which are at equilibrium with a liquid in a closed container.

viscosity Viscosity is the resistance to flow of liquids.

volume percent The volume percent of the solution is the volume of the solute divided by the volume of the solution and multiplied by 100% to generate the percentage.

VSEPR theory The VSEPR (valence shell electron-pair repulsion) theory says that the electron pairs around a central atom will try to get as far as possible from each other in order to minimize the repulsive forces. This theory is used to predict molecular geometry.

water dissociation constant, K_w The water dissociation constant is the equilibrium constant associated with the ionization of pure water.

wave function The wave function is a mathematical description of the electron's motion.

wavelength, λ Wavelength is the distance between two identical points on a wave.

weak acid A weak acid is an acid that only partially ionizes in water.

weak base A weak base is a base that only partially ionizes in water.

weak electrolytes Weak electrolytes only partially ionize or dissociate in water.

About the Authors

John Moore grew up in the foothills of western North Carolina. He attended the University of North Carolina–Asheville, where he received his bachelor's degree in chemistry. He earned his master's degree in chemistry from Furman University in Greenville, South Carolina. After a stint in the United States Army he decided to try his hand at teaching. In 1971 he joined the faculty of Stephen F. Austin State University in Nacogdoches, Texas, where he still teaches chemistry. In 1985 he started back to school part-time, and in 1991 received his doctorate in education from Texas A&M University. For the last five years he has been coeditor, along with one of his former students, of the *Chemistry for Kids* feature of *The Journal of Chemical Education*. In 2003 his first book, *Chemistry for Dummies,* was published.

Richard Langley grew up in southwestern Ohio. He attended Miami University in Oxford, Ohio, where he earned bachelor's degrees in chemistry and mineralogy and a master's degree in chemistry. He next went to the University of Nebraska in Lincoln, where he received his doctorate in chemistry. He took a postdoctoral position at Arizona State University in Tempe, Arizona, then became a visiting assistant professor at the University of Wisconsin–River Falls. He has taught at Stephen F. Austin State University in Nacogdoches, Texas, since 1982. For the past several years, he has been a grader for the free-response portion of the AP Chemistry exam.